A Study of Denominations

Ethan R. Longhenry

DeWard™

for your journey

A Study of Denominations
© 2015 by DeWard Publishing Company, Ltd.
P.O. Box 6259, Chillicothe, Ohio 45601
www.deward.com

Cover design by Eric Wallace

Printed in the United States of America.

ISBN: 978–1–936341–79–5

Contents

Preface

This book represents, in some small way, my attempt to understand the religious world around me and to present a defense for the hope that is in me (1 Peter 3.15). It is the fruit of much discussion and study.

I have tried to assist others in their attempts to defend and promote the faith in their own lives. The idea of this book originated in a series of lessons I presented in 2000 before the brethren of the Hessville church in Hammond, Indiana, and the substance of the book materialized in a class I taught on denominations in 2001–2002 for the church in Rantoul, Illinois. The final revision (and expansion) was undertaken while teaching a similar class for the church in Norwalk, Ohio, in 2007.

Acknowledgements

This book would never have come about if it were not for the assistance and encouragement of many people. I would like to thank all the brethren from the Hessville church in Hammond for their encouragement while I worked through and presented lessons on denominations there, and also the brethren in Rantoul and in Norwalk for encouraging me while writing the material and giving me the chance to present and test what was written. A word of thanks also goes to my parents, John and Carol, who were willing to finance the purchasing of many of the resources that are used in this study. I would like to thank my wife, Sarah, who encouraged me throughout the process of studying, defending, preaching, and teaching, who bore with me patiently while I spent much time writing the material, and who proved a willing sounding board for my ideas. I would like to thank Dan Watt and Raja Sandor for their work on designing the charts found within the study and for all those at DeWard Publishing for getting this work in print. Finally, all thanks, glory, and honor must go to God the Father and His Son Jesus Christ, without whom there would be no salvation and no faith to defend.

In the end, I hope that you will find this study to profit you and encourage you in the faith. I hope that you gain a better understanding of the beliefs of many denominations and that which the Scriptures teach.

Notes

All Scriptures, unless indicated otherwise, are quoted from the American Standard Version (ASV). "LORD" has been substituted for "Jehovah."

Dates are given according to the Before the Common Era (BCE) and Common Era (CE) format. The dates are identical to "Before Christ" (BC) and "In the Year of our Lord/Anno Domini" (AD) format. This choice was made because the latter system is inaccurate (Jesus was born in 4 BCE, and the Kingdom was not inaugurated until 30 CE), Jesus never commanded such a thing, and the system comes from the sixth century CE, not the New Testament.

Introduction

> But and if ye should suffer for righteousness' sake, blessed are ye: and fear not their fear, neither be troubled; but sanctify in your hearts Christ as Lord: being ready always to give answer to every man that asketh you a reason concerning the hope that is in you, yet with meekness and fear. *(1 Peter 3.14–15)*

We live in a world of religious confusion. There are all kinds of religions which teach and practice all kinds of things, and plenty of people who profess to have no religion whatsoever.

Furthermore, confusion reigns among all the various groups who profess Christianity. All kinds of denominations exist today, all of them teaching different doctrines and practices, and all claiming to present God's truth.

In this climate of confusion, many ask difficult questions. What is the truth? Can it even be known? How tragic it is that so many despair of ever knowing the truth of God!

I believe that the truth can be known, and the truth is present completely and infallibly in the revealed Word of God, the Bible. I will attempt in the study that follows to present what God has revealed to be the truth.

Before we begin this journey, however, I would like to present some explanations of this study and some general thoughts.

Structure of the Study

Any attempt to synthesize and explain the various beliefs of hundreds of groups presents many logistical challenges. The study has been divided into four parts. Part I involves discussions of denominations. Part II speaks of the various movements that have developed within Christianity, especially in the past two centuries, since many movements now transcend denominational boundaries. Part III represents certain practices and doctrines that come up consistently. Part IV involves early movements in Christianity, and demonstrates how history tends to repeat itself.

In each entry in parts I and II, there is a section entitled "general considerations" referring you to the associated movements, doctrines, and practices of the denomination that are covered in other parts. The "general considerations" section also will cover doctrines and practices of a denomination covered in the section of another denomination.

Some denominations have their own sections; many other times, however, different denominations who share the same heritage, beliefs, and practices on the whole are addressed together.

What this Book Is and Is Not

This study presents basic information on denominational beliefs and practices, basic responses to these beliefs and practices, and basic defenses for the teachings of the Scriptures. This study does not present an exhaustive history and background of the denominations, nor does it set out to present everything that every denomination believes and teaches. You will notice that matters of marriage, divorce, and remarriage are not even addressed in this book; that is a study in and of itself, and that just among churches of Christ, let alone among other groups. Other issues are left unaddressed.

This book is intended to be a handy reference book and general guide for Christians as they strive to talk to people in their lives about matters of faith. It would take a large series of books to fully treat every denomination with its beliefs and practices and to present a full refutation. I freely encourage you to seek out other resources, written both by myself and others, to provide further and more in-depth guidance in speaking with members of denominations. To this end, a bibliography is presented to direct you to these good resources.

This study is "a" study of denominations, not "the" study of denominations. In the end, this study is my study into denominations and their beliefs and practices, and represents my views. I have attempted to make sure that what I present in here concords to the message of the Scriptures, but that does not mean that you should take my word for it. I encourage you to also seek out these things in the Scriptures and see what is so (cf. Acts 17.10–11). I do not, nor ever would, presume to speak for churches of Christ in general, or even for the local church of which I am a part. I speak only as myself based on my research and experiences in defending the faith and promoting the truth.

This study presents what denominations say they believe in their official literature. Just as members of churches of Christ dispute over various contentious matters, so also many matters are under dispute in various denominations. Furthermore, just as many members of churches of Christ do not really know what they believe or do not practice what they believe (to their shame), even more members of denominations do not really know what they believe or do not practice what they believe. I have done the best that I can through my research to present accurately what the denominations teach; do not assume, however, that just because a person you know is, say, a Lutheran, that they even know what the Lutheran church teaches on a given subject. Knowing the material present in this book will help you be able to communicate with members of denominations, but it is not wise to presume that since a person goes to a particular denominational church that they believe everything that denomination teaches.

This study is designed to demonstrate how teachings of denominations diverge from the Scriptures; it is not my place to judge.

> For it is written, "As I live, saith the Lord, to me every knee shall bow, And every tongue shall confess to God."
> So then each one of us shall give account of himself to God. *(Romans 14.11–12)*

> One only is the lawgiver and judge, even he who is able to save and to destroy: but who art thou that judgest thy neighbour? *(James 4.12)*

We are called upon to test the spirits (1 John 4.1), and not to accept that which is false (Revelation 2.2). God, however, is the Judge of mankind, and only He has the prerogative to redeem or to condemn. We can encourage members of denominations to consider our defense and exhort them to consider the Scriptures, but in the end God will judge them as He will judge us. Will members of denominations be going to Hell for what they have believed and taught? That is God's decision, not mine or yours or anyone else's.

The study is designed to encourage and instruct Christians. It will benefit you little if it is not used. Furthermore, it may assist you in your understanding, but if you do not take the knowledge gained and use it profitably to help instruct those around you, then the study is not reaching its full potential.

Let us now begin the journey of exploration into denominations by seeing the big picture: a historical overview of denominations.

Historical Overview

Introduction

By some counts, there are over 2,000 denominations in the United States alone. Modern "Christendom" is full of the names of different people and groups spanning two millennia. How did we get to this point? Where did all of these groups come from? We will strive to partially untangle the web of denominational history here.

We will examine denominational history in four phases for easier understanding; there are charts provided for each of the four phases. We will also consider many modern movements.

As the Preacher says,

> That which hath been is that which shall be; and that which hath been done is that which shall be done: and there is no new thing under the sun *(Ecclesiastes 1.9).*

This statement especially holds true for Christianity; we will see that there are many doctrines and beliefs that continually return in different forms. Let us now examine the history of the denominations in "Christendom."

Phase I: to 1054

The first phase begins with the church as established in Christ by the Apostles to the end of the "catholic" church in the division of 1054. A large number of the denominations that began in this period are no more; nevertheless, many of their doctrines abound in denominations today.

The first such groups even existed during the time of the Apostles.

The "Judaizers": We use the term "Judaizers" today to describe groups of Jewish Christians, especially those who had previously been Pharisees, in the first century who taught that Gentiles who converted to Christ should observe part or all of the Law of Moses. This belief system

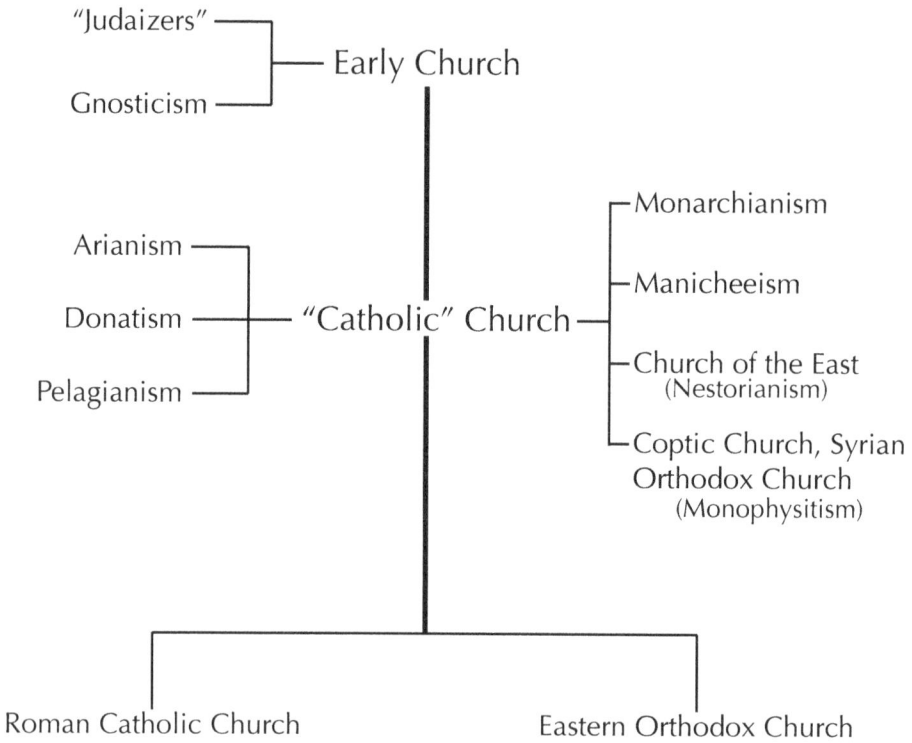

"Judaizers" —
Gnosticism — — Early Church

Arianism —
Donatism — — "Catholic" Church —
Pelagianism —

— Monarchianism

— Manicheeism

— Church of the East
(Nestorianism)

— Coptic Church, Syrian
Orthodox Church
(Monophysitism)

Roman Catholic Church   Eastern Orthodox Church

Chart, Phase I: to 1054

gained traction in Jerusalem in the years after God accepted the Gentiles into the faith (ca. 40–50), and the doctrine was the subject of an Apostolic council sometime between 48–50 (Acts 15). The determination was made by the Holy Spirit that the Gentile converts should not be bound by the Law of Moses (Acts 15.22–29). Nevertheless, many continued to teach these doctrines, and we see Paul confronting such teachings in Galatia, Corinth, and Colossae. The destruction of Jerusalem in 70 and the attendant cessation of the covenant between God and Israel curtailed this movement; later movements of Jewish Christians, such as the Ebionites, were small and not long-lasting.

Gnosticism: A term from the Greek word *gnosis*, which means "knowledge," Gnosticism is a broad term used to describe the various groups of individuals in the latter first century through the sixth century who seem to have infused Christian belief with Hellenistic philosophy to create entirely new brands of religion. The Gnostics are known to believe in a strictly dualistic world and for rejecting the God of the Old Testament, believing Him to be an inferior god compared to the Son. Gnostics were notable docetists, believing that Jesus was never "in the flesh," but only the appearance thereof (hence, docetism, from the Greek *dokeo*, "to seem"). The beginnings of this group can be seen as early as the Colossian letter, where Paul warns against such philosophy in Colossians 2.8. Gnosticism proper seems to originate by the 90s, when John explicitly writes in his Gospel and his letters that Christ was in the flesh. These Gnostics were most prevalent in the middle of the second century, with one Gnostic in particular, Valentius, almost elected "bishop" of Rome. When so-called "orthodox" Christianity triumphed in the Roman Empire in the fourth century, Gnosticism *per se* declined sharply. Nevertheless, Gnostic influence can be seen in later groups such as the Manichaeans, Paulicians, Bogomils, and the Cathars.

All of the Apostles had died by 100; therefore, direct connections to Jesus the Christ had become few and far between. The main bulk of Christianity began to slowly but surely stray from the truth, accepting too many conventions from the world around them. A distinction was soon made between "elders" and "bishops," with a bishop presiding over a group of elders, and from there a bishop without necessarily having the elders present. "Bishops" of larger metropolitan areas began exercising more influence over the surrounding lands. Pagan festivals celebrating the spring equinox and the winter solstice were "Christianized" into Easter and Christmas, respectively. Many of these developments and changes had developed throughout the second and third centuries, yet they had certainly crystallized a new denomination by 312, when the "Catholic" church received official sanction from the Roman Empire. This entity would develop and last until 1054, when the western and eastern Mediterranean churches split, the former becoming the Roman Catholic Church, the latter, the Eastern Orthodox Church.

The period of 100–1054 saw many divisions and dissensions over multiple issues, mostly concerning the nature of God, the Father, the Son, and the Holy Spirit.

Marcionism: Marcionism owed its existence to Marcion, an individual who gained popularity in Rome in 140–144. His theology was influenced heavily by the Gnostics, and he denied the power of the God of the Old Testament. He promulgated the use of a limited form of the New Testament, including Luke's Gospel and Acts, and many of the Pauline epistles, the former since Luke was a Gentile and the latter since he was sent to preach to the Gentiles. He found the God of the Old Testament contradictory and inhumane. The "orthodox" Christianity of the time rejected his argumentation, upheld the value of the Old Testament, and dutifully began the work of canonization of the Old and New Testaments. The specter of Marcion loomed large enough so as to merit refutation by Tertullian at the end of the second century; nevertheless, Marcion's movement mostly died out or assimilated into other Gnostic groups.

Montanism: Montanism receives its name from its founder, Montanus, a Phrygian and a former priest of Cybele. Around 172, he believed that he, along with the prophetesses Prisca and Maximilla, was given a dispensation of the Spirit, and uttered prophecies without control over his faculties. They believed that they were the last manifestation of the Paraclete (the Comforter), and that the battle of Armageddon would be fought soon and the "new Jerusalem" would come to earth in the small village of Pepuza in Phrygia. This movement was highly charismatic; one of the "church fathers," Tertullian, eventually joined the North African branch of this movement. Even though apocalyptic hopes of the Montanists were left unfulfilled, this movement endured in some places for three hundred years.

Monarchianism: A term meaning "rule of one," this doctrine permeated Christianity in the second and third centuries. This doctrine claims that there is one authority involved with God. One form was "dynamistic" monarchianism, espoused first by the Theodotians (from around 190 until the fourth century) and later by Paul of Samosata around 260 and the adoptionist movement in Spain around 782. "Dynamistic" monarchianism involved the belief that Jesus was born a man and became God (thus, "adopted") at His baptism. Another form of this belief system, "modalistic" monarchianism, was presented by Sabellius (around 215), suggesting that God is inherently unknowable, and that only through manifestations can He be seen. Therefore, according to such a view, the Father, the Son, and the Holy Spirit are the same person in different manifestations. Its opponents branded the doctrine as "patripassianism," the "suffering of the Father," since it demanded that the Father and the Spirit suffered on the cross as well since the form of God known as Christ was on the cross. "Modalistic" monarchianism is also known as modalism. Monarchian concepts would later be found in Nestorianism and possibly in the Paulicians. Overall, however, the movements failed to gain ground in "orthodox" Christianity.

Manichaeism: Manichaeism, or the Manichees, comes from Mani, an eastern mystic, who believed that he was the manifestation of the Christ, God on Earth. Around 250, he developed his theology, which included tenets of Zoroastrianism, Buddhism, and Gnosticism, and was a blatant attempt to combine Western and Eastern religions. Manichees believed in reincarnation with an eventual deliverance from life, and that good and evil came from a primeval war between light and darkness. This doctrine persevered for awhile; Augustine's first contact with religion was Manichaeism in north Africa in the fourth century. The infiltration of Islam overall tempered the growth of Manichaeism; nevertheless, a small group of Mani's followers in Iran, calling themselves Mandeans, have persevered to the modern day. Manichaeism does have direct influence on the later Paulician movement, and by extension the Bogomils and the Cathars.

Donatism: The term comes from one Donatus, a "bishop" who was one of the founders of the movement. They stood for holiness and purity in the church. They refused to recognize "bishops" or any religious authorities who handed over (Latin *traditio*) Scriptures during the persecution. Donatists are known primarily for their position on the Lord's Supper: the one giving it to the people must be free from sin or the blessings are not provided. They are also known for their position on the church, believing that the individual was the focus, not the organization: the church should be simply the collective of individual Christians, not a hierarchical organization. The group suffered constant oppression and persecution from religious and secular authorities, but only died out along with the Catholic church in northern Africa with the Islamic invasions of the seventh century.

Arianism: Named from Arius, a bishop who disagreed with the theology of the catholic church and believed that regardless of His glory, the Son is a created being and therefore cannot be considered part of the eternal Godhead. This belief began in the early fourth century, and was condemned as heretical at the Council of Nicaea in 325. Nevertheless, Arianism remained prevalent, with many leading bishops holding to the belief in the fourth century. In the fifth century, Arians converted many of the German tribes that overran the Roman empire. Arianism began to falter, however, when Justinian re-conquered the Italian peninsula for the Eastern Roman Empire in the sixth century, and was all but extinguished when Charlemagne gained control over most of central Europe in the eighth century.

Nestorianism: The name derives from Nestorius, a bishop of Constantinople. In 428, he condemned the popular use of the title "Mother of God" (*Theotoktos*) for Mary, since the title seemed to give credence to the idea that the divine could be born of a human, or that God could be a baby. To him, Jesus as man and God was not an "essential union" but a merging of wills. His belief was declared heretical at the Council of Chalcedon; however, his doctrines persevered. To this day, there are Nestorian churches (known as the Church of the East) in central Asia. There is also some Nestorian influence upon the Paulicians of the sixth century.

Monophysitism: This term derives from Greek words meaning "one nature." Monophysitism is generally considered to be a reaction to the Nestorian movement, initiated by another bishop named Cyril of Alexandria, who posited that Christ had one nature, which was manifested as flesh and as God. This was codified in the council in Ephesus in 449. Further clarification regarding this position was necessary, since the language was being used to support two sides of an argument: the council of Chalcedon interpreted the council of Ephesus in such a way as to preserve the two natures of Christ in 451, and schism was inevitable. Reconciliation was attempted, especially by the eastern emperor Justinian and his wife Theodora, with the philosophy of Monothelitism, the idea that while Christ had two natures He had only one will. This combination of Chalcedon and Ephesus was unsuccessful; Monothelitism was soundly denounced, and the eastern church split into Catholic and Monophysite factions. Monophysitism remained prevalent in many places until around the eighth century; today, the only Monophysite groups left are the Syrian Jacobites and the Coptic church of Egypt.

Pelagianism: The term comes from Pelagius, an individual from England who around 411 questioned the doctrine of original sin and believed that man was responsible for only his own sins, also denying the total depravity of man. While the eastern "catholic" church heard his views and found little with which to disagree, Augustine in the west hotly pursued Pelagius and his doctrines; in the end Pelagius was killed for his positions. The debate between the two positions, however, was by no means over: the Roman Catholic church debated for hundreds of years and in the end affirmed a more middle position, the belief that man has free will but God is the source of faith and belief. One can also see the debates in the sixteenth century and beyond concerning free will vs. total depravity in the Pelagian/Augustinian controversy.

Paulicians: The Paulicians originated in Armenia in the sixth century, first associated with Nestorianism, but by the next century seen further west and demonstrably as their own movement. The Paulicians derive their name from the Apostle Paul, whose writings were held as inspired along with the Gospels; the rest of the Bible, they claimed, came from an evil spirit. The Paulicians seem to have been heavily influenced by Marcionism, the "dynamistic" monarchianism of Paul of Samosata, and Gnostic/Manichaean philosophy. The group reached the height of its power in 844 with the formation of a Paulician state in modern-day Turkey, but soon afterward persecution from the Eastern Roman Empire intensified. In 970, many of the Paulicians of Syria were deported to the Balkan region of Europe, where they converted many of the local Bulgars (then called the Bogomils) to their views. A group of Paulicians remained in Armenia until around the eleventh century.

Bogomils: The Bogomils were active in the area around Bulgaria beginning in around the ninth century. They inherited a dualist theology from the Gnostics through the Manichaeans and the Paulicians. Harassed by the Roman Catholic and Eastern Orthodox churches, the Bogomils were eventually wiped out by the expansion of Islam into the Balkan region in the fifteenth century. Some Bogomil missionaries, however, traveled to southern France in the twelfth century and helped to establish the Cathars there.

After the sixth century, the real schism between the western and eastern factions of the catholic church became more and more apparent. For the next four hundred years, the two entities drifted further apart, due to linguistic and cultural differences and political boundaries. A controversy over how the Spirit was imparted, through the Father alone (which the east believed) or through either the Father or the Son (as the west believed) proved to be the final straw; in 1054, the bishop of Rome sent a bull of excommunication to the Patriarch of Constantinople, who responded in kind. This act effectively created the Roman Catholic Church in the west, and the Eastern Orthodox Church in the east.

Phase II: 1054 to 1500

Let us now examine the period from the schism between east and west to just before the period of the Reformation in the west. The Eastern Orthodox Church did not go through any major alterations after the eleventh century; the church would eventually be organized on national lines, but all affirm the same doctrines. The Roman Catholic church was continually beset by many divisions and schisms even before the Reformation.

Waldensians: The Waldensians come from Peter Waldo, a wealthy merchant around 1175 who sold all of his property and urged a return to "apostolic poverty." The group that eventually followed him was called the Poor Men of Lyons, and was later deemed the Waldensians. The Roman Catholic church at first accepted the group, but later the preaching of the Waldensians led to persecution. The group survived, however, and

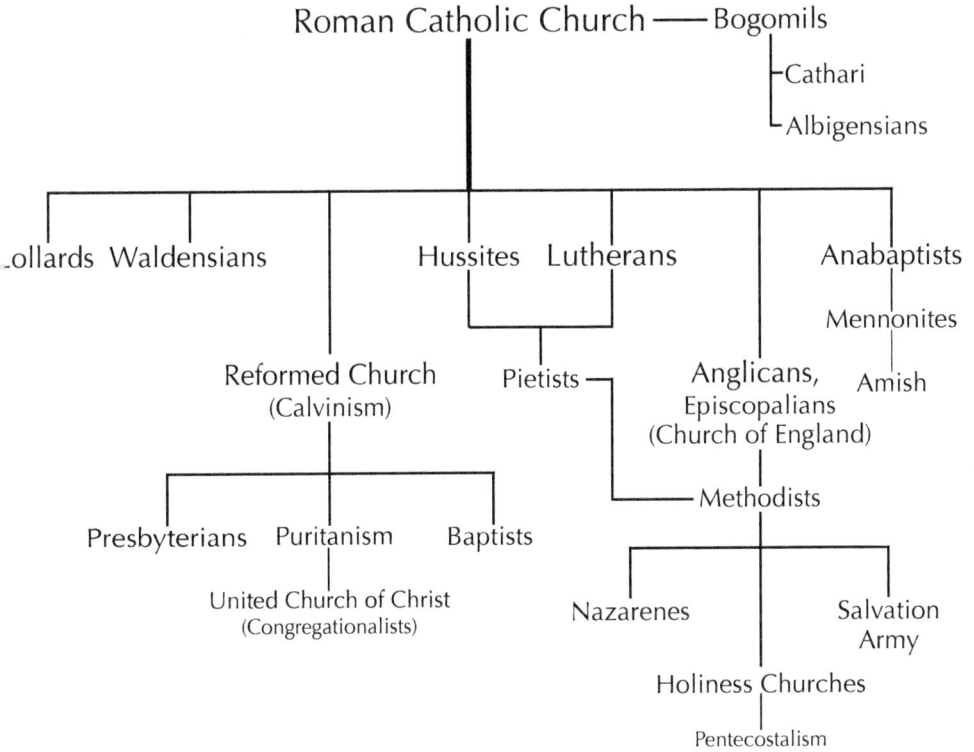

Chart, Phase II: 1054 to 1500

in the sixteenth century agreed to combine with the Reformed Church in the Calvinist tradition.

Cathars: The Cathars, or the "Cleansed," began as a group around the same time as the Waldensians, in southern France. They were also named the Albigensians, from the city of Albi, where many such Cathars lived. The Cathars were heavily influenced by the Bogomils, and held to an essentially Gnostic theology. By 1200, the Cathars were poised to take over southern France; nevertheless, the Roman Catholic church began to persecute them heavily in the late twelfth and early thirteenth centuries with a crusade and an inquisition, and severely curtailed the movement.

It may also be noted that there is also some evidence that around the eleventh century in southern France, the truth of the Gospel was being preached.

There were also some groups that were established because of the groundbreaking work of certain individuals, known today as the "pre-Reformers."

John Wycliffe and the Lollards: An English priest of the fourteenth century, John Wycliffe taught that Christ is the only King of men and rested his authority in the Bible. He began the work of translating the Bible into English, and for both his preaching and his actions, he was strongly denounced by the Roman Catholic officials. The Lollards followed after him for some time, although the movement dies out within the fourteenth century. After the "heresy" of Jan Hus, Roman Catholic officials dug up Wycliffe's bones and burned them.

Jan Hus and the Hussites: In the Holy Roman Empire, the portion of which we now call the Czech Republic, Jan Hus also began to question the Roman Catholic church's practices in the early fifteenth century. Many of his difficulties with the Roman Catholic church would be echoed by Luther about a hundred years later. Hus was burned at the stake in 1415; his followers, the Hussites, were strongly persecuted; however, they were able to survive, recognized later as the Moravian Brethren, affiliated with the Pietist movement of the seventeenth century.

Phase III: 1500 to 1800

Let us now examine the time of the Reformation, beginning proper in 1519 with Luther's quarrels with the Roman Catholic church and ending in the eighteenth century with Wesleyanism, the reformation of theology that occurred within the Church of England.

By the sixteenth century, the trials of the medieval world had faded. Western Europe was in the middle of what is deemed the Renaissance, a time of philosophical and theological regeneration. The invention of the printing press in 1450 by Johann Gutenburg allowed knowledge to be spread and read quickly and easily. Literacy rates increased, and soon after, many began to question the Roman Catholic church's positions and stances on theology. The first to question was Desiderius Erasmus, who wished to change the way the church was acting; however, it would be up to his friend Martin Luther to activate change in Europe.

Lutheranism: Lutheranism derives from Martin Luther, the original reformer. The Roman Catholic practice of indulgences (the belief that giving a specific donation to the Roman Catholic church would free one's soul from purgatory), among other things, troubled Luther. He established 95 theses about the church's practice and nailed them to the door of the church in Wittenberg, Germany, in 1519. After a debate with the local Catholic bishop on these things, Luther's ideas gained popularity. Although Luther only wished to reform the Roman Catholic church, reconciliation proved impossible in 1525 when Luther was excommunicated. Seeing no other viable alternative, Luther split from the Roman Catholic church, thus forming his own organization. Within the next century, Luther and his theology of "faith alone" would spread throughout many portions of the Holy Roman Empire and all of Scandinavia.

Anabaptism: Anabaptism ("baptism again") derives its name from the belief that one must be baptized as an adult believer, thus requiring many individuals who were "baptized" as infants to be baptized "again." This belief gained popularity in the Switzerland/southern Germany area in 1525 with the group named the "Swiss Brethren." Many Anabapists followed after Menno Simons, who in 1536 began preaching the need to be baptized as an adult, and this group was named after him: the Mennonites. Many smaller divisions occurred in the Anabaptism movement, yet there is one that stands out: in 1697, Jacob Amman split from the

Mennonite group because of his more conservative views on fellowship, thereby forming the Amish. The Anabaptists were heavily persecuted by Roman Catholic and Protestant alike. Many sought refuge in Russia, Germany, and later in North America as well.

Calvinism: In 1536, John Calvin, a native Frenchman, established his theology in Geneva, Switzerland, with his work *The Institutes of Christian Religion.* Calvin's theology, heavily influenced by Augustine, was predicated on a belief that God has already determined the fate of every man, and therefore that God's grace alone saved men. This hyper-Augustinianism persuaded many, and many of Calvin's disciples went out to spread his message. One such follower, John Knox, took Calvinism to Scotland, where the Presbyterian church was founded in the 1570s. In the seventeenth century, Calvinism took root in England in the form of Puritanism, which then took root in America. Today's Congregational church (also referred to as the United Church of Christ) is the descendant of the Puritans. Calvin's message was also taken to the area of the Netherlands in the early seventeenth century, leading to the formation of the Reformed Church.

Anglicanism: Also known as the Church of England, this church began in 1537, when King Henry VIII of England split from the Roman Catholic church since the latter would not grant an annulment to his marriage with Catherine of Aragon. After suffering persecution under Mary Tudor, the Anglican church was firmly established as England's church under Elizabeth I in the latter half of the sixteenth century. Anglicanism is still in existence in England and is known as the Episcopalian church in America.

Baptists: The Baptist movement began in England, and in its beginning, preached and taught the need for immersion in water for the remission of sin (hence, called the Baptists). "Officially" began by John Smythe in 1608, the movement spread quickly to America, where it took root and grew. Doctrinally, however, many moved toward Calvinistic beliefs regarding salvation and baptism, where most stand today. Many Baptists are affiliated with the Evangelical line of thinking, which represents a broad range of conservative Protestants, with uniform belief on the ideas of salvation and eschatology.

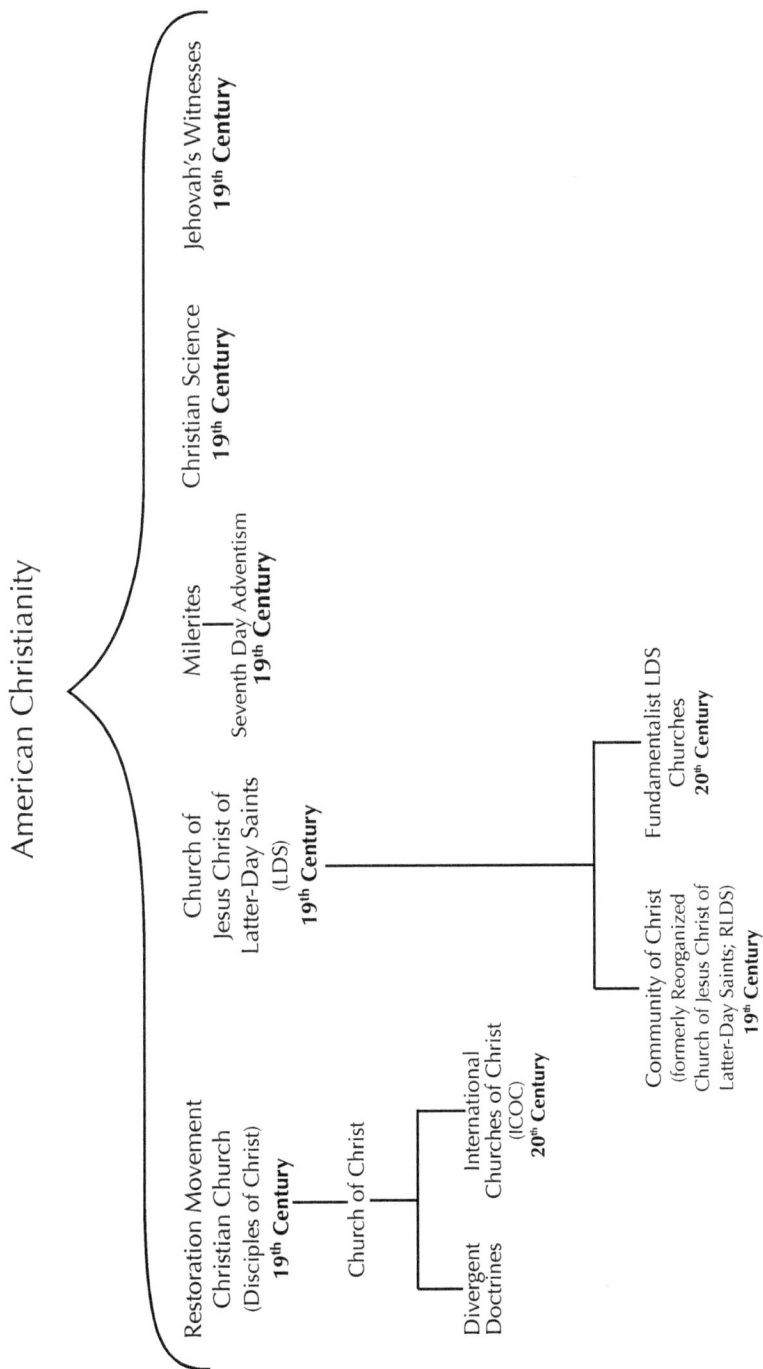

American Christianity

- Restoration Movement
  Christian Church
  (Disciples of Christ)
  19th Century
  - Church of Christ
    - International
      Churches of Christ
      (ICOC)
      20th Century
    - Divergent
      Doctrines

- Church of
  Jesus Christ of
  Latter-Day Saints
  (LDS)
  19th Century
  - Community of Christ
    (formerly Reorganized
    Church of Jesus Christ of
    Latter-Day Saints; RLDS)
    19th Century
  - Fundamentalist LDS
    Churches
    20th Century

- Milerites
  |
  Seventh Day Adventism
  19th Century

- Christian Science
  19th Century

- Jehovah's Witnesses
  19th Century

Religious Society of Friends (Quakers): The Religious Society of Friends began with one George Fox in England in 1648 as the result of supposed "revelations" given to him. He urged for reform in the thinking of Christians away from the concept of the "church" to a concept of a "society," a group of Christians who held each other in equal or better standing. The group's members received the term "Quakers" on account of the reports of people shaking with emotion in their assemblies. His movement was often persecuted, and is best known for its colony in Pennsylvania in America.

Pietism: Pietism is a movement that began within the Lutheran church in Germany in the seventeenth century. The members of this group desired to have a deeper personal faith as opposed to the often cold liturgical faith of the Lutheran establishment. Although many Pietists remained within the Lutheran fold, many others branched out and founded churches of their own. The Moravian Brethren are the supposed founders of the movement, dating back to the time of Jan Hus in the 1450s, although it is possible that the Hussites adopted the Pietist philosophies in the seventeenth century. The Church of the Brethren, the Brethren in Christ, and many other churches came out of this Pietist movement. There is also a group of Pietists which combined with some Mennonites, and are now known as the Mennonite Brethren.

Wesleyanism: Wesleyanism derives from John and Charles Wesley, members of the Anglican church. In 1729, they performed missionary work in America, and on the trip back to England, John learned of the faith of the Moravian Brethren. When back in England, the brothers founded a Methodist society and began to speak about the need of personal faith, sanctification, and "personal holiness," the continual development of maturity in Christian faith. The brothers desired to preach the need for personal faith within the Church of England, attempting to reform it. This worked well in England, but when the message spread to America, the Methodists split off from the Church of England and formed their own church. Wesleyan holiness theology was very persuasive in nineteenth century America, and many "holiness churches" were founded. Many of these churches consolidated in the twentieth century to form the Church of the Nazarene.

Phase IV: 1800 to the Present

The nineteenth century saw the rise of America as a power in the world, the first government founded on the principles of freedom. The freedom of religion enjoyed in America led to a vast number of new ideas and thus divisions, and the story of these groups will occupy the majority of the rest of the history of denominations.

Plymouth Brethren: The Plymouth Brethren began in 1827 in Ireland by four individuals who did not agree with the denominational attitudes of the "churches" around them and thus worshiped by themselves. This mentality spread, and the group (who simply are known to each other as the Brethren) had a large following in the town of Plymouth in England, and thus received their name. They are notable for the dispensational/pre-millennial belief system that would pervade much of nineteenth century American Christianity along with the modern Evangelical movement.

The Restoration Movement: The Restoration Movement fully began in the 1820s in America by the preaching of Thomas and Alexander Campbell and Barton Stone. These men recognized that denominations had departed from the message of the Scriptures with their creeds and doctrines and therefore desired to return to the faith of the Apostles. To this end, the Campbells established the Disciples of Christ, and Stone the Christian Church. These two groups soon merged, forming the Christian Church (Disciples of Christ). In the 1920s, as a response to what was viewed as growing liberalism in the Christian Church (Disciples of Christ) congregations, many split off to form what are now known as independent Christian Churches.

By the end of the nineteenth century, many within the Restoration Movement began to question some of the doctrines of the Christian Church (Disciples of Christ), especially regarding missionary societies and instrumental churches, and these Christians thus returned to the faith of the Apostles as given in the New Testament and took on the description of the Churches of Christ. Unfortunately, in the middle of the twentieth century, many such churches reverted to many doctrines of denominations, and many divisions have occurred as a result.

Mormonism: Officially the Church of Jesus Christ of Latter-Day Saints (LDS), Mormonism began with Joseph Smith, who claimed to receive a special vision in upper New York state in the 1820s, but the official beginning of the denomination was in 1830. Smith supposedly found plates written in "Reformed Egyptian" and tools by which to translate these plates. The resulting work was the *Book of Mormon*, used as additional Scripture by the LDS. Smith would later write other works, *The Pearl of Great Price* and *The Doctrines and Covenants*. The LDS believe in continuing revelation through their leaders; however, at the death of Joseph Smith and the declaration of Brigham Young as President, many Mormons departed from that denomination and established groups based either solely on the works of Smith or on the works of Smith combined with revelation given to their leaders. The most significant such group is the Reorganized Church of Jesus Christ of Latter-Day Saints (RLDS), now known as the Community of Christ, which uses only the texts of Smith.

Seventh-Day Adventism: The Seventh-Day Adventists began with some of those deemed Millerites, individuals who believed in the prophecies of William Miller, who believed the world would end in 1844. When 1844 came and went, many deemed this the "Great Disappointment." One such adherent, Ellen White, believed that she was given a prophetic gift and urged men and women to still prepare for the second coming of Christ (the Second Advent). Seventh-Day Adventism is also known for holding to many portions of the Law of Moses, including the Sabbath and dietary restrictions.

Christian Science: Beginning in the 1860s, a woman named Mary Baker Eddy believed that she was having revelations of truths kept silent since the Apostles concerning the illusion of reality and the superiority of "Mind" and spirit. Her work, *Science and Health with Key to the Scriptures*, posited that pain, illness, and even reality are merely mental conditions and that through correct discipline and training, one could control illness and disease. Through these beliefs she established "Christian Science" and the "Church of Christ, Scientist".

Jehovah's Witnesses: Jehovah's Witnesses (officially the Watch Tower Bible and Tract Society) originated around 1872 with Charles Taze Russell, who created the Watchtower Society to promote his beliefs. They derive their name from their practice of witnessing to others concerning the power in the "name" of God, the Tetragrammaton (YHWH) incorrectly translated as "Jehovah." The New World Translation of the Scriptures was made by the Jehovah's Witnesses to support their doctrines concerning the name of God, the lesser divinity of Jesus Christ, the lack of person of the Holy Spirit, and the perpetual existence of the earth.

The Salvation Army: The Salvation Army was established by William Booth in England in 1865 as essentially a modified form of Wesleyan Methodism, focusing on the need for benevolence while literalizing the metaphors in the Bible concerning "military" organization within the church.

Pentecostalism/The Charismatic Movement: Pentecostalism originated in the beginning of the twentieth century from the Wesleyan Holiness movement of the nineteenth. It was believed in 1901 that a woman received the "baptism of the Holy Spirit," since she supposedly spoke in tongues and demonstrated the gifts of the Holy Spirit as seen in the time of the Apostles. In 1904, this movement took off in Los Angeles with a revival in a building on Azusa Street, and many individuals were strongly impacted by the "baptism of the Holy Spirit" that occurred there. Many denominations, such as the Church of God in Christ (COGIC), the Assemblies of God, many of the Churches of God, and others began around this time because of these events.

Some of these Pentecostals began to believe around 1914 that baptism ought to be administered in the name of Jesus alone, since all of the features of God may be found in Christ alone. These individuals became known as the Oneness Pentecostals, and the United Pentecostal Church and some other groups are a part of this movement.

Beginning in the 1950s and 1960s, many members of other denominations began seeking the "baptism of the Holy Spirit" and many found it, and began to preach the ability to have the gifts in their own denominations. This was to be known as the Charismatic Movement, from the Greek word *charis*, meaning "gift."

Finally, in the later years of the twentieth century, many televangelists and others began to synthesize the gifts of the Holy Spirit with standard Evangelical-type theology, creating the "third wave" of Pentecostalism. This is seen especially with the proliferation of televangelism and also many churches such as the Vineyard Association of Churches.

International Church of Christ: Also known as the Boston Movement or the Crossroads Movement, the International Church of Christ began with Kip McKean, who, in 1979, established a congregation near Boston, Massachusetts, based upon his teachings, which were a combination of the doctrines of the Crossroads movement (which taught the idea of "discipling") and his own beliefs. Originally tenuously accepted by other congregations of churches of Christ, the growing radicalism of McKean's doctrines led to a clear division between "mainstream" churches of Christ any any group associated with the Boston Movement. The ICOC has gone through significant tumult since 2002 after the dissolution of the head leadership and the departure of Kip McKean; he has recently begun the "Portland Movement," attempting to return to the original concepts within the ICOC. These churches may go by the name "International Church of Christ" or "International Christian Church" (ICC).

Movements

During the twentieth and twenty-first centuries we have seen a large growth in movement-based Christianity. The popularity of ecumenism in this postmodern environment has led many to cross denominational boundaries and establish trans-denominational movements that are very popular.

Evangelicalism: The Evangelical movement finds its origins in the eighteenth century with the impetus to go out and promote the Gospel (or evangelize) that was shared by many denominations. Wesleyanism, Baptists, some Calvinists, and some Anglicans initially took part. The movement has continued to the present day. The Evangelical movement is based mostly on a "faith only" belief system, with most believing in some form of the "once saved, always saved" doctrine. Evangelicals tend to be dispensational/premillennial in eschatology, and at different times have been instruments for progress and conservatism in politics.

Ecumenism: The ecumenical movement was first organized in 1910 at the International Missionary Conference in Edinburgh, Scotland. The movement attempts to unify divergent Christian denominations by emphasizing shared beliefs while minimizing differences. The movement is best manifest in the World Council of Churches and the National Council of Churches, organizations devoted to inter-denominational dialogue and action. As postmodernism and relativism have grown in popularity in the past fifty years, more and more denominations are becoming a part of the ecumenical movement.

Fundamentalism: Fundamentalism is a movement within Evangelicalism that began in the late nineteenth century as a reaction to the "liberal" tendencies in many Protestant denominations that undermined confidence in the inspiration of the Bible. Other evangelicals and fundamentalists parted ways in the 1940s; today, fundamentalism is marked by passionate defenses of the perceived "fundamentals" of the faith, often involving as much tradition as it does substantive Biblical truth.

The Community Church Movement: Community churches are first seen explicitly in the 1920s, although financial necessity may have compelled various members of denominations in small villages to meet together in times past. The Community Church movement is a consequence of the evangelical and ecumenical movements: if denominational boundaries are not going to be considered important anymore, the impetus is there to have an organization without any such denominational affiliation, and therefore we have community churches. While community churches profess having no denomination, the doctrines of denominations, particularly those present within the Evangelical movement, abound.

The House Church Movement: While Christians have met in houses since the beginning (cf. Philemon 1.2), and there is no stigma to meeting in houses *per se*, in the latter part of the twentieth century there has been a movement to rid churches of many of the vestiges of traditionalism, and many such persons have established "house churches". The difficulties with such movements are not in meeting in houses *per se*, but the other doctrines that tend to go with such groups.

The Megachurch Movement: While there have been many churches of large size before the modern day, beginning in the 1950s, America and other "Christianized" countries saw the emergence of very large churches having many thousands of members, now called "megachurches". Half of existing megachurches are not affiliated with a particular denomination but have connections to the Evangelical and Charismatic movements. Many megachurches develop as cults of personalities surrounding popular preachers. Megachurches tend to emphasize services heavily influenced by modern forms of entertainment and focus on self-empowerment through small groups and inspirational literature. Mega-churches are also known for their large buildings, support groups, coffeehouses, bookstores, and other forms of marketing and materialism.

The Emergent Movement: The twenty-first century has seen the birth of the emergent movement, a diverse group of individuals, mostly of the Evangelical movement, who seek to communicate to the postmodern world using postmodern conceptualizations of Christianity. While the members of the movement would like to bridge the divide between "liberal" and "conservative" branches of Protestantism, there is much concern regarding their wholehearted embrace of postmodernism and its ideals.

Conclusion

We have now reached the present time and can see, if only quickly and without exhaustive detail, the development of the denominations and movements that exist in the "Christian" world today. The path is difficult to determine and very confusing, yet we can see that the majority of these denominations were established on the basis of new ideas of men and those who would follow them. The rest of the study will focus on these ideas and doctrines to determine whether or not they are in harmony with the teachings of the Scriptures.

Part I: Denominations

Roman Catholicism, I: Authority

Overview

The Roman Catholic church was formed in 1054 after the bishop of Rome sent a bull of excommunication to the patriarch of Constantinople, effectively splitting what is deemed the "catholic" church. The Roman Catholic church, headed by the pope and other bishops within what is called the Magisterium, is a constantly evolving church, continuously re-evaluating doctrinal positions and philosophies. Our consideration will focus primarily on the current doctrines of the Roman Catholic church, speaking of past doctrines only to demonstrate the inconsistencies and contradictions inherent in the tradition.

Variants

The Roman Catholic church has two forms of divisions within it, one involving different variants in worship while holding to the Roman Catholic authority, and one group that split off in the nineteenth century. There are differences in the way that certain practices of the church are performed in various areas, specifically concerning the mass and the sacraments. These variants are called "rites," and they tend to be divided by geographical regions. The current major rites recognized by the Roman Catholic church are as follows: Latin, Byzantine, Alexandrian (or Coptic), Syriac, Armenian, Maronite, and Chaldean.[1] Former Eastern Orthodox who converted to Roman Catholicism have also been given certain privileges, and they are known as the Eastern Rite Catholic Church. Further, after the Roman Catholic Church's Vatican Council of 1870, many Roman Catholics disagreed with the doctrine of papal infallibility that was approved in that council, and formed what is known as the "Old Catholic" churches [these churches include the Mariavite Old Catholic Church, North American Old Roman Catholic Church, and Old Roman Catholic Church (English Rite)]. From these groups, the Liberal Catholic church split off around

1916. There is also the Polish National Catholic Church of America, organized mostly to allow immigrant communities full ownership of their cathedrals, *et al.*, and a measure of autonomy.

General Considerations

Part I
- *Eastern Orthodoxy: The Problem With Petrine Authority*
- *Lutheranism: The Lord's Prayer*
- *Wesleyanism: The Church and Social Responsibility*

Part II
- *Ecumenism*

Part III
- *Baptism: Infant Baptism and "Original Sin"; Baptism is Immersion; Tripartite Baptism*
- *The Church Treasury, I: Benevolence: Church Benevolence to Non–Saints; The Missionary Society*
- *The Church Treasury, II: Other Considerations: Hospitals; Centers of Education; Kitchens/Fellowship Halls; Business Enterprises*

Concerning Observances:
- *Observances Concerning the Lord's Birth: Advent, Christmas*
- *Observances Concerning the Lord's Death: Ash Wednesday, Lent, Holy Thursday, Good Friday, Easter*
- *Other Observances: Ascension/Pentecost, Epiphany, Annunciation, Days Concerning Saints*
- *Creeds: The Apostles' Creed ; The Nicene Creed; The Athanasian Creed*
- *Instrumental Music*
- *Judaic Practices: The Ten Commandments and the "Moral Law"; Tithing*
- *The Lord's Supper: The Nature of the Emblems; The Bread and the Fruit of the Vine; When Should the Lord's Supper Be Observed? Part A: Weekly*
- *Positions of Authority: A Hierarchy of Bishops; Priests; Ordination Synods, Councils, Conventions, and Other Meetings*

The Papacy

The Roman Catholic church has at its head the pope, an individual appointed by a college of bishops, and who rules for life. He sits on what is called the "see of Peter," the chair whose occupant holds the authority given to Peter. The pope and the bishops around him make up the Magisterium, which determines the faith of the Roman Catholic church through the interpretation of Scripture and the use of tradition.[2] The statements of doctrine made by the Magisterium are deemed to be infallible.[3] This authority is believed to have been derived from Peter himself, who is attested as being a pope. Let us examine whether Peter was a pope and then whether the magisterial system of authority is truly valid in the eyes of God.

Scriptural Considerations

The main Scripture concerning Peter is his confession in Matthew 16.15–19:

> He saith unto them, "But who say ye that I am?"
> And Simon Peter answered and said, "Thou art the Christ, the
> Son of the living God."
> And Jesus answered and said unto him, "Blessed art thou, Simon
> Bar-jonah: for flesh and blood hath not revealed it unto thee, but
> my Father who is in heaven. And I also say unto thee, that thou
> art Peter, and upon this rock I will build my church; and the gates
> of Hades shall not prevail against it. I will give unto thee the keys
> of the kingdom of heaven: and whatsoever thou shalt bind on
> earth shall be bound in heaven; and whatsoever thou shalt loose
> on earth shall be loosed in heaven."

It is upon this verse that the Roman Catholic church asserts that Christ established His church on Peter[4] and that the one who sits on the chair of Peter has authority to determine matters of faith. But is this what Jesus intends for us to understand from this text?

While it is true that Jesus is presenting a play on words, calling Simon "Peter" (Greek *petros*) and speaking of building His church on "this rock" (Greek *petra*), there is nothing in the text that requires Jesus to be speaking about the same "rock." As we see from all the evidence available in the New Testament, the best interpretation of this passage is to recognize that Jesus has two different rocks in mind: Peter (and by extension the other eleven), who will do great things in the church, but it is upon the rock of Peter's confession that Jesus builds His church. Let us consider Matthew 18.18 in terms of Peter's authority:

> "Verily I say unto you, what things soever ye shall bind on earth shall be bound in heaven; and what things soever ye shall loose on earth shall be loosed in heaven."

This is the same statement made by Jesus in Matthew 16.19, and this time it cannot be denied that Jesus is speaking to the twelve disciples (Matthew 18.1). The Roman Catholic church does not deny this, yet states that the apostles are given all authority for binding and loosing, while only Peter has the keys to the Kingdom.[5] This statement made by Christ, however, demonstrates that He was speaking to the twelve in Matthew 16, and that the promise of the foundation of the church was for all of them (Cf. Acts 2, Ephesians 2.20).

It must also be stated that the Roman Catholic church believes that Peter and the other Apostles were given the authority to determine doctrine because of Jesus' statement that "whatsoever you bind shall be bound in Heaven, and whatsoever you loose shall be loosed in Heaven."[6] However, this statement is inaccurate according to the Greek: the text reads correctly, "whatsoever you bind shall have been bound in Heaven, and whatsoever you shall loose shall have been loosed in Heaven." This proves that the work of the Apostles was not performed on their own initiative but on the initiative of their Father in Heaven.

There is also reason to believe that the name given to Simon by Christ was not necessarily given to him first at his confession, for we read the following in John 1.41–42:

> He findeth first his own brother Simon, and saith unto him, "We have found the Messiah" (which is, being interpreted, Christ). He brought him unto Jesus. Jesus looked upon him, and said, "Thou art Simon the son of John: thou shalt be called Cephas" (which is by interpretation, Peter).

This is at the beginning of Christ's ministry; the events of the latter part of John chapter one correlate with the time period of Matthew chapters three and four, long before the confession in Matthew 16. Thus, the name Peter was given long before the account in Matthew 16 and is not a special title demonstrating his authority in the Kingdom.

The Scriptures themselves show that the idea that Peter is the singular foundation of the church is incorrect. Paul states the following in 1 Corinthians 3.11 and Ephesians 2.20:

> For other foundation can no man lay than that which is laid, which is Jesus Christ.

> Being built upon the foundation of the apostles and prophets, Christ Jesus himself being the chief corner stone.

We see that Paul states emphatically that the foundation of the church is much more than Peter. Chief of all is Jesus the Christ, the cornerstone, without whom there would be no church. The foundation also includes the apostles and prophets; Peter is therefore a part of the foundation, but yet is not the foundation by himself.

Historical Considerations

History also speaks against Peter being a pope. There is no text that states that he ever filled that position; his presence in Rome is only based on tradition. The argument that Peter had the authority from Christ and that it then was continued through a succession, based on Matthew 16.18, was not even used until Pope Stephen I in 250, almost two hundred years after the death of Peter.

Furthermore, history as seen through the Scriptures also speaks against the supposed authority of Peter. We read the following in Matthew 20.20–24:

> Then came to him the mother of the sons of Zebedee with her sons, worshipping Him, and asking a certain thing of him.
> And He said unto her, "What wouldest thou?"
> She saith unto Him, "Command that these my two sons may sit, one on Thy right hand, and one on Thy left hand, in Thy kingdom."
> But Jesus answered and said, "Ye know not what ye ask. Are ye able to drink the cup that I am about to drink?"
> They say unto Him, "We are able."
> He saith unto them, "My cup indeed ye shall drink: but to sit on My right hand, and on My left hand, is not Mine to give; but it is for them whom it hath been prepared of My Father."

> And when the ten heard it, they were moved with indignation
> concerning the two brethren.

Why would the ten, including Peter, be indignant with the two brothers?
The two brothers asked to obtain the authority before they did! Furthermore, had it been made clear by Jesus in Matthew 16 that Peter was to
be the foundation of the Kingdom, why would the mother of the sons of
Zebedee ever dare ask Christ for her sons to have this authority? Why do
they seem to be willing partners in this request? If the authority of Peter were as valid as the Roman Catholic church declares, the other elev-
en apostles would have recognized it. Matthew 20.20–24 demonstrates,
however, that this was not the case.

Character Considerations

The Scriptures also speak of the character of Peter, and they show a different kind of character than what we see in the papacy today.

First, Peter was married. This is made clear by Matthew 8.14 and 1
Corinthians 9.5:

> And when Jesus was come into Peter's house, He saw his wife's
> mother lying sick of a fever.

> Have we no right to lead about a wife that is a believer, even as
> the rest of the apostles, and the brethren of the Lord, and Ce-
> phas?

Here we see that Peter was married not only while a disciple of Christ,
but even while being one of His Apostles! This is in complete harmony
with his position as an elder in 1 Peter 5.1 and the need for an elder to
be married in 1 Timothy 3.2. This marriage is not in harmony with the
Roman Catholic teachings concerning the pope and all ecclesiastical authorities, who are to remain celibate.[7]

We also see a great humility being displayed by Peter, especially in
Acts 10.25–26:

> And when it came to pass that Peter entered, Cornelius met him,
> and fell down at his feet, and worshipped him.
> But Peter raised him up, saying, "Stand up; I myself also am a man."

This humility is fitting for a servant of the Lord Jesus Christ (Luke 18.14); however, this humility is not seen in the papacy today, wherein the pope receives much reverence to the point of being worshiped.

We also see that Peter is content with being "one among many," as seen in 1 Peter 5.1–3:

> The elders among you I exhort, who am a fellow-elder, and a witness of the sufferings of Christ, who am also a partaker of the glory that shall be revealed: Tend the flock of God which is among you, exercising the oversight, not of constraint, but willingly, according to the will of God; nor yet for filthy lucre, but of a ready mind; neither as lording it over the charge allotted to you, but making yourselves examples to the flock.

Here, Peter declares himself to be a "fellow elder." If Peter were given some form of higher authority, he would emphasize it here. He does not, however; all he does is say that he is an elder among other elders. This attitude is not seen in the bishop of Rome; he was not content to be an elder among fellow elders, especially in 1054, when the actions of the pope separated the "catholic" church.

Concerning infallibility, it is clear that Peter was far from infallible. We read the following in Galatians 2.11–13:

> But when Cephas came to Antioch, I resisted him to the face, because he stood condemned. For before that certain came from James, he ate with the Gentiles; but when they came, he drew back and separated himself, fearing them that were of the circumcision. And the rest of the Jews dissembled likewise with him; insomuch that even Barnabas was carried away with their dissimulation.

These are the same people who Peter declares are now accepted by God in the apostolic council of Acts 15.7–11, and now, he separates himself from them—a clear error in doctrine. Yet the papacy receives their infallibility from him?

It is therefore clear that Peter is not the only part of the foundation of the church: Jesus is the principal part of the foundation, being the chief corner stone, while Peter resides with the other eleven Apostles along with the prophets as the rest of the church's foundation. It is also clear that Peter was not a pope, but just an elder among elders in a local congregation, either in Antioch or in Jerusalem, in the middle of the first century. Peter's character also contrasts sharply with the characteristics of the papacy today.

Apostolic Succession

The other fundamental tenet of the authority system in the Roman Catholic church is that the authority given to Peter and the apostles was handed down to the pope and bishops of first the "catholic" church and then the Roman Catholic church, even to this day.[8] This is justified by appealing to the system of evangelists and elderships instituted in the early church, as seen in Matthew 28.20 and Titus 1.5.[9] Is this truly the practice of the early church?

We can see in **Positions of Authority: A Hierarchy of Bishops**, that the Apostles and their fellow evangelists did establish an eldership, but the eldership was set up to be a plurality of elders in a single congregation (cf. Philippians 1.1). There is no indication from the Scriptures that any gift of the Holy Spirit concerning knowledge or interpretation was given to them alone. Furthermore, the role of the evangelist was delineated from a position of authority in Romans 12.7. Another blow to the idea that the powers held by the Apostles were able to be handed down can be seen in Acts 8.14–17, where we see that Peter and John had to come to Samaria from Jerusalem to bestow the gift of the Holy Spirit upon the Samaritans; Philip clearly could not do so. It is clear that the Apostles could give the gift of the Holy Spirit, but there is no indication that others could do the same.

The argument of apostolic succession developed to justify the truth of what was being presented by later Christians. They would say that since their church had an unbroken succession of leaders back to the Apostles, then their teachings could therefore be certified as true. Yet this is never a guideline in the Scriptures for legitimacy; many churches were founded by Apostles and yet believed falsely (cf. 1/2 Corinthians, Galatians). Truth was and is based in what God has revealed (2 Timothy 3.16–17, 1 John 4.1).

Thus, we can see that the Scriptures do not teach that there is an "apostolic succession" from Peter and the Apostles through a system of a pope and bishops through the ages. The Scriptures do show us a pattern of shepherds, a plurality of elders for each local congregation, as seen in

Positions of Authority. Therefore, the system of authority promulgated by the Roman Catholic church is without Scriptural validity.

Notes

1: *Catechism of the Catholic Church*, Pt. II, par. 1203 (listed as Roman numeral and paragraph number for the rest of the notes)

2: Ibid., I. 100; I. 877; 880

3: Ibid., III. 2035

4: Ibid., I. 552–553

5: Ibid., I. 553

6: Ibid., I. 881

7: Ibid., II. 1579

8: Ibid., I. 100; II. 1555–1557

9: Ibid., I. 860–861

Roman Catholicism, II: Tradition

Apostolic Tradition

The Roman Catholic church holds dearly to what they call Apostolic Tradition. They believe that the Apostles entrusted the church with the Scriptures and "oral teachings," or traditions.[1] This belief is justified using verses like 2 Thessalonians 3.6:

> Now we command you, brethren, in the name of our Lord Jesus Christ, that ye withdraw yourselves from every brother that walketh disorderly, and not after the tradition which they received of us.

Let us examine this assertion.

First, if there is a tradition from the Apostles, there must be proof of its origin. The Roman Catholic church must prove that the traditions that they hold to came down as an oral tradition from the Apostles. So far, no such evidence has been presented.

The one piece of evidence we have from the Apostles is the New Testament. We see within it in 2 Timothy 3.16–17:

> Every scripture inspired of God is also profitable for teaching, for reproof, for correction, for instruction which is in righteousness. That the man of God may be complete, furnished completely unto every good work.

The Scriptures themselves say that they are inspired, and they will make the man of God "adequate," and he will be "equipped for every good work." Therefore, it can be concluded that there is no good work that can be done that is not authorized in the Scriptures.

It is often said in response to this that when Paul wrote 2 Timothy, the New Testament had not yet been formed. This is only half-true. Paul, in 1 Timothy 5.18, quotes Luke in Luke 10.7 as a "Scripture," so it is certain that Paul knew of some of what would become the New Testament canon. The Scriptures themselves attest to their own sufficiency.

Some will also say that the Scriptures themselves testify that they do not include all matters of faith, based upon John 20.30–31 and John 21.25:

> Many other signs therefore did Jesus in the presence of the disciples, which are not written in this book: but these are written, that ye may believe that Jesus is the Christ, the Son of God; and that believing ye may have life in His name.

> And there are also many other things which Jesus did, the which if they should be written every one, I suppose that even the world itself would not contain the books that should be written.

This does affirm that the Scriptures do not contain the information concerning all of the works and deeds of Christ and His Apostles. Yet John states in John 21.25 that the world itself could not contain such information! Surely if the information was too vast for Scripture, no tradition could even contain all of it. The answer to this claim is seen in John 20.31, that the Scriptures are written so that "you may believe that Jesus is the Christ, the Son of God"; what else is necessary concerning the Gospel? No one would say that the Scriptures contain every fact that could be known about Christ or His Apostles; the Scriptures do, however, affirm that within their pages will be found all the information that is necessary for salvation.

The Scriptures do speak of tradition as we saw in 2 Thessalonians 3.6, but what exactly are these traditions? The only sure evidence of Apostolic traditions comes from the Scriptures themselves. There certainly are traditions that we can see in the Scriptures, including the practice of baptism for remission of sins (Acts 2.38), the partaking of the Lord's Supper (Acts 20.7; 1 Corinthians 11), and many other such things. We even see that there are traditions concerning Christ which made it into the Scriptures. John 7.53–8.11 presents the story of Jesus with the adulterous woman. The earliest texts of the New Testament do not contain this section in this location; furthermore, within the structure of the Gospel, it seems to clearly be an addition, for John 7.52 and John 8.12 seem to be connected. Yet few will doubt the authenticity of the story. This narrative, then, represents a tradition concerning Jesus that was made a part of the Scriptures. Likewise, there is the statement of Paul in Acts 20.35:

"In all things I gave you an example, that so laboring ye ought to
help the weak, and to remember the words of the Lord Jesus, that
He Himself said, 'It is more blessed to give than to receive.'"

This statement of Jesus is not recorded in any of our Gospel narratives.
Does this mean it is not true? By no means! Here is another example of
a tradition concerning Jesus that is now part of the Scriptures. The statement is clearly in harmony with the nature of Jesus, so there is no contradiction in the matter.

There is not necessarily a problem with tradition, as long as it is a part
of the commandments of God, not the traditions of men, as Christ established in Mark 7.8–9:

"Ye leave the commandment of God, and hold fast the tradition of
men."
And He said unto them, "Full well do ye reject the commandment
of God, that ye may keep your tradition."

The only way to truly examine the claims of apostolic tradition made by
the Roman Catholic church is to compare them to the commandments
made by the Word of God. Let us do so now.

Traditions Concerning the Scriptures

The Roman Catholic church teaches that the Scriptures were determined
by tradition, and that one must read the Scriptures in the context of tradition.[2] Is this verified by history?

We have already seen above that Paul quoted Luke's Gospel as Scripture, and surely one would not say that the Scriptures were determined
by tradition found within the Scriptures. Furthermore, in 2 Peter 3.15–
17, Peter gives his endorsement to the letters of Paul.

Beyond even this, the historical record shows clearly that the vast majority of the New Testament was accepted as authoritative within years
of the death of their authors. The "church fathers" of the early second
century demonstrate familiarity with twenty of the books of the New
Testament; by the end of that century, all but three were agreed upon,
and two of those not due to their authoritativeness, but because one of
those had no author listed (Hebrews) and the other's prophecy was too
often misused by the heretics (Revelation). Historically, it is clear that

no tradition determined Scripture, but the knowledge that the works contained in the New Testament were written by the Apostles and their followers.

The Roman Catholic church also accepts nine apocryphal works of the second century BCE as a part of the Old Testament: Tobit, Judith, 1 Maccabees, 2 Maccabees, the extended version of Esther, additions to Daniel, Wisdom of Solomon, Sirach, and Baruch.[3] Are these inspired works, directed by God's hands?

First of all, it is important to note that the Roman Catholic church did not accept all apocryphal works from this time period; the Septuagint, the Greek version of the Old Testament from which all of these books were derived, also included 1 Esdras, Epistle of Jeremiah, 3 Maccabees, 4 Maccabees, and the Prayer of Manasseh. Not one of these apocryphal works were ever quoted or clearly referred to in the words of Christ and the writings of the Apostles, despite their familiarity with the Septuagint.

They did not quote or refer to them for good reason. Three of the historical works (Tobit, Judith, and the extended Esther) are historically inconsistent with known facts, as shown below:

Tobit: In Tobit 1.15, the author refers to the change of Assyrian kingship from Shalmaneser to Sennacherib. Let the note from the Roman Catholic church's authorized English translation of the Bible, the New American Bible, speak for itself:

> Sennacherib (705–681 BCE): the son of Sargon (722–705 BCE); neither was descended from Shalmaneser. Inconsistencies such as this point to the fact that Tobit is a religious novel.[4]

Even the Roman Catholic authorities admit that this work is "religious fiction!"

Judith: In Judith 1.1, the author refers to Nebuchadnezzar as "king of Assyria," even though he is always known as the king of Babylon in the Scriptures. There is also Judith 4.1–3:

> When the Israelites who dwelt in Judea heard of all that Holofernes, commander in chief of Nebuchadnezzar, king of the Assyrians, had done to the nations, and how he had despoiled all their temples and

destroyed them, they were in extreme dread of him, and greatly alarmed for Jerusalem and the temple of the LORD, their God. Now, they had lately returned from exile, and only recently had the people of Judea been gathered together, and the vessels, the altar, and the temple been purified from profanation.

This whole passage is historically inconsistent and anachronistic; we know that Sennacherib king of Assyria threatened Judea under the reign of Hezekiah (2 Chronicles 32), that later Nebuchadnezzar king of Babylon conquered Judea (2 Chronicles 36.6–21), and during the reign of Cyrus I of Persia, the Israelites returned to Judea from their exile (2 Chronicles 36.22–23). These historical inconsistencies point to the fictional nature of this story.

The extended Esther: Esther, when giving an address in Esther chapter E, verse 14, speaks of how one Haman attempted to turn the Persian rule over to the Macedonians. This statement would make a lot of sense about a hundred and twenty-five years after Esther was alive, for at that time the Macedonians overran the Persian Empire. However, at the time of Esther (the era of Xerxes I), Macedonia was a Greek backwater, easily overtaken in Xerxes' rush to conquer Greece.

1 Maccabees: The final, and most condemning, evidence comes from 1 Maccabees. The author of 1 Maccabees indicates numerous times that there are no prophets in the land, and establishes that there has been the passage of some time since prophets had been in the land (1 Maccabees 4.46, 9.27, 14.41). This indicates that the author of 1 Maccabees did not consider himself a prophet or anyone else of his own day as prophets. How, then, can inspired Scripture be written when no one is being guided by the Holy Spirit (cf. 2 Peter 1.20)? Since there is no good evidence for the inspiration of any of the authors of these books, along with the numerous inconsistencies within them, we can establish that they are not Scripture. There is profit in reading them to understand intertestamental Judaism, but the works are not at the level of Scripture.

The reading of Scripture in the context of tradition would not be a problem unless the traditions upheld were inconsistent with the Scriptures. As we see and will see, it does appear that the tradition upheld by the

Roman Catholic church is inconsistent with the truths of Scripture, thus, we should not attempt to read Scripture in the context of errors.

Finally, many Roman Catholics will argue that the Scriptures are impossible for an individual to understand and to be able upon which to render judgment. On account of this, it is necessary to have someone with authority to interpret the Scriptures to assist in the knowledge of Christ. They appeal to 2 Peter 3.15–16 for their evidence:

> And account that the longsuffering of our Lord is salvation; even as our beloved brother Paul also, according to the wisdom given to him, wrote unto you; as also in all his epistles, speaking in them of these things; wherein are some things hard to be understood, which the ignorant and unstedfast wrest, as they do also the other scriptures, unto their own destruction.

It should be noted that Peter does not say here that Paul's writings are impossible to understand, merely that "some parts" are "hard to understand." We do not see any indication in the New Testament that an "authority" was required for the understanding of Scripture. We do see that elders ought to shepherd the flock and that they must be able to teach (1 Timothy 3.1–2), but Paul never declares that the elders are to interpret the Scriptures for the flock or to determine matters of doctrine by themselves. Paul actually commands us to study the Word diligently, as seen in 2 Timothy 2.15:

> Give diligence to present thyself approved unto God, a workman that needeth not to be ashamed, handling aright the word of truth.

Therefore, we can see that in the Scriptures, it is the responsibility of the individual to study the Word of God and to determine the truths of Scripture, and not to just accept what has been taught to them by a superior.

Traditions Concerning the Sacraments

The Roman Catholic church teaches that there are seven "sacraments," particular actions that are considered holy. These seven are baptism, confirmation, Eucharist, Penance, Anointing of the Sick, Holy Orders, and Matrimony.[5] The only considerations concerning baptism are that the Roman Catholic church baptizes infants and allows for pouring, as discussed in **Baptism**. The Eucharist and the difficulties inherent in the doctrine of transubstantiation are addressed in **The Lord's Supper: The Nature of the Emblems: Transubstantiation**. Certain aspects of the Holy Orders are mentioned in **Positions of Authority: A Hierarchy of Bishops,** demonstrating that a hierarchy of bishops was not present in the New Testament church. There is no problem with matrimony, and even though it is not often practiced, there is nothing in the Scriptures against the anointing of the sick. Penance will be discussed below in **Traditions Concerning Sin.** Let us, then, speak of the final sacrament, confirmation.

Confirmation is the anointing of an individual who has been baptized into the Roman Catholic church yet has not partaken of the Eucharist.[6] For those baptized as infants, this sacrament is performed at the "age of discretion," or, if a child is in danger of death, immediately.[7] Catechumens, or adult converts to Roman Catholicism, receive confirmation immediately after baptism.[8]

We see no such practice in the Scriptures; however, the Roman Catholic church declares that confirmation today is seen in the "laying on of hands" of the New Testament.[9] Does the use of "laying on of hands" conform to the sacrament of confirmation?

The laying on of hands in the New Testament is most often seen immediately after baptism as the giving of the Holy Spirit. This was done only by the authority of the Apostles; we see this in Acts 8.14, since Peter and Paul had to come to Samaria to give the recent converts the gift of the Holy Spirit, for such power was not in the hands of Philip. Even though the Roman Catholic church asserts that only a bishop can perform a confirmation,[10] and that the bishops receive authority from the Apostles, we have shown earlier that this is not the case. Without this authority, there is no transfer of the Holy Spirit in the laying on of hands.

We must also see the natural progression for the need of confirmation. When infants began to be baptized, some seal was required for their faith once they attained the age of maturity. The New Testament teaches that the only seal of Christ and the Holy Spirit is for a believer to be baptized in water for the remission of their sins (Acts 2.38); confirmation, therefore, is an addition made necessary by the practice of baptizing infants. We conclude, therefore, that the Scriptures teach that people enter into Christ through baptism and have no need of any such "confirmation."

Traditions Concerning the Church

The Roman Catholic church has a very institutional view of the church; it even goes so far as to call the church the "mother" of its members.[11] Is this view consistent with the nature of the church of the New Testament?

In Romans 12 and 1 Corinthians 12, the church is considered to be like a body, with different parts working to the betterment of the whole. This idea is completely inconsistent with the notion that the church is as a mother—how can a body have its origin in itself? The only founder of the church is Christ Jesus, who purchased it with His blood (1 Corinthians 3.11). To assert that the church has any other founder would be blasphemy.

While the New Testament does demonstrate an informal relationship between members of different churches, particularly in the same Roman districts, the New Testament betrays no knowledge of any organization or structure beyond the local congregation. According to the New Testament, one is saved by being in Christ and therefore part of His Church, not being part of His Church and therefore saved (cf. Acts 2.47). There is no New Testament precedent, therefore, for the highly structured and institutional view of the Roman Catholic organization.

Traditions Concerning History

The Roman Catholic church considers its history as the following:

> As the First Vatican Council noted, the "Church herself, with her marvelous propagation, eminent holiness, and inexhaustible fruitfulness in everything good, her catholic unity and invincible stability, is a great and perpetual motive of credibility and an irrefutable witness of her divine mission." [12]

Does this statement conform to any objective understanding of history?

Time and space would fail if we were to examine every instance wherein the Roman Catholic church acted in a manner most unsuited to a body bearing the name of Christ. Let us consider a few examples:

The Donation of Constantine: This document supposedly came from Constantine, and it ceded the power of the western Roman Empire to the bishop of Rome. This document was officially presented to Pepin, king of France, in 754, and accepted as legitimate.[13] For the next five hundred years, the pope used this document to effectively control western Europe. In the thirteenth century, scholars within the Roman Catholic church itself proved the document to be a forgery, composed not long before it was presented to Pepin.

The Crusades: Called for by Pope Urban II in 1095 when the Muslims closed Jerusalem to all foreigners, the Crusades have few parallels in bloodiness and savagery. Roman Catholic knights from throughout western Europe traveled to Asia Minor and Israel, sacking and plundering the cities of Eastern Orthodox and Muslims alike, raping women and slaughtering all of the men, all in the name of Christ.

The Fourth Crusade: In 1204, another Crusade was called, this time for Egypt. Assembling in Constantinople, the Crusaders began to get involved with the political intrigues of the Byzantines. Losing patience quickly, the Crusaders turned on Constantinople and conquered the city, killing thousands of the Eastern Orthodox. This action firmly divided the Eastern Orthodox church from the Roman Catholic church.

The Reformation: The excesses of the Roman Catholic church in the fifteenth and sixteenth centuries led many to become greatly dissatisfied with the Roman Catholic church. These excesses include popes who had secret affairs, a pope using his position of power to help install his son as ruler of Florence (Alexander VI), and "pope" Julius II, known as the "Warrior Pope," who was bent on conquering more of the Italian peninsula for his own territory, and lavishly funded such structures as the Basilica of St. Peter in Rome with indulgence money obtained throughout Europe.

Martin Luther's nailing of the ninety-five theses on the door in Wittenberg began the Reformation, after which ensued bloody conflict for the next century. Much blood was shed throughout Europe due to this division. While no attempt is being made to exonerate the Protestants from the blood that they shed, the actions of the Roman Catholic church to suppress this division did not conform to the pattern established by the First Vatican Council.

There are many, however, who will strive to entirely exonerate the Roman Catholic organization from any of this and will attempt to pin the blame on the secular authorities of the day. Historically, such is a desperate attempt to use a technicality to distort reality: while secular authorities had much to do with the Crusades and the Spanish Inquisition, it is not as if Rome was unaware of what was going on. Such events occurred with the approval of the Roman Catholic authorities and oftentimes were encouraged by them. Attempting to shift the blame does not change the reality of the matter.

Nevertheless, some will confess the difficulties of these actions, but will say that they are the result of the sins of men, and that the church cannot be blamed for the deeds of men. We must establish that it is not as if we strive to hold the Roman Catholic organization to any other level than it would seem to hold itself: if they recognize that terrible actions have been done in its name to its own shame, they should confess as much without striving to portray its history as consistently excellent. Furthermore, the majority of these and other actions were approved by the popes and the bishops of these time periods, and the Roman Catholic church teaches that ordained individuals cannot be separated from the church;[14] therefore, the church also cannot be separated from the deeds of those ordained.

The first Crusade, for instance, was called for by the pope, preached in the parishes by the bishops and priests, affirmed by the ruling classes and the soldiery, and performed by the soldiers who were a part of the Roman Catholic church. To say that the Roman Catholic church was not responsible for this would be like saying that the President of the United States declared war on a country, it was affirmed by Congress, and the military affirmed and carried it out, but the United States was not responsible for the war. The Roman Catholic church is surely guilty of many indecent and worldly actions which caused much harm and grief not only to many parts of the world, but also to the One in whose name these deeds were performed, Jesus the Christ. The Roman Catholic church is surely not the paragon of purity that the First Vatican Council has declared.

Traditions Concerning Mary

The Roman Catholic church thinks very highly of Mary, the mother of Jesus; to them, she "illumines" the faith in Christ.[15] They teach that she was not liable to original sin, having been conceived without sin, and was sinless,[16] she was a perpetual virgin,[17] and was assumed at death.[18] She has special roles concerning the church in the belief system of the Roman Catholic church, as she is deemed to be the mother of the church,[19] that she aided the early church with prayers and continues to be the main "pray-er" for the church,[20] and she is the "exemplary realization" of the church;[21] thus, Mary is often prayed to by Roman Catholics to intercede on their behalf in the presence of Christ.[22] Finally, the teachings of the Roman Catholic church can be summed up with the following: "she is mother wherever He is Savior and head of the Mystical Body."[23] Do these teachings conform to what we see regarding Mary in the New Testament?

In the New Testament, Mary is surely blessed, being the mother of the Son of God (Luke 1.28). She helps to raise Him, and He makes sure that she is taken care of at His death (John 19.26–27). She is nowhere mentioned, however, as being the "mother" of the church, or an intercessor in prayer, or having any role whatsoever in the New Testament church.

Jesus speaks of His mother in Matthew 12.46–50:

> While He was yet speaking to the multitudes, behold, His mother and His brethren stood without, seeking to speak to him.
> And one said unto Him, "Behold, Thy mother and Thy brethren stand without, seeking to speak to Thee."
> But He answered and said unto him that told Him, "Who is My mother? and who are My brethren?"
> And He stretched forth His hand towards His disciples, and said, "Behold, My mother and My brethren! For whosoever shall do the will of My Father who is in heaven, he is My brother, and sister, and mother."

Jesus surely respects His mother as the one who bore Him. Nevertheless, He wishes to make it known that only those who do the will of His Father can be considered to be part of the family of Jesus (cf. 1 John 1.1–4). It would be difficult for us to create an entire system of reverence for Mary when the Scriptures remain quite silent on her life, especially in view of what Jesus has said.

She is called a perpetual virgin; the Roman Catholic church thus denies that James and Jude are His brothers, but believes that they are the children of the sister of Mary.[24] The Scriptures, however, portray a different story. We begin with Matthew 1.24–25:

> And Joseph arose from his sleep, and did as the angel of the Lord commanded him, and took unto him his wife; and knew her not till she had brought forth a Son: and he called His name Jesus.

The significant word in this passage is "until": until denotes the idea of a change of state. For Matthew to say that Mary was kept a virgin until she bore Christ demonstrates that she was most probably not a virgin after that time.

We have already examined Matthew 12.46–50; let us consider Matthew 13.54–57:

> And coming into his own country He taught them in their synagogue, insomuch that they were astonished, and said, "Whence hath this man this wisdom, and these mighty works? Is not this the carpenter's son? Is not his mother called Mary? And his brethren, James, and Joseph, and Simon, and Judas? And his sisters, are they not all with us? Whence then hath this man all these things?"
> And they were offended in Him. But Jesus said unto them, "A prophet is not without honor, save in his own country, and in his own house."

It is contended that the term "brothers" in this passage and also in Matthew 12 signify cousins, but this makes no sense in the context of the passage. The Nazarenes see Christ teaching, and wonder where He received all of this information; after all, He grew up there and was known to them all. Surely the Nazarenes would know the relationship that Jesus had with James and the rest of His kin, and the combination seen here demonstrates that James, Joseph, Simon, Judas, and some sisters are all the siblings of Christ. Had they been the children of Jesus' aunt, the Nazarenes would have mentioned this also. Likewise, it is not as if the Greek language is devoid of words to describe the relationship between cousins: if Matthew desired to indicate such a relationship, he would have used *suggeneis*, not *adelphoi*. Therefore, the idea that Mary was a perpetual virgin is inconsistent with the teachings of Scripture.

Likewise, no Scripture exists that would attest to Mary's sinlessness. The only individual we are told that was without sin was Christ Himself (Hebrews 4.15).

According to Paul in Romans 3.23,

> ...for all have sinned, and fall short of the glory of God.

Furthermore, we have Mary's own witness in Luke 1.47:

> "And my spirit hath rejoiced in God my Saviour."

From what has God "saved" Mary? What deliverance will be wrought through her Son? Mary here demonstrates that she also needs a Savior, and therefore had sin like the rest of us.

Mary is called the Mediatrix by the Roman Catholic church; yet the Scriptures establish that only Jesus the Christ functions as Mediator in 1 Timothy 2.5:

> For there is one God, one mediator also between God and men, Himself man, Christ Jesus.

As sure as we are that there is one God, there thus can only be one mediator, that is, Jesus Christ. Therefore, Mary cannot be a mediatrix. We are also told nothing of prayer toward her, but to pray to the Father, for we have fellowship with Him and His Son (1 John 1.3). We are further told nothing of her death and any assumption that may have taken place; we only know of Enoch and Elijah being taken up (Genesis 5.24; 2 Kings 2.1). These views have all been compounded upon traditions entirely foreign to the New Testament.

Therefore, we have seen that the Roman Catholic teachings concerning Mary have little foundation in the Scriptures, and many contradict the teachings of Christ. Finally, we have the witness of Christ in Luke 11.27–28, where we see a woman praising whomever may be His mother:

> And it came to pass, as He said these things, a certain woman
> out of the multitude lifted up her voice, and said unto Him,
> "Blessed is the womb that bare Thee, and the breasts which Thou
> didst suck."
> But He said, "Yea rather, blessed are they that hear the word of
> God, and keep it."

Therefore, it is evident that while Mary is worthy of honor and praise for bearing the Son of God, she has been given no authority in heaven or on earth and required the death of Jesus for her sins like every other human that has walked on the earth.

Traditions Concerning the Saints

The Roman Catholic church teaches that some of its members who have led very pious lives may be eligible for a process deemed "canonization," which is the path by which they are determined to be saints after their death. This process involves a thorough examination of the life of the individual, taking into account every good and bad deed performed by him or her. It is also required for this person to have worked miracles, especially after his or her death. If one passes these examinations, one is "beatified," and later, with more evidence for the person's sanctity, one is "canonized," and becomes a "saint," officially recognized by the Roman Catholic church and given a place in the church calendar and a mass in his or her honor.[25] Do the Scriptures speak of this process? Who are saints in the New Testament?

In the New Testament, the saints were those who were a part of the Body of Christ, and the term refers to those still living, as seen in Philippians 1.1 and Philippians 4.21:

> Paul and Timothy, servants of Christ Jesus, to all the saints in Christ Jesus that are at Philippi, with the bishops and deacons.

> Salute every saint in Christ Jesus. The brethren that are with me salute you.

There is no mention of any process which the Apostles or anyone else used to determine who were and who were not saints beyond their obedience to the will of God. Paul even calls the brethren in Corinth "saints" (1 Corinthians 1.2), and yet his letter to them is full of rebukes for the many difficulties present within that church!

As to the process of canonization, we have the witness of James in James 4.12:

> One only is the Lawgiver and Judge, even He who is able to save and to destroy: but who art thou that judgest thy neighbor?

There is only One who can save, the man Christ Jesus. The church has never been given the authority to determine of its deceased members who can be considered a "saint" and who cannot. This determination can only be made by God.

The Roman Catholic church also believes that these "saints" in Heaven can intercede for the church and its members.[26] The Roman Catholic church allows for the practice of revering relics, or various body parts or possessions of saints, which are often used to consecrate altars. What do the Scriptures say about such things?

We saw in the discussion of Mary that Christ Jesus is the Mediator, and that we have the opportunity to pray directly to God (1 John 1.9). Why, then, would we need such intercessors if we can petition the Father directly?

Concerning the body parts of various saints, we can remember well the end of the first letter of John, 1 John 5.21:

> My little children, guard yourselves from idols.

We know from 1 Corinthians 15 that the flesh is perishable, and that only that which is transformed into incorruptibility will remain; therefore, to revere a piece of a dead man or his possessions would be holding to something which in itself is not holy. What is the difference between a man honoring a statue of a god and a man honoring a piece of a saint? Such provides the honor due to the Creator to the creation, the very thing condemned by Paul in Romans 1.22–23.

Traditions Concerning Sin

The Roman Catholic church teaches that there are two kinds of sins, mortal and venial. Mortal sins "turn men away from God," while venial sin "allows charity to exist."[27] Mortal sins are considered to be those of grave matter, those condemned by the Ten Commandments, and done purposely.[28] Venial sins are considered to be the "less serious" sins, those either not of grave matter or those of grave matter not done purposely.[29] This separation of the kinds of sin is based on 1 John 5.16–17:

> If any man see his brother sinning a sin not unto death, he shall ask, and God will give him life for them that sin not unto death. There is a sin unto death: not concerning this do I say that he should make request. All unrighteousness is sin: and there is a sin not unto death.

Does this mean that there are different levels of sin? By no means! No sins are actually being defined here, nor is sin being referred to in any other way than in abstraction. John here is exhorting Christians to ask forgiveness of their sins, as seen also in 1 John 1.9. The only "sin leading to death" is the sin not confessed. Nowhere in the Bible do we see God establishing a hierarchy of sins, that one sin is greater or lesser than another. Sin is simply lawlessness (1 John 3.4), a violation of the will of God; we do not see that one violation is deemed greater than another one. The Bible presents many lists of kinds of sins (cf. 1 Corinthians 6.9–10, Galatians 5.19–21, etc.), and yet nowhere do we see anyone saying that one is greater or lesser than another.

The Roman Catholic church also teaches that it can forgive sins,[30] and that penance is required because of sin.[31] This penance is performed as confession to a priest, and this is deemed essential.[32] After hearing the confession of sin, the Roman Catholic church asserts that it has the right to determine what deeds are necessary for satisfying the sin or sins.[33] Do we see these practices within the Scriptures?

The Roman Catholics appeal to James 5.16 to defend their sacrament of penance:

> Confess therefore your sins one to another, and pray one for another, that ye may be healed. The supplication of a righteous man availeth much in its working.

This verse comes before the discussion of how to assist a man who is ill, and that prayer is necessary so that his sins may be forgiven. It is certainly good to confess our sins to one another so that we may be healed; however, we do not see that confession to each other is a requirement for private sins, and public sins are to be confessed only so that all may recognize the change of that individual from his previous course of action. Likewise, the confession of sin is "one to another"; will the priest confess his sins to the parishioner? The Bible does not show that we are to confess sins to any authority or to any one man, nor does it say that the church can forgive any sin, but establishes the following in 1 John 1.9:

> If we confess our sins, he is faithful and righteous to forgive us our sins, and to cleanse us from all unrighteousness.

We are to confess our sins to God, and He will forgive us of them. He is the only one having the authority to do so!

Furthermore, the Scriptures provide no requirement in terms of making satisfaction for sin as established by some church hierarchy. It is certainly good and commendable for one to be like Zacchaeus in Luke 19, who, having dined with Christ, promised the following in Luke 19.8:

> And Zacchaeus stood, and said unto the Lord, "Behold, Lord, the half of my goods I give to the poor; and if I have wrongfully exacted aught of any man, I restore fourfold."

However, nowhere in the Scriptures is recompense mandated. We are to ask for the forgiveness of our sins from any against whom we have sinned, as we are to forgive any who sin against us (Matthew 18.21–35), but we are never told that more is necessary. When a sin is forgiven, the sin is forgiven—in what other way can the debt be canceled?

Penance for sin is often done in the form of Hail Marys and prayer, but also was done in the form of pilgrimages. As pilgrimages became increasingly difficult because of political tensions in the Middle East, the Roman Catholics began building copies of pilgrimage sites in Italy and western Europe. Today, each parish has a way of pilgrimage called the Way of the Cross, or the Stations of the Cross, a path made in the parish in which one can become closer to Christ. Furthermore, for those who cannot get to the parish, meditation on Christ for a half an hour will suffice.[34] This is just one example of the many things that the Roman Catholic church has instituted to do what only God can do through His will, the shed blood of His Son on the cross, the forgiveness of sin. According to God, the only way that a sin can surely be forgiven is to repent of it and to "sin no more" (John 8.11). The danger of believing that works that we can do will allow the forgiveness of sin is grave indeed.

Traditions Concerning Prayer

We have already seen the Roman Catholic teachings concerning prayer to Mary and to the saints; furthermore, the Roman Catholic church teaches that prayer can be assisted with the usage of religious art,[35] all prayer is actually prayer "of the Church,"[36] that the church was taught to pray to Jesus,[37] that there should be a prayer rhythm,[38] and that there are specific places where prayer ought to take place.[39] Are these ideas in harmony with the Scriptures?

The Scriptures teach us to pray and to do so often (1 Thessalonians 5.17), yet do not show us necessarily how to pray. The Lord's Prayer in Matthew 6 and Luke 11 are good examples, yet it is clear that Christ's Kingdom has already come (cf. Matthew 6.10; Luke 11.2) in the form of the church. We are not told that individual prayer is actually a prayer of the church, for as we have seen above, the church is simply the collective of the individual Christians; we cannot deduce that since a part of the Body is praying, that prayer is a prayer of that Body.

The Scriptures do teach that prayer is to be to the Father, the one who can forgive sins (1 John 1.9), and the one to whom Christ said to pray toward (Matthew 6.9, Luke 11.2). Praying in a rhythm is not necessarily wrong in itself, but falls dangerously close to the category of the Gentiles in Matthew 6.7–8, who prayed in meaningless repetition. We are told to "pray in secret" in Matthew 6.6–7, and we are to understand that our prayers should always have the singular focus of petitioning God to assist us, and not to pray to be seen by men or to appear outwardly pious. Prayer is not limited to any location.

Many difficulties arrive with the inception of religious art. We see the clear delineation between the physical and spiritual nature of man in 1 Corinthians 15.35–49, and we recognize that in Christ, the emphasis is squarely on the spiritual man, for he is made in the image of God (Genesis 1.27), while no man has seen God (John 1.18). The use of physical objects or art to help bring one closer to a spiritual goal is rather contradictory, and resembles greatly the idolatry of the Jews before the exile and the Gentiles of the time of Christ. John urges us to guard ourselves from idolatry in 1 John 5.21, and we must constantly use spiritual things to guide us on our journey in Christ, striving to avoid confusing the Creator and the creation. Iconography only too often leads to idolatry, despite vehement denials by Roman Catholics.

Traditions Concerning Consecration

The Roman Catholic church teaches that consecration, or the taking of vows of chastity and possibly a vow of poverty, is a noble thing, approved in the church.[40] This consecration normally leads to what is deemed "religious life," seen most often in monasteries and convents.[41] It is required for anyone wishing to serve in the ministry, from the position of the priest to the pope, to take the vow of chastity.[42] Do we see this in the New Testament?

The New Testament shows us by example that many well-respected Christians had wives. We read the following in 1 Corinthians 9.5:

> Have we no right to lead about a wife that is a believer, even as the rest of the apostles, and the brethren of the Lord, and Cephas?

We see that Cephas is an "elder among elders" in 1 Peter 5.1 and that one of the "brothers of the Lord," James, was an elder in the church in Jerusalem (Acts 15). These men held positions of authority from which the Roman Catholic church asserts to be descended, yet they had no such vow. In reality, such a vow would entirely invalidate such persons from the position which they would profess, for Paul establishes that bishops are to be married and have children in 1 Timothy 3.1–8 and Titus 1.5–7! Furthermore, the entire practice of binding chastity is condemned by Paul in 1 Timothy 4.1–3:

> But the Spirit saith expressly, that in later times some shall fall away from the faith, giving heed to seducing spirits and doctrines of demons, through the hypocrisy of men that speak lies, branded in their own conscience as with a hot iron; forbidding to marry, and commanding to abstain from meats, which God created to be received with thanksgiving by them that believe and know the truth.

It should be noted in this context that as seen in *Concerning Observances: Lent*, the Roman Catholic church also forbids the eating of meat during the Fridays in Lent.

The "religious life" advocated by the monks and nuns of the Roman Catholic church also includes many who are hermits, living in seclusion to become closer to God, and were approved by the church.[43] These forms of asceticism are deemed by Paul to be the following, seen in Colossians 2.20–23:

> If ye died with Christ from the rudiments of the world, why, as though living in the world, do ye subject yourselves to ordinances, "Handle not, nor taste, nor touch"
> (all which things are to perish with the using), after the precepts

and doctrines of men? Which things have indeed a show of wisdom in will-worship, and humility, and severity to the body; but are not of any value against the indulgence of the flesh.

Such asceticism is of no use to their ultimate aim, to combat the desires of the flesh; this has been only too clearly made evident in the recent priest sex abuse scandals that have plagued the Roman Catholic organization. We can see, therefore, that such consecration is not as it is claimed to be before God, and that the "narrower path" the Roman Catholic church believes these people follow does not concord to that which is established in the New Testament.[44]

Traditions Concerning the Afterlife

The Roman Catholic church teaches that there are three levels in the afterlife: Heaven, Purgatory, and Hell.[45] Let us examine some of these teachings now.

The Roman Catholic church teaches that those found righteous immediately go to Heaven, and has determined that Paradise and Heaven refer to the same place. Do the Scriptures teach this?

The Scriptures certainly teach that the righteous will go to Heaven, but it seems that this destination is reached after the Judgment (Matthew 25.31–40; Revelation 20.11–21.27). Concerning Paradise, the Scriptures teach that it cannot be Heaven, for Christ promised the thief on the cross in Luke 23.43:

> And He said unto him, "Verily I say unto thee, To-day shalt thou be with Me in Paradise."

Yet on the third day, after Christ was resurrected, He says to Mary in John 20.17:

> Jesus saith to her, "Touch Me not; for I am not yet ascended unto the Father: but go unto My brethren, and say to them, 'I ascend unto My Father and your Father, and My God and your God.'"

If Jesus was in Paradise with the thief, yet had not ascended to the Father, and the Father is in Heaven, it seems clear that Paradise is not the same as Heaven.

Some believe that this is refuted by 2 Corinthians 12.2–4:

> I know a man in Christ, fourteen years ago (whether in the body, I
> know not; or whether out of the body, I know not; God knoweth),
> such a one caught up even to the third heaven. And I know such a
> man (whether in the body, or apart from the body, I know not; God
> knoweth), how that he was caught up into Paradise, and heard un-
> speakable words, which it is not lawful for a man to utter.

Regarding such matters, however, we must remember that the ancients
saw multiple layers of the "heavens," including the atmosphere, the universe, and then the Heaven where the Father resides. The phrase "the
third heaven" does not necessarily equal "the Heaven where the Father
is," but simply a demonstration of where this man was taken. It could be
said that the first heaven is the atmosphere, the second the universe, the
third Paradise, and the fourth Heaven, but we cannot be sure. It seems
evident, however, that Paradise is not where the Father resides.

The Roman Catholic church also teaches that there is a place called
Purgatory, where one goes if one has followed Christ but still has some
sins left to cover.[46] The existence of this location is based on the Councils
of Florence and Trent and a reference in 2 Maccabees 12.46:[47]

> Thus he made atonement for the dead that they might be freed
> from this sin.

Do we see the existence of Purgatory in the New Testament?

In the New Testament, we see no mention of any such place. We are
told that those who follow Christ and obey the will of His Father will go
to Heaven, and those who do not, to Hell (Matthew 25.31–33, 2 Thessalonians 1.6–9). Even if we were to accept 2 Maccabees as canonical, it
is still a part of the Old Testament; even though the Roman Catholic
church denies that the Law was abolished,[48] we have seen in *Judaic Practices* that the Law was fulfilled. Even then, the statement made in Maccabees does not clearly lend itself to the idea of Purgatory as imagined by
the Roman Catholic church.

The idea of Purgatory also rests on the idea that one can be purified of
his or her sins after death, yet purification can come only through Christ
alone (Hebrews 9.15). The saving work was done "once for all" (Hebrews
7.26), and we are found either righteous or not righteous (cf. Matthew
25). The Scriptures teach nothing of Purgatory.

Inconsistency within Tradition

The "Apostolic Tradition" of the Roman Catholic Church would span two millennia and would encapsulate the views promoted by all kinds of persons from all kinds of different backgrounds. While the Roman Catholic Church would like to present their tradition as solidly consistent over time, history and recent events prove otherwise.

An ancient example of the tradition conundrum is found within the writings of Irenaeus, "bishop" of Lyons at the end of the second century. He is highly esteemed overall within Roman Catholicism, for he himself appeals to the idea of apostolic tradition in his writings. Oddly, however, he appeals to apostolic tradition to substantiate the idea that the ministry of Christ lasted for about ten years after His baptism, going to some length to explain such, as seen in *Against Heresies* 2.22.3:

> On completing His thirtieth year He suffered, being in fact still a young man, and who had by no means attained to advanced age. Now, that the first stage of early life embraces thirty years, and that this extends onwards to the fortieth year, every one will admit; but from the fortieth and fiftieth year a man begins to decline towards old age, which our Lord possessed while He still fulfilled the office of a Teacher, even as the Gospel and all the elders testify; those who were conversant in Asia with John, the disciple of the Lord, [affirming] that John conveyed to them that information. And he remained among them up to the times of Trajan. Some of them, moreover, saw not only John, but the other apostles also, and heard the very same account from them, and bear testimony as to the [validity of] the statement. Whom then should we rather believe? Whether such men as these, or Ptolemaeus, who never saw the apostles, and who never even in his dreams attained to the slightest trace of an apostle?

One cannot confuse Irenaeus' message: Jesus ministered for ten years, and it is based upon apostolic tradition. Only a few years later, however, Clement of Alexandria, who also believed in apostolic tradition, taught that Jesus' ministry lasted but one year (*The Stromata*, 1.21). The Roman Catholic Church does not itself teach that Jesus ministered for one year or ten years; on a historical level a ten-year ministry is rendered impossible by the chronological system that can be reconstructed from the Gospels, Acts, and Pauline epistles. Few, if any, believe that Jesus ministered for ten years. We must ask, therefore: if apostolic tradition is supposed to be trustworthy, what shall we do with Irenaeus and his account? His attention to detail cannot be ignored. The best conclusion of the matter is that Irenaeus found little Biblical support for his idea and therefore he attempted to establish it with the "weight" of tradition. How can we trust "tradition" if it is abused so?

Other examples can be seen in more modern times. Despite a long history within the writings of the "church fathers" establishing that the Jews are separated from Christ, the Roman Catholic organization has reached out fraternally to Jews. Vatican II opened up the liturgies to vernacular languages when such had been decried in times before.

It is clear, then, that "Apostolic Tradition" is neither consistent nor uniform, and seems to change whenever it is socially advantageous for the organization.

Progression of Tradition

As we have seen, "Apostolic Tradition" poses many problems. When the above difficulties are brought up, many will say that "the church is continually developing in its traditions, thanks to the continual revelations from God" or "the church has developed in the understanding of its traditions." Are these valid arguments concerning the changes in the traditions over time?

Let us again examine Paul's exhortation to the Thessalonians about tradition in 2 Thessalonians 3.6:

> Now we command you, brethren, in the name of our Lord Jesus
> Christ, that ye withdraw yourselves from every brother that walketh
> disorderly, and not after the tradition which they received of us.

The Greek word for "received" in this text is in one of the past tenses; therefore, Paul affirms to the Thessalonians that the traditions they are to hold to have already been given. Therefore, if the church or any person attempts to hold fast to the traditions of God, he must find those traditions that are from the Apostles, and no one else.

But is it possible for Christians for 2,000 years to still need to develop in the understanding of that which has already been given? We are told the following by Paul in Ephesians 5.17 and 2 Timothy 2.15:

> Wherefore be ye not foolish, but understand what the will of the Lord is.

> Give diligence to present thyself approved unto God, a workman that needeth not to be ashamed, handling aright the word of truth.

The Christian has the responsibility to read the Word of God and understand it, and it appears from these verses that it is not impossible to understand the things of God. We are, in fact, commanded to understand the will of the Lord. If we do not have the understanding but need to "develop in it," how can Paul command the Ephesians in the first century to understand these things?

The argument that the Roman Catholic church has needed to "develop in understanding of the traditions that have been given" demonstrates, if nothing else, the implicit admission that the traditions used in the first few centuries after the death of Christ are not the same as the traditions now used in the Roman Catholic church. This statement is also an admission that the traditions that were used in the past were not as "developed" as they ought to have been and therefore flawed. It is not difficult see within this argument the reality at hand: the Roman Catholic church has not developed in understanding but has actually strayed from the message of the Gospel of Jesus Christ in its "development of tradition." Further, if the Roman Catholic church has needed to develop in its understanding over the past 2,000 years, what of the next 2,000, if we are allotted this much time on the Earth? Will the Roman Catholic church still need to "develop in its understanding?" If this is true, then the current teachings of the Roman Catholic church are themselves error-prone and may not reflect the best understanding of the traditions supposedly given to them. If this is the case, is not the Roman Catholic church fallible in its understanding and doctrine, and therefore has not received its doctrines from their supposed source?

We may see that the Christian has no need to fear, for the Hebrew author states in Hebrews 13.8:

> Jesus Christ is the same yesterday and to-day, yea and for ever.

The teachings and traditions that were truly handed down by the Apostles are understandable and have been understood since the first century.

There has been no need to add to them or "develop in the understanding" of them since the first century.

We have thus seen that many of the traditions of the Roman Catholic church are not in harmony with the teachings of the Apostles in the Scriptures, and we can thus determine that the traditions of the Roman Catholic church are the traditions of men, and not God. We must strive to follow the Word of God and the Word of God alone. The Scriptures demonstrate that the Roman Catholic organization, along with its traditions, do not represent the New Testament church.

Notes

1: *Catechism of the Catholic Church*, I. 84

2: Ibid., I. 120; I. 113

3: Ibid., I. 120

4: *The New American Bible*, note on Tobit 1.15, p. 429

5: *Catechism of the Catholic Church*, II. 1113

6: Ibid., II. 1289

7: Ibid., II. 1307

8: Ibid., II. 1290

9: Ibid., II. 1288

10: Ibid., II. 1318

11. Ibid., I. 757

12. Ibid., I. 812

13: Norman Cantor, *The Civilization of the Middle Ages*, p. 176

14: *Catechism of the Catholic Church*, II. 1593

15: *Catechism of the Catholic Church*, I. 487

16: Ibid., I. 491; I. 722; I. 493

17: Ibid., I. 499

18: Ibid., I. 966

19: Ibid., I. 963

20: Ibid., I. 965; IV. 2679

21: Ibid., I. 967

22: Ibid., IV. 2675

23: Ibid., I. 973

24: Ibid., I. 500

25: Kevin Johnson, *Why Do Catholics Do That?*, pp. 144–149

26: *Catechism of the Catholic Church*, IV. 2683

27: Ibid., III. 1855

28: Ibid., III. 1858–1859

29: Ibid., III. 1862

30: Ibid., I. 982

31: Ibid., III. 2042

32: Ibid., II. 1456

33: Ibid., II. 1448

34: Kevin Johnson, *Why Do Catholics Do That?*, pp. 91–95

35: *Catechism of the Catholic Church*, IV. 2705

36: Ibid., IV. 2655

37: Ibid., IV. 2665

38: Ibid., IV. 2698

39: Ibid., IV. 2691

40: Ibid., I. 919

41: Ibid., I. 924

42: Ibid., II. 1472

43: Ibid., I. 918

44: Ibid., I. 932

45: Ibid., I. 1022

46: Ibid., I. 1030

47: Ibid., I. 1031–1032

Eastern Orthodoxy

Overview

The Eastern Orthodox church began in 1054 with the dissolution of the "catholic" church by the actions of the bishop of Rome. Eastern Orthodoxy is a denomination highly fractured by nationalism, prevalent in the Balkan peninsula of Europe, Russia, and also having small numbers in the Near East. Although very similar to Roman Catholicism, Eastern Orthodoxy has grown apart from the other portion of the "catholic" church, having faced severe persecution from both Muslims and Communists since the fourteenth century. The belief system of the Eastern Orthodox can be summed up in the decisions of the Seven Ecumenical Councils that were called in the first millennium CE.

Variants

The Eastern Orthodox church is a confederation of many national churches, all having the same doctrinal positions yet governed separately. Nominally, the lands in Eastern Orthodoxy are divided amongst the four historic Patriarchates (the main heads of the Eastern Orthodox church): in Constantinople (now Istanbul), Alexandria, Antioch, and Jerusalem. There are nine other "autocephalous," or self-governing, churches, in Russia, Serbia, Romania, Bulgaria, Georgia, Cyprus, Greece, Poland, and Albania. There are also five churches which are deemed "autonomous," as mostly independent and mostly self-governed, but do not yet have full independence, in the Czech Republic/Slovakia, Sinai, Finland, and China.[1] There are also many Orthodox living in America and in western Europe, and at this time, they tend to still hold to the specific church of their nationality.

General Considerations

Part I

- *Lutheranism: The Lord's Prayer*

Part II

- *Ecumenism*

Part III

- *Baptism: Infant Baptism and "Original Sin"; Baptism is Immersion; Tripartite Baptism*

- *The Church Treasury, I: Benevolence: Church Benevolence to Non-Saints; The Missionary Society*

- *The Church Treasury, II: Other Considerations: Hospitals; Centers of Education*

Concerning Observances:

- *Observances Concerning the Lord's Birth: Advent; Christmas*

- *Observances Concerning the Lord's Death: Ash Wednesday; Lent; Palm Sunday; Holy Thursday; Good Friday; Easter*

- *Other Observances: Ascension-Pentecost; Epiphany; Annunciation; Days Concerning Saints*

- *Creeds: The Apostles' Creed; The Nicene Creed; The Athanasian Creed*

- *Judaic Practices: The Ten Commandments and the "Moral Law"*

- *The Lord's Supper: The Nature of the Emblems; The Bread and the Fruit of the Vine*

- *Positions of Authority: A Hierarchy of Bishops; Female Deacons [Deaconesses]; Priests; Ordination; Synods, Councils, Conventions, and Other Meetings*

Eastern Orthodoxy and Roman Catholicism

The Eastern Orthodox church and the Roman Catholic church share many views and doctrines on account of their shared heritage in the "catholic" church; nevertheless, many differences also exist. Let us now examine briefly the various traditions discussed concerning Roman Catholicism and their similarities and differences with the traditions of the Eastern Orthodox church.

Traditions Concerning the Scriptures: The Eastern Orthodox use a translation of the Septuagint for their Old Testament, and all the works included in the original. Some, however, do not accept 4 Maccabees.[2] The church is still considered the ultimate interpreter of the Scriptures.[3]

Traditions Concerning the Sacraments: The Eastern Orthodox church has essentially the same seven sacraments (although the terminology is different) as the Roman Catholic church, except the Roman Catholic confirmation is chrismation in the Eastern Orthodox church, and it is always performed immediately after baptism (unless one converts to Eastern Orthodoxy and was already baptized; then they are simply chrismated when they join).[4]

Traditions Concerning the Church: The Eastern Orthodox church has not gone so far as to say that the church is their "mother," but do regard highly their church as an institution.[5]

Traditions Concerning History: The Eastern Orthodox church has not made any claim to a pure history, and many in it recognize the abuses that some of its members have committed in times past.

Traditions Concerning Mary: The Eastern Orthodox also regard Mary very highly, holding to the same traditions as the Roman Catholic church.[6]

Traditions Concerning Saints: "Saints" are held in high esteem within Eastern Orthodoxy as in Roman Catholicism, although in Eastern Orthodoxy saints are chosen by popular opinion and the council of each autocephalous church. Prayer to these "saints" and relics concerning them are likewise accepted.[7]

Traditions Concerning Sin: The Eastern Orthodox church does not bind penance as necessary, yet urges its members strongly to do so. The confession is done face to face, and there is more humility on the role of the priest than in Roman Catholicism, but it still places a man in the wrong position (1 John 1.9).[8]

Traditions Concerning Prayer: The Eastern Orthodox have a "Jesus Prayer," a prayer said constantly like a meditative chant, which is an attempt to reach higher spiritual levels.[9] This is likewise not seen in the Scriptures, and is inconsistent with Matthew 6.7.

Traditions Concerning Consecration: The Eastern Orthodox bishops need to be celibate in order to obtain their position, but priests are not bound to celibacy as in the Roman Catholic church (unless they desire the priesthood while single; in that situation, they must remain celibate).[10] The emphasis on monasticism and asceticism is also present.[11]

Traditions Concerning the Afterlife: The Eastern Orthodox deny the concept of Purgatory.

Theosis

The Eastern Orthodox church has formulated the idea of *theosis*, or "becoming god." The belief is that through spiritual maturation, humans can actually become divinities, and they use Psalm 82.6, quoted in part by Jesus in John 10.34–36, as justification:[12]

> I said, "You are gods, and all of you are sons of the Most High."

> Jesus answered them, "Has it not been written in your Law, 'I said, you are gods'? If he called them gods, to whom the word of God came (and the Scripture cannot be broken), do you say of Him, whom the Father sanctified and sent into the world, 'You are blaspheming,' because I said, 'I am the Son of God'?

Do the Scriptures truly teach that we can become gods through spiritual maturity? By no means! The Psalmist uses the present tense; if such people are to "be" gods, they must be this way already! The Psalmist is perhaps best understood as making a more sarcastic form of comment, especially when we see that he continues in verse 7 by saying that these "gods" will "die like men." Jesus' use of the passage serves as a demonstration that it is possible for God to come in the form of a man, as He Himself does, and should not be extended to indicate the divinity of the persons to whom the Psalm was addressed. The very "oddity" of the idea that Jesus was God in the flesh should indicate to us that the idea of man becoming as a god was not a common view in Jesus' day.

We also have the witness of Isaiah in Isaiah 55.9:

> "For as the heavens are higher than the earth, so are My ways
> higher than your ways and My thoughts than your thoughts."

God is much, much higher than man is, and we cannot attain to His level of maturity or anything near it. Does man obtain maturity similar to that which God has? Surely, for through God we receive the fruit of the Spirit and chiefly love (Galatians 5.22–23, 1 Corinthians 13). To say, however, that we can become gods takes the Biblical doctrine of spiritual maturity too far. We have the opportunity to share in attributes of God, but never can it be said that by them we can become as God.

Iconography

The Eastern Orthodox believe highly in icons, religious art painted on wood displaying a spiritual message. They give great reverence to these icons, similar to the Roman Catholic church and its relics, going so far as to kiss these icons and bow in front of them.[13] They even treat Bibles in the same manner, kissing them also.[14] This all comes out of the belief that we must remember the humanity of Christ somehow, and therefore there are these icons, and they must be used.[15] Is this an idea present in Scripture?

The Lord, before His death, did give us a memorial of His physical life in His Supper (cf. Matthew 26.26–29, the other Gospel accounts). Paul goes so far to call it the proclamation of His death in 1 Corinthians 11.26. There is within the Scriptures therefore a fitting memorial for the life of our Lord in the bread and the fruit of the vine.

Concerning icons, it is, along with the Roman Catholic church's practices concerning relics, too close to idolatry to be fit for Christian worship, especially in light of 1 Corinthians 8. It would be too easy for many to forget that the icon is just a tool to be used in prayer and service, and to begin praying to and bowing before the icon itself. We could also see the examples given in the Old Testament concerning the Jews making shapes of wood and stone and His reaction against them (cf. especially the deeds of Jeroboam, 1 Kings 12.25–13.5).

Especially in some of the eastern European countries in which Eastern Orthodoxy is prevalent, the argument is often made that the icon is only two-dimensional and therefore cannot be an idol. On the other hand, God never mentions how many dimensions a figure must have before it becomes an idol, for God even calls things which technically have no form idols, as seen in Colossians 3.5:

> Therefore consider the members of your earthly body as dead
> to immorality, impurity, passion, evil desire, and greed, which
> amounts to idolatry.

An idol, then, is not defined by its dimensions; an idol is defined as anything that takes the full attention of an individual away from God. If the icon is placed before God, then it is an idol in His sight.

The Problem with Petrine Authority

The Eastern Orthodox church is governed nominally by five Patriarchs, sitting in seats in Constantinople (Istanbul), Alexandria, Antioch, Jerusalem, and Moscow. Their desire is to have the bishop in Rome (i.e., the Pope) restored to that association, if he would recognize that "first among equals" means primacy, not supremacy.[16] This is not the supremacy that the bishop in Rome now believes he has.[17] The Eastern Orthodox church believes that all bishops are collectively the successors of Peter, not just the one in Rome, although he has a "special claim" to being such.[18] Where the papacy claims infallibility, the Eastern Orthodox says the church has infallibility when met in a council,[19] and there is a much greater emphasis on a more oligarchical system of governing (many bishops meeting in councils to determine doctrine) over the more monarchical system in Roman Catholicism (the pope determining doctrine with the assent of some bishops). Finally, both churches claim to be the "true church," founded on Peter, the "rock."[21]

The implications of the schism between the Roman Catholic and the Eastern Orthodox churches show most clearly how Peter is not the true source of authority. It should be said first that members of both churches will often appeal to all of the disagreement over what the Bible says about various issues of faith, and point to the vast number of denominations in the world today. This certainly is tragic, however, no one denies the source of faith, the Word of God. The Word is fairly objective, because all can appeal to it as an authority for issues of doctrine. This is not so for those holding to a system of Petrine authority, especially since there are two groups claiming this authority.

Let us use an example to illustrate: the main doctrinal issue that divided these two churches, the presence of the *filioque* in the Nicene Creed.[22] If one were to ask the pope in Rome if the Holy Spirit proceeds from the Son, he would say that it does, and that his judgment is true because he sits on Peter's chair in Rome. Now, if one would go before a council of the patriarchs of the Eastern Orthodox church and ask if the Holy Spirit proceeds from the Son, they will say that the Holy Spirit only proceeds from the Father and that their judgment is true because it was the doctrine promoted within the original Nicene Creed as agreed upon by that particular ecumenical council, and that council's determination is inspired by the Holy Spirit through apostolic succession. Who is right? They both claim the same authority and yet have come to completely different answers; to what should one turn?

The Roman Catholic church answers that since Peter is one man, only one man can have his authority. This is all well and good if they wish to say that they have only had Peter's authority since 1054, since before then the bishop in Rome had at least nominally accepted the existence of the bishops in Constantinople, Alexandria, Antioch, and Jerusalem, and there was much communication and work done between them, especially in the earlier centuries. The implications of this argument are vast—the Roman Catholic church would be forced to admit that they had communion with heretics between 150–1054, and that they have esteemed some heretics as their "church fathers," such as Athanasius, Origen, and many others, who were members of the eastern churches. The Roman Catholic church has not made any such move; therefore, they contradict their own argumentation. The system of authority grounded in Peter is still divided.

There would be only one place that one could turn to in order to answer the question above or any question similar to it. It cannot be tradition, nor the pope, nor the councils of the Eastern Orthodox, but the Word of God as seen in the Holy Scriptures. No one within "Christendom" questions the authority of its authors, nor can anyone claim that its authority can be compromised by division. Authority vested within men has proven itself to avail nothing, and has been compromised by division. Authority for the Christian's deeds and beliefs, therefore, can only be found in the Scriptures.

Notes

1: From Timothy Ware, *The Orthodox Church*, p. 5

2: Ibid., p. 200

3: Ibid., p. 201

4: Ibid., pp. 278–279

5: Ibid., pp. 199, 239

6: Ibid., pp. 257, 260

7: Ibid., p. 256

8: Ibid., pp. 288–289

9: Ibid., p. 65

10: Ibid., p. 291

11: Ibid., pp. 36–37

12: Ibid., p. 219

13: Ibid., p. 32

14: Ibid., p. 201

15: Ibid., p. 33

16: Ibid., p. 27

17: Ibid., p. 27

18: Ibid., p. 28

19: Ibid., p. 239

20: Ibid., p. 15

21: Ibid.

22: *Filioque* is a Latin term meaning "and the son." In around the eighth century CE, the "catholic" churches in the west began to add this phrase in the Nicene Creed in the article concerning the Holy Spirit, signifying that the Holy Spirit proceeds from both the Father and the Son. The eastern churches considered this as heretical, believing that the Holy Spirit proceeds only from the Father, and through the Son. There is still great dissension over this word in the creed. For more, please see *Creeds: The Nicene Creed*.

Lutheranism

Overview

The Lutheran church has its roots in Martin Luther, a Roman Catholic monk who, in 1517, posted 95 theses on a church door in Wittenberg, Germany, questioning the Roman Catholic church's teaching concerning indulgences. He desired to reform the teachings of the Roman Catholic church; the Roman Catholics did not share that vision. Luther was officially excommunicated from the Roman Catholic church at the Diet of Worms in 1521, and he left to begin the church now known as the Lutheran church. The Lutheran church holds many of the important Protestant doctrines—grace alone, faith alone, and the Scriptures alone—but also maintains many of the doctrines of Roman Catholicism.

Variants

The Lutheran church is not divided on the main precepts of their faith. There are, however, many variants of Lutheranism; some are based on nationalities, especially in Scandinavia, but most in America are based on a few disagreements concerning the Scriptures and organization beyond the church. In America, the main groups are the Evangelical Lutheran Church of America (ELCA), the Lutheran Church-Missouri Synod (LCMS), the Wisconsin Evangelical Lutheran Synod (WELS), the American Association of Lutheran Churches, the Association of Free Lutheran Churches, the Church of the Lutheran Brethren of America, and the Evangelical Lutheran Synod.

General Considerations

Part I
- *Roman Catholicism, II: Tradition: Traditions Concerning Sacraments [Confirmation]; Traditions Concerning Sin; Traditions Concerning the Afterlife [Heaven]*
- *Wesleyanism: The Church and Social Responsibility*

A Study of Denominations

Part II
- *Evangelicalism*
- *Ecumenism*
- *Emergism*

Part III
- *Baptism: Infant Baptism and "Original Sin"; Baptism=Immersion; Baptism is for Remission of Sin and is Necessary for Salvation*
- *The Church Treasury, I: Benevolence: Church Benevolence to Non-Saints; The Missionary Society*
- *The Church Treasury, II: Other Considerations: Hospitals; Centers of Education; Kitchens/ Fellowship Halls; Gymnasiums; Business Enterprises*

Concerning Observances:
- *Observances Concerning the Lord's Birth: Advent; Christmas*
- *Observances Concerning the Lord's Death: Ash Wednesday; Lent; Palm Sunday; Maundy Thursday; Good Friday; Easter*
- *Other Observances: Ascension-Pentecost; Epiphany; Annunciation; Days Concerning Saints*
- *Creeds: The Apostles' Creed; The Nicene Creed; The Athanasian Creed*
- *Instrumental Music*
- *Judaic Practices: The Ten Commandments and the "Moral Law"; Tithing*
- *The Lord's Supper: The Nature of the Emblems; The Bread and the Fruit of the Vine; When Should the Lord's Supper Be Observed? Part A: Weekly*
- *Positions of Authority: Who is the Pastor?; A Hierarchy of Bishops [ELCA]; Female Deacons [Deaconesses]; Female Evangelists; Ordination; Synods, Councils, Conventions, and Other Meetings*

Faith Alone

The main tenet of the Lutheran faith is the doctrine of "faith alone." Lutherans believe that God gives the gift of faith to individuals by the Holy Spirit; this leads to salvation.[1] God does this through the act of baptism, which is considered to be administered by God Himself.[2] This is justified with 1 Corinthians 2.14 and Ephesians 2.8:[3]

> Now the natural man receiveth not the things of the Spirit of God: for they are foolishness unto him; and he cannot know them, because they are spiritually judged.

> For by grace have ye been saved through faith; and that not of yourselves, it is the gift of God.

Is this what the Scriptures truly teach?

While it is true that the Scriptures make a distinction between believers and unbelievers, indicating that believers can accept and understand spiritual truths while unbelievers do not (Romans 8.1–11, 1 Corinthians 2.6–16), such by no means proves that God gives the gift of faith to believers but not unbelievers. The New Testament makes it clear that these are not "hard and fast" rules: 1 Thessalonians 1.8–10 indicates how the Thessalonians turned from unbelief to belief to serve God, and Paul goes on to say in 1 Corinthians 3.1–3 that the Corinthian brethren themselves are "carnal" or "worldly." It is not that the Thessalonians could not understand what Paul was saying, and Paul still calls the Corinthians "saints" despite their "carnality" (cf. 1 Corinthians 1.2). Cornelius in Acts 10 was considered righteous and one who was God-fearing (Acts 10.1–2), yet he was a Gentile and at the time had not heard the word of God concerning His Son! We will not deny that God can and has led individuals to faith in Him, most notably Saul in Acts 9, but the agency of faith is never told to be within God: even Saul had to himself believe in the vision that he saw. Instead, Paul reveals that belief (faith) comes by hearing the Word of God in Romans 10.17:

> So belief cometh of hearing, and hearing by the word of Christ.

To say that faith is a gift of God in Ephesians 2.8 is a misinterpretation of the Scriptures. In the Greek, the word "that" ("...that not of yourselves, it is the gift of God") refers to "[being] saved," not "faith." The relative pronoun *touto* ("this") is in the neuter gender, and therefore cannot refer to the feminine *pistis* ("faith"), but the salvation that is under discussion. Salvation is indeed offered by grace, but it must be accepted by faith. Faith, therefore, represents the medium by which grace is received ("For by grace you have been saved through faith"), not the gift of God itself. Therefore, it can be conclusively determined that the Scriptures do not teach that faith is a gift of God; instead, faith is the response of the belief in God and the works He has done, seen clearly on the day of Pentecost in Acts 2. Man still has control over his ability to receive the gifts of God freely given to us.

It should be noted that the one place in the New Testament which speaks of "faith alone," or even "justification by faith alone," is James 2.24:

> Ye see that by works a man is justified, and not only by faith.

The only time the concept is even mentioned in the Scriptures, then, is a refutation of the very idea! While many have attempted to dismiss James' witness because of these matters, it goes to show us that Paul's messages in Romans cannot be read within a vacuum. Paul's message of salvation by faith does not negate the need for obedience (cf. Romans 6); therefore, to take Paul's arguments establishing that no one can be saved by works of merit and thus earn salvation and to twist them to claim "faith alone" is a manifest abuse of the Scriptures and an over-extension of the Apostle's argument.

The witness of the Scriptures testifies to the need for believers not to just have faith, but to obey the Lord Jesus (Matthew 7.21–27, Matthew 10.22, Hebrews 11.6, 1 Peter 1.22, 1 John 2.1–6, Revelation 2.10, Revelation 12.11, Revelation 19.8). Let us remember that both those who do not know God and those who do not *obey* the Gospel of our Lord Jesus Christ will suffer eternal torment and destruction!

> But wilt thou know, O vain man, that faith apart from works is barren? *(James 2.20).*

Scripture Alone

The Lutheran church teaches that the Scriptures alone are to be used.[4] Yet we see in their belief system the usage of three creeds—the Apostles', the Nicene, and the Athanasian—along with *The Book of Concord* as books of religious instruction and training.[5] Is it not inconsistent to hold to Scripture alone and yet use three creeds and a book of instruction?

It may be said to this that the books are used to supplement the Scriptures and therefore the Scriptures remain the primary authority. We recognize that many resources can aid and assist people in understanding God's Word, and there is no problem in using such resources. The matter at hand, however, is establishing creeds or books of men as authoritative for teaching: upon whose authority do these books rest? Resources are well and good, but where do we get the idea from the New Testament to vest anything but the Bible with such authority?

The Lord's Prayer

The Lutheran church, like its predecessors the Roman Catholic church and the Eastern Orthodox Church along with the Protestant churches that developed later, places a strong emphasis on the Lord's Prayer. The Lord's Prayer is used as a prayer and as a way of instruction.[6] Is this in harmony with the Scriptures?

We can see from the Scriptures that Jesus gave it to show the disciples a method by which one could pray. It was a "model prayer," not *the* prayer to pray: Jesus tells His disciples to pray *like* "this" in Matthew 6.9, not to recite it. Our prayers and petitions should surely incorporate many of the aspects of the Lord's Prayer, yet to bind it as necessary is troublesome, for it could fall under the realm of meaningless repetition, condemned by Jesus in Matthew 6.7–8, right before the Lord's Prayer:

> "And in praying use not vain repetitions, as the Gentiles do: for they think that they shall be heard for their much speaking. Be not therefore like unto them: for your Father knoweth what things ye have need of, before ye ask Him."

Therefore, we are not bound to pray the Lord's Prayer.

Confession and Sin

The Lutheran church also accepts Luther's teaching concerning confession and sin, that a pastor can be the vehicle of the forgiveness of sin, that one is not a Christian if one does not confess their sins in this way, and that the church itself can forgive sin (the Office of the Keys).[7] What do the Scriptures teach concerning this?

We have addressed the issue of an individual being able to forgive sins in **Roman Catholicism, II: Tradition: Traditions Concerning Sin,** and the conclusions there apply here. Luther introduces John 20.22–23 as evidence of the church being able to forgive sins:[8]

> And when He had said this, He breathed on them, and saith unto them, "Receive ye the Holy Spirit: whose soever sins ye forgive, they are forgiven unto them; whose soever sins ye retain, they are retained."

Does this mean that the church can forgive sins? The difficulty with this conclusion is that the church is not mentioned here in John 20. We see in verses 19 and 20 that this is a secret meeting of the risen Jesus and His disciples save Thomas. Therefore, the disciples are the ones receiving this benefit, not the church. This benefit is seen clearly in the acts of Peter concerning Ananias and Sapphira in Acts 5.1–11, when Peter condemned them to death by the witness of the Holy Spirit. The Apostles were given a measure of the Spirit not seen today; therefore, to say that any individual or even the collective church can hold the same powers as the Apostles did would be in direct contradiction with 1 Corinthians 13.8–10.

The charge in John 20.22–23, however, is also much like the ones given to these disciples concerning binding and loosing in Matthew 16.19 and Matthew 18.18; it may be observed that the Apostles, and the church after them, had the ability through the preaching of the Gospel to lead men to salvation or to have them condemned in their unbelief. The actions taken by the Apostles (and also by the church) were done in accordance with the will of and by the agency of God, not by any declaration they made on their own. Thus, it is inaccurate to say that the church has the power to remit sins based on the Apostles' ability to do so. Just as we have seen that no one has the authority to claim the Apostles' ability to bind and loose, no one can claim their ability to loose or retain sin.

Notes

1: Martin Luther, *Luther's Small Catechism, With Explanation*, pp. 15, 147
2: Ibid., p. 208 (question 253)
3: Ibid., p. 147 (157)
4: From http://www.lcms.org/introlcms.html
5: Ibid.
6: Martin Luther, *Luther's Small Catechism, With Explanation*, p. 174
7: Martin Luther, *The Large Catechism*, part VI, paragraphs 15, 28–29; *Luther's Small Catechism, With Explanation*, p. 27
8: Martin Luther, *Luther's Small Catechism, With Explanation*, p. 27

Anabaptism

Overview

The Anabaptist movement began in central Europe around 1525 with the desire of some to return to the faith expressed in the Scriptures. They saw that the death of Christ truly inaugurated a new covenant, and therefore the old law was not to be followed or used for doctrinal purposes. This stood in stark contrast to many other Protestant groups, who held that many of the laws under the covenant with Moses were still valid, either in their pure form or in a more "Christ-like" form. It was for this reason that they denied the need for infant baptism and stressed the need for what is known as "believer's baptism," that the individual is only baptized after believing in Christ himself. They were thus given the name "anabaptist," or "re-baptizers."

As discussed below, the Anabaptist movement began with three groups, the largest of which was named "Mennonite" after one of its most influential evangelists, Menno Simons, around the year 1536. Near the end of the seventeenth century, division occurred within one of the groups when Jacob Amman left the church because of perceived laxity concerning the "ban" on excommunicated members.[1] The group that followed him was known as the Amish, and these two groups represent the greatest portion of the Anabaptist movement today.

There is great diversity within the Anabaptist movement, especially concerning conformity (or the lack thereof) to technological and sociological developments and the interaction between church members and the state government. The Anabaptist movement is united, however, in its desire to conform to the pattern of the New Testament church. We can applaud the Anabaptists for their desire to return to the church of the New Testament; we appreciate this desire, although the goal was not fully met.

Variants

The Anabaptist movement and its variants are exceedingly complex; therefore, a chart has been provided to assist in the understanding of the changes that have gone on since the sixteenth century.

The Anabaptists began in three different communities, the oldest of which is known as the Swiss Brethren. This group began in 1525, and it stressed the unity within the group (calling themselves brethren and not a church), the need for "believer's baptism," and nonconformity. Persecution by Calvinists and Roman Catholics kept this group very small. The Swiss Brethren still have a following today, although it is rather small compared to the other Anabaptist groups. The second group began as just the "Anabaptists," when some from the Swiss Brethren began preaching in Germany. Three groups of these "Anabaptists" eventually developed and did so on cultural lines: the Dutch, the Frisian, and the Flemish. These are the groups that took on the name "Mennonite" after the 1530s because of the popularity of Menno Simons. The third group is known as the Hutterian Brethren, from Hans Hut, who preached in Germany in around 1528. His group emphasized the need for communal living and the sharing of property and goods for the welfare of the whole; this teaching would catch on in many Anabaptist groups in later times. The Hutterian Brethren is the only Anabaptist group that has not suffered schism, and many colonies exist today.

The first real division in an Anabaptist group came in 1697 between the Swiss Brethren and Jacob Amman, who believed that the "ban" on excommunicated members needed strict adherence. His opinion was not popular among the Brethren, and he left. Many followed him, and took on his name, coming to be known as the Amish.

The sixteenth and seventeenth centuries saw little division because of the persecution that the Anabaptist churches faced. They taught doctrines that did not conform to either church or state: infants need not be baptized, since adults do; Anabaptists should not go to war or cause any form of pain on anyone, since Jesus taught that one should turn the other cheek. The churches of the time, both Roman Catholic and Protestant, did not want to consider the loss of infant baptism, for then the future is not as secure; furthermore, the states of the time did not wish to support individuals who would not support the state militarily. The persecutions were the worst in the cities; therefore, the majority of the Anabaptists

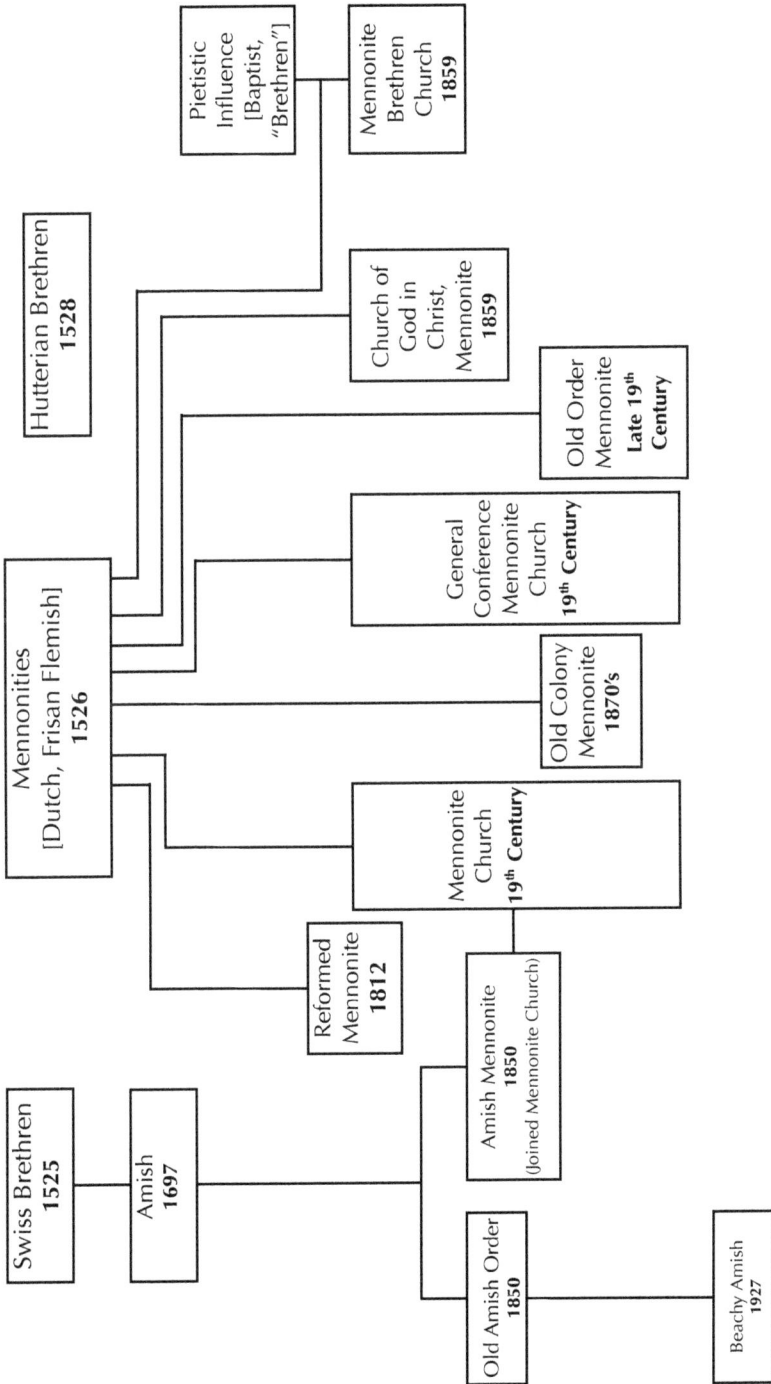

fled to rural areas, and became adept at farming. In order to survive, most Anabaptist groups either lived communally or made up the vast majority of the population in certain areas.

The eighteenth and nineteenth centuries saw easing of the persecution, and tensions began to form. By this time, many of the Anabaptist groups had moved to North America, in Canada and the United States, and the tolerance provided to them caused internal conflict. The Anabaptists no longer needed to live separately in their own communes or cities, and some groups resisted conformity within new societies. This caused division in both the Amish and the Mennonite churches: among the Amish, many churches drifted from the former patterns and became the "Amish Mennonite" church in the latter half of the nineteenth century, while the "conservative" Amish became known as the "Old Order" Amish. Another wave of separation occurred in the early twentieth century when Moses Beachy did not disassociate from Amish who left to become part of the Mennonite churches; this group is known as the Beachy Mennonite Amish.

In the end, the Amish Mennonites had fewer problems with English or the technology of the nineteenth century, and all eventually joined the Mennonite Church. The Mennonite division came in the 1870s, with the "Old Colony" and "Old Order" Mennonites splitting off due to their allegiance to the communal way of life and the use of German. Both the Old Order Amish and the Old Colony Mennonites are known for their simplistic way of living, their farming ability, and their embrace of community over technology.

Another division within the Mennonite body came from external sources. The eighteenth century saw the creation of the Pietist movement in Germany, which focused on the spirit in man. They placed emphasis not on Scripture alone, but also on the conversion process within the individual and the work of the Spirit within him afterward. Some of the preachers of this movement began to preach to some in the Mennonite groups in Russia, and some of these began to add the Pietistic beliefs to their Mennonite heritage. This group also had contact with the Baptists, who believed that baptism was immersion; they added this to their belief also. This group is known as the Mennonite Brethren Church, began officially in 1859.

Other divisions occurred in this time over external doctrines and internal schism, creating the smaller Reformed Mennonite Church and

Church of God in Christ, Mennonite. The end of the nineteenth century saw the formation of two groups that would eventually represent the majority of the Mennonite church, the Mennonite Church (MC) and the General Conference Mennonite Church (GCMC). The difference between the two groups is based on evangelism, with the GCMC placing greater emphasis on it than the MC.

General Considerations

Part I
- *Pietism: Foot Washing [Amish]*

Part II
- *Evangelicalism*
- *Fundamentalism*

Part III
- *Baptism: Baptism=Immersion [save Mennonite Brethren Church]*
- *The Church Treasury, I: Benevolence: Church Benevolence to Non-Saints; The Missionary Society*
- *The Church Treasury, II: Other Considerations: Hospitals; Centers of Education; Kitchens/ Fellowship Halls*
- *Concerning Observances: Observances Concerning the Lord's Birth: Christmas; Observances Concerning the Lord's Death: Easter*
- *Instrumental Music*
- *The Lord's Supper: The Bread and the Fruit of the Vine; When Should the Lord's Supper Be Observed? Part A: Weekly*
- *Positions of Authority: Who is the Pastor?; Elders Determining Doctrine? [Amish]; Ordination; Synods, Councils, Conventions, and Other Meetings*

Nonresistance

One of the practices that unite many of the Anabaptist groups is nonresistance.[2] Nonresistance is the belief that one should not physically fight against an opponent, but should be at peace with all men. This is based on the teaching of Jesus in Matthew 5.38–39:

"Ye have heard that it was said, 'An eye for an eye, and a tooth for a tooth:' but I say unto you, resist not him that is evil: but whosoever smiteth thee on thy right cheek, turn to him the other also."

There is certainly no problem with not wishing to fight against another; unfortunately, however, some Anabaptists have taken this belief to the point of withholding their tax money because of the warlike actions of the state.[3] Concerning the government, Paul says the following in Romans 13.7

Render to all their dues: tribute to whom tribute is due; custom to whom custom; fear to whom fear; honor to whom honor.

We see no evidence that Paul is telling Christians to only pay taxes when the funds do not go for the expenses of war; likewise, we can be confident that the money that Paul and the early Christians would have paid in taxes went to the building up of the Roman army. Nevertheless, we are still to pay taxes, so that our earthly protector in the government may continue.

Communalism

Some Anabaptist groups, particularly the Hutterites, practice communalism, which represents having all believers living in a commune, having all goods and possessions in common. This belief is based on the early church in Acts 2 that did the same and also the political condition of the Anabaptists in the sixteenth and seventeenth centuries: excluded from society and/or persecuted, many groups had to come together in order to survive. There is nothing wrong with a communal lifestyle; unfortunately, their self-imposed isolation has made many exclusionary, looking at all outsiders as threats, and some have the belief that the communistic life is the only life to live.[4] What do the Scriptures teach?

As Christians, we do have a responsibility not to be conformed to this world, as Paul says in Romans 12.1–2:

I beseech you therefore, brethren, by the mercies of God, to present your bodies a living sacrifice, holy, acceptable to God, which is your spiritual service. And be not fashioned according to this world: but be ye transformed by the renewing of your mind, and ye may prove what is the good and acceptable and perfect will of God.

We are not supposed to be completely excluded from the world, however, or else no one else would be saved, emphasized by Jesus in Matthew 5.14–16 and Paul in 1 Corinthians 5.9–10:

> "Ye are the light of the world. A city set on a hill cannot be hid. Neither do men light a lamp, and put it under the bushel, but on the stand; and it shineth unto all that are in the house. Even so let your light shine before men; that they may see your good works, and glorify your Father who is in heaven."

> I wrote unto you in my epistle to have no company with fornicators; not altogether with the fornicators of this world, or with the covetous and extortioners, or with idolaters; for then must ye needs go out of the world.

The true Christians will live so as to glorify God to all mankind, and not live apart, viewing non-members as outsiders that pose a threat.

Concerning communalism in the New Testament, we see that it was done in Jerusalem after Pentecost, most probably because the former Jews who heard the Gospel while visiting Jerusalem for Pentecost had nowhere to stay and little money to survive, and it was necessary to support them with the goods of the other Christians. We know that this situation was temporary, for we see the following in Acts 8.1:

> And Saul was consenting unto his death. And there arose on that day a great persecution against the church which was in Jerusalem; and they were all scattered abroad throughout the regions of Judaea and Samaria, except the apostles.

This is the last that we hear of a communal living environment in the Scriptures. Christians had strong bonds with each other and would help each other in a time of need (cf. the famine in Judea, 1 Corinthians 16.1–2, 2 Corinthians 8–10), but did not hold all things in common. Communal living is therefore not the only pattern of life that the Christian has been given in the Scriptures, and God has never bound communal living upon His children as a necessity.

Ultra-Conservatism

Some parts of the Anabaptist movement, the "Old Orders" especially (Old Order Amish, Old Order Mennonite, Old Colony Mennonite), have clung to many traditions concerning dress, lifestyle, language, and other factors.[5] Many believe that their way of life is simpler and thus more "biblical" than modern life and appreciate their traditions: they wish to keep the old languages (generally German), to wear the clothing worn in the seventeenth centuries, and to use the machinery used then. For others, the choices are made on the basis of maintaining community and to remain distinct from the outside world. If all members consent to such a lifestyle, there is nothing inherently wrong with it; unfortunately, those who attempt to leave this system are often excommunicated and banned over these traditions.

We do have Scriptural commentary on such things. Paul says the following in Romans 14.1–4:

> But him that is weak in faith receive ye, yet not for decision of scruples. One man hath faith to eat all things: but he that is weak eateth herbs. Let not him that eateth set at nought him that eateth not; and let not him that eateth not judge him that eateth: for God hath received him. Who art thou that judgest the servant of another? To his own lord he standeth or falleth. Yea, he shall be made to stand; for the Lord hath power to make him stand.

Paul here is discussing the division in Rome over the cleanliness of certain foods, but the principle is the same: in issues where God has not bound, one has the liberty to perform the action or to not perform the action, but the one who does not perform the action (the "weak") does not have the right to judge the one who does (the "strong"). By not accepting those who do not accept their old traditions, these groups are working against Paul's prayer in Romans 15.5–7:

> Now the God of patience and of comfort grant you to be of the same mind one with another according to Christ Jesus: that with one accord ye may with one mouth glorify the God and Father of our Lord Jesus Christ. Wherefore receive ye one another, even as Christ also received you, to the glory of God.

Acceptance needs to be based on righteousness, peace, and joy in the Holy Spirit (Romans 14.17), not on the language used or the clothes worn. It would be good to remember the words of John in 2 John 1.9:

> Whosoever goeth onward and abideth not in the teaching of Christ, hath not God: he that abideth in the teaching, the same hath both the Father and the Son.

The focus of many of these groups on community and the Christian life is commendable in many ways, yet the means by which these goals are accomplished are at odds with the greater mission of Christians in Christ. Jesus indicates not only that Christians are to be lights of the world and a city set on a hill but also a light on a lampstand for all to see (Matthew 5.13–16). Christians, as much as they are able, also ought to emulate Paul in being "all things to all men, that by all means [we] may save some" (1 Corinthians 9.22). If we demonstrate ourselves as so distinct in matters of liberty so that we have no common ground with our fellow man, how can we win them over? The overall failure of many of these conservative communities to engage in evangelism proper demonstrates the Biblical difficulties with this lifestyle (Matthew 28.18–20, Romans 1.16). We indeed are to not be of the world and we are not to be conformed to the world (1 John 2.15–17, Romans 12.2); nevertheless, we have a responsibility to remain within the world so as to lead others to salvation (1 Corinthians 5.10). This is a difficult path to follow, but going to either extreme will not help us conform to Jesus!

Notes

1: The "ban" refers to the ban on fellowship with excommunicated individuals according to 1 Corinthians 5. Mennonites have wavered many times on the strictness of the ban, whether it dealt with complete ostracization or if family members could still hold to their physical ties despite one breaking the spiritual tie.

2: from Cornelius Dyck, *An Introduction to Mennonite History*, pp. 412–413

3: an example is in ibid., p. 143

4: an example is in ibid., p. 407

5: Ibid., pp. 238, 307

Calvinism

Overview

Calvinism originated in John Calvin, a French theologian who moved to Geneva, Switzerland, in 1536, where he published his *Institutes of Christian Religion*. Calvin's theology was similar to Luther's, yet highly influenced by Augustinianism, especially in terms of God's sovereignty and predestination. Calvin held strongly to the belief that God had already determined who was and who was not going to be saved, that all things are under the direct control of God; man does not have free will since he "fell" into sin. Only God's grace can lead to salvation for man. His belief system caught on, and Geneva soon became a Calvinistic theocracy. Calvinism spread throughout Europe and has greatly influenced Protestant theology for almost 500 years.

Variants

Variants of Calvinism are seen in three main groupings: Reformed churches, Presbyterian churches, and Congregational churches.

Reformed churches originated as the continental European Calvinist churches, especially popular in the Netherlands. In North America, the Reformed Church in America represents one such group; more conservative groups include the Christian Reformed Church of North America and United Reformed Churches of North America.

Presbyterian churches owe their origins to John Knox, who studied under Calvin in the 1550s and desired to establish churches governed by the elder system (elder, in Greek, is *presbuteros*, hence "Presbyterian"). The Scottish government affirmed his Scottish Confession of Faith in 1560, but it is the Westminster Confession of Faith (written in England in 1646) that provides the basis of Presbyterian belief. In America today, the Presbyterian Church in America and the Presbyterian Church (USA) (also known as PCUSA) represent the largest such bodies, although they have denied limited atonement and are rather liberal in many areas; more conservative groups include the Associate Reformed Presbyterian Church, Evangelical Presbyterian Church, and The Orthodox Presbyterian Church (not affiliated with Eastern Orthodoxy). There is also the Cumberland Presbyterian Church, representing a group that rejected most tenets of Calvinism but maintained a presbyterian system of governance.

Congregational churches are the descendants of the Puritan or Separatist movement that came out of England in the seventeenth century. Congregational churches are so named on the basis of their belief that each congregation should govern its own affairs; thus they distinguished themselves from Anglicans and Presbyterians. The Puritans were mostly Calvinist in their theology, and Calvinist concepts remain in such bodies today. The largest and most liberal group of Congregational churches is the United Church of Christ (UCC); more conservative groups include Congregational Christian Churches (National Association) and the Conservative Congregational Christian Conference.

General Considerations

Part I

- *Roman Catholicism, II: Tradition: Traditions Concerning Sacraments [Confirmation]*
- *Lutheranism: The Lord's Prayer*
- *Wesleyanism: The Church and Social Responsibility*

Part II

- *Evangelicalism*
- *Ecumenism*
- *Fundamentalism*
- *Community Church Movement*
- *House Church Movement*
- *Megachurch Movement*
- *Emergism*

Part III

- *Baptism: Infant Baptism and "Original Sin"; Baptism=Immersion; Baptism is for Remission of Sin and is Necessary for Salvation*

- *The Church Treasury, I: Benevolence: Church Benevolence to Non-Saints; The Missionary Society*
- *The Church Treasury, II: Other Considerations: Hospitals; Centers of Education; Kitchens/Fellowship Halls; Gymnasiums; Business Enterprises*

Concerning Observances:
- *Observances Concerning the Lord's Birth: Christmas*
- *Observances Concerning the Lord's Death: Palm Sunday; Good Friday; Easter*
- *Other Observances: Epiphany; Days Concerning Saints*

- *Creeds: The Apostles' Creed; The Nicene Creed; The Athanasian Creed*

- *Instrumental Music*

- *The Lord's Supper: The Bread and the Fruit of the Vine; When Should the Lord's Supper Be Observed? Part A: Weekly*

- *Positions of Authority: Who is the Pastor?; A Hierarchy of Bishops; Female Deacons [Deaconesses]; Female Elders; Female Evangelists; Homosexual Evangelists [disputed among liberal groups]; Ordination; Synods, Councils, Conventions, and Other Meetings*

- *Judaic Practices: The Ten Commandments and the "Moral Law"; Tithing*

TULIP

The basic theology of Calvin was the concept of predestination and election, later summarized in the acrostic TULIP: Total Depravity, Unconditional Election, Limited Atonement, Irresistible Grace, and the Perseverance of the Saints.[1] Essentially, this doctrine states that due to his sinful nature, man cannot come to God; rather, God must come to him. God has already determined who He will save and who He will condemn, and therefore, His Son only died for those who are the saved, otherwise known as the "elect." The members of the "elect" cannot help to be saved, for God will bring them to Himself; because of this, those who are truly the elect must be saved and cannot fall away. Let us now examine each of these tenets separately to see if they correspond to the teachings of the Scriptures.

T – Total Depravity

The first teaching in the TULIP acrostic is total depravity. Total depravity can be defined as man's inability to come to God by his own means. Since man was born with original sin and cannot help but live in a fallen state, there is no way that he can perform any good deed; the only way he can be saved or to do anything good is if God works within him.[2] "Original sin" is addressed in **Baptism: Infant Baptism and "Original Sin"**. Likewise, the view that God must provide the individual with all things necessary for salvation, including faith, is considered in **Lutheranism: Faith Alone,** since Calvinists also use 1 Corinthians 2.14 and Ephesians 2.8–9 to justify their belief. This belief is further justified with verses such as Romans 8.6–8 and 2 Corinthians 3.5:[3]

> For the mind of the flesh is death; but the mind of the Spirit is life and peace: because the mind of the flesh is enmity against God; for it is not subject to the law of God, neither indeed can it be: and they that are in the flesh cannot please God.

> …not that we are sufficient of ourselves, to account anything as from ourselves; but our sufficiency is from God.

Are these claims true? On the one hand, it is true that man has sinned and that all have fallen short of God's glory (Romans 3.23), but on the other hand, this does not necessitate that man is completely unable to do any good thing and is unable to come to God.

The context of Romans 8.6–8 demonstrates that Paul is speaking about the differences between the man in sin and the man in Christ, as is made clear when examining a broader look at the chapter, Romans 8.5–9:

> For they that are after the flesh mind the things of the flesh; but they that are after the Spirit the things of the Spirit. For the mind of the flesh is death; but the mind of the Spirit is life and peace: because the mind of the flesh is enmity against God; for it is not subject to the law of God, neither indeed can it be: and they that are in the flesh cannot please God. But ye are not in the flesh but in the Spirit, if so be that the Spirit of God dwelleth in you. But if any man hath not the Spirit of Christ, he is none of his.

We can understand Paul clearly in his proper context: Paul is explaining that the man who is in sin will be against the teachings of God, for he has chosen the world, not the Father (cf. 1 John 2.15–17). The man who lives by the Spirit will be in fellowship with God, for he has chosen wisely. Furthermore, Paul speaks of the Corinthians in 1 Corinthians 3.1–2 as the following:

> I fed you with milk, not with meat; for ye were not yet able to bear it: nay, not even now are ye able; for ye are yet carnal: for whereas there is among you jealousy and strife, are ye not carnal, and walk after the manner of men?

Paul says that the Corinthians are still "carnal" and yet calls them "saints" in 1 Corinthians 1.2. How can it be, then, that "carnal" people can be "in Christ" if we interpret Romans 8 to mean that the carnal ones of the flesh are consigned to hellfire without a chance?

Romans 8.6–8, therefore, is Paul's attempt to encourage Christians to walk by the Spirit and is not an attempt to demonstrate that humans are totally depraved.

Concerning 2 Corinthians 3.5, Paul is explaining the difference between the Old Covenant and the New Covenant; the discussion concerning the lifelessness of stone versus the life in the Spirit (verses 7–8) attests to this. Paul is confirming to the Corinthians that the Gospel, the plan of salvation instituted by God, came not from man, but from God. All truth and really all existence come from God, not from ourselves; nevertheless, our ability to perform deeds that are good in the eyes of God is not negated by this.

The Scriptures have many examples of individuals performing good works, despite their not being in the fold of God. In Matthew 8.5–13, we read of the centurion who wished for Jesus to heal his servant. This man had the faith that Jesus could perform this deed by the word of His power, and exclaimed that he was "not worthy for [Jesus] to come under [his] roof," (verse 8). Jesus marveled at this, proclaiming that "I have not found such great faith in anyone of Israel," (verse 10). This man was a Gentile during God's covenant with the Israelites, yet he had greater faith than they did. We also have the example of Cornelius in Acts 10.1–2, of whom it says:

> Now there was a certain man in Caesarea, Cornelius by name, a centurion of the band called the Italian band, a devout man, and one that feared God with all his house, who gave much alms to the people, and prayed to God always.

Here is a devout man who at this time was a Gentile and had heard not the news of Christ, yet he is determined to be "a devout man and one that feared God." How can this be if those who are not saved cannot do good works? That God worked in them? Yet these men were not a part of the fold of God, and thus God would be a hypocrite! Surely even the unsaved can do good works, but they are still in their sins, and have not been cleansed by the blood of Christ. Only then can they be deemed truly righteous in God's eyes.

Furthermore, we have the witness of passages such as Philippians 2.12 and 1 Peter 1.22, among others, that attest to the role of our obedience in our salvation:

> So then, my beloved, even as ye have always obeyed, not as in my presence only, but now much more in my absence, work out your own salvation with fear and trembling.

> Seeing ye have purified your souls in your obedience to the truth unto unfeigned love of the brethren, love one another from the heart fervently.

It is manifest, then, that while God has done the greater part by giving us of His Son, our response of obedient faith in Him is necessary for salvation. According to the Scriptures, the response comes from man on the basis of what God has done.

U – Unconditional Election

We now move on to unconditional election, the belief that God has already elected (or predestined) whom He desires to be saved, and predestined those who would be condemned.[4] Romans 9.15; 21, Ephesians 1.4–8, Ephesians 2.10, and 2 Timothy 1.9 are used to justify this belief:[5]

> For he saith to Moses, "I will have mercy on whom I have mercy, and I will have compassion on whom I have compassion,"...

Or hath not the potter a right over the clay, from the same lump
to make one part a vessel unto honor, and another unto dishonor?

...even as he chose us in him before the foundation of the world,
that we should be holy and without blemish before him in love:
having foreordained us unto adoption as sons through Jesus Christ
unto himself, according to the good pleasure of his will, to the
praise of the glory of his grace, which he freely bestowed on us in
the Beloved: in whom we have our redemption through his blood,
the forgiveness of our trespasses, according to the riches of his grace,
which he made to abound toward us in all wisdom and prudence.

For we are his workmanship, created in Christ Jesus for good
works, which God afore prepared that we should walk in them.

...who saved us, and called us with a holy calling, not according
to our works, but according to his own purpose and grace, which
was given us in Christ Jesus before times eternal.

As we begin to analyze the claims made, we must again consider the
context in terms of Romans 9.15, 21; Paul is discussing the Jews and the
choices God made concerning them (verses 1–13). His conclusion is that
God has the right to decide to whom He will open the doors of salvation
(verses 14–24). Is Paul saying here that God has already decided who
will be saved and who will not? By no means! Paul is declaring God's
ability to do so, and how that ability was exercised in the Old Testament.
Romans 9.22–33 declares that God has now opened the doors of salvation to all, Jew and Gentile alike:

What if God, willing to show his wrath, and to make his power
known, endured with much longsuffering vessels of wrath fitted
unto destruction: and that he might make known the riches of his
glory upon vessels of mercy, which he afore prepared unto glory,
even us, whom he also called, not from the Jews only, but also
from the Gentiles? As he saith also in Hosea,
"I will call that my people, which was not my people; And her
beloved, that was not beloved. And it shall be, that in the place

> where it was said unto them, 'Ye are not my people,' There shall
> they be called sons of the living God."
> And Isaiah crieth concerning Israel, "If the number of the chil-
> dren of Israel be as the sand of the sea, it is the remnant that shall
> be saved: for the Lord will execute his word upon the earth, fin-
> ishing it and cutting it short."
> And, as Isaiah hath said before, "Except the Lord of Sabaoth had
> left us a seed, We had become as Sodom, and had been made like
> unto Gomorrah."
> What shall we say then? That the Gentiles, who followed not after
> righteousness, attained to righteousness, even the righteousness
> which is of faith: but Israel, following after a law of righteousness,
> did not arrive at that law. Wherefore? Because they sought it not
> by faith, but as it were by works. They stumbled at the stone of
> stumbling; even as it is written,
> "Behold, I lay in Zion a stone of stumbling and a rock of offence:
> And he that believeth on him shall not be put to shame."

God has declared that all men—not only Jews—may come to Him now
for salvation. This is what Paul says in Romans 9, not that God has already determined exactly who will be saved.

In order to understand what Paul means in Ephesians 1, we must also
consider Romans 8.29–30:

> For whom he foreknew, he also foreordained to be conformed to
> the image of his Son, that he might be the firstborn among many
> brethren: and whom he foreordained, them he also called: and
> whom he called, them he also justified: and whom he justified,
> them he also glorified.

As Paul writes to encourage the brethren in Rome and Ephesus, he does
establish that God has predestined them for conformity to the image of
the Son and adoption. This predestination is not on the basis of God's
predetermined sovereign choice, as Calvinists contend; as Paul says in
Romans 8.29, it is based in His foreknowledge of the choices man will
make. God predestines those whom He foreknows, but that knowledge
does not impede man's free will, lest God be the author or cause of any
kind of sin (cf. James 1.13, 1 Timothy 2.4).

Ephesians 2.10 is used to demonstrate that we do not perform good works, but that God works through us. This is not explicitly stated; however, God is said to have established the good works to be performed, which He most certainly has in His Word. Such does not mean that God performs the works. The actual performance of the work is left to us (Titus 3.8)! We have been created to perform good works and have been given the parameters of good works according to Ephesians 2.10 (and that the Scriptures equip us for all these good works, 2 Timothy 3.16–17); this does not require, however, that God also performs the works. James 2.14–26 also establishes that we are the ones who perform the work.

Finally, 2 Timothy 1.9 is a further explanation of the works done for our salvation, that Christ was crucified for our sins (cf. John 3.16). We affirm that we cannot work for salvation in the sense that by deeds alone we can be saved. We must have the grace of God, manifested in that sacrifice of His Son, in order to be saved; this is what Paul affirms in 2 Timothy 1.9. In order to receive this sacrifice, however, it is abundantly evident that a response is necessary, and whatever response is given is necessarily a work (cf. 2 Thessalonians 1.6–9, Philippians 2.12). We cannot earn our salvation, but we must be obedient if we wish to go to Heaven.

Unconditional Election, therefore, has not been justified from the Scriptures. The problems with this doctrine are many; if God has predestined the elect for salvation by His sovereign choice alone, that necessitates that God has predestined the rest for condemnation in the same way. This violates the Biblical precept found in Romans 2.11:

...for there is no respect of persons with God.

If God arbitrarily decides who will be saved and who will be condemned, this demonstrates partiality; if we accept the doctrine of original sin, there is thus no real difference between one who would be elected versus one who would be condemned except for God's choice.

Some will say in response to this that Paul is only establishing that the sovereign choice of God is arbitrary: when God makes the choice, He does not take race, culture, ethnicity, birth, economic status, etc., into consideration. The text does not require such a limitation on the interpretation, however, and such a limitation is not consistent with the message Paul provides immediately before making the statement in question, as can be seen in Romans 2.5–10:

> But after thy hardness and impenitent heart treasurest up for thyself wrath in the day of wrath and revelation of the righteous judgment of God; who will render to every man according to his works: to them that by patience in well-doing seek for glory and honour and incorruption, eternal life: but unto them that are factious, and obey not the truth, but obey unrighteousness, shall be wrath and indignation, tribulation and anguish, upon every soul of man that worketh evil, of the Jew first, and also of the Greek; but glory and honour and peace to every man that worketh good, to the Jew first, and also to the Greek.

Paul here clearly defines the standard by which men shall be judged; it is not God's sovereign arbitrary choice, but on the basis of whether one was found obedient or disobedient to God. This is equally true of the Jew and the Greek. It is clear, therefore, that Paul demonstrates that God's judgment is not based on some predetermined arbitrary judgment, but based upon the fidelity of each individual.

Furthermore, if God has already determined who will be saved and who will be condemned, this would even negate the need for the last Judgment, defined clearly in the following passages:

> "For by thy words thou shalt be justified, and by thy words thou shalt be condemned" *(Matthew 12.37).*

> "For the Son of man shall come in the glory of his Father with his angels; and then shall he render unto every man according to his deeds" *(Matthew 16.27).*

> "But when the Son of man shall come in his glory, and all the angels with him, then shall he sit on the throne of his glory: and before him shall be gathered all the nations: and he shall separate them one from another, as the shepherd separateth the sheep from the goats; and he shall set the sheep on his right hand, but the goats on the left" *(Matthew 25.31–33).*

> "The times of ignorance therefore God overlooked; but now he commandeth men that they should all everywhere repent: inas-

much as he hath appointed a day in which he will judge the world in righteousness by the man whom he hath ordained; whereof he hath given assurance unto all men, in that he hath raised him from the dead" *(Acts 17.30–31)*.

And I saw a great white throne, and him that sat upon it, from whose face the earth and the heaven fled away; and there was found no place for them. And I saw the dead, the great and the small, standing before the throne; and books were opened: and another book was opened, which is the book of life: and the dead were judged out of the things which were written in the books, according to their works. And the sea gave up the dead that were in it; and death and Hades gave up the dead that were in them: and they were judged every man according to their works. And death and Hades were cast into the lake of fire. This is the second death, even the lake of fire. And if any was not found written in the book of life, he was cast into the lake of fire *(Revelation 20.11–15)*.

The Judgment is spoken of as a real event, wherein every man will be judged on the basis of his life and his relationship with Christ. Why would this event be written about if God had already determined its outcome?

The main problem with unconditional election involves the Calvinist (and Augustinian) perspective on the nature of God Himself. While there is much regarding the nature of God which we do not understand (Isaiah 55.9–10), we can understand that which He has revealed to us. When we consider the Scriptures, we do not find evidence that God's sovereignty demands His predetermination of all events; instead, we see times in which God's will is not accomplished, along with times where God's determination is changed based upon changes in circumstance. Examples include God's predictions to David regarding Saul in Keilah (1 Samuel 23), changes in plans based on the repentance of Ahab and the Ninevites (1 Kings 22, Jonah 1–3), and the changes of fortune in Paul's journey (Acts 27). Matthew 19.8 is also quite instructive: Jesus Himself establishes that the Israelites were not really following God's original intention for marriage when they were given the ability to divorce their wives, yet God still suffered them to do so.

We have no quarrel with the fact that God is omnipotent and sovereign—in fact, we will not impose on Him any form of "logical" necessity! God's omnipotence and sovereignty does not *demand* that God function in any given way—instead, He reveals for our benefit part of His nature so that we can serve Him. That nature is not the tyrannical God presented in Augustinian Calvinist theology; instead, God calls all men through the Gospel, and it is up to them to choose to serve Him or not, and reap the consequences (Romans 1.16; 6.17–23; 10.14–17, 2 Thessalonians 1.6–9, 1 Timothy 2.4). Man's fate was not arbitrarily predetermined before his existence!

Therefore, it can be determined that unconditional election of each saint is not established in the Scriptures, for God now allows all men to come to Him.

L – Limited Atonement

The next doctrine in the TULIP acrostic is limited atonement, the belief that Jesus Christ died only for those in the elect. John 17.9 and Matthew 26.28 are used to justify this belief:

> "I pray for them: I pray not for the world, but for those whom Thou hast given Me; for they are Thine."

> "…for this is My blood of the covenant, which is poured out for many unto remission of sins."

Do these teach that Christ died only for some? Let us examine these passages.

John 17.9 is a part of what is called Jesus' "High Priestly" prayer; the first part of this prayer concerns the disciples of Christ, as seen in verses 6–7:

> "I manifested Thy name unto the men whom Thou gavest Me out of the world: Thine they were, and Thou gavest them to Me; and they have kept Thy word. Now they know that all things whatsoever Thou hast given Me are from Thee."

We see that in verse 9, Jesus is saying that He is praying for "these". Exactly who is under discussion is made evident in verse 11:

> "And I am no more in the world, and these are in the world, and I come to Thee. Holy Father, keep them in Thy name which Thou hast given Me, that they may be one, even as We are."

Then, in the end, Jesus prays in verses 20–21 for all who would believe:

> "Neither for these only do I pray, but for them also that believe on
> Me through their word; that they may all be one; even as Thou,
> Father, art in Me, and I in Thee, that they also may be in Us: that
> the world may believe that Thou didst send Me."

Therefore, we can conclude that Jesus is not saying in verse 9 that God
has given to Him only some, but that during His lifetime, the twelve
plus the seventy given to Him have learned of Him. His prayer is clearly
being given on behalf of all or any who will believe in Him and in His
Father, as seen in verses 20 and 21.

Matthew 26.28 says that Christ's was poured out for "many" to receive
the forgiveness of sins. Does this mean that Christ's blood is limited to a
few? We have the witness of the Hebrew writer in Hebrews 9.11–12:

> But Christ having come a high priest of the good things to come,
> through the greater and more perfect tabernacle, not made with
> hands, that is to say, not of this creation, nor yet through the blood
> of goats and calves, but through his own blood, entered in once for
> all into the holy place, having obtained eternal redemption.

His sacrifice was performed "once for all," and the all is not qualified.
Therefore, the Hebrew author is telling us that Christ's blood was sacrificed for all men. How can these two statements agree?

It is inaccurate to say that Christ died to cleanse the sins of a few or
for many; Christ died to cleanse all men of sin. Not all men are cleansed
of sin, however, for they do not accept Christ's sacrifice and/or declaration. Therefore, in the end, Christ's blood will cleanse those who have
accepted Him of their sins. Christ did die for all men to be saved; however, since only a few will accept that sacrifice, it is effective only for
those who do. The agent of the limitation is not God but man, for it is
up to him to accept or reject the work of God through Jesus Christ.

I – Irresistible Grace

The next tenet of TULIP is irresistible grace, the belief that God calls
those whom He has elected with His grace and that the elect cannot
help but to heed the call. This belief is justified with John 6.37, John
6.44, and Romans 8.14:

"All that which the Father giveth Me shall come unto Me; and him that cometh to Me I will in no wise cast out."

"No man can come to Me, except the Father that sent Me draw him: and I will raise him up in the last day."

For as many as are led by the Spirit of God, these are sons of God.

Let us now examine these Scriptures.

John 6 is the discussion between Jesus and the Jews concerning spiritual matters. He declares that the Father has drawn men, which He has, and that those will come to Him. How are men drawn? We see this in Romans 10.13–14:

...for, "Whosoever shall call upon the name of the Lord shall be saved."
How then shall they call on him in whom they have not believed? and how shall they believe in him whom they have not heard? and how shall they hear without a preacher?

God draws men to Him through the preaching of the Gospel and the acceptance thereof. Jesus is not saying that the elect will be forced to come to Him because of the Father's will, but that those who will heed the call of the Father will come.

The statement in Romans 8.14 is not making a declaration concerning how men are called; it is a simple statement of fact: if you are led by the Spirit, you are a son of God. He has accepted you. This verse makes no comment concerning how the Spirit was bestowed upon you, whether God has forced Him upon you or if you received it by desire. The multiple conversion stories in the Acts of the Apostles point clearly to the desire of man to follow the Gospel call as seen in the day of Pentecost (Acts 2), those who believed when the lame man was healed (Acts 3), the Samaritans and the Ethiopian eunuch (Acts 8), and many, many more. God certainly calls, but as Paul explains in Romans 10.16–17, man may not answer; if one does answer the call, he has faith in Him:

But they did not all hearken to the glad tidings. For Isaiah saith, "Lord, who hath believed our report?"

So belief cometh of hearing, and hearing by the word of Christ.

Furthermore, if God calls irresistibly by grace, why is it that Christians are called to go out and preach the Gospel (Matthew 28.18–20)? What need is there for the "preacher" of Romans 10.13–14 if God will call them, preacher or no?

It is true that some people were called more strongly or clearly than others. We can think of Saul on the road to Damascus in Acts 9, or Matthew in Matthew 9.9: both received personal and specific calls. Nevertheless, both still had to obey the call: Saul needed to be baptized (Acts 22.16), and Matthew had to leave what he had to follow Jesus (Matthew 9.9). Had Saul not believed the vision, or had Matthew not left his post, would they have received salvation? We have no reason to believe that they would!

"Irresistible grace," then, is at odds with the way the Gospel was promoted in the New Testament.

P – Perseverance of the Saints

The final doctrine in the TULIP acrostic follows logically from the first four: if man cannot come to God, but God has determined to come to some through the death of His Son Jesus Christ and such individuals have no choice but to come to Him, it logically follows that those individuals must be saved and cannot be lost. This final idea is known as the perseverance of the saints. Romans 8.28–39 is often used to justify this:

> And we know that to them that love God all things work together for good, even to them that are called according to his purpose. For whom he foreknew, he also foreordained to be conformed to the image of his Son, that he might be the firstborn among many brethren: and whom he foreordained, them he also called: and whom he called, them he also justified: and whom he justified, them he also glorified. What then shall we say to these things? If God is for us, who is against us? He that spared not his own Son, but delivered him up for us all, how shall he not also with him freely give us all things? Who shall lay anything to the charge of God's elect? It is God that justifieth; who is he that condemneth? It is Christ Jesus that died, yea rather, that was raised from the dead, who is at the right hand of God, who also maketh interces-

sion for us. Who shall separate us from the love of Christ? shall tribulation, or anguish, or persecution, or famine, or nakedness, or peril, or sword? Even as it is written,

"For thy sake we are killed all the day long; We were accounted as sheep for the slaughter."

Nay, in all these things we are more than conquerors through him that loved us. For I am persuaded, that neither death, nor life, nor angels, nor principalities, nor things present, nor things to come, nor powers, nor height, nor depth, nor any other creature, shall be able to separate us from the love of God, which is in Christ Jesus our Lord.

Does this mean that those who are saints must be saved? Let us examine this and other Scriptures.

Romans 8 is a very wonderfully comforting passage, for Paul is confirming for us that no external power can separate us from Christ. Even though Christians may go through no end of persecution, pain, and suffering, Christ will always be there for us. There is one significant variable, however, that Paul does not address here: one's own choice. It is true that no external force can separate us from the love of Christ; our own hardness of heart, however, can. Paul says of Demas in 2 Timothy 4:10a:

…for Demas forsook me, having loved this present world, and went to Thessalonica.

He has loved the world and has therefore left the fold of Christ. Did any power separate him from the love of Christ? No, but his own desire for the present world severed him from Christ again. We have further commentary on this in Hebrews 6.4–6:

For as touching those who were once enlightened and tasted of the heavenly gift, and were made partakers of the Holy Spirit, and tasted the good word of God, and the powers of the age to come, and then fell away, it is impossible to renew them again unto repentance; seeing they crucify to themselves the Son of God afresh, and put him to an open shame.

The Hebrew writer here explains quite clearly that if one falls away, one may never return to the fold. Thus, one who was a saint may fall away and be lost.

To this many will turn to 1 John 2.19 and say that John establishes that such individuals were really never with us; therefore, they were merely hypocrites, who attended services and performed service to God but were never saved. Let us consider the passage:

> They went out from us, but they were not of us; for if they had been of us, they would have continued with us: but they went out, that they might be made manifest that they all are not of us.

John does say that these individuals were really not of us, for if they had been, they would still be in the fold. This is, in fact, true: one can only fall away if there is a deficiency in the faith of that individual. This does not mean, however, that they never were saved or any such thing. We saw in Hebrews 6.4 that these individuals had "once been enlightened and [had] tasted of the heavenly gift and [had] been made partakers of the Holy Spirit, and [had] tasted the good word of God and the powers of the age to come." How can one have been enlightened, have been a partaker of the Holy Spirit, and have known the good word of God and yet not have been saved? Peter demonstrates in Acts 2.38 that through baptism, the remission of sins, one receives the gift of the Holy Spirit. If we are to have trust in God and His promises, we will see that these individuals were at one point saved, but they did not endure, and thus fell away from the faith. Jesus describes these as the seeds who fell in the rock in Matthew 13.20–21:

> "And he that was sown upon the rocky places, this is he that heareth the word, and straightway with joy receiveth it; yet hath he not root in himself, but endureth for a while; and when tribulation or persecution ariseth because of the word, straightway he stumbleth."

Likewise, the Hebrew author speaks of Christians who flagrantly sin without repentance in Hebrews 10.26–31:

> For if we sin wilfully after that we have received the knowledge of the truth, there remaineth no more a sacrifice for sins, but a certain fearful expectation of judgment, and a fierceness of fire which shall devour the adversaries. A man that hath set at nought Moses' law dieth without compassion on the word of two or three witnesses: of how much sorer punishment, think ye, shall he be

> judged worthy, who hath trodden under foot the Son of God, and
> hath counted the blood of the covenant, wherewith he was sanctified,
> an unholy thing, and hath done despite unto the Spirit of grace?
> For we know him that said, "Vengeance belongeth unto me, I will
> recompense."
> And again, "The Lord shall judge his people."
> It is a fearful thing to fall into the hands of the living God.

Does the Hebrew author give the impression that the persons who did such things were never saved? He indicates that they "received the knowledge of the truth" and that for such persons there no longer remains a sacrifice for sin. He speaks of these persons in the first person plural: it could be us ourselves! Such a one was "sanctified" by the "blood of the covenant". If one can have knowledge of the truth, be considered part of the church, and sanctified by the blood of the covenant, yet in reality were never saved in the first place, how can any of us cherish the hope of eternal life?

In the end, this exposes a great difficulty with the entire TULIP system: no one can ever *really* know whether they represent part of the elect. The possibility always exists that one was always a reprobate. The assumption is made, of course, that those who are part of Calvinist churches are the "elect", but such ones will even admit that such may not be the case for each individual. We can contrast this with the message of the Scriptures, where God establishes in 1 Peter 1, Hebrews 10.26–31, 2 Peter 2.20–22, and other passages, that many are initially saved and strive in hope to obtain the final salvation, and yet some will sin so as to fall away without obtaining that final salvation.

We can thus see that one can be saved and then fall away. The TULIP theology of Calvinism may be logical, but it does not conform to the teachings of the Scriptures.

Concerning Ministers

Many Calvinist groups also teach that ministers must be called and elected according to the standards in 1 Timothy 3 and Titus 1.[6] They also teach that the minister is the only one to administer the "sacraments," baptism and the Lord's Supper,[7] that he holds the keys described in Matthew 16.19,[8] and that he is to administer church discipline.[9] Are these teachings in harmony with God's Word?

In the discussion in **Positions of Authority: Who Is the Pastor?**, it is determined that the Scriptures speak of an office known as the overseer, the elder, the presbyter, the bishop, or the pastor, and a completely different office of the evangelist, or minister. Thus a minister may be an elder if he meets the qualifications of 1 Timothy 3 and Titus 1 and the congregation accepts him as such, but being a minister does not necessitate being an elder/pastor.

Most Calvinists have missed this distinction in the Scriptures and thus state that the minister is also a pastor/elder/overseer/bishop. This is not consistent, for even the examples in the Scriptures demonstrate that a minister need not be also an elder, etc. Paul says the following in 1 Corinthians 7.5–7:

> Defraud ye not one the other, except it be by consent for a season, that ye may give yourselves unto prayer, and may be together again, that Satan tempt you not because of your incontinency. But this I say by way of concession, not of commandment. Yet I would that all men were even as I myself. Howbeit each man hath his own gift from God, one after this manner, and another after that.

He thus states that he is not married, yet he commands the following concerning elders in 1 Timothy 3.2:

> The bishop therefore must be without reproach, the husband of one wife, temperate, sober-minded, orderly, given to hospitality, apt to teach...

Here he says that an overseer must be the husband of one wife. Finally, there is Colossians 1.24–25:

> Now I rejoice in my sufferings for your sake, and fill up on my part that which is lacking of the afflictions of Christ in my flesh for his body's sake, which is the church; whereof I was made a minister, according to the dispensation of God which was given me to you-ward, to fulfil the word of God.

He calls himself a minister, yet is not married despite the fact that he says all overseers must be the husband of one wife. There is only one conclusion that we can possibly draw from these three statements made by Paul: there is a difference between the evangelist/minister/preacher and the elder/overseer/bishop/presbyter/pastor. They are not one and the same.

Do the Scriptures require an evangelist/minister to baptize and to offer the Lord's Supper? The Scriptures make no such commandment. We even see examples in the New Testament that contradict this notion in Acts 9.10–12 and Acts 22.12–16, concerning Saul and Ananias:

> Now there was a certain disciple at Damascus, named Ananias; and the Lord said unto him in a vision, "Ananias."
> And he said, "Behold, I am here, Lord."
> And the Lord said unto him, "Arise, and go to the street which is called Straight, and inquire in the house of Judas for one named Saul, a man of Tarsus: for behold, he prayeth; and he hath seen a man named Ananias coming in, and laying his hands on him, that he might receive his sight."

> "And one Ananias, a devout man according to the law, well reported of by all the Jews that dwelt there, came unto me, and standing by me said unto me,
> 'Brother Saul, receive thy sight.'
> And in that very hour I looked up on him.
> And he said, 'The God of our fathers hath appointed thee to know his will, and to see the Righteous One, and to hear a voice from his mouth. For thou shalt be a witness for him unto all men of what thou hast seen and heard. And now why tarriest thou? arise, and be baptized, and wash away thy sins, calling on his name.'"

Paul states that Ananias baptized him, but we have not been told that Ananias was a minister, but simply a disciple of Christ. We see Christians baptizing individuals into Christ, but that serves as our only valid example from the Scriptures. Therefore, to determine that only ministers/evangelists can administer baptism and the Lord's Supper is not a doctrine supported by the Scriptures.

Do ministers hold the keys to the Kingdom as described in Matthew 16.19? Let us examine this Scripture:

> "I will give unto thee the keys of the kingdom of heaven: and whatsoever thou shalt bind on earth shall be bound in heaven; and what-

soever thou shalt loose on earth shall be loosed in heaven."

This is the same idea that was presented by Luther concerning confession, which was discussed in *Lutheranism: Confession and Sin*, that the church has been given the keys (thus, the Office of the Keys). The Calvinists have determined that the ministers, not the church, have this capacity. As before, however, this is not so. We discussed in *Roman Catholicism, I: Authority: Apostolic Succession* that the correct translation of this passage demonstrates that God has done the binding and the loosing, and that the Apostles, to whom this gift is given, are the agents of proclaiming this binding and loosing. Thus, the power is not their own, but is of God. Furthermore, there is no evidence that this power was retained after the death of the Apostles by any evangelist.

We must also ask the question, "What are the keys of the Kingdom of Heaven?" We should not think that Jesus refers to literal keys. The best understanding, from the Scriptures, is that the Gospel is the key to the Kingdom of Heaven, and therefore the preaching of the Gospel by the Apostles opened up the Kingdom to those who hear. Since evangelists are entrusted with preaching the Gospel (cf. 2 Timothy 4.4), they are to promote the Kingdom of Heaven; on the other hand, the charge to promote the Gospel is given to all Christians (Matthew 28.18–20). Therefore, we can determine that it is not the minister's duty to hold the keys to the Kingdom of Heaven; that responsibility was found with the Apostles in the first century and is now seen through the preaching and acceptance of the Word of God.

Finally, is it the minister's obligation only to perform church discipline? We read the following in 1 Corinthians 5.9–13:

> I wrote unto you in my epistle to have no company with fornicators; not at all meaning with the fornicators of this world, or with the covetous and extortioners, or with idolaters; for then must ye needs go out of the world: but as it is, I wrote unto you not to keep company, if any man that is named a brother be a fornicator, or covetous, or an idolater, or a reviler, or a drunkard, or an extortioner; with such a one no, not to eat. For what have I to do with judging them that are without? Do not ye judge them that are within? But them that are without God judgeth. Put away the wicked man from among yourselves.

This Scripture says that the wicked man needs to be removed from among "yourselves." This is our example from the Scriptures of church discipline, and it appears that the obligation falls upon the collective body, not just an evangelist. We as a group are to remove the wicked man from among ourselves; the minister is certainly included in this, although it is not his obligation alone.

Notes

1: The acrostic is explicitly discussed at http://www.reformed.org
2: *The Second Helvetic Confession*, Chapter IX, pargraph 45 (IX, 45)
3: Ibid.
4: Ibid, IX. 52
5: Ibid.
6: *The Second Helvetic Confession*, XVIII. 150
7: Ibid., XVIII. 156
8: Ibid., XVIII. 159
9: Ibid., XVIII. 165

Anglicanism/Episcopalianism

Overview

Anglicanism (from the Latin term for "English"), formally known as the Church of England, began in the 1530s under King Henry VIII. He was unhappy that the pope in Rome would not grant him an annulment of his marriage with Catherine of Aragon; this, along with political and economic reasons, led Parliament to enact legislation effectively dissolving England's ties to the Roman Catholic church. Parliament also determined that the King of England was to be the head of the Church of England, and this was the effective beginning of the Anglican church. Over the next fifty years, certain doctrinal changes were introduced, most of them coming from the Reformation occurring on the European continent, along with the introduction of the *Book of Common Prayer*, which is still used today as the order for services in the Church of England. When England began to colonize other parts of the world, they brought Anglicanism along with them: in America, after the Revolution, the "Anglican" church there felt it better to be known as the Episcopalian church (from the Greek word *episkopos*, or "bishop," since the church is headed by bishops), as it is known today. The Church of England is a mixture of Roman Catholic/Eastern Orthodox traditions along with the ideas presented in the Reformation, a synthesis not fully accepted by either side.

Variants

The Anglican church, as a collective, is known as the Anglican Communion, which is comprised of the different national churches, each headed by its own archbishop. There are Anglican churches in Australia, Canada, New Zealand, South Africa and many other countries in Africa and Asia, and most are governed within those states. Anglicanism in America is primarily seen in the Episcopal Church (USA), and while they have bishops of dioceses, the hierarchical structure generally ends there. The heads of these Anglican churches meet with each other in Canterbury, England, regarding the challenges of the church at the time. The church is thus in name united, but has autonomous groupings in various countries around the world.

Furthermore, there is the distinction between the "high church," which holds more strongly to ritual and tradition and is therefore more "Catholic," and the "low church," which is more evangelical and therefore more "Protestant." The high church/low church distinction is especially evident in the United Kingdom, yet also exists in the United States.

In America, however, there have also been a few spinoffs from the Episcopal church. The Reformed Episcopal Church in America is more Protestant-minded, the Episcopal Orthodox Christian Archdiocese of America is more conservative, and the Anglican Catholic Church is "catholic" in terms of being "universal" and sees itself as more aligned with Roman Catholicism and Eastern Orthodoxy.

General Considerations

Part I

- *See below for comparisons and contrasts with Roman Catholicism and Protestant groups.*
- *Wesleyanism: The Church and Social Responsibility*
- *The Charismatic Movement [some churches/individuals]*

Part II

- *Evangelicalism [some individuals, especially in the "low church"]*
- *Ecumenism*
- *Emergism*

Part III

- *Baptism: Infant Baptism and "Original Sin"; Baptism=Immersion; Baptism is for Remission of Sin and is Necessary for Salvation*
- *The Church Treasury, I: Benevolence: Church Benevolence to Non-Saints; The Missionary Society*
- *The Church Treasury, II: Other Considerations: Hospitals; Centers of Education; Kitchens/Fellowship Halls; Gymnasiums; Business Enterprises*

Concerning Observances:

- *Observances Concerning the Lord's Birth: Advent; Christmas*
- *Observances Concerning the Lord's Death: Ash Wednesday; Lent; Palm Sunday; Maundy Thursday; Good Friday; Easter*
- *Other Observances: Ascension-Pentecost; Epiphany; Annunciation; Days Concerning Saints*
- *Creeds: The Apostles' Creed; The Nicene Creed; The Athanasian Creed*
- *Instrumental Music*
- *The Lord's Supper: The Nature of the Emblems; The Bread and the Fruit of the Vine; When Should the Lord's Supper Be Observed? Part A: Weekly*
- *Positions of Authority: A Hierarchy of Bishops; Female Deacons [Deaconesses]; Female Elders; Female Evangelists; Homosexual Evangelists [Episcopal Church USA]; Priests; Ordination; Synods, Councils, Conventions, and Other Meetings*
- *Judaic Practices: The Ten Commandments and the "Moral Law"; Tithing*

Anglicanism and Roman Catholicism

The Church of England separated itself from Roman Catholicism not so much on the basis of doctrine but because of political reasons. Therefore, we see that Anglicanism shares much in common with Roman Catholicism, while also maintaining some traditions seen more clearly in Eastern Orthodoxy. Let us examine these now.

Apostolic Succession: The Anglican church has a system of bishops and archbishops, who (they assert) have authority similar to that of the Apostles', but makes no comment concerning authenticity as has the Roman Catholic church.

Traditions Concerning the Scriptures: The Anglicans are more akin to the Eastern Orthodox, using all of the Apocrypha (save 3 and 4 Maccabees); the Anglicans also say that the Apocrypha is placed in a lower level of emphasis than the Old Testament.[1]

Traditions Concerning Sacraments: The Anglicans are between the Roman Catholics and the rest of Protestantism concerning sacraments: they believe that there are two sacraments of necessity, baptism and the Lord's Supper, yet still hold that the other five sacraments of the Roman Catholic church, confirmation, matrimony, holy orders, anointing of the sick, and confession, are "sacramentals," good to do but not as necessary as baptism and the Lord's Supper.[2]

Traditions Concerning History: The Anglican church accepts the history of the English church, even those portions under the pope in Rome. It has not made any comment, however, on the sanctity of its history.

Traditions Concerning Mary: The Anglicans do not place as much emphasis on Mary as the Roman Catholics do, although she is still looked upon as the mother of the church, among other titles.

Traditions Concerning the Saints: The Anglican church accepts the existence of saints, although the process of canonization is not practiced. The notion of relics and other such things is rejected.[3]

Traditions Concerning Sin: The Anglican church believes that a priest/bishop has the authority from God to remit sins, and allows for its members to give confession to the priest. This action is not required to continue within the church as it is in Roman Catholicism.[4]

Traditions Concerning Consecration: The Anglican church has monks and nuns, although celibacy is not required for the clergy.[5]

Anglicanism and Protestantism

Even though the Church of England shares much in common with Roman Catholicism, it did not turn a blind eye to the doctrines developed on the European continent in Lutheranism and Calvinism. Let us examine these similarities now.

Lutheranism: Faith Alone: The Anglican church accepts the idea that we are saved by faith alone and that the work performed is done by God.[6]

Lutheranism: The Lord's Prayer: The Anglicans believe in the prayer's use as a part of their liturgy and personal life.[7]

Calvinism: Total Depravity: The Anglicans agree that man has fallen short and can do nothing to come to God; man cannot do any good work.[8]

The Book of Common Prayer

The Church of England has used a version of *The Book of Common Prayer* to guide its spiritual life since 1549. *The Book of Common Prayer* is essentially a handbook to all things Anglican: within its pages one will find the order and manner of the worship service; the prayers and the meditations (called collects) to be used at specific times of the year; the liturgies for the various observances and seasons; special ceremonies for baptism, the Lord's Supper, confirmation, the consecration of bishops/priests/deacons, the consecration of a church; prayers; thanksgivings; a catechism; and historical documents of the church. It is held by many Anglicans that while a Bible may be considered helpful to have at an Anglican/Episcopalian service, *The Book of Common Prayer* is indispensable. *The Book of Common Prayer* is also considered to be the source of unity among Anglicans: all kinds of diversity are tolerated, but all agree on the value of *The Book of Common Prayer*. Is this in harmony with the Word of God? God has not mandated a specific way to serve Him in the assembly, but to have your assembly confined to the pages of a book, even if just a guideline, could easily lead to the type of activity condemned by Jesus in Matthew 6.7–8:

> And in praying use not vain repetitions, as the Gentiles do: for they think that they shall be heard for their much speaking. Be not therefore like unto them: for your Father knoweth what things ye have need of, before ye ask him.

Rigid order easily leads to coldness and a loss of meaning. We can certainly commend the Anglicans for taking seriously the command of Paul for order to reign in the church in 1 Corinthians 14.40, but we should be wary to quench the Spirit by merely reciting words from a page with no life and no heart within them.

Notes

1: *The Book of Common Prayer*, "Historical Documents: Articles of Religion," VI

2: Ibid, "Catechism: Other Sacramental Rites"

3: e.g., Ibid., "Collects: Contemporary: The Common of Saints"

4: Ibid., "The Reconciliation of a Penitent;" "Morning Prayer I: Confession of Sin"

5: Ibid., "Prayers: 16: For Monastic Orders and Vocations"

6: Ibid., "Historical Documents: Articles of Religion," X-XIII

7: Ibid., "The Holy Eucharist: Decalogue I;" "Morning Prayer I: The Prayers"

8: Ibid., "Historical Documents: Articles of Religion," X

Baptists

Overview

The Baptist movement began in Holland in 1609 with an English Separatist, John Smythe, who preached the need for immersion in water as baptism and that it was for believers, not infants. The movement was brought to England two years later and quickly began to spread. By the middle of the seventeenth century, the movement was on American shores, where the Baptists would eventually grow to be one of the largest groups of "Christians" in North America. Baptists have developed and accepted many doctrines over the past four hundred years, with much evidence of Calvinist and premillennial influence. The movement has since diversified, and very few groups of Baptists have much in common; very few generalizations can hold true across the board.

Variants

The study of the variants in the Baptist movement is a study within itself, for there are hundreds of different groups ascribing to different sets of beliefs. In general, Baptist groups range from being outright Calvinist to those teaching more accurately concerning baptism, salvation, and God's final Judgment. The general considerations and topics of discussion will be accurate for a large number of Baptists but can by no means be attributable to all.

Some of the general terms used to describe different types of Baptists ought to be defined. "General" Baptists are those who believe that the blood of Christ was shed for all men, and so salvation is generally available to all men. "Particular" Baptists are more influenced by Calvinism and accept the concept of limited atonement. "Freewill" Baptists reject many aspects of Calvinism and believe that men have free will. "Landmark" Baptists believe that the local church is the expression of the universal assembly in a given area, to the exclusion of any others. "Primitive" Baptists seek to return to the primitive faith of the New Testament.

Major groups include the American Baptist Association, American Baptist Churches in the USA, Baptist General Conference (emerging from Pietism), General Association of General Baptist Churches, General Association of Regular Baptist Churches, National Association of Free Will Baptists, National Baptist Convention of America, National Primitive Baptist Convention, New Testament Association of Independent Baptist Churches, North American Baptist Conference, Primitive Baptists, Progressive National Baptist Convention, Reformed Baptist Church, and the Southern Baptist Convention.

General Considerations

Part I
- *Lutheranism: Faith Alone*
- *Calvinism: P- Perseverance of the Saints*
- *Plymouth Brethren: Dispensationalism; Premillennialism*

Part II
- *Evangelicalism*
- *Fundamentalism*
- *Community Church Movement*
- *House Church Movement*
- *Megachurch Movement*
- *Emergism*

Part III
- *Baptism: Baptism is for Remission of Sin and is Necessary for Salvation*
- *The Church Treasury, I: Benevolence: Church Benevolence to Non-Saints; The Missionary Society*
- *The Church Treasury, II: Other Considerations: Hospitals; Centers of Education; Kitchens/ Fellowship Halls; Gymnasiums; Business Enterprises*

Concerning Observances:
- *Observances Concerning the Lord's Birth: Christmas*
- *Observances Concerning the Lord's Death: Palm Sunday; Good Friday; Easter*

- *Instrumental Music*

- *Judaic Practices: The Ten Commandments and the "Moral Law"*

- *The Lord's Supper: The Bread and the Fruit of the Vine; When Should the Lord's Supper Be Observed? Part A: Weekly*

- *Positions of Authority: Who is the Pastor?; Ordination; Synods, Councils, Conventions, and Other Meetings*

"Once Saved, Always Saved"

Many Baptist groups hold to a doctrine rather similar to Calvinism's **P–Perseverance of the Saints**, called "Once Saved, Always Saved" (hereafter OSAS). Essentially, many Baptists have taken the Calvinist notion of "perseverance of the saints" exclusively, omitting the rest of the TULIP belief system. The belief is that once you have been saved, no matter what you do, you will still be saved. OSAS is based on Romans 8.35–39 (discussed in **Calvinism: P–Perseverance of the Saints**), and verses like Acts 16.31:

> And they said, "Believe on the Lord Jesus, and thou shalt be saved, thou and thy house."

Verses like these, which state that belief will lead to salvation, are used to say that salvation must come. Do the Scriptures teach this?

The Scriptures do teach that we can be sure of our salvation as we walk in the light (1 John 1.7). Nevertheless, our salvation is dependent on our continued obedience to God and His Word, as He Himself has made evident in Matthew 10.22:

> "And ye shall be hated of all men for My name's sake: but he that endureth to the end, the same shall be saved."

The Scriptures do make it clear that we can lose our salvation, as seen in Hebrews 6.4–6 and Hebrews 10.26–31 in **Calvinism: P–Perseverance of the Saints**, and also in Hebrews 3.12–14 and 2 Peter 2.20–22:

> Take heed, brethren, lest haply there shall be in any one of you an evil heart of unbelief, in falling away from the living God: but exhort one another day by day, so long as it is called To-day; lest any one of you be hardened by the deceitfulness of sin: for we are

become partakers of Christ, if we hold fast the beginning of our confidence firm unto the end.

For if, after they have escaped the defilements of the world through the knowledge of the Lord and Saviour Jesus Christ, they are again entangled therein and overcome, the last state is become worse with them than the first. For it were better for them not to have known the way of righteousness, than, after knowing it, to turn back from the holy commandment delivered unto them. It has happened unto them according to the true proverb, "The dog turning to his own vomit again," and,

"the sow that had washed to wallowing in the mire."

There are many that take issue with these verses, especially 2 Peter 2.20–22. They will say that Peter is discussing "false teachers" and that they were never saved. It is true that Peter is discussing false teachers, as seen in 2 Peter 2.1, but this does not necessitate that they were never saved. These individuals are said to have "escaped the defilements of the world by the knowledge of the Lord and Savior Jesus Christ." Mere comprehension of the Lord and Savior Jesus Christ does not lead to the escape of the defilements of the world, for we see many individuals who heard and understood (cf. Felix in Acts 24), yet still were defiled by the world. It is evident that these individuals were thus in the fold of Christ and then departed from it, having been again "entangled in [the world's defilements] and overcome."

In attempting to defend OSAS, many will say that since we cannot work to gain our salvation, we can do nothing to lose it. This argument is based on a false premise, that what cannot be gained by work cannot be lost by it. It is true that we cannot gain salvation by any deed that we can do, for Christ's death on the cross is sufficient (John 3.16). No one will deny, however, that salvation must be accepted. We must accept the truth that Christ died on the cross for our sins and that through Him we will be saved. We must then confess His name, repent of our sins, and be immersed in water for the forgiveness of our sins, for this is the method that He has demonstrated for us to show our acceptance of His sacrifice (Matthew 10.32, Romans 10.9–10, Acts 2.38). This is not the end of our demonstration of acceptance, for we are told that we also must make sacrifice in Romans 12.1–2:

> I beseech you therefore, brethren, by the mercies of God, to present your bodies a living sacrifice, holy, acceptable to God, which is your spiritual service. And be not fashioned according to this world: but be ye transformed by the renewing of your mind, and ye may prove what is the good and acceptable and perfect will of God.

Furthermore, we have the witness that obedience to God's will must exist if we are not to be condemned in 2 Thessalonians 1.6–9:

> If so be that it is righteous thing with God to recompense affliction to them that afflict you, and to you that are afflicted rest with us, at the revelation of the Lord Jesus from heaven with the angels of his power in flaming fire, rendering vengeance to them that know not God, and to them that obey not the gospel of our Lord Jesus: who shall suffer punishment, even eternal destruction from the face of the Lord and from the glory of his might.

It is thus true that we have not gained salvation by our deeds, but we have surely accepted salvation by our deeds. And it is very true that if we accept salvation by our deeds, we can then reject it by our deeds.

It is also said by those defending OSAS that the Bible clearly says that our belief will save us. While this is true, the Bible also says clearly that confession will save us in Romans 10.9–10:

> Because if thou shalt confess with thy mouth Jesus as Lord, and shalt believe in thy heart that God raised him from the dead, thou shalt be saved: for with the heart man believeth unto righteousness; and with the mouth confession is made unto salvation.

Furthermore, baptism also will save us in 1 Peter 3.21:

> which also after a true likeness doth now save you, even baptism, not the putting away of the filth of the flesh, but the interrogation of a good conscience toward God, through the resurrection of Jesus Christ.

Finally, the Bible is clear that our continued obedience also will save us, as Jesus said in Matthew 10.22:

> "And ye shall be hated of all men for My name's sake: but he that
> endureth to the end, the same shall be saved."

This long list of Scriptures is given to prove an argument also made in **Baptism: Baptism is for Remission of Sin and is Necessary for Salvation**: the Bible says what is necessary for salvation, but never says in any one place all the things necessary for salvation. Will we deny that belief is necessary because Romans 10.9–10 says that confession also saves us? Or will we deny the need for belief, confession, repentance, and baptism because Jesus said in Matthew 10.22 that our endurance will allow us to be saved? By no means! We see that belief is necessary because of Acts 16.31, that confession is necessary by Matthew 10.32, and so on, and that all of these criteria need to be met, not just the ones we pick and choose. Therefore, our final salvation is dependent on our ability to endure.

We have already discussed many Scriptures that show the need for obedience for salvation; there are other arguments that can be used to show the difficulties with OSAS:

1. **Satan.** In the belief system of OSAS, no matter what we do, we are saved. Therefore, why should we fear Satan? If we can be saved regardless of what we do, there is nothing that Satan can do to us. If this is so, why then does Peter say the following in 1 Peter 5.8?

    > Be sober, be watchful: your adversary the devil, as
    > a roaring lion, walketh about, seeking whom he
    > may devour.

2. **Sin.** If we are saved no matter what we do, as is said in OSAS, then what if we commit a terrible sin? Let us say that a Christian loses his composure and kills a man, and will not repent of the sin. Then what?

    It is often said that a true Christian would not do such a thing. This is so, but all Christians will falter at some point, as John says clearly in 1 John 1.8–10:

    > If we say that we have no sin, we deceive ourselves,
    > and the truth is not in us. If we confess our sins, he

is faithful and righteous to forgive us our sins, and
to cleanse us from all unrighteousness. If we say
that we have not sinned, we make him a liar, and
his word is not in us.

"We" in this context refers to Christians, and thus we would be
making Christ a liar if we would say that we have not sinned since
becoming children of God.

Normally, the response will be made that if a Christian were
to do such a thing, he would still be saved, but he would not go to
Heaven. There are many variants of this response, with the person
not going to Heaven or losing fellowship with God or losing their
"testimony." Regardless, the principle is the same: salvation is being
differentiated from going to Heaven or having fellowship with the
Father. There is only one response that can be given to this: where did
God ever separate "salvation" from going to Heaven/having fellowship with Him/having a "testimony"? He does no such thing!

The implication of this argument is enormous. If I can be "saved"
but will not go to Heaven, what is the value of salvation? Salvation is
made almost worthless if the promises of Heaven and peace do not
go along with it. Furthermore, where do those who are "saved" but
cannot enter Heaven go? God has never made such distinctions, and
therefore, neither should we.

This argument shows the inherent flaw in OSAS, for it is based
on the premise that salvation is immediate and permanent. The
Scriptures, especially in 1 Peter 1, make it clear that there are two
levels of salvation: initial salvation, obtained when one becomes a
child of God, and final salvation, which will be made manifest
in the resurrection. While we have obtained initial salvation, we
strive toward our final salvation, which will be based on our endurance in the truth. This is why God makes it evident that salvation is only possible for those who continue in His truth. Our salvation is only permanent when we have left this Earth and have
returned to our Master.

Religious Society of Friends (Quakers)

Overview

The Religious Society of Friends (most commonly referred to as Quakers) began around 1648 with revelations supposedly given to George Fox in England. For the rest of his life he went around England, Wales, Scotland, Ireland, and even America and Holland, preaching concerning the revelations given to him. The Quakers have separated the practice of Christianity from having doctrines, and prefer to follow the former; they have removed any physical event of importance (including baptism and the Lord's Supper) to focus on the spiritual life. The New Testament, according to Friends theology, should not be taken as the final revelation of God; it is just as possible to receive revelations today as it was in the first century. Quakers are known for plain dress, respectful greeting to all, and being rather informal in meetings.

Variants

Quaker groups are divided mostly in terms of conferences, including the Friends General Conference, the Friends United Meeting, and the Evangelical Friends International. The Religious Society of Friends (Conservative), having perceived the overall movement toward Evangelical beliefs, has maintained more traditional Quaker beliefs.

General Considerations

Part I

- *Anabaptism: Nonresistance*

Part II

- *Evangelicalism*
- *Ecumenism*

Part III

- *Baptism: The Need for Baptism; Baptism=Immersion; Baptism is for Remission of Sin and is Necessary for Salvation*
- *The Church Treasury, I: Benevolence: Church Benevolence to Non-Saints; The Missionary Society*
- *The Church Treasury, II: Other Considerations: Hospitals; Centers of Education*
- *The Lord's Supper: The Need for the Lord's Supper; When Should the Lord's Supper Be Observed? Part A: Weekly*
- *Positions of Authority: Female Evangelists; Synods, Councils, Conventions, and Other Meetings*

Physical and Spiritual Natures

The Quakers are known for their concept of "practicing" Christianity, believing in "living" Christianity rather than having "doctrinal" Christianity.[1] This emphasis is complete, for the Quakers do not practice baptism, the Lord's Supper, or any physical rite; instead, they believe in the "baptism of the Spirit" and having meetings where the communion is in the unity of the Spirit.[2] Quaker theology is essentially the working of the Spirit, with little to be left for the physical nature: man comes to God by the working of the Spirit, and his only comprehension of God can be through the Spirit.[3] Is this what the Scriptures teach?

It is certainly true that the Spirit is to work within us and that there are important spiritual natures to such things as baptism and the Lord's Supper. Nevertheless, we do not see evidence that the physical aspects of these practices are to be omitted. Christianity was never meant to be a purely physical religion, but it also was never meant to be a religion without any physical action. We have positive commandments to be immersed in water for the remission of our sin and for the partaking of the Lord's Supper (see **Baptism** and **The Lord's Supper** for these commandments), and we see them being performed physically by Christ and His disciples. The Quakers were correct in condemning the attitudes of other denominations of the time, which treated these acts as physical rites with no spiritual value within them; the reaction of completely rejecting the physical nature of baptism and the Lord's Supper, however, is just as unjustifiable.

We certainly will not reject the Spirit's work in the conversion of man from sinner to Christian; however, we see that the agency of the Spirit is extremely similar to the agency of the Word of God. Both assist in convicting the sinner of his sin (John 16.8; Titus 1.9), sanctifying man (1 Corinthians 6.11; John 17.17), calling mankind out of sin (Revelation 22.17; 2 Thessalonians 2.14), and finally, in the need to be born again (John 3.5; 1 Peter 1.23). We therefore hear the words of Paul in Romans 10.17:

So belief cometh of hearing, and hearing by the word of Christ.

The Quakers deny this, saying that the Scriptures cannot be understood without the revelation of the Spirit and that the Spirit still teaches today beyond the Scriptures.[4] Yet we have the words of Jude in Jude 1.3:

Beloved, while I was giving all diligence to write unto you of our common salvation, I was constrained to write unto you exhorting you to contend earnestly for the faith which was once for all delivered unto the saints.

The faith was handed down "once for all." Where do we see this faith originate? From the word of Christ, in Romans 10.17. How do we have the word of Christ? We are told in John 14.26 the following concerning the Apostles:

"But the Comforter, even the Holy Spirit, whom the Father will send in My name, he shall teach you all things, and bring to your remembrance all that I said unto you."

The Spirit's work in the Apostles was to have them remember the word of Christ, which they then faithfully wrote in the Scriptures, evidenced in 2 Timothy 3.16–17:

Every scripture inspired of God is also profitable for teaching, for reproof, for correction, for instruction which is in righteousness. That the man of God may be complete, furnished completely unto every good work.

The Scriptures will equip us for every good work; what else can?

Finally, we are told the following concerning revelation in 1 Corinthians 13.8–10:

> Love never faileth: but whether there be prophecies, they shall be done away; whether there be tongues, they shall cease; whether there be knowledge, it shall be done away. For we know in part, and we prophesy in part; but when that which is perfect is come, that which is in part shall be done away.

As Jude told us that the faith was delivered "once for all," surely we see that the revelation of God to man, the "perfect," has come as the Scriptures. There has not been knowledge since the time of the Apostles; are we to believe the Quakers that the Spirit of God did not give knowledge for the 1,500 year period between them and the Apostles? We would make God a liar, for the promise was made in Matthew 28.20:

> "and lo, I am with you always, even unto the end of the world."

Furthermore, we know that the Spirit will not preach a Gospel contrary to the one already given, seen in Galatians 1.6–9:

> I marvel that ye are so quickly removing from him that called you in the grace of Christ unto a different gospel; which is not another gospel only there are some that trouble you, and would pervert the gospel of Christ. But though we, or an angel from heaven, should preach unto you any gospel other than that which we preached unto you, let him be anathema. As we have said before, so say I now again, if any man preacheth unto you any gospel other than that which ye received, let him be anathema.

If we see that Paul preaches the necessity of baptism (cf. Galatians 3.27; Acts 22.16) and the partaking of the Lord's Supper (1 Corinthians 11.17–30), yet the Quakers do not and further propose to have revelation from God, whom are we to believe? The Scriptures have spoken.

It is good to have a religion where its tenets are practiced, and we will not fault the Quakers for this. They were right to condemn the "religious" among them who spoke righteousness but did not perform it. To completely reject doctrine, however, is just as wrong as holding only to it. Christianity can and must be a religion of spirit and truth, where one holds to the faith delivered once for all and practices the pure religion of James 1.27, to visit orphans and widows in distress and to keep oneself unstained from the world. Neither portion is optional.

Perfectionism

The other main tenet of Quakerism (among many other movements of the seventeenth century) is perfectionism, that God can make man perfect, without sin. George Fox, the founder of the Quakers, declared himself to be without sin.[5] Do the Scriptures teach that man can be perfect on Earth?

Many will point to Matthew 5.48 to prove this belief:

"Ye therefore shall be perfect, as your heavenly Father is perfect."

We certainly will not disagree with this verse; we are to strive to be perfect (in the Greek, mature or complete), as our heavenly Father is perfect/mature/complete. We do have the witness of Paul, however, about our Christian path, in Philippians 3.12–16:

> Not that I have already obtained, or am already made perfect: but I press on, if so be that I may lay hold on that for which also I was laid hold on by Christ Jesus. Brethren, I could not myself yet to have laid hold: but one thing I do, forgetting the things which are behind, and stretching forward to the things which are before, I press on toward the goal unto the prize of the high calling of God in Christ Jesus. Let us therefore, as many as are perfect, be thus minded: and if in anything ye are otherwise minded, this also shall God reveal unto you: only, whereunto we have attained, by that same rule let us walk.

Paul says that he has not yet become perfect, but he strives for this perfection, and then calls upon "us…as many as are perfect," to have this attitude! Perfection is clearly aimed to be a level of maturity, not complete perfection, but maturity in Christ, as contrasted with a babe in Christ.

We can surely see that if Paul himself said he was not perfect and yet was an apostle of the Lord Jesus Christ, how could George Fox claim perfection? The Scriptures are clear in showing that even after becoming children of God, we will sin; fortunately, we can obtain forgiveness, as seen in 1 John 1.8–10:

> If we say that we have no sin, we deceive ourselves, and the truth is not in us. If we confess our sins, he is faithful and righteous to forgive us our sins, and to cleanse us from all unrighteousness. If we say that we have not sinned, we make him a liar, and his word is not in us.

The Christian will not live a life of sin (cf. 1 John 1.6), but will continually strive to be sinless. We surely should develop in the faith and therefore sin less as we grow in Christ, but never will we reach a point of utter sinlessness before our glorification. The Scriptures show that to say that one is sinless makes Christ a liar, and His Word is not in him.

Notes

1: From Jessamyn West, *A Quaker Reader*, p. 17

2: Ibid., p. 8

3: Ibid., pp. 15–16

4: Robert Barclay, "Turn Thy Mind into the Light," from *A Quaker Reader*, p. 232

5: George Fox, *The Journal*, ed. Nigel Smith, p. 48.

Pietism

Overview

Pietism, or the Pietist movement, saw its origin in Jan Hus, the pre-Reformation preacher in the modern day Czech Republic, in the 1450s; more specifically, the movement originated in Germany in the seventeenth century within the Lutheran church with a group of Lutherans interested more in the working of the Spirit and a personal faith than the institutional type faith of the church at that time. Many such Lutherans stayed within Lutheranism; some of these "Pietists," however, were disenchanted with the attitudes in the Lutheran church, and began their own churches, most of them involving the term "Brethren," of which the Church of the Brethren is the oldest and one of the largest. John Wesley was influenced greatly by the Pietists, and many consider him to be a Pietist. These groups are known for a focus on individual faith with the workings of the Spirit and a very literal reading of New Testament practices, including foot washing and the holy kiss.

Variants

The Moravian Brethren, called as such by the region of their origin, trace their history back to the 1450s with Jan Hus and his preaching. Otherwise, the Pietist movement has many members within the Lutheran churches, but by the beginning of the eighteenth century, some groups began to separate, starting with the Schwarzenau Brethren, now known as the Church of the Brethren, in 1708. The Old German Baptist Brethren separated from the Church of the Brethren in 1881 over the adaptations in dress and custom in the nineteenth century; in 1921, an even more conservative faction of the Old German Baptist Brethren split off, calling themselves the Old Order German Baptist Brethren.

On the other side of the Church of the Brethren, the "Progressive" Brethren split off in 1882 over the lack of adaptation to some of the innovations of the nineteenth century. They formed the Brethren Church (Ashland, Ohio), which would split again in 1939 with the formation of the Fellowship of Grace Brethren Churches. Finally, another smaller division occurred within the Church of the Brethren in 1926 with the departure of the Dunkard Brethren.

The Pietist movement also came to America. The Brethren in Christ Church formed on the basis of revivalistic preaching heavily influenced by Pietism and Anabaptism in Pennsylvania in the late eighteenth century. In 1767, some of those who were influential in establishing the Brethren in Christ Church diverged and formed the United Brethren. The United Brethren were split in the late 1860s by one George Hoffman, whose followers were known first as the "Hoffmanites" and later as the United Christian Church. In 1889, another division occurred in the United Brethren, with a portion of the more liberal members joining the Evangelical Church (another sect of German Pietists) to form the Evangelical United Brethren Church, which in 1968 joined the Methodists to form the United Methodist Church.

Meanwhile, many Swedish Lutherans who were caught up in the Pietist movement immigrated to the United States and formed the Evangelical Covenant Church and also what would become the Evangelical Free Church of America. These two groups tend to be more loosely Pietist.

Another group of note is the Mennonite Brethren Church, discussed in **Anabaptism: Variants**.

The Church of God (Anderson, Indiana) is sometimes considered part of the Pietism movement, having come out of the holiness emphasis of both Pietism and Wesleyanism.

General Considerations

Part I
- *Lutheranism: Faith Alone*
- *Anabaptism: Nonresistance*
- *Religious Society of Friends (Quakers): Physical and Spiritual Natures*

Part II
- *Evangelicalism*
- *Ecumenism*

Part III
- *Baptism: Tripartite Baptism; Baptism is for Remission of Sin and is Necessary for Salvation*
- *The Church Treasury, I: Benevolence: Church Benevolence to Non-Saints; The Missionary Society*
- *The Church Treasury, II: Other Considerations: Hospitals; Centers of Education; Kitchens/Fellowship Halls*

Concerning Observances:
- *Observances Concerning the Lord's Birth: Christmas*
- *Observances Concerning the Lord's Death: Palm Sunday; Good Friday; Easter*

- *Instrumental Music*

- *The Lord's Supper: When Should the Lord's Supper Be Observed? Part A: Weekly*

- *Positions of Authority: Who Is the Pastor?; Synods, Councils, Conventions, and Other Meetings*

Foot Washing

One of the practices of note of the Pietist movement is foot washing, the practice of washing another's feet as a sign of servitude. The Scriptures used to justify this are John 13.12–15 and 1 Timothy 5.9–10:

> So when he had washed their feet, and taken his garments, and
> sat down again, he said unto them,
> "Know ye what I have done to you? Ye call me, Teacher, and, Lord:
> and ye say well; for so I am. If I then, the Lord and the Teacher, have
> washed your feet, ye also ought to wash one another's feet. For I have
> given you an example, that ye also should do as I have done to you."

> Let none be enrolled as a widow under threescore years old, hav-
> ing been the wife of one man, well reported of for good works;
> if she hath brought up children, if she hath used hospitality to
> strangers, if she hath washed the saints' feet, if she hath relieved
> the afflicted, if she hath diligently followed every good work.

Do these mean that we must wash the feet of others? Not necessarily. We certainly do not condemn the Pietists for practicing foot washing, for there is clear Scripture showing that it can be performed. The practice itself is not mandated, however, and we can see this by understanding the words of Christ and Paul.

Christ is teaching His disciples the lesson of servitude in John 13. He takes the most extreme example, the washing of feet, which was generally considered a despicable work because it was one done by slaves. Foot washing was necessary because the ancients walked either barefoot or with hard sandals; either way, their feet were sure to be callused after any journey of distance. By washing the disciples' feet and telling them to do the same, He teaches them that they ought to serve one another. This is brought out even more clearly by Paul in 1 Timothy 5.10, who uses foot washing as a qualification of a widow being placed on the "list." It is interesting to note that Paul never says that she "served the saints;" he says that she has "washed the saints' feet." Paul clearly uses foot washing to represent her serving the saints, for it would make no sense for the widow to need to help the afflicted and show hospitality to strangers but nothing for the saints beyond mere foot washing!

Therefore, we can see that "foot washing" was a symbol for the practice of saints assisting one another. If one wishes to wash another's feet today, he is surely able to do so. To interpret this practice so literally as to bind it as necessary for proper obedience to God, however, is not Biblically justifiable.

Love Feast

Pietists also practice the *agape* or "love feast," a dinner before the Lord's Supper. The evidence for this is Mark 14.22 and 1 Corinthians 11.20–21:

> And as they were eating, he took bread, and when he had blessed,
> he brake it, and gave to them, and said,
> "Take ye: this is my body."

> When therefore ye assemble yourselves together, it is not possible
> to eat the Lord's supper: for in your eating each one taketh before
> other his own supper; and one is hungry, and another is drunken.

Do these verses justify a feast before the Lord's Supper? The entirety of the Scriptures does not support this. It is true that Jesus most certainly partook of an evening meal (the Passover meal, in fact) before He instituted the Lord's Supper; we see, however, that He only made commandment to observe the Lord's Supper itself, as seen in Luke 22.19–20 and 1 Corinthians 11.23–26:

> And he took bread, and when he had given thanks, he brake it,
> and gave to them, saying,
> "This is My body which is given for you: this do in remembrance
> of Me."
> And the cup in like manner after supper, saying,
> "This cup is the new covenant in My blood, even that which is
> poured out for you."

> For I received of the Lord that which also I delivered unto you,
> that the Lord Jesus in the night in which he was betrayed took
> bread; and when he had given thanks, he brake it, and said,
> "This is My body, which is for you: this do in remembrance of Me."
> In like manner also the cup, after supper, saying,
> "This cup is the new covenant in My blood: this do, as often as ye
> drink it, in remembrance of Me."
> For as often as ye eat this bread, and drink the cup, ye proclaim
> the Lord's death till he come.

We see, therefore, that the memorial instituted was the breaking of the bread and the dividing of the cup, not the meal that occurred beforehand. We can take this understanding to 1 Corinthians 11.20–21, which shows clearly that Paul is discussing the Lord's Supper, for the Corinthians had not come together for the purpose of remembering the Lord as much as to eat and drink. Paul in fact says the following about eating of meals in 1 Corinthians 10.22:

> What? have ye not houses to eat and to drink in? or despise ye the
> church of God, and put them to shame that have not? What shall
> I say to you? shall I praise you in this? I praise you not.

The solution to the class divisions manifest in the eating of meals among the Corinthians, therefore, is not to eat such meals in the assembly, but to eat and drink at home. This demonstrates quite clearly that a meal before the Lord's Supper is not justified.

Therefore, there is no commandment to partake of a "love feast" before the Lord's Supper. More information on these subjects can be seen in **The Lord's Supper** and **The Church Treasury, II: Kitchens/Fellowship Halls**.

The Holy Kiss

Pietists also observe the holy kiss, as seen in Romans 16.16:

> Salute one another with a holy kiss. All the churches of Christ salute you.

It is certainly justifiable if one wishes to greet one another in this fashion; to bind it on others, however, is Biblically unjustifiable. It was customary in ancient Roman and Greek society (and in many European and Asian societies today) to greet one another with kisses, and Paul here determines that the kiss must be "holy." Our custom in America today is to shake hands or to give a slight hug, and by doing so we share with one another the same affection and warmth that was demonstrated in Roman times with a kiss.

Wesleyanism

Overview

Wesleyanism, manifest today in Methodist and Holiness churches, is named for its founders, John and Charles Wesley. In 1736, these men traveled to the Georgia colony in America as missionaries for the Church of England; they left rather disheartened at what they saw. Both men then had "religious experiences," especially John in 1738, being greatly influenced by the Pietist movement. They began to organize a movement within the Church of England to focus on personal faith and holiness, and they succeeded. John Wesley took the Reformation churches to task over the nature of sanctification, the process by which a believer is made to conform to the image of Christ, and in many ways restored the New Testament teachings regarding the work of God and the believer in sanctification. The movement did well within the Church of England in Britain, but when the movement crossed the ocean into America, it took on a form of its own, finally being established as the Methodist Episcopal Church in 1784. The Wesleyan churches are very similar to Anglicanism, yet have added a strong emphasis on personal faith and personal experience.

Variants

The Wesleyan movement began as a reform movement within the Church of England, and in many places, it remains as such. In some places, especially in America, the movement separated itself from its "mother church" and became known as the Methodist Episcopal Church. Many divisions occurred within the Methodist Episcopal Church in the nineteenth century, mostly over first the slavery question and later the inclusion of African-Americans. Some of these schisms healed in the early twentieth century, and many of the splinter Methodist groups came together to form The Methodist Church by 1939. In 1968, the Methodist Church joined with the Pietist Evangelical United Brethren

Church to form The United Methodist Church, the largest Methodist church in America. Other groups include the African Methodist Episcopal Church, Christian Methodist Episcopal Church, the Congregational Methodist Church, the Evangelical Church of North America, the Evangelical Congregational Church, the Evangelical Methodist Church, the Free Methodist Church of North America, and the Southern Methodist Church.

In the nineteenth century, a dissension arose over the nature of sanctification. Those who saw sanctification as a never completed progressive task, true to Wesley's teachings, remained within the Methodist churches; others, however, having been influenced by revivalist Evangelicalism, believed in instantaneous sanctification that could be perfected. Those who followed this line of thought began the various Holiness churches, including the Church of Christ (Holiness) USA, Church of God (Holiness), the Churches of Christ in Christian Union, and the Wesleyan Church, which are present today. In the nineteenth century, there were many other Holiness groups; many of these groups became the foundation for the Pentecostal movement. Other Holiness groups that rejected the Pentecostal movement merged to form the Church of the Nazarene, perhaps the most prevalent Holiness denomination.

General Considerations

Part I

- *Roman Catholicism, II: Tradition: Traditions Concerning Sacraments [Confirmation]*
- *Lutheranism: Faith Alone*
- *Calvinism: T–Total Depravity*

Part II

- *Evangelicalism*
- *Ecumenism*
- *Fundamentalism*
- *Community Church Movement*
- *House Church Movement*
- *Megachurch Movement*
- *Emergism*

Part III
- *Baptism: Infant Baptism and "Original Sin"; Baptism=Immersion; Baptism is for Remission of Sin and is Necessary for Salvation*
- *The Church Treasury, I: Benevolence: Church Benevolence to Non-Saints; The Missionary Society*
- *The Church Treasury, II: Other Considerations: Hospitals; Centers of Education; Kitchens/ Fellowship Halls; Gymnasiums; Business Enterprises*

Concerning Observances:
- *Observances Concerning the Lord's Birth: Advent; Christmas*
- *Observances Concerning the Lord's Death: Ash Wednesday; Lent; Palm Sunday; Good Friday; Easter*
- *Other Observances: Ascension-Pentecost; Epiphany*
- *Creeds: The Apostles' Creed; The Nicene Creed*
- *Instrumental Music*
- *Judaic Practices: The Ten Commandments and the "Moral Law"; Tithing*
- *The Lord's Supper: When Should the Lord's Supper Be Observed? Part A: Weekly*
- *Positions of Authority: Who Is The Pastor?; A Hierarchy of Bishops; Female Deacons [Deaconesses]; Female Elders; Female Evangelists; Homosexual Evangelists [disputed]; Ordination; Synods, Councils, Conventions, and Other Meetings*

The Church and Social Responsibility

The Wesleyan churches teach that the church has responsibilities in the society surrounding it, notably, that the gospel contains "relevant social concerns,"[1] and, specifically:

> It is our conviction that the good news of the Kingdom must judge, redeem, and reform the sinful social structures of our time.[2]

Are these teachings in harmony with the Scriptures? In order to determine this, we must see whether or not the Christians in the apostolic era preached a gospel containing social concerns.

Paul speaks of the relationship of Christians to others in 1 Timothy 2.1–4:

> I exhort therefore, first of all, that supplications, prayers, intercessions, thanksgivings, be made for all men; for kings and all that are in high place; that we may lead a tranquil and quiet life in all godliness and gravity. This is good and acceptable in the sight of God our Saviour; who would have all men to be saved, and come to the knowledge of the truth.

Paul says that Christians do have the responsibility to pray to God concerning all those who are in the world; does he say that we have a responsibility to reform the social structures around us?

There are no Scriptures in the New Testament that teach that the Christian is to attempt to reform the social structures in which he lives. The Christian can surely assist those in distress (James 1.27), and is most certainly commissioned to preach the good news of Christ to all men (Matthew 28.18–20), yet no mention is made of the Christian changing society.

The Bible does have the following to say, however, about the Christian and the world, in Romans 12.1–2:

> I beseech you therefore, brethren, by the mercies of God, to present your bodies a living sacrifice, holy, acceptable to God, which is your spiritual service. And be not fashioned according to this world: but be ye transformed by the renewing of your mind, and ye may prove what is the good and acceptable and perfect will of God.

Thus, we see that we are not to conform to the world. Are we to expect the world to conform to us? Jesus spoke the following to His disciples about their relation to the world:

> "And brother shall deliver up brother to death, and the father his child: and children shall rise up against parents, and cause them to be put to death. And ye shall be hated of all men for my name's sake: but he that endureth to the end, the same shall be saved," *(Matthew 10.21–22).*

> "Think not that I came to send peace on the earth: I came not to send peace, but a sword. For I came to set a man at variance

against his father, and the daughter against her mother, and the daughter in law against her mother in law: and a man's foes shall be they of his own household," *(Matthew 10.34–36)*.

Are these the words of a man expecting to change society? By no means! Jesus warned His disciples that they would be persecuted for the sake of the Word, not accepted for it. If the message prepared was going to be seen as hostile, how could anyone expect it to change a society?

Perhaps we can learn by the example of Jesus Himself. We see the following in John 6.15:

> Jesus therefore perceiving that they were about to come and take him by force, to make him king, withdrew again into the mountain himself alone.

And further in John 18.36–37:

> Jesus answered, "My kingdom is not of this world: if my kingdom were of this world, then would my servants fight, that I should not be delivered to the Jews: but now is my kingdom not from hence."
> Pilate therefore said unto him, Art thou a king then? Jesus answered, Thou sayest that I am a king. To this end have I been born, and to this end am I come into the world, that I should bear witness unto the truth. Every one that is of the truth heareth my voice."

Jesus never meant for His Kingdom to be an earthly kingdom. Had His desire been to reform society, what better capacity can there be to do so than the kingship? Yet He would not have it. His Kingdom is not of this earth; it is a spiritual kingdom, attempting to reform the heart of each individual member. It is in stark contrast with the kingdom of this world, as seen in 1 John 2.15–17:

> Love not the world, neither the things that are in the world. If any man love the world, the love of the Father is not in him. For all that is in the world, the lust of the flesh and the lust of the eyes and the vain glory of life, is not of the Father, but is of the world. And the world passeth away, and the lust thereof: but he that do-

eth the will of God abideth for ever.

What, then, is the Christian's relationship to his society?

We have already examined Romans 12.1–2, and we can see further from 1 Corinthians 5.12–13 that the judgment of those outside the church is left to God:

> For what have I to do with judging them that are without? Do not ye judge them that are within? But them that are without God judgeth. Put away the wicked man from among yourselves.

We are told to observe some rules of society, as seen in Romans 12.17–18:

> Render to no man evil for evil. Take thought for things honorable in the sight of all men. If it be possible, as much as in you lieth, be at peace with all men.

Yet as Christians, we are asked to make a different kind of impact on the world. We are told concerning this in Matthew 5.13–16:

> "Ye are the salt of the earth: but if the salt have lost its savor, where-with shall it be salted? it is thenceforth good for nothing, but to be cast out and trodden under foot of men. Ye are the light of the world. A city set on a hill cannot be hid. Neither do men light a lamp, and put it under the bushel, but on the stand; and it shineth unto all that are in the house. Even so let your light shine before men; that they may see your good works, and glorify your Father who is in heaven."

The Christian's example in living should reflect the love of Jesus within him and should shine to the world, beckoning all to come to Him. We should not suppose that we can judge, redeem, and reform our social structures; in-stead, by being examples of Christ, we may bring some in those social structures to be redeemed and reformed by Christ Jesus Himself.

The individual Christian, if he will live a life pleasing to God, must have concern for the poor, the disenfranchised, and other needy persons in society (Galatians 2.10, Galatians 6.10, James 1.27). Nevertheless, the only way of deliverance from sin and death is obedience to God (Romans 6.23), and the only hope that we have to reform society is for each individual to come to faith in Christ Jesus and act accordingly. We cannot establish the Kingdom by reforming society; we can only hope to reform society by promoting the Kingdom.

Notes

1: *The Book of Discipline of the United Methodist Church*, 1996 ed., p. 47

2: Ibid.

Plymouth Brethren

Overview

The Plymouth Brethren, or simply "Brethren," began around 1827 with four individuals in Ireland who assembled by themselves since they had difficulties with the "professed" churches of the day. They did not see the Scripture for the doctrines of the churches around them and thus began preaching this to other individuals. Many "gatherings" grew up throughout the United Kingdom, with the most well-known group being founded in Plymouth, England, from which the name "Plymouth Brethren" is derived. The Brethren are known for simplicity in meeting and a "non-denominational" approach to their church; they are, however, best known for the origin in John Darby of the dispensational/premillennial belief system, incorporated today in much of Evangelical teaching.

Variants

The Plymouth Brethren have had some division, notably over the nature of church discipline, whether a disciplinary action by one church was binding on all congregations or only those affected. The exclusive group, believing that the action was binding on all congregations, has in its ranks the best known teachers, including John Darby; their position, however, led to more divisions that have since been healed. The open group, believing that the action was only for those groups that were affected, is known more for their evangelism and such things.

General Considerations

Part I

- *Lutheranism: Faith Alone*
- *Calvinism: P–Perseverance of the Saints*
- *Baptists: "Once Saved, Always Saved"*

Dispensationalism

The Plymouth Brethren are well known for the doctrinal system which they believed to have "restored," known as Dispensationalism/Premillennialism. Dispensationalism is the determination of different periods of time in the history of God's involvement with humanity, called "dispensations."[1] To the Dispensationalists, there are three main periods:

1. The Mosaic Law;
2. The Time of Grace;
3. The Millennial Kingdom.[2]

These can be further broken down into seven dispensations:

1. Innocence (the Garden);
2. Conscience (between Adam and Noah);
3. Government (Noah to Abraham; so named because of the determination of eating meat and the "death penalty" in Genesis 9);
4. Promise (Abraham to Moses on Sinai);
5. Law (Moses to Christ)
6. Grace (Christ to the Millennial Kingdom)
7. Millennial Kingdom (1,000 year reign of Christ in Jerusalem).[3]

The dispensational theology further says that its system shows God's progressive development in His dealings with mankind and that God will deal with not only the church but also Israel in the end times.[4]

Dispensationalism goes hand in hand with premillennialism, for dispensationalism attempts to show God's plan through the ages which will reach a climax in the millennial kingdom; premillennialism attempts to explain exactly how we will reach this "millennial kingdom." Dispensationalism requires the premillennial theology in order to exist—specifically, the idea that we must interpret all prophecy literally, and then direct it to concern the "end times." We will see in our study of premillennialism that many of these prophecies have already been fulfilled, and the literal use of some of the prophetic language of the Bible is not consistent with other truths described in Scripture. We surely agree that there have been different covenants made by God with man in history, notably with Adam, Noah, Abraham, Isaac, Jacob, Moses, and Christ. Since then, the Scriptures demonstrate that God's judgment will take place in a day (cf. Acts 17.30, 2 Peter 3.7–10), we will see that the idea of a literal, physical "millennial kingdom" is not in harmony with the Scriptures.

Premillennialism

Premillennialism is a doctrine that was purportedly "restored" by John Darby, one of the founders of the Plymouth Brethren. It has since grown in popularity, and the majority of those in the Evangelical movement adhere to its tenets. "Premillennialism" means "before a thousand years," and it refers to the belief that we are currently living in the period before Christ returns to reign for a thousand years on earth. The premillennial system of belief, however, tends to go beyond the mere belief in a thousand-year period to come. Premillennialists have developed a belief system concerning the "end times," or the period of time just before the coming of Christ to establish said kingdom, by adapting Old Testament and New Testament prophecies to fit within the frame of the Revelation, all of which are taken "literally."[5] Premillennialists believe that there will be a period of seven years just before the millennial kingdom known as the "tribulation," when the judgments of God as seen in the Revelation will be fulfilled literally.[6] The premillennialists believe that the church will be "raptured," or taken up to be with Christ, at some point during this period; it is internally debated whether it will be before the Tribulation, in the middle of it, or at its conclusion.[7] Finally, they believe that Christ will return and establish His millennial kingdom on earth, at the conclusion of which all evildoers will be thrown into the lake of fire and the righteous will live in the "new Jerusalem" as described in Revelation 21 and 22.[8] Is this belief system in harmony with the Scriptures? Let us examine the tenets of premillennialism.

Premillennialism = Literal Teaching?

That dispensational premillennialism represents the "literal" understanding of Biblical prophecy is one of its foundational principles.[9] Others, in their view, have "allegorized" the prophecies, leading to apostasy.[10] Is this an accurate analysis?

It should be noted here that premillennialism is not a belief system that takes every prophecy concerning the end of time literally. We have two Scriptures which speak concerning the return of Christ, and neither is accepted literally in premillennialism—Acts 17.30–31 and 2 Peter 3.10:

> "The times of ignorance therefore God overlooked; but now he commandeth men that they should all everywhere repent: inasmuch as he hath appointed a day in which he will judge the world in righteousness by the man whom he hath ordained; whereof he hath given assurance unto all men, in that he hath raised him from the dead."

> But the day of the Lord will come as a thief; in the which the heavens shall pass away with a great noise, and the elements shall be dissolved with fervent heat, and the earth and the works that are therein shall be burned up.

Premillennialists hold to the belief that the "day of the Lord" as described in these two passages is not a literal 24-hour period, but rather the time of the tribulation, God's judgments upon the earth.[11] Why can this period not be a 24-hour period as we recognize a "day?" If this were so, it would completely uproot the whole premillennialist belief in the tribulation period and the millennial kingdom, so they allegorize the term "day" in Acts 17.30 and 2 Peter 3.9.

Therefore, it is evident that premillennialists consciously determine which Scriptures they will interpret literally and which ones they will interpret symbolically or allegorically in order to fit their belief system. As we will see, there are other ways of looking at Scriptures concerning Christ's return that by no means necessitate the premillennial system of belief.

Prophetic Language

Another founding premise of premillennial theology is the literal rendering of prophecy, using the following guideline:

> When the plain sense of Scripture makes common sense, seek no other sense, but take every word at its primary, literal meaning unless the facts of the immediate context clearly indicate otherwise.[12]

We certainly agree that as often as possible, the literal meaning of a text should be used; however, the premillennialists have missed an important criterion: we should read the text so that it is in harmony with the text as a whole. Many times, if we were to interpret all texts literally, we would have a contradiction: a good example was used previously, with the "day of the Lord" in Acts 17.30 and 2 Peter 3.9 versus the "millennial kingdom" of Revelation 20.4. In these situations, then, how are we to understand what to interpret literally and what to interpret symbolically/allegorically?

For our considerations dealing with Christ's return, we must understand that God has used prophetic language since the days of old to communicate the events of the future. We can recognize that much prophetic language, especially in an eschatological context, is language full of symbolism and allegory used to help facilitate the understanding of future events in a way not immediately obvious. Even the premillennialists understand this use of prophetic language, since many of the figures of the Revelation require non-literal interpretation. An example is the first horseman of Revelation 6.2:

> And I saw, and behold, a white horse, and he that sat thereon had a bow; and there was given unto him a crown: and he came forth conquering, and to conquer.

Does this mean that there will appear a man on a white horse with a bow and a crown conquering? By no means! The language used demonstrates to us that this individual will be given authority to conquer. The question, therefore, is not whether we interpret prophetic language literally or figuratively, but how we understand the referent of the language.

Probably the best text to use to demonstrate the differences between literal and prophetic language is Acts 2.16–21:

> "But this is that which hath been spoken through the prophet Joel:
> 'And it shall be in the last days,' saith God, 'I will pour forth of
> My Spirit upon all flesh: And your sons and your daughters shall
> prophesy, And your young men shall see visions, And your old men
> shall dream dreams: yea and on My servants and on My handmaid-
> ens in those days Will I pour forth of My Spirit; and they shall
> prophesy. And I will show wonders in the heaven above, And signs
> on the earth beneath; Blood, and fire, and vapor of smoke: The sun
> shall be turned into darkness, And the moon into blood, Before the
> day of the Lord come, That great and notable day. And it shall be,
> that whosoever shall call on the name of the Lord shall be saved.'"

Peter is quoting Joel 2.28–32 here; we will be discussing this verse below as
it pertains to the arguments of the premillennialists. We see, however, that
Peter, filled with the Holy Spirit as seen in Acts 2.4, says that "this," the
apostles speaking in the tongues of those present, "is what was spoken of by
the prophet Joel." If we accept the literal words of Peter, we must believe that
the whole of what is quoted from Joel was fulfilled on the day of Pentecost.
It may be said, however, that the sun did not turn to darkness, nor the moon
to blood on that day, and literally, this is true. If we were to take the literal rendering of this whole text, we would have a contradiction indeed. Yet,
there is prophetic language full of imagery here: the darkening of the sun
and the moon into blood can refer to the fall of kingdoms and the destruction of rulers, and one can see that the preaching of Jesus as Lord and Christ
establishes His Kingdom on earth above all others. Therefore, in our study
of prophecy, we should always strive to recognize when figurative language
is used, and at what level that language must be interpreted.

The Nature of Prophecy

Another distinction within prophecy must be made before the discussion of the premillennialist view of prophecy. We must understand that
predictive prophecy takes on two forms within the Scriptures: prophecy by word and prophecy by sign/vision. Prophecy by word is exactly
that, when one prophecies or receives revelation by word. The Scriptures
abound in examples of these, including the "Olivet Discourse" of Matthew 24 and 25, Acts 17.30, 2 Peter 3.9–11, and as an Old Testament ex-

ample, Daniel 11. These prophecies are somewhat easier to interpret, for we can look at the events of history and to events in the future and see what historical/future events would most closely parallel with the language presented by these prophets. Daniel 11 is a good example: Daniel comforts king Darius of Persia concerning the kings that will rule after him (Daniel 11.1); the rest of the chapter is devoted to the kings ruling after Darius. We can look back into history and see the fulfillment of all of these prophecies, from the kings of Persia to Alexander the Great to the kings of Seleucia and Egypt.

Prophecy by sign/vision is more difficult to follow. These prophecies come about when God shows a sign or gives a vision to a prophet, sometimes with explanation, sometimes not. These prophecies require more interpretation than the prophecies by word, for the signs and the vision require deeper analysis. The vision in Daniel 7 of the four beasts is a good example; we do not doubt that Daniel literally saw the four beasts, but no one would assert that we are to expect the four beasts coming out of the water to be a historical event. This vision is explained in Daniel 7.15–28, which helps to alleviate doubt about the meaning of the vision.

Another relevant example of this type of prophecy is the Revelation given to John. We do not doubt that John was given a vision of heaven with the four beasts and the twenty-four elders, and all the rest of the visions given to him. Does this mean, however, that we are to interpret these things literally, that there are literally four beasts in heaven along with twenty-four elders, and the whole of Revelation is a glimpse of actual historical events? This would not be consistent with the rest of prophecies given by signs and visions.

Having established these matters, let us now examine some of the prophecies used by premillennialists and their interpretation.

Old Testament Prophecy

Premillennialists will often use some of the Old Testament prophecies and assign them to the "end times." Let us examine some of these prophecies now.

Daniel 2: The Dream of Nebuchadnezzar

Premillennialists use the dream of Nebuchadnezzar and Daniel's interpretation of it to describe the tribulation period and the millennial kingdom.[13] Is this an accurate way of interpreting this passage?

Here are the portions of the text in question, Daniel 2.31–35, 40–45:

> "Thou, O king, sawest, and, behold, a great image. This image, which was mighty, and whose brightness was excellent, stood before thee; and the aspect thereof was terrible. As for this image, its head was of fine gold, its breast and its arms of silver, its belly and its thighs of brass, its legs of iron, its feet part of iron, and part of clay. Thou sawest till that a stone was cut out without hands, which smote the image upon its feet that were of iron and clay, and brake them in pieces. Then was the iron, the clay, the brass, the silver, and the gold, broken in pieces together, and became like the chaff of the summer threshing-floors; and the wind carried them away, so that no place was found for them: and the stone that smote the image became a great mountain, and filled the whole earth."

> "And the fourth kingdom shall be strong as iron, forasmuch as iron breaketh in pieces and subdueth all things; and as iron that crusheth all these, shall it break in pieces and crush. And whereas thou sawest the feet and toes, part of potters' clay, and part of iron, it shall be a divided kingdom; but there shall be in it of the strength of the iron, forasmuch as thou sawest the iron mixed with miry clay. And as the toes of the feet were part of iron, and part of clay, so the kingdom shall be partly strong, and partly broken. And whereas thou sawest the iron mixed with miry clay, they shall mingle themselves with the seed of men; but they shall not cleave one to another, even as iron doth not mingle with clay. And in the days of those kings shall the God of heaven set up a kingdom which shall never be destroyed, nor shall the sovereignty thereof be left to another people; but it shall break in pieces and consume all these kingdoms, and it shall stand for ever. Forasmuch as thou sawest that a stone was cut out of the mountain without hands, and that it brake in pieces the iron, the brass, the clay, the silver, and the gold; the great God hath made known to the king what shall come to pass hereafter: and the dream is certain, and the interpretation thereof sure."

It is generally acknowledged that the gold refers to Babylon, the silver to

Persia, the bronze to Greece, and the iron to Rome, yet there is disagreement on the iron mixed with clay. The premillennialists believe that the kingdom of the iron mixed with clay will be a democracy in the future, at the time in which the end shall come.[14] Does this interpretation fit the text?

If we look at the interpretation itself, some clues are given. It is notable to see that each kingdom is given a distinct metal: gold is for Babylon, silver for Persia, bronze for Greece, iron for Rome…and then "iron mixed with clay." Daniel does not call it "another" kingdom, but a "divided" kingdom. Furthermore, all of the kingdoms that are listed exist one after another in direct succession: the Persians overthrow the Babylonians, who are themselves overturned by the Greeks, who are finally dethroned by the Romans. There is no mention of a separation between the times of any kingdom, and yet we are to believe that there is a 1,600+ year separation between the "iron" Rome and the "iron mixed with clay" of later times?

Finally, concerning the kingdom established after the time of the "iron mixed with clay," we are told by Daniel that this kingdom will last forever (verse 44), yet the millennial kingdom is just that—a millennium. A much more sound interpretation that fits the events that Daniel describes would be that the "iron" kingdom refers to the Roman Republic and the "iron mixed with clay" refers to the Roman Empire, whose internal strength was always compromised by the tension among the emperor, army, senate, and subjects. During this period, the Son of God, Jesus the Christ, was born, and He established a kingdom that will last forever and one that is far greater than any kingdom created by man.

Daniel 7: The Beasts

Daniel 7 is another passage referred to by the premillennialists to demonstrate the "end times." Let us examine the passage now, Daniel 7.1–8, 15–28:

> In the first year of Belshazzar king of Babylon Daniel had a
> dream and visions of his head upon his bed: then he wrote the
> dream and told the sum of the matters. Daniel spake and said,
> "I saw in my vision by night, and, behold, the four winds of heaven
> brake forth upon the great sea. And four great beasts came
> up from the sea, diverse one from another. The first was like a
> lion, and had eagle's wings: I beheld till the wings thereof were
> plucked, and it was lifted up from the earth, and made to stand
> upon two feet as a man; and a man's heart was given to it. And,

behold, another beast, a second, like to a bear; and it was raised up on one side, and three ribs were in its mouth between its teeth: and they said thus unto it, Arise, devour much flesh. After this I beheld, and, lo, another, like a leopard, which had upon its back four wings of a bird; the beast had also four heads; and dominion was given to it. After this I saw in the night-visions, and, behold, a fourth beast, terrible and powerful, and strong exceedingly; and it had great iron teeth; it devoured and brake in pieces, and stamped the residue with its feet: and it was diverse from all the beasts that were before it; and it had ten horns. I considered the horns, and, behold, there came up among them another horn, a little one, before which three of the first horns were plucked up by the roots: and, behold, in this horn were eyes like the eyes of a man, and a mouth speaking great things."

"As for me, Daniel, my spirit was grieved in the midst of my body, and the visions of my head troubled me. I came near unto one of them that stood by, and asked him the truth concerning all this. So he told me, and made me know the interpretation of the things. These great beasts, which are four, are four kings, that shall arise out of the earth. But the saints of the Most High shall receive the kingdom, and possess the kingdom for ever, even for ever and ever. Then I desired to know the truth concerning the fourth beast, which was diverse from all of them, exceeding terrible, whose teeth were of iron, and its nails of brass; which devoured, brake in pieces, and stamped the residue with its feet; and concerning the ten horns that were on its head, and the other horn which came up, and before which three fell, even that horn that had eyes, and a mouth that spake great things, whose look was more stout than its fellows. I beheld, and the same horn made war with the saints, and prevailed against them; until the ancient of days came, and judgment was given to the saints of the Most High, and the time came that the saints possessed the kingdom. Thus he said, The fourth beast shall be a fourth kingdom upon earth, which shall be diverse from all the kingdoms, and shall devour the whole earth, and shall tread it down, and break it in pieces. And as for the ten horns, out of this kingdom shall ten kings arise: and another shall arise after them; and he shall be diverse from the former, and he shall put down three kings. And he shall speak words against the Most High, and shall wear out the saints of the Most High; and he shall think to change the times and the law; and they shall be given into his hand until a time and times and half a time. But the judgment shall be set, and they shall take away his dominion, to consume and to destroy it unto the end. And the kingdom and the dominion, and the greatness of the kingdoms under the whole heaven, shall be given to the people of the saints of the Most High: his kingdom is an everlasting kingdom, and all dominions shall serve and obey him. Here is the end of the matter. As for me, Daniel, my thoughts much troubled me, and my countenance was changed in me: but I kept the matter in my heart."

There is not much discussion over the first three beasts, nor really the beginning of the fourth; they represent the same kingdoms as did the statues of Nebuchadnezzar, Babylon, Persia, Greece, and Rome. The premillennialists believe, however, that the little horn that comes from the fourth beast is the Antichrist.[15] Is this consistent with the text?

The most accurate way of placing this prophecy within a temporal context can be seen in Daniel 7.9–14:

"I beheld till thrones were placed, and one that was ancient of days did sit: his raiment was white as snow, and the hair of his head like pure wool; his throne was fiery flames, and the wheels thereof burning fire. A fiery stream issued and came forth from before him: thousands of thousands ministered unto him, and ten thousand times ten thousand stood before him: the judgment was set, and the books were opened. I beheld at that time because of the voice of the great words which the horn spake; I beheld even till the beast was slain, and its body destroyed, and it was given to be burned with fire. And as for the rest of the beasts, their dominion was taken away: yet their lives were prolonged for a season and a time. I saw in the night-visions, and, behold, there came with the clouds of heaven one like unto a son of man, and he came even to the ancient of days, and they brought him near before him. And there was given him dominion, and glory, and a kingdom, that all the peoples, nations, and languages should serve him: his dominion is an everlasting dominion, which shall not pass away, and his kingdom that which shall not be destroyed."

We have already seen from Daniel 2 that the future of the world could not possibly be complete without the mention of Jesus and His Kingdom, represented in Roman times. Therefore, in a parallel account in Daniel 7, why should we expect any less? This kingdom, as with the one in Daniel 2, will last forever—how, then, can it refer to a thousand-year kingdom? The Kingdom in Daniel 7 is no different from the kingdom in Daniel 2—Christ's spiritual kingdom, manifested on earth by His church. Knowing this, that the fourth beast and all of its outgrowths come before Christ does, we can be sure that the ten-horned beast represents Rome, most probably the Roman Republic, and thus the "little horn" perhaps the emperor of the Roman Empire, who would become a great persecutor of the truth in Christ Jesus. Furthermore, as the text indicates, the "one like a son of man" must come up to Heaven to receive the Kingdom (Daniel 7.13–14), not to "go down" to receive it on earth. Daniel 7 is an important text in regards to the first advent of Christ and His vindication in 70 CE with the destruction of Jerusalem; therefore, there is neither need nor contextual ability to assign the role of the "little horn" to the supposed "Antichrist" of the "end times."

Daniel 9: The Duration of Israel

Daniel 9 is one of the two pivotal prophecies of the premillennialists outside of the Revelation. Daniel 9 supposedly gives the "time frame" of the tribulation and the end times: the "seventieth week" at the beginning of this period with the Antichrist's pact with Israel for the latter to build a third temple, leading to the violation of that pact in the middle of the period.[16] Let us examine the prophecy now.

The prophecy in question is in Daniel 9.20–27:

> And while I was speaking, and praying, and confessing my sin and the sin of my people Israel, and presenting my supplication before the LORD my God for the holy mountain of my God; yea, while I was speaking in prayer, the man Gabriel, whom I had seen in the vision at the beginning, being caused to fly swiftly, touched me about the time of the evening oblation. And he instructed me, and talked with me, and said,
>
> "O Daniel, I am now come forth to give thee wisdom and understanding. At the beginning of thy supplications the command-

ment went forth, and I am come to tell thee; for thou art greatly
beloved: therefore consider the matter, and understand the vision.
Seventy weeks are decreed upon thy people and upon thy holy
city, to finish transgression, and to make an end of sins, and to
make reconciliation for iniquity, and to bring in everlasting righteousness, and to seal up vision and prophecy, and to anoint the
most holy. Know therefore and discern, that from the going forth
of the commandment to restore and to build Jerusalem unto the
anointed one, the prince, shall be seven weeks, and threescore and
two weeks: it shall be built again, with street and moat, even in
troublous times. And after the threescore and two weeks shall the
anointed one be cut off, and shall have nothing: and the people of
the prince that shall come shall destroy the city and the sanctuary; and the end thereof shall be with a flood, and even unto the
end shall be war; desolations are determined. And he shall make
a firm covenant with many for one week: and in the midst of the
week he shall cause the sacrifice and the oblation to cease; and
upon the wing of abominations shall come one that maketh desolate; and even unto the full end, and that determined, shall wrath
be poured out upon the desolate."

When we examine this prophecy, we must first recognize to what this
prophecy refers, and our answer is in verse 24: "your people and your
holy city." This without doubt refers to the Jews and Jerusalem, respectively; thus, the prophecy relates to the future of the Jews and Jerusalem.
"Seventy weeks" have been given for them to finish their iniquity; in the
Hebrew, the term "weeks" is literally "sevens," so "seventy sevens" have
been given. What does this mean?

"Seven" was understood to be the number of perfection or completion.
"Seventy sevens" seems to be an indefinite period. This is used by Jesus in
Matthew 18.21–22 to explain the need for forgiveness:

> Then came Peter and said to him, "Lord, how oft shall my brother
> sin against me, and I forgive him? until seven times?"
> Jesus saith unto him, "I say not unto thee, Until seven times; but,
> Until seventy times seven."

Would anyone declare that Jesus is telling us to forgive our brother only

490 times in this passage? Yet we are to understand that the "seventy sevens" of Daniel 9 are literal? It is evident from the Scriptures that this "seventy sevens" refers to an indefinite period of time in which all things will be completed.

We see that this period of "seventy sevens" is broken down further: there are "seven sevens" until the Temple is rebuilt, and then "sixty-two sevens" until the Messiah will come. Premillennialists will point to history to show that the Temple was rebuilt in forty-nine years, yet their evidence is that since all the rest of prophecy was fulfilled, this one must have been also.[17] This circular logic proves nothing; we can be sure that the Temple was rebuilt in the first section, deemed "complete," the "seven sevens." The "sixty-two sevens" refers to the period between the Temple and Christ, as universally admitted. The premillennialists then say that there is a significant gap of time and then the "one week" will be initiated by the Antichrist signing a pact with the Jews.[18] Is this consistent with the text?

We see that the first sixty-nine "sevens" are in order. We are not told of any temporal separation between the events of the first "sixty-nine sevens" and the "one week" of verse 27. The most significant evidence will be discussed in more detail later, but is seen in the words of Jesus in Matthew 24.15:

> "When therefore ye see the abomination of desolation, which was spoken of through Daniel the prophet, standing in the holy place" (let him that readeth understand).

We thus can say that whatever Jesus is discussing in Matthew 24, this is what the abomination of desolation will be. Our study below will show conclusively that the topic of conversation in this part of Matthew 24 refers to the destruction of Jerusalem in 70 CE, which included the destruction of the Temple and the cessation of the Mosaic form of worship. This period of time truly does allow the Jews "to finish transgression, and to make an end of sins, and to make reconciliation for iniquity, and to bring in everlasting righteousness, and to seal up vision and prophecy, and to anoint the most holy," as declared by Gabriel in Daniel 9.24.

Daniel 11: Historical Prophecy

Premillennialists also use Daniel 11 to provide prophecy concerning the "Antichrist," specifically, Daniel 11.36–45:

And the king shall do according to his will; and he shall exalt himself, and magnify himself above every god, and shall speak marvellous things against the God of gods; and he shall prosper till the indignation be accomplished; for that which is determined shall be done. Neither shall he regard the gods of his fathers, nor the desire of women, nor regard any god; for he shall magnify himself above all. But in his place shall he honor the god of fortresses; and a god whom his fathers knew not shall he honor with gold, and silver, and with precious stones, and pleasant things. And he shall deal with the strongest fortresses by the help of a foreign god: whosoever acknowledgeth him he will increase with glory; and he shall cause them to rule over many, and shall divide the land for a price. And at the time of the end shall the king of the south contend with him; and the king of the north shall come against him like a whirlwind, with chariots, and with horsemen, and with many ships; and he shall enter into the countries, and shall overflow and pass through. He shall enter also into the glorious land, and many countries shall be overthrown; but these shall be delivered out of his hand: Edom, and Moab, and the chief of the children of Ammon. He shall stretch forth his hand also upon the countries; and the land of Egypt shall not escape. But he shall have power over the treasures of gold and of silver, and over all the precious things of Egypt; and the Libyans and the Ethiopians shall be at his steps. But tidings out of the east and out of the north shall trouble him; and he shall go forth with great fury to destroy and utterly to sweep away many. And he shall plant the tents of his palace between the sea and the glorious holy mountain; yet he shall come to his end, and none shall help him.

Premillennialists believe that these verses refer to the Antichrist and his desire to have people worship him and a "world war" in the middle of the tribulation.[19] Is this in harmony with the text?

In order to understand Daniel 11, we must see first to whom it is directed, and this is said in Daniel 11.1:

And as for me, in the first year of Darius the Mede, I stood up to confirm and strengthen him.

Daniel is speaking to Darius, attempting to "confirm and strengthen him;" essentially, Daniel is letting Darius know that he will rule over a prosperous empire, and so will some of his descendants.

Then, Daniel begins his discussion in Daniel 11.2–4:

> And now will I show thee the truth. Behold, there shall stand up yet three kings in Persia; and the fourth shall be far richer than they all: and when he is waxed strong through his riches, he shall stir up all against the realm of Greece. And a mighty king shall stand up, that shall rule with great dominion, and do according to his will. And when he shall stand up, his kingdom shall be broken, and shall be divided toward the four winds of heaven, but not to his posterity, nor according to his dominion wherewith he ruled; for his kingdom shall be plucked up, even for others besides these.

Daniel speaks of the final kings of the Persian Empire, and its fall to Alexander the Great. He then goes on to relate the death of Alexander and the distribution of his empire amongst his four generals, of whom Ptolemy and Seleucus concern us.

Now Daniel focuses in on the future of the area around Israel in Daniel 11.5–6:

> And the king of the south shall be strong, and one of his princes; and he shall be strong above him, and have dominion; his dominion shall be a great dominion. And at the end of years they shall join themselves together; and the daughter of the king of the south shall come to the king of the north to make an agreement: but she shall not retain the strength of her arm; neither shall he stand, nor his arm; but she shall be given up, and they that brought her, and he that begat her, and he that strengthened her in those times.

Here we are introduced to the "king of the south" and the "king of the north," who will occupy the rest of the discussion in Daniel 11. The "king of the south" refers to Ptolemy and his descendants on the throne of Egypt; these rulers were powerful and often exerted much influence over the areas to the north. The "king of the north" refers to Seleucus and his descendants, the Seleucid rulers of Syria. The history of the power transfers between these groups is discussed in the body of Daniel 11; the king under discussion around verses 36–45 is Antiochus IV Epiphanes of Seleucia. From Josephus, a Jewish historian of the first century CE, we learn that this Antiochus Epiphanes conquered Jerusalem and plundered the temple, designed to destroy the Jews, and did act most impiously, sacrificing swine on the altar in the Temple.[20] It was at this time that the Maccabees revolted against the rule of the Seleucids, and were successful; thus, this Antiochus makes a fitting end to Daniel's comfort of Darius, for he has prophesied the future of the foreign rulers of the land of Israel until they would rule themselves again.

The account of Josephus concerning Antiochus IV Epiphanes and the record in Daniel about this "king of the north" coincide greatly. We can see that the context of Daniel 11 does not facilitate a gap in time between the actions of the same "king of the north" of over 2000 years, and since we have historical witness consistent with the events described by Daniel, we have no need to look any further than Antiochus Epiphanes to see our final "king of the north" over the Jews.

Joel 2: The Gift of the Holy Spirit

The premillennialists will often quote Joel 2.28–32 in reference to the "end times:"

> And it shall come to pass afterward, that I will pour out my Spirit upon all flesh; and your sons and your daughters shall prophesy, your old men shall dream dreams, your young men shall see visions: and also upon the servants and upon the handmaids in those days will I pour out my Spirit. And I will show wonders in the heavens and in the earth: blood, and fire, and pillars of smoke. The sun shall be turned into darkness, and the moon into blood, before the great and terrible day of the LORD cometh. And it shall come to pass, that whosoever shall call on the name of the LORD shall be delivered; for in mount Zion and in Jerusalem there shall be those that escape, as the LORD hath said, and among the remnant those whom the LORD doth call.

The premillennialists say that Joel speaks partially on the day of Pentecost in Acts 2 and more completely as the giving of the Spirit upon the evangelists of the tribulation period.[21] Is this what the Scriptures teach?

There should be no question about this prophecy and its fulfillment. Peter says the following in Acts 2.16–21:

"But this is that which hath been spoken through the prophet Joel:
'And it shall be in the last days, saith God, I will pour forth of
My Spirit upon all flesh: And your sons and your daughters shall
prophesy, And your young men shall see visions, And your old men
shall dream dreams: Yea and on My servants and on My hand-
maidens in those days Will I pour forth of My Spirit; and they shall
prophesy. And I will show wonders in the heaven above, And signs
on the earth beneath; Blood, and fire, and vapor of smoke: The sun
shall be turned into darkness, And the moon into blood, Before the
day of the Lord come, That great and notable day. And it shall be,
that whosoever shall call on the name of the Lord shall be saved.'"

Peter here says definitively that "this **is** what was spoken of by the prophet Joel" (emphasis mine; Acts 2.16). If we follow the text "literally" as
the premillennialists say we must, then it is evident that the whole of the
prophecy was fulfilled.

Against this it is said that none of the signs in heaven and on earth were
seen on the day of Pentecost. While it is true that they were not literally
seen, Peter does say that the day of Pentecost **was** the fulfillment of this
prophecy. In this scenario, we have three possible answers to accept:

1. Peter was not accurate when he said that "this is what was spoken of by the prophet Joel."

2. Peter quoted too much of Joel.

3. The day of Pentecost was the fulfillment of Joel 2.28–32, with
   the signs in heaven and earth being fulfilled in a symbolic way.

If we accept the Bible as inspired and inerrant, the only choice we can
take is number three. It is sometimes seen that the sun turning to darkness is a sign of a change of power, and the moon turning to blood represents the destruction of a kingdom. These things can be seen, especially considering the language of Daniel 2 and 7 above, as the inauguration
of Christ's kingdom, which was certainly on the day of Pentecost.

Peter demonstrated the referent of the prophecy, and that should be
the end of it. There is absolutely no need to have Joel 2.28–32 refer to the
"tribulation soul harvest."

Malachi 4: Elijah

It is argued by premillennialists that the prophecy in Malachi 4.5–6 concerning the return of Elijah corresponds to the witnesses of God in Revelation 11.13.[22] They argue that this cannot be John the Baptist, as the Scripture says, because John himself said that he was not.[23] Let us examine Malachi 4.5–6 and John 1.21:

> Behold, I will send you Elijah the prophet before the great and terrible day of the LORD come. And he shall turn the heart of the fathers to the children, and the heart of the children to their fathers; lest I come and smite the earth with a curse.

> And they asked him, "What then? Art thou Elijah?"
> And he saith, "I am not."
> "Art thou the prophet?"
> And he answered, "No."

Does this mean, then, that John the Baptist is not Elijah? We have the witness of Jesus in Matthew 11.13–14:

> "For all the prophets and the law prophesied until John. And if ye are willing to receive it, this is Elijah, that is to come."

Are we to reject the words of Jesus because of the humility of John? We must accept Jesus' words, that John the Baptist was the Elijah of Malachi 4.5–6, lest we be guilty of rejecting the words of God.

New Testament Prophecies

The premillennialists also discuss many New Testament prophecies in connection with the "end times." Let us examine these prophecies now.

Matthew 24–25: The "Olivet Discourse"

Matthew 24–25 is the "backbone" of premillennial theology. It is called the Olivet Discourse, since it takes place on the Mount of Olives outside of Jerusalem. The premillennialists consider it to be the outline of the happenings of the end times: deception, war, tribulation, and finally, the return of Christ.[24] Is this what Jesus is saying?

A Study of Denominations

Let us examine first the text of Matthew 24.1–36:

> And Jesus went out from the temple, and was going on his way; and his disciples came to him to show him the buildings of the temple. "But he answered and said unto them, See ye not all these things? verily I say unto you, There shall not be left here one stone upon another, that shall not be thrown down."
>
> And as he sat on the mount of Olives, the disciples came unto him privately, saying, "Tell us, when shall these things be? and what shall be the sign of thy coming, and of the end of the world?"
>
> And Jesus answered and said unto them, "Take heed that no man lead you astray. For many shall come in my name, saying, 'I am the Christ;' and shall lead many astray. And ye shall hear of wars and rumors of wars; see that ye be not troubled: for these things must needs come to pass; but the end is not yet. For nation shall rise against nation, and kingdom against kingdom; and there shall be famines and earthquakes in divers places. But all these things are the beginning of travail. Then shall they deliver you up unto tribulation, and shall kill you: and ye shall be hated of all the nations for my name's sake. And then shall many stumble, and shall deliver up one another, and shall hate one another. And many false prophets shall arise, and shall lead many astray. And because iniquity shall be multiplied, the love of the many shall wax cold. But he that endureth to the end, the same shall be saved. And this gospel of the kingdom shall be preached in the whole world for a testimony unto all the nations; and then shall the end come. When therefore ye see the abomination of desolation, which was spoken of through Daniel the prophet, standing in the holy place (let him that readeth understand), then let them that are in Judaea flee unto the mountains: let him that is on the housetop not go down to take out things that are in his house: and let him that is in the field not return back to take his cloak. But woe unto them that are with child and to them that give suck in those days! And pray ye that your flight be not in the winter, neither on a sabbath: for then shall be great tribulation, such as hath not been from the beginning of the world until now, no, nor ever shall be. And except those days had been shortened, no flesh would have been saved: but for the elect's sake those days shall be shortened. Then if any man shall say unto you, 'Lo, here is the

Christ,' or, 'Here;' believe it not. For there shall arise false Christs, and false prophets, and shall show great signs and wonders; so as to lead astray, if possible, even the elect. Behold, I have told you beforehand. If therefore they shall say unto you, Behold, he is in the wilderness; go not forth: Behold, he is in the inner chambers; believe it not. For as the lightning cometh forth from the east, and is seen even unto the west; so shall be the coming of the Son of man. Wheresoever the carcase is, there will the eagles be gathered together. But immediately after the tribulation of those days the sun shall be darkened, and the moon shall not give her light, and the stars shall fall from heaven, and the powers of the heavens shall be shaken: and then shall appear the sign of the Son of man in heaven: and then shall all the tribes of the earth mourn, and they shall see the Son of man coming on the clouds of heaven with power and great glory. And he shall send forth his angels with a great sound of a trumpet, and they shall gather together his elect from the four winds, from one end of heaven to the other. Now from the fig tree learn her parable: when her branch is now become tender, and putteth forth its leaves, ye know that the summer is nigh; even so ye also, when ye see all these things, know ye that he is nigh, even at the doors. Verily I say unto you, This generation shall not pass away, till all these things be accomplished. Heaven and earth shall pass away, but my words shall not pass away. But of that day and hour knoweth no one, not even the angels of heaven, neither the Son, but the Father only."

What, then, are we to do with this prophecy? Our first goal is to recognize what Jesus is discussing. In the account in Matthew, the discussion begins as follows, in Matthew 24.1–2:

And Jesus went out from the temple, and was going on his way; and his disciples came to him to show him the buildings of the temple. But he answered and said unto them, "See ye not all these things? verily I say unto you, There shall not be left here one stone upon another, that shall not be thrown down."
And as he sat on the mount of Olives, the disciples came unto him privately, saying, "Tell us, when shall these things be? and what shall be the sign of thy coming, and of the end of the world?"

The disciples ask Jesus two questions: when and with what signs will the Temple be destroyed, and the nature of the end of the world. How can we be sure about these being the two questions? We see the parallel passage in Mark, Mark 13.1–4:

> And as he went forth out of the temple, one of his disciples saith unto him, "Teacher, behold, what manner of stones and what manner of buildings!"
> And Jesus said unto him, "Seest thou these great buildings? there shall not be left here one stone upon another, which shall not be thrown down."
> And as he sat on the mount of Olives over against the temple, Peter and James and John and Andrew asked him privately, "Tell us, when shall these things be? and what shall be the sign when these things are all about to be accomplished?"

The rest of the passage in Mark 13 parallels almost exactly Matthew 24.4–36. The same is true for the account in Luke, Luke 21.5–36. The premillennialists focus on the last question in Matthew concerning the "end times," but nothing of the sort is mentioned in Mark and Luke! Therefore, we can conclude by textual evidence that the questions concerning Jesus and the signs of the destruction of the Temple comprise Matthew 24.1–41, and when we examine the historical accounts of the destruction of Jerusalem, especially from Josephus, we see the fulfillment of these prophecies. We will find that Jesus discusses preparation for the coming trials in 70 CE and in the future for His return in Matthew 24.42–25.30, and gives us a full picture of the Judgment in Matthew 25.31–46. Indeed, this story is vastly different from the picture portrayed in premillennialism!

This demonstrates clearly the error of premillennialism: the tribulation, the witness of the Gospel to the whole world, and the false Christs do not belong to the "end times," but to 33–70 CE; furthermore, the "abomination of desolation" of Daniel 9 is also fulfilled in this event, therefore, the "one week" of Daniel 9.27 is not the "Antichrist" signing a pact with Israel, nor does the Temple need to be rebuilt in the future. Therefore, the whole structure of the premillennial viewpoint has no basis in Scriptural fact.

2 Thessalonians 2: The "Man of Sin"

The premillennialists also use 2 Thessalonians 2 to represent the deeds of the Antichrist, described by Paul as the "man of sin."[25] Let us examine the text, 2 Thessalonians 2.1–12:

> Now we beseech you, brethren, touching the coming of our Lord Jesus Christ, and our gathering together unto him; to the end that ye be not quickly shaken from your mind, nor yet be troubled, either by spirit, or by word, or by epistle as from us, as that the day of the Lord is just at hand; let no man beguile you in any wise: for it will not be, except the falling away come first, and the man of sin be revealed, the son of perdition, he that opposeth and exalteth himself against all that is called God or that is worshipped; so that he sitteth in the temple of God, setting himself forth as God. Remember ye not, that, when I was yet with you, I told you these things? And now ye know that which restraineth, to the end that he may be revealed in his own season. For the mystery of lawlessness doth already work: only there is one that restraineth now, until he be taken out of the way. And then shall be revealed the lawless one, whom the Lord Jesus shall slay with the breath of his mouth, and bring to nought by the manifestation of his coming; even he, whose coming is according to the working of Satan with all power and signs and lying wonders, and with all deceit of unrighteousness for them that perish; because they received not the love of the truth, that they might be saved. And for this cause God sendeth them a working of error, that they should believe a lie: that they all might be judged who believed not the truth, but had pleasure in unrighteousness.

Is Paul speaking of the Antichrist in this passage? It is highly doubtful, since Paul says that the mystery of this lawlessness was already in action at the time of the writing of the letter (verse 7); it is difficult to believe that the man has not yet been revealed after well over 1,900 years. It may refer to a series of individuals perverting the truth since the time of the Apostles, and we can think of many that thus have done. This seems to be more consistent with the suggestion of the passage: this perdition had originated in the first century CE, and we are still here over nineteen centuries later with similar perdition still around us.

Revelation: Cornerstone of Prophecy

The Revelation of Jesus Christ to His Apostle John is the primary and foundational text used by those advocating premillennialism. It is not my desire to examine all of the different signs and visions in Revelation and examine the various interpretations of them; Revelation is a work that each individual must study and arrive at his or her own conclusions. It is necessary, however, to examine portions of the Revelation that we can gauge their meaning with accuracy.

The Revelation begins as follows, Revelation 1.1–3:

> The Revelation of Jesus Christ, which God gave him to show unto his servants, even the things which must shortly come to pass: and he sent and signified it by his angel unto his servant John; who bare witness of the word of God, and of the testimony of Jesus Christ, even of all things that he saw. Blessed is he that readeth, and they that hear the words of the prophecy, and keep the things that are written therein: for the time is at hand.

The Revelation also ends on a similar note, in Revelation 22.6–7, 12, 20:

> And he said unto me, "These words are faithful and true: and the Lord, the God of the spirits of the prophets, sent his angels to show unto his servants the things which must shortly come to pass. And behold, I come quickly." Blessed is he that keepeth the words of the prophecy of this book.

> "Behold, I come quickly; and my reward is with me, to render to each man according as his work is."

> He who testifieth these things saith, "Yea: I come quickly." Amen: come, Lord Jesus.

Here we have the declaration, five times, that the things discussed in the Revelation were to "shortly come to pass." One may quibble over how "short" time must be to be qualified as "shortly," yet according to premillennialism, the time has not yet arrived for these things to begin. It is very difficult to believe that 2,000+ years can be considered as a "short" time. The idea that the Revelation would begin shortly does coincide with a more historical understanding of the Revelation.

A fundamental problem with the premillennial view of Revelation involves its placement within the New Testament. It would seem, from the way that premillennialists interpret Revelation, that Revelation stands out in marked contrast to the rest of the inspired writings. Are we really to believe that the humble Savior of the World, who strove to promote peace and well-doing both during His earthly ministry and afterward (cf. Matthew 5, Romans 12), all of a sudden acts like a despotic ruler?

When such a viewpoint portrays Revelation entirely apart from the rest of the New Testament, we should give pause. More telling is that within Revelation, Jesus is referred to as the "Lamb" throughout the majority of the book, represented as the "Lion of Judah" but once (Revelation 5.5; cf. 5.6). Does a story of great violence correspond with the image of Jesus as the Lamb of God?

Any likely reading of Revelation will complement the rest of the New Testament, not stand against it. John is writing concerning the revelations Jesus gave to him to the seven churches of Asia Minor in the late first century; to truly understand Revelation in context, then, we should seek to understand how the vision would provide comfort and understanding to persecuted Christians of the first century. When viewed in this light, the premillennial interpretation falls flat.

There are many other difficulties with the premillennial view of Revelation:

1. The "seven churches." Many premillennialists believe that the "seven churches" of Revelation refer to those churches and also as the "seven periods" of church history. They believe that the "Ephesian Age" was from 30–100, "Smyrna" from 100–312, "Pergamum" from 312–606, "Thyatira" from 606-present, "Sardis" from 1520-present, "Philadelphia" from 1750-present, and "Laodicea" from 1900-present.[26] They believe that the commendation and condemnation of each church also represents a portion of church history, the positives and negatives of each.[27]

   This philosophy flies completely in the face of the whole belief of premillennialism, that Scripture must be read at its literal level. Furthermore, while the connection may be able to be made generally, it cannot stick completely: who wants to declare that the churches of Thessalonica and Philippi had "left their first love" because they were in the Ephesian Age? Is it not rather convenient that the age of the Philadelphian church happened to coincide with the Evangelical movement? If the periods were so well-determined, how come the last four still exist?

In the end, we must see that there are applications of the "seven churches" beyond the seven specific churches mentioned. We have said before that the number seven represents completion; it makes much sense to say that the situations within the seven churches are the situations which churches will deal with. If we honestly examine any congregation, we will be able to place it within the context of one of the seven churches to which John writes. To go further and dictate that the seven churches represent historical periods is subjective and a demonstration of unsound exegesis.

2. The church in Revelation. Premillennialists help support their theory on the rapture, discussed below, by showing that the church is never referred to in the book of Revelation after chapter 328. Corresponding to that, they then say that the Jewish nation is under discussion for the rest of the book due to the extensive use of terms referring to the Jews29. Is this a valid assertion?

If we examine the New Testament, we will often see language that was once used to refer to the Jews redefined to refer to Christians. We see this in James 1.1:

> James, a servant of God and of the Lord Jesus
> Christ, to the twelve tribes which are of the
> Dispersion, greeting.

Will we say that James is addressing the Jews, and the whole book is not of value to Christians? By no means! He uses language of the "chosen people" to refer to the "chosen people" of his time.

We further have Romans 2.28–29 and Philippians 3.3:

> For he is not a Jew who is one outwardly; nei-
> ther is that circumcision which is outward in
> the flesh: but he is a Jew who is one inwardly;

> and circumcision is that of the heart, in the
> spirit not in the letter; whose praise is not of
> men, but of God.

> For we are the circumcision, who worship by
> the Spirit of God, and glory in Christ Jesus, and
> have no confidence in the flesh.

Paul here shows that we are a part of the chosen people of God, the "true circumcision" (cf. also Galatians 4.21–31, Galatians 6.16), and thus as "Jews" or "Israel".

Therefore, we can see clearly that the Revelation can speak of the church and its members using the language that once referred to physical Israel and now refers to the spiritual Israel, the Church of Christ. God's dealings with physical Israel were irreparably ended with the destruction of Jerusalem, seen in Daniel 9.24–27; His only dealings are with those who have called upon the name of His Son.

3. Futurist interpretation. The premillennialists believe that all of the events of the Revelation will occur in the future30. They base this on Revelation 1.19:

> "Write therefore the things which thou sawest,
> and the things which are, and the things which
> shall come to pass hereafter."

John here is surely commanded to write the following:

- "which you have seen:" the Revelation so far, the lampstands and the Christ

- "things which are:" the status of the seven churches in Asia, present reality

- "things which shall come to pass hereafter:" the events of the future

The question must be, therefore, "when is hereafter?" The only answer possible is the period of time after John. As we have seen above, John said that the events of the Revelation were to "short-ly come to pass"; therefore, it is most feasible to examine the text of Revelation as a series of events, many of which have already occurred, with final stages yet to occur.

The book of Revelation, therefore, does not support the main premillennial doctrines.

The Resurrection

Premillennialism teaches that there will be three resurrections, the first for the saints of the "church age," which will be raptured according to 1 Thessalonians 4.13–18.[31]

> But we would not have you ignorant, brethren, concerning them that fall asleep; that ye sorrow not, even as the rest, who have no hope. For if we believe that Jesus died and rose again, even so them also that are fallen asleep in Jesus will God bring with him. For this we say unto you by the word of the Lord, that we that are alive, that are left unto the coming of the Lord, shall in no wise precede them that are fallen asleep. For the Lord himself shall descend from heaven, with a shout, with the voice of the archangel, and with the trump of God: and the dead in Christ shall rise first; then we that are alive, that are left, shall together with them be caught up in the clouds, to meet the Lord in the air: and so shall we ever be with the Lord. Wherefore comfort one another with these words.

The second resurrection is for the Old Testament saints, according to Daniel 12.1–2.[32]

> And at that time shall Michael stand up, the great prince who standeth for the children of thy people; and there shall be a time of trouble, such as never was since there was a nation even to that same time: and at that time thy people shall be delivered, every one that shall be found written in the book. And many of them that sleep in the dust of the earth shall awake, some to everlasting life, and some to shame and everlasting contempt.

The final resurrection is for the "tribulation saints," which is inferred from Revelation 6.9–11 and 20.4, in which these "saints" are told, supposedly, to wait to be resurrected, but are resurrected before the millennium.[33]

Further, there is a second distinction made with the resurrections, the resurrection of the believers and the resurrection of the unbelievers, termed the "first" and the "second" resurrections, the second of which is seen in Revelation 20.7–15.[34]

> And when the thousand years are finished, Satan shall be loosed out of his prison, and shall come forth to deceive the nations which are in the four corners of the earth, Gog and Magog, to gather them together to the war: the number of whom is as the sand of the sea. And they went up over the breadth of the earth, and compassed the camp of the saints about, and the beloved city: and fire came down out of heaven, and devoured them. And the devil that deceived them was cast into the lake of fire and brimstone, where are also the beast and the false prophet; and they shall be tormented day and night for ever and ever. And I saw a great white throne, and him that sat upon it, from whose face the earth and the heaven fled away; and there was found no place for them. And I saw the dead, the great and the small, standing before the throne; and books were opened: and another book was opened, which is the book of life: and the dead were judged out of the things which were written in the books, according to their works. And the sea gave up the dead that were in it; and death and Hades gave up the dead that were in them: and they were judged every man according to their works. And death and Hades were cast into the lake of fire. This is the second death, even the lake of fire. And if any was not found written in the book of life, he was cast into the lake of fire.

Are these teachings in accordance with the Scriptures?

First of all, let it be said that there are no Scriptures that speak of the "resurrection" of the "tribulation saints;" it is inferred from "evidence" within Revelation. We have seen from Matthew 24 that the tribulation that the premillennialists speak of is not even in the proper time setting. Daniel 12 is perhaps the most concrete Old Testament referent to the resurrection; its phraseology, in fact, conforms to the view that there will be one resurrection of both the righteous and the unrighteous, along with 1 Thessalonians 4.13–18. We see further proof of this in John 5.28–29:

> "Marvel not at this: for the hour cometh, in which all that are in the tombs shall hear his voice, and shall come forth; they that have done good, unto the resurrection of life; and they that have done evil, unto the resurrection of judgment."

How can one say that there will be two resurrections, one for the "believing," and one for the "unbelieving," when Jesus says quite clearly that the "hour" will come in which the good have the "resurrection of life" and the evil have the "resurrection of judgment?"

We have further evidence in 1 Corinthians 15.51–53:

> Behold, I tell you a mystery: We all shall not sleep, but we shall all be changed, in a moment, in the twinkling of an eye, at the last trump: for the trumpet shall sound, and the dead shall be raised incorruptible, and we shall be changed. For this corruptible must put on incorruption, and this mortal must put on immortality.

According to these accounts, we will rise when Christ returns and we shall be changed. This is the Scriptural "rapture," the term favored by the premillennialists; it will not be people shedding even their clothes to be with Christ in the air, but the transformation of the corruptible body into the incorruptible, as seen in 1 Corinthians 15.51–53. At that one resurrection, all will be resurrected, and the Judgment following will take place. The concept of three resurrections of believers and one for the unbelievers is not in harmony with the teachings of the Scriptures.

The Judgment

Premillennialism teaches that there are three judgments: the first comes at the rapture, when Christ will judge those who have been raptured according to 2 Corinthians 5.10:[35]

> For we must all be made manifest before the judgment-seat of Christ; that each one may receive the things done in the body, according to what he hath done, whether it be good or bad.

The second is Christ's judgment of nations at the "Glorious Appearing," seen supposedly in Matthew 25.31–46.[36] The third and final judgment is for the unbelievers, according to Revelation 20.11–15.[37]

And I saw a great white throne, and him that sat upon it, from whose face the earth and the heaven fled away; and there was found no place for them. And I saw the dead, the great and the small, standing before the throne; and books were opened: and another book was opened, which is the book of life: and the dead were judged out of the things which were written in the books, according to their works. And the sea gave up the dead that were in it; and death and Hades gave up the dead that were in them: and they were judged every man according to their works. And death and Hades were cast into the lake of fire. This is the second death, even the lake of fire. And if any was not found written in the book of life, he was cast into the lake of fire.

Will there be three judgments? Let us examine the Scriptures.

The concept of three judgments is necessitated by the four resurrections of the premillennialist system. The three texts quoted above represent one single judgment:

1. 2 Corinthians 5.10: at the Judgment, "all" will be recompensed for their deeds in the body: where is the qualifier that shows definitively that only Christians will appear before this seat, especially when Jesus makes the same type of statement in Matthew 16.27?

    > For the Son of man shall come in the glory of his
    > Father with his angels; and then shall he render unto
    > every man according to his deeds.

2. Matthew 25.31–46: This is the definitive text for the Judgment. Is Christ literally judging nations, or is He judging the members of all nations? In the text itself, the qualification of righteousness versus unrighteousness is the assistance of those in need: is this done collectively or individually? Christ says above in Matthew 16.27 that every MAN will be judged according to his deeds. Matthew 25 is in complete harmony with this: Christ will judge every man according to his deeds. The fact that He will gather all nations demonstrates clearly that there is one judgment, not many.

3. Revelation 20.11–15: This text can be seen as quite similar to the scene in Matthew 25, with the book of life representing the judgment of Christ. The text itself says that "every one of them were judged according to their deeds," (Revelation 20.13), the same language of Matthew 16. The language of verse 15 is to be noted also: the fact that it is a conditional (if anyone's name was not found…thrown into the lake of fire), and is not causal (since their names were not found…thrown into the lake of fire). If this judgment is to condemn all unbelievers, why is the conditional used? This is not consistent with the textual evidence.

    We are also told the following about the Judgment in Acts 17.30–31 and 2 Peter 3.9–11:

    > "The times of ignorance therefore God overlooked; but now he commandeth men that they should all everywhere repent: inasmuch as he hath appointed a day in which he will judge the world in righteousness by the man whom he hath ordained; wherof he hath given assurance unto all men, in that he hath raised him from the dead."

    > The Lord is not slack concerning his promise, as some count slackness; but is longsuffering to youward, not wishing that any should perish, but that all should come to repentance. But the day of the Lord will come as a thief; in the which the heavens shall pass away with a great noise, and the elements shall be dissolved with fervent heat, and the earth and the works that are therein shall be burned up.

These verses also clearly point to a singular judgment in one day, wherein all will be judged according to their deeds and the earth and heavens will be destroyed.

As there is no need to have four resurrections, there is no need to have three judgments. If the "rapture" and the "glorious appearing" are really a part of the same event, the return of Christ to judge the world, there is simply no need for more than one judgment. 2 Corinthians 5.10, Matthew 25.31–46, Revelation 20.11–15, and many other Scriptures all refer to the same event which will happen in the future.

The Nature of Christ's Kingdom

The fundamental principle of premillennialism, as exhibited in its name, is the belief in the 1,000-year reign of Christ on earth. This belief is based in a reading of Revelation 20.1–6.[38]

> And I saw an angel coming down out of heaven, having the key of the abyss and a great chain in his hand. And he laid hold on the dragon, the old serpent, which is the Devil and Satan, and bound him for a thousand years, and cast him into the abyss, and shut it, and sealed it over him, that he should deceive the nations no more, until the thousand years should be finished: after this he must be loosed for a little time. And I saw thrones, and they sat upon them, and judgment was given unto them: and I saw the souls of them that had been beheaded for the testimony of Jesus, and for the word of God, and such as worshipped not the beast, neither his image, and received not the mark upon their forehead and upon their hand; and they lived, and reigned with Christ a thousand years. The rest of the dead lived not until the thousand years should be finished. This is the first resurrection. Blessed and holy is he that hath part in the first resurrection: over these the second death hath no power; but they shall be priests of God and of Christ, and shall reign with him a thousand years.

Does this mean that Christ will return to Earth and rule for a thousand years? Let us examine the complete body of Scripture to see if it is so.

Christ spoke much about His Kingdom; almost every parable He spoke related to that Kingdom. He does speak about its existence, nature, and inauguration. We hear of this Kingdom in Luke 17.20–21:

> And being asked by the Pharisees when the kingdom of God cometh, he answered them and said, "The kingdom of God cometh not with observation: neither shall they say, 'Lo, here!' or, 'there!' for lo, the kingdom of God is within you."

We are told more about this Kingdom in John 18.36:

Jesus answered, "My kingdom is not of this world: if my kingdom were of this world, then would my servants fight, that I should not be delivered to the Jews: but now is my kingdom not from hence."

It is spoken of in terms of a present reality in Colossians 1.13:

Who delivered us out of the power of darkness, and translated us into the kingdom of the Son of his love.

This is the same Kingdom prophesied of by Daniel in Daniel 2.44 and 7.14:

And in the days of those kings shall the God of heaven set up a kingdom which shall never be destroyed, nor shall the sovereignty thereof be left to another people; but it shall break in pieces and consume all these kingdoms, and it shall stand for ever.

And there was given him dominion, and glory, and a kingdom, that all the peoples, nations, and languages should serve him: his dominion is an everlasting dominion, which shall not pass away, and his kingdom that which shall not be destroyed.

This Kingdom was instituted on the day of Pentecost, prophesied by Joel in Joel 2.31–32 and confirmed by Peter in Acts 2.20–21:

"The sun shall be turned into darkness, And the moon into blood, Before the day of the Lord come, That great and notable day. And it shall be, that whosoever shall call on the name of the Lord shall be saved."

We can see clearly the nature of this Kingdom: it is spiritual, it is everlasting, and it exists today. There is a sense in which, of course, the Kingdom is not yet present, since Christ has not yet returned in Judgment and returned the rule back to His Father (cf. 1 Corinthians 15), yet the future aspect of the Kingdom in no way necessitates the premillennialist view. Furthermore, how can a kingdom described as "everlasting" be construed to fit a period of 1,000 years? The only conclusion that we are able to make with the Scriptures supporting us is that the 1,000 years of Revelation 20 refers to a general period of time of considerable length. The Kingdom is at hand; the only thing left to be done is the final Judgment of God of all men, believer and unbeliever together, the final separation of the wheat and the tares, the former entering eternal life, the latter, eternal punishment. In a sense, the truth about the "millennium" and the "end times" is that we are in the "millennium" and the "end times," for we know not when Jesus will return to judge the world. Such illustrates the real danger of premillennialism: many are deceived into thinking that there will be future chances in this "tribulation" period when Jesus clearly demonstrates that at His return there will be no more chances, clearly seen in Matthew 25.1–12:

> "Then shall the kingdom of heaven be likened unto ten virgins, who took their lamps, and went forth to meet the bridegroom. And five of them were foolish, and five were wise. For the foolish, when they took their lamps, took no oil with them: but the wise took oil in their vessels with their lamps. Now while the bridegroom tarried, they all slumbered and slept. But at midnight there is a cry, 'Behold, the bridegroom! Come ye forth to meet him.'
> Then all those virgins arose, and trimmed their lamps. And the foolish said unto the wise, 'Give us of your oil; for our lamps are going out.'
> But the wise answered, saying, 'Peradventure there will not be enough for us and you: go ye rather to them that sell, and buy for yourselves.'
> And while they went away to buy, the bridegroom came; and they that were ready went in with him to the marriage feast: and the door was shut. Afterward came also the other virgins, saying, 'Lord, Lord, open to us.'
> But he answered and said, 'Verily I say unto you, I know you not.' Watch therefore, for ye know not the day nor the hour."

Let us be constantly diligent in our service to God, expecting His return at any moment (1 Thessalonians 5.1–10)!

Notes

1: From http://www.dispensationalism.com

2: Ibid.

3: Ibid.

4: Ibid.

5: Tim LaHaye, *Revelation Unveiled*, pp. 9, 12–13, 18 [It should be noted that Tim LaHaye is not a member of the Plymouth Brethren, but is acknowledged as a spokesperson for the premillenialist belief system]

6: Ibid., pp. 135–136, 138–139, 141

7: Tim LaHaye and Jerry Jenkins, *Are We Living in the End Times?*, pp. 106–112

8: Ibid., pp. 234, 244–245, 249; *Revelation Unveiled*, p. 357 9: *Are We Living in the End Times?*, p. 6

10: Ibid., p. 238

11: *Revelation Unveiled*, p. 344

12: Dr. David L. Cooper, qt. in *Are We Living in the End Times?*, p. 5

13: Ibid., pp. 130, 162, 164

14: Ibid., p. 164

15: Ibid., p. 166

16: Ibid., pp. 122, 127, 277; *Revelation Unveiled*, pp. 136, 139

17: Ibid., p. 135

18: Ibid., p. 139

19: Ibid., p. 201, 210

20: Flavius Josephus, *Antiquities of the Jews*, 13.8.2

21: *Revelation Unveiled*, p. 151; *Are We Living in the End Times?*, pp. 308–309

22: *Revelation Unveiled*, p. 186

23: Ibid.

24: *Are We Living in the End Times?*, pp. 29–43

25: *Revelation Unveiled*, pp. 210, 215

26: Ibid., pp. 24, 35–36

27: Ibid.

28: Ibid., p. 100

29: Ibid.

30: Ibid., p. 21

31: Ibid., p. 325

32: Ibid., p. 326

33: Ibid.

34: Ibid., p. 328

35: *Are We Living in the End Times?*, p. 102

36: Ibid., p. 103

37: Ibid., p. 250

38: Ibid., pp. 235–236

Christian Church (Disciples of Christ)

Overview

The Christian Church (Disciples of Christ) is the combination of two separate churches of the "restoration movement," the Christian Church, and the Disciples of Christ. The "restoration movement" was established in the late eighteenth century; its members who left the largest impact came in the 1820s with Barton Stone, Thomas and Alexander Campbell, and Walter Scott, all Presbyterians who wished to "restore" the principles of Christianity as seen in the New Testament. Barton Stone believed that there needed to be unity in faith, desiring to be rid of the denominational attitudes of his day. He organized his group of believers as the Christian Church. Meanwhile, Thomas and Alexander Campbell, father and son, also desired to return to a more unified Christianity, without creeds or clergy. They believed that baptism needed to be done for adults by immersion, and that the Lord's Supper ought to be served weekly. They named those within their group the Disciples of Christ, and called their congregations the churches of Christ. In 1832, the two groups merged. The Christian Church (Disciples of Christ) is known for its positions on baptism and the Lord's Supper, and was close to the church of the New Testament, yet unfortunately fell short.

Variants

The "Restoration Movement" first divided in the latter half of the nineteenth century over the use of "missionary societies" and other forms of parachurch organizations; many "independent Christian Churches" at this time became distinct from the Christian Church (Disciples of Christ). Another division occurred the end of the nineteenth century, for many had recognized the need to go further and remove instruments from the church building (among other things) and return to the church of the New Testament. They took on the name of the church of Christ, finding a designation of the church that was present in Scripture. Many have argued that the "church of Christ" is a denomination that began at this time—it can be proven, however, that the "church of Christ" does not have its origin in the "Restoration Movement," but has existed throughout history, with evidence for its existence in many places. Many just discovered the truths of the Scriptures in the late nineteenth century and practiced Christianity as seen in the New Testament.

Since the nineteenth century, the members of the churches of Christ have divided over many issues, all of them hearkening back to denominational tendencies: giving benevolence to non-saints, instrumental music within the worship service, growing acceptance of the Evangelical belief system, and others. It is our hope that all members of the church of Christ return to the teachings of the New Testament.

General Considerations

Part II
- *Evangelicalism*
- *Ecumenism*
- *Fundamentalism*
- *Emergism*

Part III
- *The Church Treasury, I: Benevolence: Church Benevolence to Non-Saints; The Missionary Society; The Sponsoring Church Arrangement*
- *The Church Treasury, II: Other Considerations: Hospitals; Centers of Education; Kitchens/Fellowship Halls; Gymnasiums*

Concerning Observances:
- *Observances Concerning the Lord's Birth: Advent; Christmas*
- *Observances Concerning the Lord's Death: Palm Sunday; Good Friday; Easter*

- *Instrumental Music*

- *Positions of Authority: Who Is the Pastor?; Female Deacons [Deaconesses]; Female Elders; Female Evangelists; Ordination; Synods, Councils, Conventions, and Other Meetings*

Mormonism, I: Authority

Overview

Mormonism (officially the Church of Jesus Christ of Latter-Day Saints; also referred to as "LDS") originated with Joseph Smith, Jr., in New York in 1830. He asserted that he had seen a vision of God and had been instructed by "exalted beings" to find and translate plates containing records of an ancient people. This translation came to be known as the *Book of Mormon*, which Smith began to distribute as "another testament of Jesus Christ." Mormonism began to grow and continually developed with supposed on-going revelation given to Joseph Smith, much of which was put forth in written form in the *Doctrine and Covenants*. When Smith was killed in 1844, the leadership of the church was passed on to Brigham Young, who would be responsible for moving a large portion of Mormons to what is now the state of Utah. The LDS church is known for its priesthood system of authority, continual revelation, and a very Judaic system of services.

Variants

There have been some divisions within Mormonism, the most significant of which occurred in 1852 in Beloit, Wisconsin, when many Mormons decided to separate from those under the leadership of Brigham Young in favor of the accession of Joseph Smith III, for they felt that Young was moving the church in a different direction from the one seen in the *Book of Mormon* and the *Doctrine and Covenants*. This group came to be known as the Reorganized Church of Jesus Christ of Latter Day Saints (RLDS) and has recently changed its official name to the Community of Christ. There are also three other splinter groups: the Church of Christ (Temple Lot), who separated from the LDS soon after the death of Smith for the same reasons as the RLDS; the Church of Jesus Christ (Bickertonites), consisting of some Pennsylvania Mormons who spoke against Young's teachings on polygamy and refused to march westward (the name comes from Bickerton, one of the elders of this group); and the Church of Jesus Christ of Latter-Day Saints (Strangite), a group in 1844 who claimed that James Strang was the successor to Joseph Smith, Junior, and followed his revelations and translations of other plates.

Many other smaller sectarian groups have developed, mostly in the Utah area, many of whom follow after a persuasive leader and who attempt to restore LDS practices from the nineteenth century.

General Considerations

Part I
- *Eastern Orthodoxy: Theosis*

Part III
- *The Church Treasury, I: Benevolence: Church Benevolence to Non-Saints; The Missionary Society*
- *The Church Treasury, II: Other Considerations: Hospitals; Centers of Education; Kitchens/ Fellowship Halls; Gymnasiums; Business Enterprises*

Concerning Observances:
- *Observances Concerning the Lord's Birth: Christmas*
- *Observances Concerning the Lord's Death: Palm Sunday; Good Friday; Easter*

- *Instrumental Music*

- *Judaic Practices: The Ten Commandments and the "Moral Law"*

- *The Lord's Supper: The Bread and the Fruit of the Vine*

- *Positions of Authority: A Hierarchy of Bishops; Priests; Ordination*

Part IV
- *The "Judaizers"*

The Mormon Scriptures

The three books of "Scriptures" that were either written or translated by Joseph Smith represent the primary authority for the LDS church. They are *The Book of Mormon* (BOM), *The Doctrine and Covenants* (D&C), and

The Pearl of Great Price (PGP). *The Book of Mormon* purports to be a history of a portion of the tribe of Joseph that traveled to America in 600 BCE until the final remnant of that group perished around 400 CE. This book contains supposedly "another testament" of Jesus Christ with prophecies from and commandments made by Him. *The Doctrine and Covenants* (the full title is *The Doctrine and Covenants of the Church of Jesus Christ of Latter-Day Saints*) is a book containing the alleged revelations of God to Joseph Smith between 1831 and 1843 along with some by later church leaders. *The Pearl of Great Price* is a collection of other works thought inspired by the LDS church, including portions of the Bible translated by Joseph Smith, a portion of his *History of the Church*, and *The Book of Abraham*, claiming to be a translation of some papyri Smith found concerning Abraham and his dealings with the Egyptians. The LDS church also affirms the validity of some of the other texts written from Smith's time to the present day, but the only sources that they believe are thoroughly inspired are these three.

It would not be sufficient to reject these works merely because they are not a part of our Scriptures; we must examine them according to Paul's criterion as established in Galatians 1.6–9:

> I marvel that ye are so quickly removing from him that called you in the grace of Christ unto a different gospel; which is not another gospel only there are some that trouble you, and would pervert the gospel of Christ. But though we, or an angel from heaven, should preach unto you any gospel other than that which we preached unto you, let him be anathema. As we have said before, so say I now again, if any man preacheth unto you any gospel other than that which ye received, let him be anathema.

We must these books in light of the gospel of Jesus Christ as given in the New Testament.

Textual Considerations

Let us first examine these texts to see if they validate Smith's claims and if they are internally consistent.

In his account in PGP called "Joseph Smith- History," Smith relates the story of his finding of the gold plates that supposedly contained *The Book of Mormon*. He says that he was given revelation of their existence and location in 1823, but was not allowed to obtain them for translation until 1828.[1] We are then told that he began to translate portions of the book, and his material was brought to New York to have the translation verified:

> I went to the city of New York, and presented the characters, with the translation thereof, to Professor Charles Anthon, a gentleman celebrated for his literary attainments. Professor Anthon stated that the translation was correct, more so than any he had before seen from the Egyptian. I then showed him those which were not yet translated, and he said that they were Egyptian, Chaldaic, Assyriac, and Arabic; and he said that they were true characters. He gave me a certificate, certifying to the people of Palmyra that they were true characters, and that the translation of such of them that had been translated was also correct...[2]

We are told in 1 Nephi 1.2 that the plates are written in the "language of the Egyptians," yet the language is considered by Smith to be a "reformed Egyptian," as admitted by the LDS church. From the evidence given above, the only Egyptian script that could fit those characteristics is hieratic, a "cursive" shorthand form of hieroglyphics used in everyday writing. This language, however, was not well known by 1827, and no translation of it could be verified as Smith has claimed. To counter this, many Mormons will argue that "reformed Egyptian" is simply a variation of Egyptian that developed because of the isolation of the Jews in America, much like the difference between American English and British English. The problem with this explanation is that the professor supposedly says that the translation was "correct, more so than any he had before seen from the Egyptian," a verification without substance since Egyptian was still not fully known during this period of time. Therefore, it is not possible for Smith's story about the text being Egyptian to be true along with the verification of the translation: either the text was originally in Egyptian and the verification cannot be substantiated, the text was in another language that could be understood, or the entire story is fiction.

These same plates were also supposedly taken back into heaven after Smith had completed his translation. Therefore, we have no way of confirming the translation made by Smith or that the plates existed. We must rely on his translation and have no basis upon which to judge its fidelity. The story seems not a little suspicious, and there are good reasons to wonder whether the entire story was manufactured by Smith to justify his claims.

There is another text that he supposedly translates, *The Book of Abraham*. Smith claims that these Egyptian papyri contain a story concerning Abraham, including revelations given to him. The book even contains facsimiles of portions of the Book of Abraham, and they appear to be no more than pages of *The Book of Breathings* and *The Book of the Dead*, Egyptian texts found in many tombs containing the itinerary of the journey of the deceased through the afterlife. Recently, Smith's originals came to light in New York, and they were demonstrated to be Egyptian texts of these sorts, and their translations were nothing like what Smith presented in *The Book of Abraham*. The LDS do not deny that the texts are Egyptian and that the characters do not represent what Smith translated. Instead, they posit that Smith received *The Book of Abraham* by inspiration while examining the papyri, and such is how the work was "translated". Such entirely goes against any prevailing view of what "translation" represents; how can anyone have any confidence in anything Smith presents as "translation" when it does not correlate to what is in the translated document? Likewise, if "translation" often has nothing to do with what is on a papyrus (or plate, or whatever Smith sees with his "seer stone"), how could any of it truly be "verified", as is claimed above, or even any attempt made at verification?

Furthermore, within the texts themselves there are discrepancies. Many may be explained away, but there is one glaring discrepancy regarding the number of wives one may have according to *The Book of Mormon*; Jacob 2.24 says the following:

> Behold, David and Solomon truly had many wives and concubines, which things was abominable to me, saith the Lord.

Yet Joseph Smith supposedly is given the following revelation in D&C 132.38–39:

> David also received many wives and concubines, and also Solomon and Moses my servants, as also many others of my servants, from the beginning of creation until this time; and in nothing did they sin save in those things which they received not of me. David's wives and concubines were given unto him of me, by the hand of Nathan, my servant, and others of the prophets who had the keys of this power; and in none of these things did he sin against me save in the case of Uriah and his wife...

What was an abomination to God in Jacob 2.24 is given to David by God in D&C 132.38–39. Either God lied to one of them, was mistaken in speaking to one of them, or did not speak to one or both of them at all. Therefore, we can determine from the evidence provided that the source of the Mormon Scriptures is doubtful and its reliability questionable; furthermore, they have inconsistencies throughout. Some of these inconsistencies can perhaps be explained, yet not ones like the above. Let us now examine the texts in their supposed historical context to see if they conform to the information we have available.

Historical Considerations

The *Book of Mormon* purports to be a record of Lehi and his sons, Laman, Lemuel, and Nephi, their journey from the Middle East to the Americas in 600 BCE, and the history of the Lamanites and Nephites, the descendants of Lehi and his sons, until 400 CE. This text is either an accurate rendering of the history of these people in the Americas in the past, or an invention of Smith. The only way that we can determine the truth of these things is to see whether there is any evidence in the Americas for the stories provided by Smith.

There is no evidence that proves any portion of *The Book of Mormon*, nor is there any evidence that would even hint at a Jewish presence in the Americas between 600 BCE and 400 CE. This does not in itself disprove *The Book of Mormon*; however, any inconsistencies between the text and current understanding about the civilizations of America at that time would further demonstrate the lack of validity of the text. Let us examine this text to see if the information given is consistent with our understanding of the Middle East and the Americas in the seventh century BCE and beyond.

First, we are told the following in 1 Nephi 1.2:

> Yea, I make a record in the language of my father, which consists
> of the learning of the Jews and the language of the Egyptians.

It is of note that we do not see any evidence in the seventh century BCE of the Israelites of Judea using Egyptian as a language; the Israelites considered the Egyptians as a group of the Gentiles, and a true follower of God would have had nothing to do with anything of the Egyptians. The language of the Israelites was Hebrew, and individuals professing Judaism would write in Hebrew, not Egyptian, as is indicated in texts discovered in Israel from this time period.

The Mormons respond by saying that it is possible for Lehi to have spoken Egyptian and that we cannot discount that possibility. It may be possible that Lehi spoke Egyptian, and no one could deny its possibility; however, we must look beyond possibility and look at the situation at hand. The Israelites who followed God were very much against any form of cultural contamination, as evidenced by the message of the prophets; therefore, it is highly implausible for any Israelite following God to use the language of the Egyptians. The criticism still stands.

There is another anachronism in the book of 1 Nephi, seen in 1 Nephi 16.18:

> And it came to pass that as I, Nephi, went forth to slay food, behold, I did break my bow, which was made of fine steel; and after I did break my bow, behold, my brethren were angry with me because of the loss of my bow, for we did obtain no food.

Nephi is supposed to have used a bow of steel in the seventh century BCE; however, there is no evidence in any portion of the world that the knowledge of refining iron to make steel existed in the seventh century BCE. Many Mormons attempt to say that it was entirely possible that someone happened upon this information and that such remains possible. We see in Ether 7.9 that steel is supposedly known before even Abraham, yet this is the time of copper, when even the combination of copper and tin to create bronze was yet unknown! Therefore, there is clearly an anachronism at play here.

Many Mormons will point to passages such as Psalm 18.34 in the KJV, showing that the Bible would also be inconsistent:

> He teacheth my hands to war, so that a bow of steel is broken by mine arms.

Yet this is no more than a translation error, introduced by the translators of the KJV, not by God. The ASV translates the passage as follows:

> He teacheth my hands to war; So that mine arms do bend a bow of brass.

This translation is even a little inaccurate, for the correct translation is "bronze." Therefore, the Bible is not inconsistent, for the language of David is accurate; the language of Smith, however, is not.

The Mormons further argue that Smith came across a word for a metal that he did not understand and therefore translated it as "steel." They point to information gathered about Mayan culture and that they had a metal that was similar to steel, yet is not known by us today. If this were true and this anachronism is no more than a translational difficulty of Smith, why did he not say that the bow was made of a metal "like steel?" Why is the language in 1 Nephi so specific as to include "steel?" This mistake could be forgiven of him had he not claimed himself that the Book of Mormon was "the most correct of any book on Earth;" if the claim were correct, "steel" would have been translated properly.

Finally, in an attempt to justify the translation of Smith, many Mormons will claim that it is entirely possible that Nephi had a bow of steel and that we cannot disprove that his bow was of steel.

We should there speak somewhat of the distinction that we must make between "possibility" and "existence," since the majority of the claims of the veracity of the *Book of Mormon* are based on possibility. The story may have happened, even though no evidence exists for it. This is very true; however, this does not mean that we should accept the *Book of Mormon*. I will give another example that has relevance.

There are some today who believe that the Sphinx of Egypt was carved around 10,000 BCE. Their evidence is that the limestone of the Sphinx shows weathering by water, which could only have occurred when Egypt was more tropical, or 12,000 years ago (it should be noted that even this is more evidence than there is for BOM). This is their only evidence. They posit that since the Sphinx is that old, there must have been a civilization that carved it. Yet there is no evidence for such a civilization. Does this mean that the Sphinx is 12,000 years old? By no means! We could say that the weathering could be caused by another agent, possibly wind, or we could even accept that the rock was weathered by rain 12,000 years ago and the Sphinx carved into it 4,600 years ago. Can we disprove that the Sphinx is 12,000 years old? That is impossible, but upon the examination of all evidence that exists, we must discount this claim because it does not have enough supporting evidence. The theory about the rock being weathered first and carved later has much more evidence, and therefore is the most accurate conclusion.

The same concept goes for the Book of Mormon and specifically the claim about steel. We do not have any evidence that anyone in the seventh century BCE understood how to refine iron to make steel. The only plausible explanation for the "steel" in the Book of Mormon is that it is an anachronism of Joseph Smith's own invention, and a demonstration that the work is of his contrivance, and not of God.

Let us now examine another text of Smith, *The Book of Abraham*. The first chapter of *The Book of Abraham* contains an account of how an idolatrous priest of the god Pharaoh attempted to sacrifice Abraham on an altar upon Potiphar's Hill. We read the following in Abraham 1.8:

> Now, at this time it was the custom of the priest of Pharaoh, the king of Egypt, to offer upon the altar which was built in the land of Chaldea, for the offering unto these strange gods, men, women, and children.

There are two difficulties with this text. First, it is claimed that Abraham himself wrote the text, yet he calls the king of Egypt "Pharaoh." This term was not applied to any king of Egypt until Amenhotep III in the 1300s BCE, who ruled between 700–1100 years after Abraham traveled to Egypt. Furthermore, Egypt never in its history had control over the land of Chaldea, let alone during the Old Kingdom, where its borders never went further than the Sinai Peninsula. There is no evidence whatsoever that any of the Chaldeans, who were actually Sumerians at this time, ever worshiped or sacrificed to a god named Pharaoh, king of Egypt. This text, which seems to be something other than what Smith translated in the first place, has major historical and geographical disparities within it.

The evidence that we have here is good evidence to show that the Mormon scriptures do not have their origin in God. The textual and historical evidence, however, is actually irrelevant to the validity of the Mormon scriptures as texts for understanding and doctrine; the texts could be consistent internally and with history and yet still be works not approved by God. Let us now examine the most important criterion: is the gospel presented by Smith in these scriptures the Gospel delivered once for all (Jude 1.3)?

Scriptural Considerations

Let us now look at the Mormon scriptures to see if they are in complete conformity with the Word of God.

Let us compare two portions of *The Book of Mormon*, 1 Nephi 5.14 and 2 Nephi 5.26:

> And it came to pass that my father, Lehi, also found upon the plates of brass a genealogy of his fathers; wherefore he knew that he was a descendant of Joseph; yea, even that Joseph who was the son of Jacob, who was sold into Egypt, and who was preserved by the hand of the Lord, that he might preserve his father, Jacob, and all his household from perishing with famine.

> And it came to pass that I, Nephi, did consecrate Jacob and Joseph, that they should be priests and teachers over the land of my people.

The Book of Mormon thus shows that priests were made out of the lineage of Joseph. Yet we read from the word of God the following in Hebrews 7.12–14:

> For the priesthood being changed, there is made of necessity a change also of the law. For he of whom these things are said belongeth to another tribe, from which no man hath given attendance at the altar. For it is evident that our Lord hath sprung out of Judah; as to which tribe Moses spake nothing concerning priests.

We also are given an example of an individual who appointed priests at will, Jeroboam, in 1 Kings 13.33–34:

> After this thing Jeroboam returned not from his evil way, but made again from among all the people priests of the high places: whosoever would, he consecrated him, that there might be priests of the high places. And this thing became sin unto the house of Jeroboam, even to cut it off, and to destroy it from off the face of the earth.

God therefore did not look kindly to the alteration of His plan to have priests of the tribe of Levi and the tribe of Levi alone. God would have not suffered members of the house of Joseph to be priests any more than He would have suffered Jeroboam's priests or the others appointed without His authority.

There is much in *The Book of Mormon* and in the other Mormon scriptures about Jesus Christ, with extremely accurate prophecies of His future life. Not much can be said of these prophecies, since one must either believe that they are valid prophecies or that they are nineteenth-century contrivances; one recurring thread in these scriptures about Jesus, however, cannot be overlooked. The Mormon scriptures posit that many individuals of the past knew about Jesus Christ, believed in Him, were immersed in water for the forgiveness of their sins in His name, and even established churches, and all of this long before He walked the Earth. It is stated that Adam called upon Christ's name,[3] that Enoch commanded baptism and was himself baptized with fire and the Holy Spirit,[4] that Noah preached baptism in the name of Jesus Christ,[5] and that many of the characters of *The Book of Mormon*, Alma, Nephi (the "third Nephi," of the first century BC), and others believed in Jesus Christ and instituted churches.[6] Does the established Word of God allow for such a possibility?

We must understand the nature of the covenants between man and God. We hear of this in Hebrews 9.15–23:

> And for this cause he is the mediator of a new covenant, that a death having taken place for the redemption of the transgressions that were under the first covenant, they that have been called may receive the promise of the eternal inheritance. For where a testament is, there must of necessity be the death of him that made it. For a testament is of force where there hath been death: for it doth never avail while he that made it liveth. Wherefore even the first covenant hath not been dedicated without blood. For when every commandment had been spoken by Moses unto all the people according to the law, he took the blood of the calves and the goats, with water and scarlet wool and hyssop, and sprinkled both the book itself and all the people, saying, "This is the blood of the covenant which God commanded to you-ward."
> Moreover the tabernacle and all the vessels of the ministry he sprinkled in like manner with the blood. And according to the law, I may almost say, all things are cleansed with blood, and apart from shedding of blood there is no remission. It was necessary therefore that the copies of the things in the heavens should be cleansed with these; but the heavenly things themselves with better sacrifices than these.

We see in this text many different points: a covenant is not in effect until the testator has died, the covenant is dedicated by blood, and the heavenly copies of things need to replace the earthly ones. We see, therefore, that it would be impossible Scripturally to place any form of redemption in Jesus Christ in His name before He died for the remission of our sins. God has determined that no covenant is in effect until the death of its testator—the covenant of God and man through Jesus Christ, therefore, did not exist until His death on the cross. This explains why the prophecies of the Old Testament point to the fulfillment of the promise in the future but the adherence to the Law at the present time: *The Book of Mormon* would have both at the same time![7] How could one sacrifice bulls and goats in adherence to the Law of Moses while recognizing that Christ is the only true sacrifice? This cannot be so! God did not speak any such thing to His children in Judah, even though many remained faithful after the Exile, yet He guided the creation of a church for His Son Jesus in America? He recognized individuals calling upon the fruit of a promise that had yet to be fulfilled? This is not in harmony with the Word of God as given in the first century.

There is another discrepancy in 3 Nephi 28.6–7:

> And he said unto them: Behold, I know your thoughts, and ye have desired the thing which John, my beloved, who was with me in my ministry, before that I was lifted up by the Jews, desired of me. Therefore, more blessed are ye, for ye shall never taste of death; but ye shall live to behold all the doings of the Father unto the children of men, even until all things shall be fulfilled according to the will of the Father, when I shall come in my glory with the powers of Heaven.

This text is one that speaks of John never dying, a belief held by the Mormons. The belief comes from John 21.21–23:

> Peter therefore seeing him saith to Jesus, "Lord, and what shall this man do?"
> Jesus saith unto him, "If I will that he tarry till I come, what is that to thee? Follow thou me."

This saying therefore went forth among the brethren, that that disciple should not die: yet Jesus said not unto him, that he should not die; but, "If I will that he tarry till I come, what is that to thee?"

The LDS church and Joseph Smith in particular have fallen into the category of "the brethren!" John here makes it evident that Jesus did not say that he would never die, but was merely asking Peter a rhetorical question. How could John have thus desired for something that there is no indication that he ever wanted or that it would be granted him?

There are many more inconsistencies that we could examine, but these are some of the most evident. It is clear, then, that the gospel presented in the Mormon scriptures is at odds with not only itself and history but also, and most importantly, with the Gospel of the Apostles. *The Book of Mormon* and its ilk are not "another testament of Jesus Christ," but a "different testament," one declared accursed by Paul.

The Priesthood System

The LDS church regards very highly the scriptures it has been given from Joseph Smith, Jr., but also holds in high esteem the succession of leadership that has continued since Smith's death. The leaders were designated as priests, either of the order of Melchizedek or of the order of Aaron.[8] The priesthood of Melchizedek is the higher order, and in their ranks are the head authorities of the LDS church: a President, who is the official head of the LDS Church;[9] high priests, who stand with the president;[10] the twelve apostles, who are messengers and create a quorum equal to that of the presidency;[11] and the seventy, 70 individuals called to preach the gospel who also form a quorum equal to the power of the twelve apostles.[12] Elders and bishops also come from the Melchizedek priesthood,[13] and the members of the Melchizedek priesthood are the ones who supposedly receive the revelations of God.[14] The priesthood of Aaron consists of individuals who have been given revelation that they are literal descendants of Aaron,[15] and they are the ones to administer the gospel to the people.[16]

It should therefore be evident that the whole system of authority in the LDS church is rooted in its priesthood system. Does this system conform to the teachings of the New Testament?

Let us first examine the claims about a priesthood of Aaron. This is also known as the Levitical priesthood, and its presence is well documented in the Old Testament. It is understood that under the Law of Moses that the Levites were the individuals chosen to be the priests of God and were to serve Him in His established rituals. But does this priesthood last beyond the Law of Moses?

Let us examine Hebrews 7.11–14:

> Now if there was perfection through the Levitical priesthood (for under it hath the people received the law), what further need was there that another priest should arise after the order of Melchizedek, and not be reckoned after the order of Aaron? For the priesthood being changed, there is made of necessity a change also of the law. For he of whom these things are said belongeth to another tribe, from which no man hath given attendance at the altar. For it is evident that our Lord hath sprung out of Judah; as to which tribe Moses spake nothing concerning priests.

The verse of importance to us is verse 12:

> For the priesthood being changed, there is made of necessity a change also of the law.

The author of the Hebrew letter is very plain in his language: the priests of the Levitical priesthood could not bring forth the perfect sacrifice; only the High Priest of the order of Melchizedek, Jesus Christ, could do so. The lack of perfection demonstrated that the priesthood was not to last—the Hebrew author states clearly that there was a change of priesthood, from the earthly Levites to the heavenly Christ. Therefore, how can one say that the priesthood of Aaron is still legitimate when the Hebrew author attests to its passing away?

We do read about a priesthood of Melchizedek in the letter to the Hebrews, but we must examine it to see if it is the same as the one now practiced by the LDS church.

First, it is interesting to note that Smith speaks of this priesthood as if it lasted since Adam, and was carried down through the ages to Melchizedek.[17] We see the specifics of this in D&C 84.14:

> Which Abraham received the priesthood from Melchizedek, who received it through the lineage of his fathers, even till Noah.

Yet the Hebrew author says the following about Melchizedek in Hebrews 7.3:

> without father, without mother, without genealogy, having neither beginning of days nor end of life, but made like unto the Son of God), abideth a priest continually.

Why should we believe that Joseph Smith received revelations kept hidden from the Hebrew author? God did not reveal to the Hebrew author the father or genealogy of Melchizedek, and this lack of information is used to make an important point—Melchizedek's priesthood is not based on lineage, as was Aaron's priesthood. Such is entirely contradictory to Smith's supposed revelation.

The Hebrew author speaks much about the character of the priesthood of Melchizedek, as we can see in Hebrews 5.5–10:

> So Christ also glorified not himself to be made a high priest, but he that spake unto him, "Thou art my Son, This day have I begotten thee:"
> as he saith also in another place, "Thou art a priest for ever After the order of Melchizedek."
> Who in the days of his flesh, having offered up prayers and supplications with strong crying and tears unto him that was able to save him from death, and having been heard for his godly fear, though he was a Son, yet learned obedience by the things which he suffered; and having been made perfect, he became unto all them that obey him the author of eternal salvation; named of God a high priest after the order of Melchizedek.

We read further in the seventh chapter, verses 11, 15–17, 23–28:

> Now if there was perfection through the Levitical priesthood (for under it hath the people received the law), what further need was there that another priest should arise after the order of Melchizedek, and not be reckoned after the order of Aaron?... And what we say is yet more abundantly evident, if after the likeness of Melchizedek there ariseth another priest, who hath been made, not after the law of a carnal commandment, but after the power of an endless life: for it is witnessed of him, "Thou art a priest for ever

After the order of Melchizedek.".…

And they indeed have been made priests many in number, because that by death they are hindered from continuing: but he, because he abideth for ever, hath his priesthood unchangeable. Wherefore also he is able to save to the uttermost them that draw near unto God through him, seeing he ever liveth to make intercession for them. For such a high priest became us, holy, guileless, undefiled, separated from sinners, and made higher than the heavens; who needeth not daily, like those high priests, to offer up sacrifices, first for his own sins, and then for the sins of the people: for this he did once for all, when he offered up himself. For the law appointeth men high priests, having infirmity; but the word of the oath, which was after the law, appointeth a Son, perfected for evermore.

We should now see a fuller picture of the nature of the priesthood of Melchizedek. It is not an order to be given to men: we see that Melchizedek himself is without origin and end (Hebrews 7.3), as also is Christ. Christ performed the function of the priesthood of Melchizedek by offering Himself as an offering for sin once for all. We read in Hebrews 7.26–28 the awesome characteristics which make Christ the perfect High Priest: He has offered up Himself for our sin, has been tempted in all ways that we have without sin, and is all holy and all powerful.

Therefore, we must ask: can any of the members of the priesthood of Melchizedek in the LDS church perform any of these practices? Have any given themselves as a sacrifice "once for all?" Are any "separated from sinners and exalted above the heavens?" Are any "holy, innocent, [and] undefiled?" This is not so, for they are mere men. It is not for mankind to hold the priesthood of Melchizedek, but to be content with the promise of Peter in 1 Peter 2.5,9:

Ye also, as living stones, are built up a spiritual house, to be a holy priesthood, to offer up spiritual sacrifices, acceptable to God through Jesus Christ…But ye are a elect race, a royal priesthood, a holy nation, a people for God's own possession, that ye may show forth the excellencies of him who called you out of darkness into his marvellous light.

We should enjoy being a "holy" and "royal" priesthood and not accept claims of any other priesthood in Christ. Christ and Christ alone is our High Priest (Hebrews 5.1–5); the priests of the LDS priesthood of Melchizedek are hard-pressed to conform to any of the qualifications that Christ fulfilled in Hebrews 7.26–28.

Mormon Elders

The LDS church also has "elders" that are sent out as missionaries. They are often in their twenties or thirties, and are mostly unmarried. Does this conform to the teaching of the New Testament?

First, it must be stated that the Greek term *presbuteros* means literally "one who is advanced in age." Thus, it is inherent in the definition that an elder is one who is advanced in age, and it is commonly accepted that 20–40 is not "advanced in age."

Beyond this, let us examine 1 Timothy 3.2, 4–5:

> The bishop therefore must be without reproach, the husband of one wife, temperate, sober-minded, orderly, given to hospitality, apt to teach…one that ruleth well his own house, having his children in subjection with all gravity; (but if a man knoweth not how to rule his own house, how shall he take care of the church of God?)

We see here that an overseer (Biblically, the same position as an elder; 1 Peter 5.1–4) must be married and have children in order to be qualified for the position. Therefore, the LDS eldership does not conform to New Testament teaching.

It is evident that the complete authority system of the LDS church, its scriptures from Joseph Smith, Jr., and its priesthood system, do not conform to the authority system of God as presented in the New Testament.

Notes

1: Joseph Smith- History (JS-H) 1.42–43, 59–60

2: Ibid., 1.64

3: Moses 5.7–8

4: Ibid., 6.52, 56

5: Ibid., 8.19, 24

6: Mosiah 18.10, 17; Helaman 10.7

7: Alma 25.15

8: Doctrine and Covenants (D&C) 107.6

9: Ibid., 107.8–9

10: Ibid., 107.22

11: Ibid., 107.23–24

12: Ibid., 107.25–26

13: Ibid., 107.5, 7

14: Ibid., 107.19

15: Ibid., 107.70

16: Ibid., 107.20

17: Ibid., 84.6–16

Mormonism, II: Doctrine

The LDS and the Scriptures

In the previous lesson, **Mormonism, I: Authority**, we examined the supposed scriptures of the Mormons. Let us now examine their attitudes toward the received Scriptures, the Old and New Testaments.

We read from the Articles of Faith of the Church of Jesus Christ of Latter-Day Saints, Article VII:

> We believe the Bible to be the word of God as far as it is translated correctly; we also believe the Book of Mormon to be the word of God.

This is the explicit statement that is seen more implicitly in many of the statements of Smith, declaring that he had received revelations concerning the "true interpretation" of the Scriptures, many of which we will examine below.

Many members of the LDS church will attempt to discredit various portions of the Bible in order to bolster their own claims about *The Book of Mormon* and their other scriptures. However, the words of Paul in 2 Timothy 3.16–17 should be sufficient:

> Every scripture inspired of God is also profitable for teaching, for reproof, for correction, for instruction which is in righteousness. That the man of God may be complete, furnished completely unto every good work.

Many Mormons will assert that this refers to the Old Testament or perhaps to some of the New Testament, but not the whole. Yet the text does not say which "scriptures" are the "Scripture" discussed except for the phrase "inspired of God." Any Scripture "inspired of God" will be profitable for equipping the man of God for every good work. Our previous examination of the Mormon scriptures (found in **Mormonism, I: Author-ity**) has demonstrated that the Mormon scriptures are not inspired of God, yet we all agree that the Old and New Testaments are "inspired of God."

Many LDS will argue the main point of the article of faith, that the Bible is only as good as its translation. They will argue that any translation will lose much of the meaning of the work and is not as reliable. They will further argue that the translations themselves are based on copies of the New Testament that were made by unreliable copiers, therefore, they are justified in saying that the Bible is the word of God "as far as it is translated correctly."

It is true that some meaning is lost in translating a work; however, there are plenty of ways to determine the meaning of the text. The Greek language is much more specific in its usage than English; further, we possess the ability to know the different meanings for various words, and we can examine the words in context in Scripture to determine the best meaning. Concerning the text of the New Testament itself, there are many sources that can be used to prove that the text we possess today is highly accurate, and we can rest assured that the New Testament we use today is very similar to the one written by the Christians of the first century.[1]

Therefore, there is no reason to add a disclaimer to our belief in the Scriptures, that they are the word of God "as far as [they are] translated correctly." We have every reason to trust the Scriptures as our source of the truth of God. Attempting to discredit the transmission of the Scriptures is extremely reckless, especially considering the wealth of attestation we now possess for the New Testament, dating as far back as 175 CE.

It is also not inappropriate to mention that *The Book of Mormon* and other LDS scriptures, which Mormons claim to be "perfect" and without such difficulties, cannot be verified. The LDS church does not even claim that Joseph Smith wrote down actual translations of his sources; instead, it is claimed that he wrote down whatever he was inspired to write down when looking upon them. There is far greater reason to cast doubt on the LDS "scriptures" than upon the Old and New Testaments.

Eternal Progression

The LDS Church has developed the doctrine of eternal progression to describe the life of man. In this system, a man's spirit exists, develops, and takes on the form of a man to gain earthly experiences; those who are exalted are able to develop into immortality and equality with God.[2] There are many aspects to this doctrine involving the nature of God, our relationship with Jesus, and the nature of our existence. Let us now examine the points of this doctrine in order to see if it is in conformity to the Scriptures.

The Nature of God the Father

Joseph Smith taught that God Himself was once a man and was exalted into His godhood.[3] He further claimed that if we were to see Him as He is, we would see a man.[4] These statements come from the King Follett Discourse, and many are verified in the D&C 130.22:

> The Father has a body of flesh and bones as tangible as man's; the Son also; but the Holy Ghost has not a body of flesh and bones, but is a personage of Spirit. Were it not so, the Holy Ghost could not dwell with us.

Are these teachings compatible with the Scriptures?

Concerning the nature of God the Father, we read in Numbers 23.19 and John 4.23–24:

> God is not a man, that he should lie; Neither the son of man, that he should repent: Hath he said, and shall he not do it? Or hath he spoken, and shall he not make it good?

> "But the hour cometh, and now is, when the true worshippers shall worship the Father in spirit and truth: for such doth the Father seek to be his worshippers. God is a Spirit: and they that worship him must worship in spirit and truth."

Jesus says here unequivocally that the Father is a spirit. However, many of the LDS will point to examples in the Old Testament where men, such as Moses or Jacob, "saw" God. Contrary to their claims, we find the following in John 1.18:

> No man hath seen God at any time; the only begotten Son, who is in the bosom of the Father, he hath declared him.

We could also examine Hosea 11.9 to see that God is most assuredly not a man. It is evident, then, that those individuals in the Old Testament perhaps saw a manifestation of God in some way, but not God Himself.

To this, sometimes Mormons will simply deny the validity of John 1.18 or try to emphasize the "anthropomorphic" Scriptures against statements indicating that God is not a man. Such attempts to create conflict within the Word of God should be assiduously avoided (Psalm 119.160).

There is also the issue of God's "exaltation," that God was a man who was exalted to godhood. This requires that there must have been a time when God the Father was not God. In fact, Smith went much further than this, claiming that there were in fact many gods, as evidenced in Abraham 3.3–4:

> And they (the Gods) said: Let there be light, and there was light. And they (the Gods) comprehended the light, for it was bright, and they divided the light, or caused it to be divided, from the darkness.

Smith went further in D&C 93.29, claiming the following:

> Man was also in the beginning with God. Intelligence, or the light of truth, was not created or made, nor indeed can be.

Do the Scriptures teach that there were gods, some before God the Father, and that man existed in the beginning with God?

We have evidence in the Scriptures in Isaiah 43.10 and 44.6–8:

> "Ye are my witnesses," saith the LORD, "and my servant whom I have chosen; that ye may know and believe me, and understand that I am he: before me there was no God formed, neither shall there be after me."

> Thus saith the LORD, the King of Israel, and his Redeemer, the LORD of hosts: "I am the first, and I am the last; and besides me there is no God. And who, as I, shall call, and shall declare it, and set it in order for me, since I established the ancient people? and the things that are coming, and that shall come to pass, let them declare. Fear ye not, neither be afraid: have I not declared unto thee of old, and showed it? and ye are my witnesses. Is there a God besides me? yea, there is no Rock; I know not any."

These passages, along with Deuteronomy 13.1–5, Isaiah 45.21–22, Galatians 4.8, and Isaiah 40.13–18, 21–28, demonstrate clearly that God is one and that there are no other gods. We also read the following in Psalm 90.2:

> Before the mountains were brought forth, Or ever thou hadst formed the earth and the world, Even from everlasting to everlasting, thou art God.

There is further evidence in Malachi 3.6:

> For I, the LORD, change not; therefore ye, O sons of Jacob, are not consumed.

Therefore, it is evident that God has not changed nor was ever created, but was the Creator. We also have evidence of man's nature in Romans 9.19–21:

> Thou wilt say then unto me, "Why doth he still find fault? For who withstandeth his will?"
> Nay but, O man, who art thou that repliest against God? Shall the thing formed say to him that formed it, "Why didst thou make me thus?"
> Or hath not the potter a right over the clay, from the same lump to make one part a vessel unto honor, and another unto dishonor?

It is evident that man is a created being; therefore, he could not have possibly been present at creation. God's nature is not changed. How can Smith thus assert that God "became" as such through exaltation? Or that other gods exist? How can man, a creation, be present in creation? These ideas are inconsistent with the Scriptures.

Joseph Smith also claimed that God did not really create the heavens and the earth, but merely organized them:

> You ask the learned doctors why they say the world was made out of nothing; and they will answer, "Doesn't the Bible say He created the world?" And they infer, from the word create, that it must have been made out of nothing. Now, the word create came from the baurau which does not mean to create out of nothing; it means to organize; the same as a man would organize materials and build a ship. Hence, we infer that God had materials to organize the world

out of chaos —chaotic matter, which is element, and in which dwells all the glory. Element had an existence from the time he had. The pure principles of element are principles which can never be destroyed; they may be organized and re-organized, but not destroyed. They had no beginning, and can have no end.[5]

Yet we read the following in Psalm 33.6,9:

By the word of the LORD were the heavens made, And all the host of them by the breath of his mouth…For he spake, and it was done; He commanded, and it stood fast.

There is further, more definitive evidence in Isaiah 44.24 and 45.18:

Thus saith the LORD, thy Redeemer, and he that formed thee from the womb: "I am the LORD, that maketh all things; that stretcheth forth the heavens alone; that spreadeth abroad the earth (who is with me?)."

For thus saith the LORD that created the heavens, the God that formed the earth and made it, that established it and created it not a waste, that formed it to be inhabited: "I am the LORD; and there is none else."

How then can we say that God did not create, but merely organized, when He says clearly that He has created the heavens and the earth?

We must see the awesome nature of God, not to be confused in any sense with humanity, as He has made perfectly evident in Isaiah 55.8–9:

"For my thoughts are not your thoughts, neither are your ways my ways," saith the LORD. "For as the heavens are higher than the earth, so are my ways higher than your ways, and my thoughts than your thoughts."

The Relationship Between Jesus and Man

Smith also asserted in his King Follett discourse that man will be "joint heirs with Christ," and that this "inheritance" is understood as the following:

...the same power, the same glory and the same exaltation, until
you arrive at the station of a God, and ascend the throne of eternal power, the same as those who have gone before.[6]

Therefore, Smith determines that we will be equal heirs with Christ. Do
the Scriptures support this conclusion?

The Scriptures do teach that we shall be joint-heirs with Christ, as
seen in Romans 8.16–17:

> The Spirit himself beareth witness with our spirit, that we are
> children of God: and if children, then heirs; heirs of God, and
> joint-heirs with Christ; if so be that we suffer with him, that we
> may be also glorified with him.

This is also seen in Galatians 3.26–29 and 4.1–7. Yet the question remains: does being a joint heir with Christ necessitate that we will be
equal heirs with Christ? The text does not support this conclusion. For
example, if my grandparents die and they will my father $100,000 and
me $20, we are both heirs of my grandparents, and could be rightly
called "joint heirs." Yet we are by no means equal heirs of my grandparents. The situation is similar with our relationship to Christ. Jesus Christ
is called the "firstborn from the dead" in Revelation 1.5, and in this
sense, we are equal heirs in Christ: we all will receive resurrection from
the dead by the power of God and we will all be granted eternal life. We
see in Ephesians 5.23–29, however, that Christ is the head of the church,
the body of Christ, and that since we are members of that body, we are
subject to Him. In this sense we are not joint heirs with Christ, for He
is the one who has been granted the authority over heaven and earth (cf.
Matthew 28.18–20), and not ourselves. Therefore, the determination that
"joint heirs" means "equal heirs" is not made evident in the Scriptures,
and we have seen that the opposite is in fact the case.

The Eternal Nature of Man

The previous discussions concerning the nature of God and our relationship with Jesus Christ all work to the end of the nature of man. It was
Smith's belief, articulated clearly later by Lorenzo Snow, that,

As man now is, God once was: As God is, man may be.[7]

This is further spoken of in D&C 132.19–20:

…and shall be of full force when they are out of the world; and they shall pass by the angels, and the gods, which are set there, to their exaltation and glory in all things, as hath been sealed upon their heads, which glory shall be a fulness and a continuation of the seeds forever and ever. Then shall they be gods, because they have no end; therefore shall they be from everlasting to everlasting, because they continue; then they shall be above all, because all things are subject to them. Then shall they be gods, because they have all power, and the angels are subject to them.

The concept of exaltation runs through this theology, for it is the idea that a man, through his righteousness and obedience to God, shall be exalted to godhood (cf. D&C 76.50–60). Do the Scriptures teach that man can become as a god?

The LDS church will often point to the Eastern Orthodoxy's concept of theosis as a justification for their belief system, for, as we have seen in **Eastern Orthodoxy: Theosis**, the Orthodox also have the belief that man can reach a level of godhood. The Eastern Orthodox, however, by no means believe that the Father was once a man nor do they accept the concept of eternal progression.

The LDS use the same Scriptures as the Orthodox do to justify their beliefs, Psalm 82.6 and John 10.33–36:

I said, "Ye are gods, And all of you sons of the Most High."

The Jews answered him, "For a good work we stone thee not, but for blasphemy; and because that thou, being a man, makest thyself God."
Jesus answered them, "Is it not written in your law, 'I said, ye are gods?' If he called them gods, unto whom the word of God came (and the scripture cannot be broken), say ye of him, whom the Father sanctified and sent into the world, 'Thou blasphemest;' because I said, 'I am the Son of God?'"

Many observations were made concerning these passages in **Eastern Orthodoxy: Theosis**, but let us also see what Asaph declares in the word of God in Psalm 82 as to whether the Jews "are" gods. It is not taught within the LDS system of eternal progression that a man may become a god while on earth. Jesus also uses this same language in John 10, that the Jews, at this time His adversaries, "are" gods; are we to believe that those who deny Jesus' position as the Son of God are "gods?"

It is evident when reading the whole of Psalm 82 that Asaph is condemning the unjust rulers of Israel, for God had placed them in their position to be like "gods," the rulers of His people. Yet they are unjust, and their end is made evident in Psalm 82.7–8:

> "Nevertheless ye shall die like men, And fall like one of the princes."
> Arise, O God, judge the earth; For thou shalt inherit all the nations.

Therefore, Jesus' usage of this passage in John 10 is made evident: the Jews of His time are acting as unjust judges like those in the time of Asaph. Jesus is by no means calling these individuals gods, but is simply declaring what they are: unjust, inconsistent judges of Him.

We do see from the Scriptures that we shall inherit eternal life (Matthew 25.31–46), but we see no indication that we will ascend to the level of God. We must always keep in mind that God is higher than we are (Isaiah 55.8–9) and that Jesus Christ is our head, our authority, and our High Priest, not our equal (Ephesians 5.23–29, Hebrews 7.26–29). We should be more than content to be able to have eternal life through fellowship with Him, for even that is far more than what we deserve.

The Nature of Marriage

Another fundamental teaching of Joseph Smith concerning exaltation was the necessity of marriage, and not only marriage, but what was deemed "celestial marriage." This marriage was deemed to be performed by God and necessary for entrance into the highest levels of exaltation and godhood.[8] The doctrine further states that this marriage will endure for an eternity if both partners live properly.[9] Do the Scriptures teach this?

We do not see in the Scriptures that marriage is necessary for entrance into Heaven. In fact, the opposite is proclaimed by Paul in 1 Corinthians 7.8–9, 32–35:

> But I say to the unmarried and to widows, It is good for them
> if they abide even as I. But if they have not continency, let them
> marry: for it is better to marry than to burn.

But I would have you to be free from cares. He that is unmarried is careful for the things of the Lord, how he may please the Lord: but he that is married is careful for the things of the world, how he may please his wife, and is divided. So also the woman that is unmarried and the virgin is careful for the things of the Lord, that she may be holy both in body and in spirit: but she that is married is careful for the things of the world, how she may please her husband. And this I say for your own profit; not that I may cast a snare upon you, but for that which is seemly, and that ye may attend upon the Lord without distraction.

We also have the words of Jesus in Matthew 19.12:

For there are eunuchs, that were so born from their mother's womb: and there are eunuchs, that were made eunuchs by men: and there are eunuchs, that made themselves eunuchs for the kingdom of heaven's sake. He that is able to receive it, let him receive it.

How could any who make themselves "eunuchs for the kingdom of heaven's sake" possibly enter into a "celestial marriage?" This concept is not in harmony with the Scriptures.

Jesus also speaks about the permanence of marriage in Matthew 22.23–32:

On that day there came to him Sadducees, they that say that there is no resurrection: and they asked him, saying, "Teacher, Moses said, 'If a man die, having no children, his brother shall marry his wife, and raise up seed unto his brother.' Now there were with us seven brethren: and the first married and deceased, and having no seed left his wife unto his brother; in like manner the second also, and the third, unto the seventh. And after them all, the woman died. In the resurrection therefore whose wife shall she be of the seven? for they all had her."
But Jesus answered and said unto them, "Ye do err, not knowing the scriptures, nor the power of God. For in the resurrection they neither marry, nor are given in marriage, but are as angels in heaven. But as touching the resurrection of the dead, have ye not read that which was spoken unto you by God, saying, 'I am the

God of Abraham, and the God of Isaac, and the God of Jacob?
God is not the God of the dead, but of the living.'"

Jesus makes it plainly evident in His refutation of the Sadducees' teachings that marriage is not present in the resurrection. Therefore, we can see that there is no Scriptural basis for a belief in a "celestial marriage," nor is there any Scripture to justify any precept of eternal progression. These doctrines of Joseph Smith are not in conformity with the teachings of God in the Old and New Testaments.

The Nature of the Afterlife

Joseph Smith taught that the afterlife consisted of four kingdoms, the celestial, terrestrial, and the telestial kingdoms, along with the "outer darkness," or hell.[10] He asserted that this information was revealed to him while he was studying John 5.29.[11] Smith claims that the celestial kingdom has three levels,[12] that a celestial marriage and baptism will guide one to the highest level,[13] and that these will receive the exaltation to godhood.[14] Any who are in the celestial kingdom are there, supposedly, because of their adherence to the "celestial law," or the law of Christ.[15] The terrestrial kingdom is given to those who could not know Jesus in this life or were deceived into not following Him, and also those members of the LDS church who are not fully devoted to God;[16] these individuals are characterized by living uprightly but not according to the standards of the sanctification of God.[17] These individuals do not receive the full glory of God, but live in "reflected glory," living for eternity but without the benefits of the "celestial kingdom."[18]

The telestial kingdom and the "outer darkness" are for those who did not live uprightly. The telestial kingdom is for the vast majority of people,[19] for this kingdom is supposedly filled with the individuals who have lived according to the guidelines of the world, called the "telestial law," freely indulging in the deeds of the flesh.[20] They will live outside of the presence of God, but not in hell proper.[21] The "outer darkness" is reserved for those deemed the "sons of perdition," or those who live in open rebellion against God, breaking even the "telestial law."[22] Do we see these "kingdoms" in the Scriptures?

Jesus gives us a picture of the Judgment in Matthew 25.31–34, 41, 46:

"But when the Son of man shall come in his glory, and all the angels with him, then shall he sit on the throne of his glory: and before him shall be gathered all the nations: and he shall separate them one from another, as the shepherd separateth the sheep from the goats; and he shall set the sheep on his right hand, but the goats on the left. Then shall the King say unto them on his right hand, 'Come, ye blessed of my Father, inherit the kingdom prepared for you from the foundation of the world...'

Then shall he say also unto them on the left hand, 'Depart from me, ye cursed, into the eternal fire which is prepared for the devil and his angels...'

And these shall go away into eternal punishment: but the righteous into eternal life."

We see two kingdoms here, not four: the righteous enter the kingdom of the Father; the unrighteous, the eternal fire. There is further evidence against the notion of two "middle" kingdoms in 2 Thessalonians 1.6–9:

If so be that it is righteous thing with God to recompense affliction to them that afflict you, and to you that are afflicted rest with us, at the revelation of the Lord Jesus from heaven with the angels of his power in flaming fire, rendering vengeance to them that know not God, and to them that obey not the gospel of our Lord Jesus: who shall suffer punishment, even eternal destruction from the face of the Lord and from the glory of his might.

We are told that any who do not know God and do not obey the gospel of the Lord Jesus will suffer punishment from God, yet Smith stated that many who did not obey the gospel would be in the "reflection" of His glory or away from His glory but not in eternal destruction. We do not see anywhere in the Scriptures where God shows mercy to any who do not obey His Son Jesus in the Judgment. An individual will either enter Heaven or be cast down into Hell. Smith's four-level kingdom structure of the afterlife does not conform to the teachings of the New Testament.

Premillennialism

The LDS church believes in premillennialism, as discussed in detail in *Plymouth Brethren: Premillennialism*, but have a few adaptations of the belief system to conform to the LDS beliefs concerning *The Book of Mormon*, the priesthood, and other such things. Let us examine some of these differences now.

The LDS church teaches that a universal apostasy occurred, requiring the gospel to be "restored" by Joseph Smith, and they point to 2 Thessalonians 2.1–4 as evidence:[23]

> Now we beseech you, brethren, touching the coming of our Lord Jesus Christ, and our gathering together unto him; to the end that ye be not quickly shaken from your mind, nor yet be troubled, either by spirit, or by word, or by epistle as from us, as that the day of the Lord is just at hand; let no man beguile you in any wise: for it will not be, except the falling away come first, and the man of sin be revealed, the son of perdition, he that opposeth and exalteth himself against all that is called God or that is worshipped; so that he sitteth in the temple of God, setting himself forth as God.

Is there any evidence here to demonstrate that the apostasy would be a universal one? That none would be left to preach the true Gospel? This would be contradicting Matthew 28.20:

> "...teaching them to observe all things whatsoever I commanded you: and lo, I am with you always, even unto the end of the world."

How can Jesus be with us "always" if there was a universal apostasy? This claim does not conform to the message of Jesus.

The LDS church also claims that the Book of Mormon was to be revealed in the "last days," as prophesied by Isaiah in Isaiah 29 and the building of a temple by Ezekiel in Ezekiel 37.[24] Is this true?

The text in Isaiah is Isaiah 29.11–14:

> And all vision is become unto you as the words of a book that is sealed, which men deliver to one that is learned, saying, "Read this, I pray thee;"
> and he saith, "I cannot, for it is sealed:"
> and the book is delivered to him that is not learned, saying, "Read this, I pray thee;"
> and he saith, "I am not learned."
> And the Lord said, "Forasmuch as this people draw nigh unto me,

and with their mouth and with their lips to honor me, but have removed their heart far from me, and their fear of me is a commandment of men which hath been taught them; therefore, behold, I will
proceed to do a marvellous work among this people, even a marvellous work and a wonder; and the wisdom of their wise men shall
perish, and the understanding of their prudent men shall be hid."

Are these "mysteries" the Book of Mormon? The evidence in the Scriptures points more to the mystery of the kingdom of Heaven, as described
by Jesus in Matthew 13.10–17:

And the disciples came, and said unto him, "Why speakest thou
unto them in parables?"
And he answered and said unto them, "Unto you it is given to
know the mysteries of the kingdom of heaven, but to them it is
not given. For whosoever hath, to him shall be given, and he
shall have abundance: but whosoever hath not, from him shall be
taken away even that which he hath. Therefore speak I to them in
parables; because seeing they see not, and hearing they hear not,
neither do they understand. And unto them is fulfilled the prophecy of Isaiah, which saith,
'By hearing ye shall hear, and shall in no wise understand; And
seeing ye shall see, and shall in no wise perceive: For this people's
heart is waxed gross, And their ears are dull of hearing, And their
eyes they have closed; Lest haply they should perceive with their
eyes, And hear with their ears, And understand with their heart,
And should turn again, And I should heal them.'
But blessed are your eyes, for they see; and your ears, for they hear.
For verily I say unto you, that many prophets and righteous men
desired to see the things which ye see, and saw them not; and to
hear the things which ye hear, and heard them not."

Here Jesus says clearly that the disciples were to understand the mystery of
the Kingdom of Heaven and that the Jews had hardened their hearts to this
mystery. Therefore, the prophecy of Isaiah stands fulfilled in Christ Jesus.
Concerning Ezekiel in Ezekiel 37, we read the following in verses 21–28:

And say unto them, "Thus saith the LORD God: Behold, I will
take the children of Israel from among the nations, whither they

are gone, and will gather them on every side, and bring them
into their own land: and I will make them one nation in the land,
upon the mountains of Israel; and one king shall be king to them
all; and they shall be no more two nations, neither shall they be
divided into two kingdoms any more at all; neither shall they defile themselves any more with their idols, nor with their detestable
things, nor with any of their transgressions; but I will save them
out of all their dwelling-places, wherein they have sinned, and
will cleanse them: so shall they be my people, and I will be their
God. And my servant David shall be king over them; and they all
shall have one shepherd: they shall also walk in mine ordinances,
and observe my statutes, and do them. And they shall dwell in
the land that I have given unto Jacob my servant, wherein your fathers dwelt; and they shall dwell therein, they, and their children,
and their children's children, for ever: and David my servant shall
be their prince for ever. Moreover I will make a covenant of peace
with them; it shall be an everlasting covenant with them; and I
will place them, and multiply them, and will set my sanctuary in
the midst of them for evermore. My tabernacle also shall be with
them; and I will be their God, and they shall be my people. And
the nations shall know that I am the LORD that sanctifieth Israel,
when my sanctuary shall be in the midst of them for evermore."

Ezekiel clearly is referring to the new covenant with Jesus Christ, of the
lineage of David (see Matthew 1.1–17). Does Ezekiel mean in verse 27
that God will build a literal tabernacle in Jerusalem? What does Paul
think in 2 Corinthians 6.16?

And what agreement hath a temple of God with idols? for we
are a temple of the living God; even as God said, "I will dwell in
them, and walk in them; and I will be their God, and they shall
be my people."

Paul here calls Christians the "temple of God," the same as spoken of in
Ezekiel 37, demonstrated explicitly in 1 Corinthians 3.16:

Know ye not that ye are a temple of God, and that the Spirit of
God dwelleth in you?

The passage in Ezekiel has spiritual ramifications, not literal ones. We can be sure, then, that the Scriptures speak nothing of any unveiling of the Book of Mormon or the building of another temple.

The LDS church also believes that the prophecy concerning the return of Elijah in Malachi 4.5–6 refers to the coming of Elijah to Joseph Smith and Oliver Cowdery in 1836.[25] We have seen, however, in **Plymouth Brethren: Malachi 4: Elijah**, that John the Baptist was the fulfillment of this prophecy, as stated by Jesus Himself. Are we to trust Jesus or Joseph Smith?

There are many other small detail changes between the premillennialism of the LDS church and the premillennialism of other denominations, especially those in the Evangelical movement, but this should suffice to demonstrate that the LDS version of premillennialism is also not in accordance with the Scriptures.

Baptism for the Dead

The LDS church practices what it calls baptism for the dead, which is a baptism performed by a living person that is done for another who is dead and who may wish to accept that baptism in order to gain a higher standing in the "kingdom" structure.[26] This practice is performed with the justification of 1 Corinthians 15.29:

> Else what shall they do that are baptized for the dead? If the dead are not raised at all, why then are they baptized for them?

Does this mean that a practice called "baptism for the dead" is legitimate? Let us examine this issue.

First, it is notable to see that there is not one example in the New Testament of anyone being baptized "for" someone else. All baptisms are performed upon an individual for remission of his sin.

Regardless, let us examine 1 Corinthians 15.29. We see that Paul is asking a question about "they" who baptize for the dead. Who represents this "they?" Paul is not issuing a command nor an example here, for he is not saying who is doing this work. Paul is not. The Corinthians are not. Who, then, is?

The Scriptures never speak about this practice nor about any group actually performing it. The only verse that mentions this is 1 Corinthians 15.29, and since Paul is not actually speaking about those who perform this act, we can conclude that Paul is merely asking a hypothetical question, reinforcing his message throughout the chapter: if Jesus has not been resurrected from the dead, all of our hopes are in vain. Therefore, it is not possible to conclude from this verse that we are to "baptize for the dead."

Furthermore, we have evidence from the Scriptures that speak of an individual being judged for what he has done himself, and not by what others have done perhaps for him, in Matthew 16.27, Acts 17.30, and 2 Thessalonians 1.6–9:

> "For the Son of man shall come in the glory of his Father with his angels; and then shall he render unto every man according to his deeds."

> "The times of ignorance therefore God overlooked; but now he commandeth men that they should all everywhere repent."

> If so be that it is righteous thing with God to recompense affliction to them that afflict you, and to you that are afflicted rest with us, at the revelation of the Lord Jesus from heaven with the angels of his power in flaming fire, rendering vengeance to them that know not God, and to them that obey not the gospel of our Lord Jesus: who shall suffer punishment, even eternal destruction from the face of the Lord and from the glory of his might.

We see in these passages (and also in many others, including Matthew 25.31–46, partially quoted above) that we will each individually be judged by the actions that we perform, and not by the actions that others may perform on our behalf.

Likewise, the Hebrew author makes it clear in Hebrews 9.27–28 that there is no "intermediate" stage of accepting Christ between death and Judgment:

> And inasmuch as it is appointed unto men once to die, and after this cometh judgment; so Christ also, having been once offered to bear the sins of many, shall appear a second time, apart from sin, to them that wait for him, unto salvation.

The LDS may argue that Jesus preached to spirits in prison as seen in 1 Peter 3.19. Yet, as is discussed in **Creeds: The Apostles' Creed**, that

Peter does not actually say where the spirits were when Jesus preached to them. There is no need to speculate that Christ preached to them in prison or that Jesus will save those who have already perished without having been justified by either the Law or through the grace of God in Christ Jesus. We have been told that we will be judged on the basis of our deeds in the flesh, no more, and no less. Therefore, the Scriptures do not teach that we must baptize for the dead.

Temple Services

The LDS church has instituted a system of temple services wherein temples are built in a locality so that all may assemble there. These temples are supposedly commanded by God in D&C 124.39–40:

> Therefore, verily I say unto you, that your anointings, and your washings, and your baptisms for the dead, and your solemn assemblies, and your memorials for your sacrifices by the sons of Levi, and for your oracles in your must holy places wherein you receive conversations, and your statutes and judgments, for the beginning of the revelations and foundation of Zion, and for the glory, honor, and endowment of all her municipals, are ordained by the ordinance of my holy house, which my people are always commanded to build unto my holy name. And verily I say to you, let this house be built unto my name, that I may reveal mine ordinances therein unto my people.

It is supposed in D&C 110.7 that God will dwell in these temples:

> For behold, I have accepted this house, and my name shall be here; and I will manifest myself to my people in mercy in this house.

Bruce McConkie, in his *Mormon Doctrine*, makes the following declaration:

> The inspired erection and proper use of temples is one of the great evidences of the divinity of the Lord's work. Without revelation they can neither be built or used. Where there are temples, with the spirit of revelation resting upon those who administer therein, there the Lord's people shall be found; where these are not, the church and kingdom and the truth of heaven are not.[27]

These are serious statements. Are we commanded to build temples according to the New Testament?

Stephen, as part of his condemnation of the hardheartedness of the Jews, says the following in Acts 7.48–50:

> "Howbeit the Most High dwelleth not in houses made with hands;
> as saith the prophet,
> 'The heaven is my throne, And the earth the footstool of my feet:
> What manner of house will ye build Me?' saith the Lord: 'Or what
> is the place of My rest? Did not my hand make all these things?'"

Stephen is here quoting Isaiah in Isaiah 66.1–2. Let us read that passage:

> Thus saith the LORD, "Heaven is my throne, and the earth is my
> footstool: what manner of house will ye build unto me? and what
> place shall be my rest? For all these things hath my hand made,
> and so all these things came to be," saith the LORD: "but to this
> man will I look, even to him that is poor and of a contrite spirit,
> and that trembleth at my word."

Isaiah makes it evident here that God looks for the heart of a man for a dwelling-place, and not a creation made with hands. Paul often refers to this, as is seen in 1 Corinthians 3.16–17, 6.19–20, and 2 Corinthians 6.16:

> Know ye not that ye are a temple of God, and that the Spirit of God
> dwelleth in you? If any man destroyeth the temple of God, him shall
> God destroy; for the temple of God is holy, and such are ye.

> Or know ye not that your body is a temple of the Holy Spirit which
> is in you, which ye have from God? and ye are not your own; for ye
> were bought with a price: glorify God therefore in your body.

> And what agreement hath a temple of God with idols? for we are
> a temple of the living God; even as God said,
> "I will dwell in them, and walk in them; and I will be their God,
> and they shall be my people."

Paul also notes that the church itself, being the individual Christians, is technically a collective temple in Ephesians 2.19–22:

> So then ye are no more strangers and sojourners, but ye are fellow-citizens with the saints, and of the household of God, being built upon the foundation of the apostles and prophets, Christ Jesus himself being the chief corner stone; in whom each several building, fitly framed together, groweth into a holy temple in the Lord; in whom ye also are builded together for a habitation of God in the Spirit.

Therefore, it is evident that in the New Testament, we do not build temples with our hands to God, for we are to be His temples. God does not dwell in a temple made with hands; and if there is no Church of Jesus Christ of Latter-Day Saints without a temple, will you follow the teachings of Joseph Smith or will you follow the God of the New Testament?

Notes

1: Some resources for the textual information are http://www.deusvitae.com/faith/matters/texts and Bruce Metzger's works *The Text of the New Testament* and *The Canon of the New Testament*.

2: Bruce McConkie, Mormon Doctrine, pp. 238–239

3: Joseph Smith, "The King Follett Discourse," 1844.

4: Ibid.

5: Ibid.

6: Ibid.

7: Popular saying among Mormons; its origin in printed form is in *Improvement Era*, a Mormon publication, in 1919.

8: D&C 132.15–20

9: Ibid.

10: See D&C 76 and 88

11: D&C 76.15–16

12: D&C 131.1–4, 132

13: Ibid.

14: Ibid.

15: Ibid., 88.16–32

16: Ibid., 76.71–80

17: Ibid., also 88.16–32

18: Ibid., 76.77, 132.17

19: Ibid., 76.81–112

20: Ibid., 88.16–32

21: Ibid., 76.112

22: Ibid., 8

23: Bruce McConkie, *Mormon Doctrine*, p. 689

24: Ibid., p. 690

25: D&C 110.13–16

26: see D&C 124.28–36, 127, 128

27: Bruce McConkie, *Mormon Doctrine*, p. 781

Seventh-Day Adventism

Overview

Seventh-Day Adventism began in 1845 with some former Millerites, a group who grew around William Miller. Miller believed that the date of the return of Jesus could be ascertained in Scripture, first suggesting He would return between March 21, 1843, and March 21, 1844, which was supposedly 2,300 years after the beginning of the prophecy in Daniel 8.14. When the spring of 1844 came and passed, many of Miller's disciples determined that the date was truly October 22, 1844. When this day also passed, the group disbanded because of differences of interpretation over what happened in the "Great Disappointment," as the event was called. One group believed that something important did happen in October 1844, that Jesus began His ministry from the Most Holy Place, which represented the beginning of the "end times." The group recognized Ellen G. White as a prophet of God, and her writings were and are held in great esteem. The name "Seventh-Day Adventist" combines two of the group's messages: that Christians are to hold to the Sabbath on the seventh day as God commanded Israel, and that the return of Jesus Christ is imminent, the "second advent." Seventh-Day Adventism is known for adhering to many portions of the Law of Moses, including the Sabbath, the tithe, and dietary ordinances, and for strong premillennial beliefs.

Variants

There are some variants of the Millerite movement from which Seventh-Day Adventism originates. The Advent Christian Church was begun in 1860 from the Millerites, and they also preach the imminent return of Jesus Christ, although they do not believe that Ellen G. White was a prophet. Although there is internal disagreement over some issues and practices, the celebration of Easter being one, there have been no variants of Seventh-Day Adventism itself.

General Considerations

Part I

- *Lutheranism: Faith Alone*
- *Pietism: Foot Washing*
- *Baptists: "Once Saved, Always Saved"*

Part III

- *Baptism: Baptism is for Remission of Sin and is Necessary for Salvation*
- *The Church Treasury, I: Benevolence: Church Benevolence to Non-Saints; The Missionary Society*
- *The Church Treasury, II: Other Considerations: Hospitals; Centers of Education; Kitchens/ Fellowship Halls; Gymnasiums*
- *Instrumental Music*
- *Judaic Practices: The Ten Commandments and the "Moral Law"*
- *The Lord's Supper: When Should the Lord's Supper Be Observed? Part A: Weekly*
- *Positions of Authority: Who is the Pastor?; A Hierarchy of Bishops [one elder per congregation]; Female Deacons [Deaconesses]; Ordination*

Part IV

- *The "Judaizers"*

The Sabbath

Seventh-Day Adventism teaches that the Sabbath, the day instituted by God for Israel to rest, is still binding upon Christians today. They believe that God instituted the commandment at creation,[1] that God never commanded Christians to do otherwise,[2] and that the Apostles observed the Sabbath.[3] Are these valid Scriptural teachings?

The commandment of God concerning the Sabbath was made in Exodus 20.9–11:

> Six days shalt thou labor, and do all thy work; but the seventh day is a sabbath unto the LORD thy God: in it thou shalt not do any work, thou, nor thy son, nor thy daughter, thy man-servant, nor thy maid-servant, nor thy cattle, nor thy stranger that is within thy gates: for in six days the LORD made heaven and earth, the

sea, and all that in them is, and rested the seventh day: wherefore the LORD blessed the sabbath day, and hallowed it.

The Sabbath was given to man as a day of rest for the reason that God rested on the seventh day. There is no evidence from the Scriptures that God commanded anyone before Moses to observe the Sabbath. Yes, God is said to sanctify the seventh day according to Genesis 2.3, but Genesis was no doubt written after the covenant was inaugurated between God and Israel, and the author demonstrates to Israel (and to us) the reasons behind the Sabbath regulation in the Law.

Likewise, there is never a commandment in the New Testament to observe the Sabbath. The Seventh-Day Adventists infer from the use of the term "sabbath" in Acts 13.14;42;44, 16.13, 17.1–2, and 18.4 that the Apostles did observe it. This inference, however, is not substantiated by the text: we see the Apostles preaching the word of God to the Jews on the Sabbath because that is when the latter came together. Paul says in Romans 1.16 that the Gospel went to the "Jew first, and then to the Greek," and this is borne out in one example, Acts 17.1–2:

Now when they had passed through Amphipolis and Apollonia, they came to Thessalonica, where was a synagogue of the Jews: and Paul, as his custom was, went in unto them, and for three sabbath days reasoned with them from the Scriptures.

Paul's custom was to reason with the Jews first in the cities he entered, and only after the Jews would not hear would he preach to the Gentiles.

It may be argued that since the term "sabbath" is used, this means that these Christians obviously observed it. This is not necessarily the case. "Christendom" recognizes December 25 as Christmas. If one speaks of doing something on Christmas day, does this necessitate that one observes Christmas as a religious observance? By no means, for it is the commonly understood term for December 25. Likewise, the early Christians recognized that the "seventh day" was the "Sabbath," calling it as much does not necessitate its observance.

Concerning God having never "changed" the Sabbath, we must understand the nature of the covenants that God has with His children. We have been told in Colossians 2.13–14 the following:

> And you, being dead through your trespasses and the uncircumcision of your flesh, you, I say, did he make alive together with him, having forgiven us all our trespasses; having blotted out the bond written in ordinances that was against us, which was contrary to us: and he hath taken it out that way, nailing it to the cross.

We also read the same message in Hebrews 7.12; 9.15:

> For the priesthood being changed, there is made of necessity a change also of the law.

> And for this cause he is the mediator of a new covenant, that a death having taken place for the redemption of the transgressions that were under the first covenant, they that have been called may receive the promise of the eternal inheritance.

The apostles of God spoke clearly that there was a change of law enacted by the death of Jesus Christ. Therefore, since there has been a change of law, the laws of the people under Moses are not by that virtue alone applicable to Christians today. There are many instances where the laws of God under Moses are the same as under Christ, but many have been changed. Colossians 2.14 makes it clear that the Law of Moses has been nailed to the cross, and any practice applicable to Christians must come from either before the Law or through the Apostles. The Sabbath does not meet either of these requirements, for the Sabbath was instituted as a practice only in the time of Moses.

Colossians 2.13–16 actually speaks of the Sabbath in this regard:

> And you, being dead through your trespasses and the uncircumcision of your flesh, you, I say, did he make alive together with him, having forgiven us all our trespasses; having blotted out the bond written in ordinances that was against us, which was contrary to us: and he hath taken it out that way, nailing it to the cross; having despoiled the principalities and the powers, he made a show of them openly, triumphing over them in it. Let no man therefore judge you in meat, or in drink, or in respect of a feast day or a new moon or a sabbath day.

The Seventh-Day Adventists argue that this commandment only speaks concerning the "seven year" Sabbath of the land, since the rest of the acts are "ritual matters."[4] Yet the text does not make any such distinction; the new moon comes monthly, and "in meat, or in drink," refers to the dietary restrictions of the Law, which are by no means "ritual matters."

We have further evidence of the change in the Sabbath in Hebrews 4.1–11:

> Let us fear therefore, lest haply, a promise being left of entering into his rest, any one of you should seem to have come short of it. For indeed we have had good tidings preached unto us, even as also they: but the word of hearing did not profit them, because it was not united by faith with them that heard. For we who have believed do enter into that rest; even as he hath said, "As I sware in my wrath, They shall not enter into my rest:"
> although the works were finished from the foundation of the world. For he hath said somewhere of the seventh day on this wise, "And God rested on the eventh day from all his works;" and in this place again, "They shall not enter into my rest."
> Seeing therefore it remaineth that some should enter thereinto, and they to whom the good tidings were before preached failed to enter in because of disobedience, he again defineth a certain day, "Today," saying in David so long a time afterward (even as hath been said before), "Today if ye shall hear his voice, Harden not your hearts."
> For if Joshua had given them rest, he would not have spoken afterward of another day. There remaineth therefore a sabbath rest for the people of God. For he that is entered into his rest hath himself also rested from his works, as God did from his. Let us therefore give diligence to enter into that rest, that no man fall after the same example of disobedience.

The Seventh-Day Adventists believe that this "rest" actually refers to the weekly Sabbath.[5] However, if we examine the text, we see that this cannot be so. The Hebrew author said in verse 8:

> If Joshua had given them rest, he would not have spoken afterward of another day.

Joshua is spoken of since he was the one who led the Israelites into the promised land and re-established the law in Joshua 8.32:

> And he wrote there upon the stones a copy of the law of Moses, which he wrote, in the presence of the children of Israel.

The rest given by Joshua was the Sabbath, yet the Hebrew author demonstrates that there "remains a sabbath rest for the people of God." He further states in verses 10 and 11 that:

> he that is entered into his rest hath himself also rested from his works, as God did from his. Let us therefore give diligence to enter into that rest, that no man fall after the same example of disobedience.

How can this rest be a weekly rest on Earth if we must "give diligence" to enter it? We are to give diligence to enter Heaven (cf. 2 Timothy 2.15), and yet are never told about diligence for a weekly rest. Therefore, it is evident from the Scriptures that the Christian sabbath represents the rest given to believers in Heaven, and our day of assembling follows the example of the Apostles in Acts 20.7:

> And upon the first day of the week, when we were gathered together to break bread, Paul discoursed with them, intending to depart on the morrow; and prolonged his speech until midnight.

Dietary Restrictions

Seventh-Day Adventism also teaches that the dietary restrictions given under the Law of Moses are still applicable today.[6] However, we have numerous Scriptures showing that they are not so, including Mark 7.19 and Romans 14.2, 14:

> "because it goeth not into his heart, but into his belly, and goeth out into the draught?" This he said, making all meats clean.

> One man hath faith to eat all things: but he that is weak eateth herbs.

I know, and am persuaded in the Lord Jesus, that nothing is unclean of itself: save that to him who accounteth anything to be unclean, to him it is unclean.

The Seventh-Day Adventists believe that Mark 7.19 was referring to the manner of the eating of foods, and not of the food itself.[7] It is true that contextually Jesus is discussing the Pharisees and their binding of external washings, yet the comment made in verse 19 is a commentary by Mark, not a statement of Jesus. It need not deal directly with the context of what Jesus is saying. Mark simply affirms that by teaching the Pharisees that food does not defile men, He also teaches that all foods are clean. They also teach concerning Romans 14 that the context simply discusses food offered to idols,[8] yet the text does not make any such distinctions. Paul says very clearly, "nothing is unclean of itself," and that "one has faith to eat all things, but he that is weak eats herbs." Nothing is spoken of concerning the nature of the foods themselves, only what they are. Paul makes it evident that all foods are clean for Christians.

The Second Advent

The other main teaching of Seventh-Day Adventism is the imminent return of Jesus Christ, or the "Second Advent." Their belief system concerning the Second Advent has many parallels with **Plymouth Brethren: Premillennialism**. We will concern ourselves only with the main differences between the two belief systems.

The principal belief of the Seventh-Day Adventists concerning the Second Advent is the "Heavenly Sanctuary." The Seventh-Day Adventists believe in a literal "Heavenly Sanctuary," where Jesus now reigns as High Priest.[9] They believe that the prophecy of Daniel 8.14 gives a 2,300 year period for the cleansing of this sanctuary:

And he said unto me, Unto two thousand and three hundred evenings and mornings; then shall the sanctuary be cleansed.

If the date of 457 BCE is accepted for the decree to restore and rebuild Jerusalem, the "seventy sevens" of Daniel 9.24, or 490 years, brings us to about 33 or 34 CE; the remaining 1,810 years brings us to 1844, or the time of the prophecy of William Miller. It is believed that the actions of Daniel 7.13–14 occurred in 1844.[10]

> I saw in the night-visions, and, behold, there came with the clouds of heaven one like unto a son of man, and he came even to the ancient of days, and they brought him near before him. And there was given him dominion, and glory, and a kingdom, that all the peoples, nations, and languages should serve him: his dominion is an everlasting dominion, which shall not pass away, and his kingdom that which shall not be destroyed.

Therefore, it is the belief of Seventh-Day Adventism that Jesus began the final phase of His ministry in 1844, preparing to return for the Second Advent.[11] Is this what the Scriptures teach?

We have seen in **Plymouth Brethren: Daniel 7: The Beasts** and **Plymouth Brethren: Daniel 9: The Duration of Israel** that the signs of Daniel point clearly to the first coming of Christ, the establishment of the church, and the destruction of Jerusalem in 70 CE. The "seventy sevens" clearly refer to the time between Daniel and the destruction of Jerusalem, and this is confirmed by Jesus in Matthew 24.15.

The nature of this prophecy hinges upon the date of 457 BCE, the date wherein it is believed the decree of which Daniel spoke of in Daniel 9.25 was given:

> Know therefore and discern, that from the going forth of the commandment to restore and to build Jerusalem unto the anointed one, the prince, shall be seven weeks, and threescore and two weeks: it shall be built again, with street and moat, even in troublous times.

It is believed that this prophecy was fulfilled in the decree of Artaxerxes in Ezra 7.11–26, when Ezra was given the authority of the king to teach the Jews the commandments of their God. Even if we were to accept that this command was the "restoration" of Israel as spoken of by Daniel, the "building" of Jerusalem was first commanded by Cyrus concerning the Temple (538 BCE – Ezra 1.1) and ultimately commanded by Artaxerxes concerning the walls of Jerusalem (444 BCE – Nehemiah 2.1). This period of "building" is a long span, long before and shortly after the decree of Artaxerxes in 457 BCE. This is another situation where individuals attempt to force history to fit prophecy, as opposed to examining prophecy in light of historical evidence. There is no evidence that the decree spoken of by Daniel conforms to a decree of Artaxerxes in 457 BCE.

It is also believed by the Seventh-Day Adventists that the "millennial reign" will be in Heaven, at the conclusion of which the saints and Christ will return to the "new earth" to live forever.[12] It is also believed that there will be two resurrections, the first for the righteous at the Second Advent, and the second for the unrighteous after the "millennium."[13] Is this taught by the Scriptures?

These beliefs are mostly based on the Revelation of John, and as we have seen in **Plymouth Brethren: The Nature of Prophecy**, the Revelation is a "prophecy by sign," and while we believe John saw everything that he wrote about, we cannot determine that what John saw will literally occur. We have seen in **Plymouth Brethren: The Nature of Christ's Kingdom**, that the Kingdom exists today, comprised of all the saints, and is not limited to a thousand years. We have been told in Matthew 25.34 the following:

> "Then shall the King say unto them on his right hand, 'Come, ye blessed of my Father, inherit the kingdom prepared for you from the foundation of the world.'"

The Kingdom for the saints has been prepared from the foundation of the world; how can this be a "new earth," created after this world is destroyed? It is evident that John is using language and signs understandable to man to describe a scene so magnificent that no comparison can be valid.

We have also seen in **Plymouth Brethren: The Judgment** that the texts in Matthew 25 and 2 Corinthians 5.10 demonstrate that the Judgment will be a one-time event, and that there will not be two judgments for two resurrections. Therefore, the teachings of the Seventh-Day Adventists concerning the Second Advent of Christ are not based in the complete message of the Scriptures.

Notes

1: *Seventh-Day Adventists Believe…: A Biblical Exposition of 27 Fundamental Doctrines*, p. 249

2: Ibid.

3: Ibid., pp. 253–254

4: Ibid., p. 254

5: Ibid., p. 258

6: Ibid., p. 285

7: Ibid., p. 292

8: Ibid.

9: Ibid., p. 314

10: Ibid., p. 324

11: Ibid.

12: Ibid., pp. 364, 367–368

13: Ibid., 358

Christian Science

Overview

Christian Science (formally the Church of Christ, Scientist) is the product of the belief system of Mary Baker Eddy, who believed that she came upon the hidden truths of God in 1866 by being instantaneously healed when Scripture was read. She then opened herself up to what she deemed the "divine Mind" and began to receive revelation. She taught the principles she derived in her main book *Science and Health With Key to the Scriptures*. She believed that God demonstrated to her that the only thing that truly exists is Truth, also known as the divine Principle, Love, or God. Everything else is illusory, especially those things deemed "material," or of this physical realm. Her "divine Science" was the action of this divine Mind, and therefore the Christian Scientist was one who practiced the will of the divine Mind in his or her life. Such was generally the demonstration of God working within someone, and manifested to others by healing with the divine Mind: in Christian Science, sin, disease, and all evils are merely illusions, deceiving what was deemed "mortal mind," or the mind in humans, and causing them suffering, sickness, and death. These teachings were accepted by many, and by the time of the death of Mary Baker Eddy in 1910, the "Cause," as Christian Science was deemed, had spread far beyond her New England roots. Christian Science is known for its neo-Gnostic conception of the duality of material and spirit, and the focus in the denomination is on the individual's development of the divine Mind within him or her. Their focus is purely spiritual, allegorizing many of the practices discussed in Scripture (including baptism and the Lord's Supper) and only having church buildings and worship services proper to cater to the "weaknesses" of man.

General Considerations

Part I
- *Lutheranism: The Lord's Prayer*
- *Religious Society of Friends (Quakers): Physical and Spiritual Natures*
- *Plymouth Brethren: Premillennialism*

Part III
- *Baptism: The Need for Baptism; Baptism=Immersion; Baptism is for Remission of Sin and is Necessary for Salvation*
- *The Church Treasury, I: Benevolence: Church Benevolence to Non-Saints*
- *The Church Treasury, II: Other Considerations: Hospitals; Centers of Education*

Concerning Observances:
- *Observances Concerning the Lord's Birth: Christmas*
- *Instrumental Music*
- *The Lord's Supper: The Need for the Lord's Supper; When Should the Lord's Supper Be Observed? Part A: Weekly*
- *Positions of Authority: Who Is The Pastor?; Ordination*

Part IV
- *Gnosticism*

Dualism: Physical versus Spiritual

The foundational concept in Christian Science theology is the dualism (having two forces at odds with one another) between what is deemed physical (or material) and what is deemed spiritual (or spirit). The only thing that truly exists is God, the divine Mind, otherwise known as Truth, Love, and Intelligence, which is manifest in what is deemed the "spiritual".[1] On the other hand, that which is physical or material is merely illusory, having no existence within itself: it is a fabrication of the senses and the "mortal mind," the human mind and its belief system.[2] Christian Science introduces these concepts as polarities: materialism and spirit are two distinct systems, having no part of each other.[3] The theology follows from this that the conditions of suffering within mankind—sin, sickness, and death—are merely illusions of the mortal mind, and do not truly exist.[4] If one has the divine Mind working within him, he will understand that all of these "material" things are delusions and have no place in "Truth"; thus, he will conquer these delusions, and be thus practicing Christian Science.[5] Is this system of belief found in the Scriptures?

We have been told in the Scriptures that God made the heavens and the earth and also man, Genesis 1.1 and Genesis 2.7:

> In the beginning God created the heavens and the earth.

> And the LORD God formed man of the dust of the ground, and breathed into his nostrils the breath of life; and man became a living soul.

The Scriptures do speak concerning the "lust of the flesh" (1 John 2.16) and the fact that the physical will be transformed into the spiritual (1 Corinthians 15). The Scriptures do not say, however, that flesh and spirit have no portion with each other; in fact, we have the words of Paul in 1 Corinthians 6.17–20 the contrary:

> But he that is joined unto the Lord is one spirit. Flee fornication. Every sin that a man doeth is without the body; but he that com-mitteth fornication sinneth against his own body. Or know ye not that your body is a temple of the Holy Spirit which is in you, which ye have from God? and ye are not your own; for ye were bought with a price: glorify God therefore in your body.

The flesh can be made to glorify God; how can it do so if it has no exis-tence or has any part with spirit? How can the body be a "temple of the Holy Spirit" if the Spirit does not exist within matter?

When God established the creation, He established that it was "very good" (Genesis 1.31); the reality of the creation around us is everywhere assumed in the Scriptures. Jesus' proof of His resurrection is that He has a body of flesh and is not only spirit (Luke 24.39). To posit an illusory reality represents neo-Gnosticism, and its attendant docetic views have no place in the Scriptures (Romans 1.18–20, Colossians 2.8–9).

The Interpretation of the Scriptures

Christian Science will answer the above arguments by attempting to demonstrate that the Scriptures are being interpreted incorrectly because they are being used in a literal sense. In Christian Science, the Scriptures are to be read for spiritual meaning and understanding.[6] Mary Baker Eddy demonstrated this concept with her exegesis on Genesis 1–3 in *Science and Health with Key to the Scriptures*, attempting to demonstrate that the "light" created in Genesis 1.5 is "Truth," the "waters" in 1.9 are "thought," and so forth and so on.[7] Therefore, in the Christian Science mentality, the creation account of Genesis 1 refers to the spiritual creation, and 1 Corinthians 6 refers to the spiritual man.

This spiritual system of exegesis may have some validity if it were not for the fact that Mary Baker Eddy repudiated portions of Scripture which would not harmonize with her belief system. For instance, she considered the creation account of Genesis 2 to be a "lie" and the "opposite of scientific truth."[8] She relied on the then-new belief that there were at least two authors of the book of Genesis, the "Yahwistic" and the "Elohistic" authors, attempting to demonstrate a "material" versus a "spiritual" form of God.[9] Eddy went further with the concept of the YHWH of the Jews being a more "material" God by proclaiming the Jewish system of religion to be limited, a "tribal religion" based on "material things," the "antithesis of Christianity," with a "man-projected God" that "gives no hint of the unchanging love of God,"[10] all comments reminiscent of the position of the Gnostics. The Scriptures, however, teach that the Scriptures are inspired and that the Jews were a people of God in 2 Timothy 3.16–17, Romans 9.1–5, and 10.1–4:

> Every scripture inspired of God is also profitable for teaching, for reproof, for correction, for instruction which is in righteousness. That the man of God may be complete, furnished completely unto every good work.

> I say the truth in Christ, I lie not, my conscience bearing witness with me in the Holy Spirit, that I have great sorrow and unceasing pain in my heart. For I could wish that I myself were anathema from Christ for my brethren's sake, my kinsmen according to the flesh: who are Israelites; whose is the adoption, and the glory,

and the covenants, and the giving of the law, and the service of God, and the promises; whose are the fathers, and of whom is Christ as concerning the flesh, who is over all, God blessed for ever. Amen.

Brethren, my heart's desire and my supplication to God is for them, that they may be saved. For I bear them witness that they have a zeal for God, but not according to knowledge. For being ignorant of God's righteousness, and seeking to establish their own, they did not subject themselves to the righteousness of God. For Christ is the end of the law unto righteousness to every one that believeth.

If Mary Baker Eddy's theology required her to consider a portion of God's Word to be a lie and to denigrate the people of God, how can her theology be consistent with the Scriptures? Therefore, we can see that the exegetical and interpretive methods of Christian Science do not harmonize with the whole message of the Scriptures. There is no good reason to deny that God created a real, physical realm in which we currently reside.

Healing and Demonstration

The main practices of Christian Science—healing and demonstration—follow from its theology: if the vestiges of materialism are non-existent, they can be conquered. The only way to determine if one is conquering materialism is to negate its effects, including sin, sickness, age, and death.[11] Therefore, the practice of healing is to Christian Science the ultimate demonstration of the work of the divine Mind.[12]

Some words must first be spoken concerning the Christian Science conception of disease and healing. In Christian Science theology, disease has no material basis but is simply a condition of mortal mind. Mortal mind believes that it is ill, and therefore it is ill, either consciously or unconsciously.[13] Drugs have no effect within themselves when it comes to fighting disease, for it is the faith in the drug that leads to a form of material healing.[14] When Jesus came to earth, He thus began the task of healing people using "divine Science," and not drugs or such things, desiring that His followers would continue to do the same.[15] In fact, it is believed that Jesus founded the church on the foundation of healing.[16] In the end, Mary Baker Eddy says that Christian Science is proven to be a valid theological system on the basis of the ability to heal.[17] Is this theology consistent with the Scriptures?

It must first be said that the mind does have a significant impact in illness and healing. The mind is able to facilitate the occurrence of either, and some of the proofs of Mary Baker Eddy are true: some people are healed by the "placebo effect," some become ill because of mental disposition to become ill (hypochondria), and so on. It is not accurate, however, to say that there is absolutely no material basis for illness and/or healing. Since the death of Mary Baker Eddy, it has been conclusively determined that disease does have a material basis: bacteria and viruses enter the body and attack cells, and the body responds to this attack, or there is an imbalance in hormones and/or brain signals that lead to psychological or some internal physiological illnesses, and so on. Therefore, illness and its symptoms are most often the result of an agent (in scientific terms, a pathogen) acting within the body and the body's reaction thereto. Furthermore, drugs do perform physical actions which facilitate healing, normally either working to destroy the pathogen itself or giving the cells of the body the knowledge required to do so. It is very true that the "mortal mind" of Christian Science does play a large role in the illness/healing process, yet there are valid physical actions going on.

It is also very true that Jesus came to this earth and healed many; to remove illness, however, was not His mission. His mission was to preach the Kingdom of Heaven, to seek and save the lost, and to sacrifice Himself on the cross for our sins, as demonstrated in Mark 1.38, Matthew 15.24, and Philippians 2.8:

> And he saith unto them, "Let us go elsewhere into the next towns, that I may preach there also; for to this end came I forth."

> But he answered and said, "I was not sent but unto the lost sheep of the house of Israel."

> And being found in fashion as a man, he humbled himself, becoming obedient even unto death, yea, the death of the cross.

Healing was a means to demonstrate His power, to perform deeds not able to be performed by men. This same attitude is found in the Apostles, who used the opportunity in Acts 3 to heal a paralytic and thus open the hearts of many to receive the Gospel. Furthermore, the method of healing—instantaneous healing through the name of Christ or by the word of Christ—is not demonstrative of the ineffectiveness of drugs but the demonstration that the healing was done by the power of God and by the power of God alone. There is neither evidence nor justification to infer any other reason from the Scriptures.

The Scriptures never speak of the preeminence of healing; in fact, by the time James wrote his epistle, prayer for healing had become customary, as seen in James 5.14–16:

> Is any among you sick? Let him call for the elders of the church; and let them pray over him, anointing him with oil in the name of the Lord: and the prayer of faith shall save him that is sick, and the Lord shall raise him up; and if he have committed sins, it shall be forgiven him. Confess therefore your sins one to another, and pray one for another, that ye may be healed. The supplication of a righteous man availeth much in its working.

Likewise, there are accounts in the Scriptures of Christians who were ill and were not automatically healed by an Apostle, as seen in Philippians 2.25–27 and 2 Timothy 4.20:

> But I counted it necessary to send to you Epaphroditus, my brother and fellow-worker and fellow-soldier, and your messenger and minister to my need; since he longed after you all, and was sore troubled, because ye had heard that he was sick: for indeed he was sick nigh unto death: but God had mercy on him; and not on him only, but on me also, that I might not have sorrow upon sorrow.

> Erastus abode at Corinth: but Trophimus I left at Miletus sick.

These are not in harmony with the Christian Science system of healing by the power of the divine Mind, but will any Christian Scientist assert that James or Paul are not disciples of Jesus Christ? This demonstrates that the statement made by Mark in Mark 16.17–18 applied to the Apostles alone, and no other, and even then by the will of God and not always realized in every instance, unlike what is said by Mary Baker Eddy:[18]

> "And these signs shall accompany them that believe: in my name shall they cast out demons; they shall speak with new tongues; they shall take up serpents, and if they drink any deadly thing, it shall in no wise hurt them; they shall lay hands on the sick, and they shall recover."

Therefore, it is evident that the mission of Jesus was not primarily to heal physically, and the witness of Paul in 1 Timothy 3.15 demonstrates that the church is not founded on healing:

> But if I tarry long, that thou mayest know how men ought to behave themselves in the house of God, which is the church of the living God, the pillar and ground of the truth.

Finally, it is interesting to note that although she taught that pain was an illusion of mortal mind and that drugs only worked inasmuch as one had faith in them, Mary Baker Eddy was known to at times take morphine for the constant pain that she faced.[19] This is justified by saying that sometimes she would have to face her physical difficulties with material methods in order to regain her spiritual understanding and to be able to further promote the "Cause," Christian Science.[20] This demonstrates a major inconsistency: if pain was merely an illusion, could not Mary Baker Eddy overcome it with the divine Mind? Even if her weakness is allowed, why morphine, if Mary Baker Eddy was so convinced that drugs had no effect save the faith therein? Could she not have had faith without morphine? How can one reject materialism and materialistic medicine and then use it when beneficial? This should demonstrate clearly that there is physical, real, material basis for both illness and drug remedy.

The Nature of God

The basis of Christian Science is that God is divine Mind, otherwise known as the divine Principle, Love, Truth, Intelligence, etc. Since this divine Mind has nothing to do with anything material, the concept of Jesus being God the Son in the flesh is unsupportable in the Christian Science belief system. This is evidenced by the teachings of Mary Baker Eddy concerning Jesus: she taught that Jesus was the reflection of Christ, the "Christ-idea," that Jesus is not synonymous with Christ, that Jesus is not God the Son but the Son of God, "one in quality, not in quantity."[21] We see this demonstrated in a portion of *Science and Health with Key to the Scriptures*:

> Christ is the ideal Truth, that comes to heal sickness and sin through Christian Science, and attributes all power to God. Jesus is the name of the man who, more than all other men, has presented Christ, the true idea of God, healing the sick and the sinning and destroying the power of death. Jesus is the human man, and Christ is the divine idea; hence the duality of Jesus the Christ.[22]

We see from the Scriptures, however, that God is one, and yet Christ was with God and yet also was God, and that Christ became flesh and dwelt among us, in Isaiah 45.5, John 1.1, John 1.14, Colossians 2.9, and 2 John 1.7:

> "I am the LORD, and there is none else; besides Me there is no God. I will gird thee, though thou hast not known Me."

> In the beginning was the Word, and the Word was with God, and the Word was God.

> And the Word became flesh, and dwelt among us (and we beheld his glory, glory as of the only begotten from the Father), full of grace and truth.

> For in him dwelleth all the fulness of the Godhead bodily.

> For many deceivers are gone forth into the world, even they that confess not that Jesus Christ cometh in the flesh. This is the deceiver and the antichrist.

We also have the confession of Peter in Matthew 16.15–16:

> He saith unto them, "But who say ye that I am?"
> And Simon Peter answered and said, "Thou art the Christ, the Son of the living God."

Notice that Simon does not say that Jesus is the "Christ-idea" or any such thing, but that He is the Christ. Therefore, we have seen from the Scriptures that Jesus is the Christ, that separation of the two is not in the Scriptures, and that Jesus is fully God as the Father is fully God.

Mary Baker Eddy also considered the role of the Holy Spirit to be something like the giving of "divine Science," for she stated that the "Comforter" of John 14 was "Divine Science."[23] This, however, is inconsistent even with Christian Science doctrine, for Mary Baker Eddy says in the same place that this Comforter is given "forever," yet she states that the church lost its "healing power" in the fourth century, not to be regained until she received revelation in the nineteenth.[24] Furthermore, it is also believed by Christian Scientists that the disciples of Christ were not able to understand the divine Science, and that the responsibility of exposing materialism was left to Mary Baker Eddy.[25] How, then, can the Comforter be given to the disciples if the Comforter is divine Science and yet the disciples did not understand divine Science? This is not even internally consistent, let alone Scripturally consistent. Therefore, the belief system of Christian Science concerning the nature of God is not consistent with the God described in the Old and New Testaments.

Notes

1: Mary Baker Eddy, *Science and Health with Key to the Scriptures*, pp. 2, 27, 143

2: Ibid., pp. 97, 145, 293–294

3: Ibid., pp. 171, 173, 182

4: Ibid., pp. 42, 152

5: Ibid., pp. 374, 423, 428

6: Ibid., p. 177; Gilbert C. Carpenter, *Mary Baker Eddy: Her Spiritual Footsteps*, pp. 60, 265

7: *Science and Health with Key to the Scriptures*, pp. 504, 506

8: Ibid., pp. 521–522

9: Ibid., pp. 523–524

10: Ibid., pp. 42, 133, 140

11: Ibid., p. 194

12: Ibid., p. 344

13: Ibid., pp. 168–169, 188, 234

14: Ibid., pp. 131, 155

15: Ibid., pp. 157, 230

16: Ibid., p. 136

17: Ibid., p. 547

18: Ibid., p. 38

19: *Mary Baker Eddy: Her Spiritual Footsteps*, p. 267 20: Ibid., pp. 269–271

21: *Science and Health with Key to the Scriptures*, pp. 316, 332, 361

22: Ibid., p. 473

23: Ibid., p. 55

24: Ibid., p. 41

25: *Mary Baker Eddy: Her Spiritual Footsteps*, p. 100

Jehovah's Witnesses

Overview

Jehovah's Witnesses (officially the Watch Tower Bible and Tract Society) was founded by Charles Taze Russell in 1872 and represents a growing movement. The Jehovah's Witnesses are noted for their strong evangelistic focus, often knocking on doors and distributing literature. The Jehovah's Witnesses believe that there is power in the name of God and that the planet Earth will never cease to exist. They have a very strong premillennial focus, meeting in buildings they call "Kingdom Halls." They are also known for incorporating many Judaic belief systems into their theology and for their non-Trinitarian views. The Jehovah's Witnesses publish their own translation of the Bible, the New World Translation (NWT), which contains alterations to the original text to fit the belief system of the Jehovah's Witnesses. They are also very well known for their prophecy of the return of Jesus Christ in 1914; when this did not occur, they adapted the belief by positing that Jesus began to rule in 1914 when Satan was cast down to earth, on account of their interpretation of Revelation 12.9.

General Considerations

Part I
- *Lutheranism: The Lord's Prayer*
- *Anabaptism: Nonresistance*
- *Calvinism: T– Total Depravity*
- *Plymouth Brethren: Premillennialism*

Part III
- *Baptism: Baptism is for Remission of Sin and is Necessary for Salvation*
- *The Church Treasury, I: Benevolence: The Missionary Society*
- *The Church Treasury, II: Other Considerations: Centers of Education*

The Name of God the Father

Jehovah's Witnesses believe strongly in calling God by the name "Jehovah," the "English" form of the Hebrew Tetragrammaton YHWH, in reality most likely pronounced "Yahweh."[1] They believe that the name must be used on account of its importance in the Old Testament, from verses like Acts 15.14, and the fact that Jesus honored the name in John 17.6, 26:

> "Symeon hath rehearsed how first God visited the Gentiles, to take out of them a people for his name."

> "I manifested thy name unto the men whom thou gavest me out of the world: thine they were, and thou gavest them to me; and they have kept thy word...and I made known unto them thy name, and will make it known; that the love wherewith thou lovedst me may be in them, and I in them."

Do these verses show that we must use the "name" of God, "Jehovah," in order to be pleasing to Him?

We must first understand what the term "name" in these contexts signifies in the New Testament. Let us examine Matthew 28.18–19 and Acts 3.6:

> And Jesus came to them and spake unto them, saying, "All authority hath been given unto me in heaven and on earth. Go ye therefore, and make disciples of all the nations, baptizing them into the name of the Father and of the Son and of the Holy Spirit."

> But Peter said, "Silver and gold have I none; but what I have, that give I thee. In the name of Jesus Christ of Nazareth, walk."

We can see here clearly that the term "name" designates the use of authority. This is no less true today; when we sign a document, we are in effect giving our authority to it. When one signs a check, one gives the bank the authority to give the amount specified to the intended receiver. We see a similar thing in Matthew 28.18–19 and Acts 3.6. Is there any intrinsic power in the words "Father, Son, and Holy Spirit" or "Jesus Christ of Nazareth?" By no means! There is great power, however, in the figures of the Father, the Son, Jesus Christ of Nazareth, and the Holy Spirit. Therefore, when one speaks or acts "in the name of" Jesus Christ, one speaks or acts on the authority of Jesus Christ.

This is exactly what is spoken of by Jesus in John 17.6, 26. Jesus manifested the authority of His Father, and He made known to the Jews the power of God that is in His name. In Acts 15.14, James is discussing the prophecy in Isaiah that some of the Gentiles would be a people for His name, or under His authority. There is no intended reference to the nomenclature said Gentiles would use to speak of God. Therefore, these verses do not demonstrate that there is a need to refer to God as "Jehovah."

Nevertheless, the Scriptures do indicate how people in New Testament times referred to God. We read the following, for instance, in Matthew 4.7:

> Jesus said unto him, "Again it is written, Thou shalt not make trial of the Lord thy God."

Jesus is here quoting Deuteronomy 6.16:

> Ye shall not tempt the LORD your God, as ye tempted him in Massah.

The Revised Version in Deuteronomy, as throughout the Old Testament, uses LORD capitalized to indicate the presence of the Tetragrammaton YHWH. In Jesus' words in the New Testament, however, there is no use of the Tetragrammaton in any form; instead, the Greek term *kurios*, or "Lord," is always used. One cannot claim that the New Testament authors never presented transliterations of anything: one need only look at Matthew 27.46, or Mark 5.41, to find evidence of transliterated Hebrew/Aramaic into Greek. If it were so important for Jesus (or for Matthew) that the name of God should be pronounced and used in Matthew 4, or in any other clear reference to the Tetragrammaton, why do they not present the transliterated YHWH in the text, but provide the translation *kurios*?

The New World Translation (NWT), produced by the Jehovah's Witnesses, will translate Matthew 4.7 with "Jehovah," which is done often, yet we never see any evidence of the Tetragrammaton in the original Greek of the New Testament. Furthermore, in the Greek Old Testament (the Septuagint, or LXX), the term *kurios* is most often used to translate the Tetragrammaton, and many New Testament authors quote this text when quoting the Old Testament. There is no justification from the manuscripts of the New Testament to translate *kurios* in the New Testament as "Jehovah".

To this, many Jehovah's Witnesses will claim that the Tetragrammaton was originally within the New Testament texts, but later scribes corrupted the text and removed reference to it. There is no textual evidence for this, which is significant, considering the geographic range and ages of the texts in our possession. Furthermore, if we are to believe that later scribes were able to so thoroughly corrupt the New Testament text that we are not able to discern it today, on what basis can we have any confidence in anything the New Testament would teach us? How do we know what else was changed? Such a claim requires too much speculation without sufficient basis in reality. It therefore poses a great danger for the foundation of the faith and gives unbelievers reason to blaspheme.

There is also evidence from the words of Jesus in Matthew 6.9 and Luke 11.2:

> "After this manner therefore pray ye. Our Father who art in heaven, Hallowed be thy name."

> And he said unto them, "When ye pray, say, Father, hallowed be thy name. Thy kingdom come."

The Jehovah's Witnesses say that Matthew 6.9 is a demonstration of Jesus honoring the name of God,[2] and they also teach that the name "Jehovah" should be used in prayer when expressing Deity.[3] Yet how can this be the case when Jesus does not use the term "Jehovah" or "YHWH" or any such thing but simply "Father" or "Our Father?"

Finally, there is the term itself. The Jehovah's Witnesses condemn the Jews for their "superstition" of not pronouncing the name of God, thus not allowing us to know definitively how the Tetragrammaton is pronounced (the original Hebrew language did not contain vowels).[4] The term "Jehovah" is most certainly not the pronunciation of the Tetragrammaton. "Jehovah" was popularized a few hundred years ago on the basis of a misunderstanding of the Jewish Masoretic tradition regarding the writing of the Tetragrammaton in the Hebrew Bible.[5] "Yahweh" is the preferred pronunciation, based on ancient evidence.[6] This whole discussion serves one purpose: how can the name of God have such great importance if we do not even know what it really is? How can the name of God be used in prayer if we do not know how to pronounce it? If God considered His name of that great importance, would not Jesus or the Apostles have demonstrated how to pronounce it? Yet there is no evidence of God ever insisting on being called by the Tetragrammaton in the New Testament. Therefore, it can be determined that the use of the Tetragrammaton to refer to God the Father is not to be bound upon New Testament Christians today.

The Nature of Jesus Christ

Jehovah's Witnesses reject the belief that God is a Trinity, with God the Father, God the Son, and God the Holy Spirit as three distinct personalities that are one.[7] They instead believe that Jesus is "a" god, simply the Son of God, not God the Son. They believe that there is evidence for this in John 14.28 and 1 Corinthians 15.28:[8]

> "Ye heard how I said to you, I go away, and I come unto you. If ye loved me, ye would have rejoiced, because I go unto the Father: for the Father is greater than I."

> And when all things have been subjected unto him, then shall the Son also himself be subjected to him that did subject all things unto him, that God may be all in all.

Do these verses teach that Jesus is not God the Son?

It should be noted that neither of these verses actually discusses the nature of Jesus Christ. We have been told the following in Matthew 28.18:

> And Jesus came to them and spake unto them, saying, "All authority hath been given unto me in heaven and on earth."

It is generally understood that the one who gives power to another is a higher authority; this does not mean, however, that the Father and Jesus are of two separate natures, merely that the Father has given power to the Son.

The main evidence that Jesus truly is God the Son is seen in John 1.1:

> In the beginning was the Word, and the Word was with God, and the Word was God.

The Jehovah's Witnesses render this verse in the following manner in the NWT:

> In the beginning the Word was, and the Word was with God, and the Word was a god.

This alteration of the text comes with absolutely no textual evidence to support it. The presence of the indefinite article is justified on the basis of the fact that John does not provide the definite article in front of "God"; nevertheless, the article in Greek is not even principally a marker of definiteness,[9] and there are many times when definite nouns do not have an article with them. The lack of article is a demonstration, in fact, that the Word is not God the Father; we should understand *theos* (God) in John 1:1c as qualitative, indicating the nature of *ho logos* (the Word).[10] This is the understanding shared by textual scholars outside of the Jehovah's Witness movement. The Jehovah's Witnesses further attempt to justify their translation by pointing to John 1.18 and saying that since man has seen Jesus Christ, Jesus Christ cannot be God, so He must be only a form of divinity:[11]

> No man hath seen God at any time; the only begotten Son, who is in the bosom of the Father, he hath declared him.

We must ask, are we justified to alter the translation of the Scriptures because we see a possible contradiction? By no means, for by doing so we invalidate the word of God! John is most probably alluding to the fact that no man has seen God as spirit. Remember, he says in John 1.14:

> And the Word became flesh, and dwelt among us (and we beheld his glory, glory as of the only begotten from the Father), full of grace and truth.

The Word, which is a spirit, as the Father is (John 4.24), "became flesh and dwelt among us." Thus, while Jesus Christ is God the Son, He has not been seen in the spirit form, only in the physical manifestation of Jesus Christ. This by no means negates John 1.1, for man has seen Jesus Christ, but did not see God the Son within Him.

There is more evidence for Jesus being God the Son in Colossians 2.9:

> For in him dwelleth all the fulness of the Godhead bodily.

The NWT, again, reads differently:

> Because it is in him that all the fullness of the divine quality dwells bodily.

This translation is again unwarranted by the Greek text: the word for Godhead is theotes, which Thayer's defines as "the state of being God."[12] Yet again, the NWT distorts the true meaning of the passage by re-translating it without sufficient textual basis.

Therefore, it is evident that the Jehovah's Witness theology requires an alteration of the Scriptures to be justified. Should we force the Scriptures to conform to our doctrine or should our doctrine conform to the Scriptures? Whenever we feel compelled to adapt the Scriptures to suit our doctrines, we must recognize that it is our doctrines that are most likely in error (Galatians 1.6–9)!

How Was Jesus Killed?

The Jehovah's Witnesses also believe that Jesus was not crucified on a cross, but hung upon a wooden stake, because of the language in Deuteronomy 21.22–23.[13]

> And if a man have committed a sin worthy of death, and he be put to death, and thou hang him on a tree; his body shall not remain all night upon the tree, but thou shalt surely bury him the same day; for he that is hanged is accursed of God; that thou defile not thy land which the LORD thy God giveth thee for an inheritance.

Does this mean that Jesus was hung on a stake? This is not conclusive evidence. A stake is made out of wood, a tree, just as much as a cross is. The Greek words used in texts concerning the death of Jesus are *stauros* and *xylon*, and while the primary definitions of both words are "stake," the term *stauros* normally refers to more complex constructions (such as a cross), and both terms can mean "cross." The definitions in the Greek are not conclusive enough to demonstrate that Jesus was crucified on a cross or hung on a stake.

We do have evidence from archaeology and ancient writers that prove conclusively that Romans did perform crucifixions with crosses; much has been found to substantiate the discussion of the crucifixion in the Gospel accounts.[14] There is also the evidence in the language of Thomas in John 20.25:

> The other disciples therefore said unto him, "We have seen the Lord."
> But he said unto them, "Except I shall see in his hands the print of the nails, and put my hand into his side, I will not believe."

If Jesus were nailed to a stake, one nail would be used to go through both hands. If this were the case, would not Thomas have asked to "see in his hands the print of the nail?" This demonstrates clearly the difference between being nailed to a stake and being nailed to a cross. Therefore, the overwhelming evidence, contrary to the translation in the NWT, is that Jesus was most certainly crucified on a cross.

The Nature of the Holy Spirit

The Jehovah's Witnesses teach that the Holy Spirit is not a person, but "Jehovah's active force," the instrument God uses to carry out His will.[15] They use many verses, such as Genesis 1.2, Acts 2.1–4, 32–33, and 2 Peter 2.20–21 to substantiate this claim:[16]

> And the earth was waste and void; and darkness was upon the face of the deep: and the Spirit of God moved upon the face of the waters.

> And when the day of Pentecost was now come, they were all together in one place. And suddenly there came from heaven a sound as of the rushing of a mighty wind, and it filled all the house where they were sitting. And there appeared unto them tongues parting asunder, like as of fire; and it sat upon each one of

them. And they were all filled with the Holy Spirit, and began to speak with other tongues, as the Spirit gave them utterance.

"This Jesus did God raise up, whereof we all are witnesses. Being therefore by the right hand of God exalted, and having received of the Father the promise of the Holy Spirit, he hath poured forth this, which ye see and hear."

Knowing this first, that no prophecy of scripture is of private interpretation. For no prophecy ever came by the will of man: but men spake from God, being moved by the Holy Spirit.

It should also be noted that in the NWT, every rendering of "the Holy Spirit" is changed to "holy spirit." Do these verses teach that the Holy Spirit is not a person?

These verses do not actually discuss the character of the Holy Spirit, but demonstrate that the Holy Spirit was present at creation and filled the apostles. We are given some evidence about the Holy Spirit, however, in John 14.26:

But the Comforter, even the Holy Spirit, whom the Father will send in my name, he shall teach you all things, and bring to your remembrance all that I said unto you.

In this text, the Holy Spirit is called the "Comforter" and is referred to as a "he." The Greek word for "Comforter" is *parakletos*, which is in the masculine gender, demonstrating that the Holy Spirit is in fact a "he," not an "it."

The presence of the Spirit in creation in Genesis 1.2, along with the descending of the Spirit upon Jesus at His baptism, with the voice of God coming from Heaven (Matthew 3.16–17), both testify to the stature of the Spirit in relation to the Father and the Son. Since the testimony of the Spirit regarding the creation and Jesus was as much present as the testimony of the Father and the Son, we can be certain that the Holy Spirit is indeed a person and part of the Godhead just as God the Father and God the Son are persons and part of the Godhead. We may not understand the exact nature of their unity, but this does not mean that the belief in the Trinity is wrong. The theology of the Jehovah's Witnesses concerning the Godhead is not in harmony with the Scriptures.

The Body and the Spirit

Jehovah's Witnesses teach that there is no such thing as a soul distinct from the flesh, but that a man is a soul, since the "life force" within him is the breath of God, which simply returns to God at death.[17] Death, therefore, is a state of rest until the resurrection at the end of time; there will be no torture, simply death for those who have done wrong and life for those who have done right.[18] The Jehovah's Witnesses use Genesis 2.7, Ezekiel 18.4, 20, and Jeremiah 7.30–31 as evidence:[19]

> And the LORD God formed man of the dust of the ground, and breathed into his nostrils the breath of life; and man became a living soul.

> Behold, all souls are mine; as the soul of the father, so also the soul of the son is mine: the soul that sinneth, it shall die...The soul that sinneth, it shall die: the son shall not bear the iniquity of the father, neither shall the father bear the iniquity of the son; the righteousness of the righteous shall be upon him, and the wickedness of the wicked shall be upon him.

> "For the children of Judah have done that which is evil in my sight," saith the LORD: "they have set their abominations in the house which is called by my name, to defile it. And they have built the high places of Topheth, which is in the valley of the son of Hinnom, to burn their sons and their daughters in the fire; which I commanded not, neither came it into my mind."

Do these Scriptures show that there is no soul?

Jeremiah 7 is used because it refers to the valley of the son of Hinnom, called later "Gehenna" by Jesus. This is the place that Jesus refers to in Matthew 5.29–30 as "hell:"

> "And if thy right eye causeth thee to stumble, pluck it out, and cast it from thee: for it is profitable for thee that one of thy members should perish, and not thy whole body be cast into hell. And if thy right hand causeth thee to stumble, cut it off, and cast

it from thee: for it is profitable for thee that one of thy members should perish, and not thy whole body go into hell."

It is thus presumed that this "Gehenna" symbolizes destruction, since refuse was burned there.[20] Thus, the Jehovah's Witnesses believe there is no torture after death.[21] We have evidence to the contrary, however, in Matthew 8.11–12 and Matthew 13.49–50:

> "And I say unto you, that many shall come from the east and the west, and shall sit down with Abraham, and Isaac, and Jacob, in the kingdom of heaven: but the sons of the kingdom shall be cast forth into the outer darkness: there shall be the weeping and the gnashing of teeth."

> "So shall it be in the end of the world: the angels shall come forth, and sever the wicked from among the righteous, and shall cast them into the furnace of fire: there shall be the weeping and the gnashing of teeth."

The idea of "weeping and the gnashing of teeth" does not demonstrate a peaceful end of existence, but rather torture and misery. Thus, there will be torture for those who have worked iniquity on this earth.

Concerning the existence of a soul, we have evidence in verses such as Matthew 10.28:

> "And be not afraid of them that kill the body, but are not able to kill the soul: but rather fear him who is able to destroy both soul and body in hell."

If the soul and the body are the same, as the Jehovah's Witnesses assert, why would Jesus tell His disciples to fear the one who can destroy both soul and body in hell?

We also have Romans 8.3–5:

> For what the law could not do, in that it was weak through the flesh, God, sending his own Son in the likeness of sinful flesh and for sin, condemned sin in the flesh: that the ordinance of the law might be fulfilled in us, who walk not after the flesh, but after

the Spirit. For they that are after the flesh mind the things of the flesh; but they that are after the Spirit the things of the Spirit.

How can there be any form of conflict between the flesh and the Spirit if the two are the same?

The Hebrew author, in speaking of the Word of God, says the following in Hebrews 4.12:

For the word of God is living, and active, and sharper than any two-edged sword, and piercing even to the dividing of soul and spirit, of both joints and marrow, and quick to discern the thoughts and intents of the heart.

How can it be that the Word of God can pierce to the division of "soul" and "spirit" if the two are in fact the same and only refer to the "life force"? It would seem that the Hebrew author considered the life force (psuche) and the soul (pneuma) as separate entities, both residing within humans!

There is also the issue concerning our existence at death. Do we simply die and merely remain "asleep" until the resurrection? What of the comments of Paul in Philippians 1.22–24?

For to me to live is Christ, and to die is gain. But if to live in the flesh—if this shall bring fruit from my work, then what I shall choose I know not. But I am in a strait betwixt the two, having the desire to depart and be with Christ; for it is very far better: yet to abide in the flesh is more needful for your sake.

If Paul understood that death meant that he would simply be asleep, why would he say that he would be with Christ at death? We see, therefore, that the Jehovah's Witnesses posit a contradiction within the Bible. We see that the passage of Genesis 2.7 and Ezekiel 18.4, 20 use the term "soul" to refer to a "man," using metonymy. There is such a thing as a soul, otherwise how could Paul immediately be with Christ, or how could our souls and body be lost to hell?

An issue closely connected to the concept of the soul being the "life force" of the body concerns blood transfusions. The Jehovah's Witnesses do not believe in receiving blood transfusions, citing the premises of Genesis 9.4 and Acts 15.28–29 as proof:[22]

But flesh with the life thereof, which is the blood thereof, shall ye not eat.

For it seemed good to the Holy Spirit, and to us, to lay upon you no greater burden than these necessary things: that ye abstain from things sacrificed to idols, and from blood, and from things strangled, and from fornication; from which if ye keep yourselves, it shall be well with you. Fare ye well.

The argument is that the term "abstain" refers to any form of contact with blood and therefore one must not receive a blood transfusion.[23] Is this a legitimate argument using the Scriptures?

The texts in the Scriptures speak of the need to abstain from blood by drinking it, for this was a practice performed by many of the pagans around them. God did not speak concerning a transfusion of blood, which allows for a continuation of life on earth, but does little to nothing for the life of the spirit. The transfusion disagreement stems from the attitude that our physical corporeal life is all there is to us, and thus blood becomes sacred. The Bible does not demonstrate this attitude toward blood in the New Testament.

The Garden of Eden

Let us now discuss the Jehovah's Witnesses' conception of the future of mankind. The Jehovah's Witnesses believe that God's intention with the creation of man was for him never to die, but to remain on the Earth forever.[24] They believe that Adam and Eve were perfect creatures while in the Garden of Eden, never to perish, and they use Deuteronomy 32.4 and Proverbs 10.22 as evidence:[25]

The Rock, his work is perfect; For all his ways are justice: A God of faithfulness and without iniquity, Just and right is he.

The blessing of the LORD, it maketh rich; And he addeth no sorrow therewith.

Do these verses teach that God desired for man to be physically immortal? They state the truth that God's work is perfect; does that necessitate immortality? We read the following in the Genesis account in Genesis 3.22–23:

> And the LORD God said, "Behold, the man is become as one of us, to know good and evil; and now, lest he put forth his hand, and take also of the tree of life, and eat, and live for ever:" Therefore the LORD God sent him forth from the garden of Eden, to till the ground from whence he was taken.

It is evident, then, that Adam and Eve would have had to partake of the tree of life in order to live forever. This necessitates that their previous existence had not been deemed immortal in their physical form.

We see, therefore, that it cannot be determined from the Garden of Eden that God intended for man to live forever in physical form. Let us now examine the process by which the Jehovah's Witnesses believe that the "regeneration" of the earth will occur.

Premillennialism

The Jehovah's Witnesses believe very strongly in the idea of God's reign for the millennium. We have already discussed many tenets of premillennialism in **Plymouth Brethren: Premillennialism**, so let us now examine the differences of the Jehovah's Witnesses' conception of the "end times."

The Jehovah's Witnesses believe that the Kingdom of Heaven was established in 1914 CE.[26] They believe that this date is correct because of prophetic statements of the Scriptures, in Daniel 4.23–25 and Revelation 12.6, 14:

> And whereas the king saw a watcher and a holy one coming down from heaven, and saying, Hew down the tree, and destroy it; nevertheless leave the stump of the roots thereof in the earth, even with a band of iron and brass, in the tender grass of the field, and let it be wet with the dew of heaven: and let his portion be with the beasts of the field, till seven times pass over him; this is the interpretation, O king, and it is the decree of the Most High, which is come upon my lord the king: that thou shalt be driven from men, and thy dwelling shall be with the beasts of the field, and thou shalt be made to eat grass as oxen, and shalt be wet with the dew of heaven, and seven times shall pass over thee; till thou know that the Most High ruleth in the kingdom of men, and giveth it to whomsoever he will.

And the woman fled into the wilderness, where she hath a place prepared of God, that there they may nourish her a thousand two hundred and threescore days…And there were given to the woman the two wings of the great eagle, that she might fly into the wilderness unto her place, where she is nourished for a time, and times, and half a time, from the face of the serpent.

They thus believe that the Revelation passage shows that three and a half "times" is equivalent to 1,260 days, and thus seven "times" is equivalent to 2,520 days.[27] If we accept that a prophetic day is a year, then we have 2,520 years from the destruction of Jerusalem in 607 BCE, believed to be the "times of the Gentiles" of Luke 21.24,[28] to the time that Christ will begin His reign. This time would be 1914 CE. The Jehovah's Witnesses first proclaimed that this would be the time of the Second Coming; when 1914 came and went, they began to use Psalm 110.2 to show that Jesus would begin His reign in the midst of His enemies:[29]

Who devise mischiefs in their heart; Continually do they gather themselves together for war.

They thus believe that in 1914 Satan was cast down to the earth, as proclaimed in Revelation 12.9:[30]

And the great dragon was cast down, the old serpent, he that is called the Devil and Satan, the deceiver of the whole world; he was cast down to the earth, and his angels were cast down with him.

They then see the events of World War I and World War II as demonstrating the fact that Satan has been brought down to Earth and is fulfilling the prophecies of Matthew 24.1–34.[31] Yet we have seen in **Plymouth Brethren: Matthew 24–25: The "Olivet Discourse"** that Jesus was discussing the destruction of Jerusalem in those verses, not the "end times." Also, how secure is their prophetic belief when it had to be altered after the original prediction was wrong? Likewise, the numbers themselves do not correlate: Jerusalem was destroyed in 586 BCE, not 603 BCE; while it is likely that Nebuchadnezzar led away some Jewish captives to Babylon in 603, the tumultuous year was 17 years in the future. Regardless, we shall see that the whole belief that Christ's reign began in 1914 is not in accordance with the Scriptures concerning His Kingdom.

The Jehovah's Witnesses further believe that the Kingdom of Heaven will soon be established after the "end times" with 144,000 faithful saints being chosen by God to become spirits and to rule with Christ for the Millennium.[32] They further believe that these rulers will be ruling over the Earth, which will contain resurrected fleshly humans along with animals.[33] They derive this belief from Revelation 7.4 and Revelation 14.1:[34]

> And I heard the number of them that were sealed, a hundred and forty and four thousand, sealed out of every tribe of the children of Israel.

> And I saw, and behold, the Lamb standing on the mount Zion, and with him a hundred and forty and four thousand, having his name, and the name of his Father, written on their foreheads.

Do these verses show that there will only be 144,000 saints in Heaven?

The Jehovah's Witnesses regard these passages highly, but do not recognize the implications of the following verses in Revelation 14, Revelation 14.2–5:

> And I heard a voice from heaven, as the voice of many waters, and as the voice of a great thunder: and the voice which I heard was as the voice of harpers harping with their harps: and they sing as it were a new song before the throne, and before the four living creatures and the elders: and no man could learn the song save the hundred and forty and four thousand, even they that had been purchased out of the earth. These are they that were not defiled with women; for they are virgins. These are they that follow the Lamb whithersoever he goeth. These were purchased from among men, to be the firstfruits unto God and unto the Lamb. And in their mouth was found no lie: they are without blemish.

If we are to take the number 144,000 literally, we must also therefore believe that these 144,000 will be male Jewish virgins. Yet the Jehovah's Witnesses believe that Simon Peter will be one of them; he is surely male and Jewish, but the Scriptures demonstrate that he was married (1 Corinthians 9.5). We find, therefore, inconsistency in application of "literal" and "figurative" understandings even within their interpretation of the passage; since this is the case, it is quite clear how John is speaking not in literal, but figurative, terms.

Furthermore, much needs to be said regarding the resurrection. We have been told the following in 1 Corinthians 15.42–53:

> So also is the resurrection of the dead. It is sown in corruption; it is raised in incorruption: it is sown in dishonor; it is raised in glory: it is sown in weakness; it is raised in power: it is sown a natural body; it is raised a spiritual body. If there is a natural body, there is also a spiritual body. So also it is written, The first man Adam became a living soul. The last Adam became a life-giving spirit. Howbeit that is not first which is spiritual, but that which is natural; then that which is spiritual. The first man is of the earth, earthy: the second man is of heaven. As is the earthy, such are they also that are earthy: and as is the heavenly, such are they also that are heavenly. And as we have borne the image of the earthy, we shall also bear the image of the heavenly. Now this I say, brethren, that flesh and blood cannot inherit the kingdom of God; neither doth corruption inherit incorruption. Behold, I tell you a mystery: We all shall not sleep, but we shall all be changed, in a moment, in the twinkling of an eye, at the last trump: for the trumpet shall sound, and the dead shall be raised incorruptible, and we shall be changed. For this corruptible must put on incorruption, and this mortal must put on immortality.

The Jehovah's Witnesses assert that this passage speaks uniquely of the 144,000, yet we do not see any language that delineates who receives this resurrection.[35] It is also sometimes argued that here Paul speaks of those who will receive immortality in their physical bodies, but this is not the case: Paul says very clearly in verses 51–52:

> Behold, I tell you a mystery: We all shall not sleep, but we shall all be changed, in a moment, in the twinkling of an eye, at the last trump: for the trumpet shall sound, and the dead shall be raised incorruptible, and we shall be changed.

We will go through some transformation, although how specifically is unsure. This fact is further demonstrated by John in 1 John 3.2:

> Beloved, now are we children of God, and it is not yet made manifest what we shall be. We know that, if he shall be manifested, we shall be like him; for we shall see him even as he is.

Paul discusses further concerning the nature of the return of Christ and the resurrection in 1 Thessalonians 4.16–17:

> For the Lord himself shall descend from heaven, with a shout, with the voice of the archangel, and with the trump of God: and the dead in Christ shall rise first; then we that are alive, that are left, shall together with them be caught up in the clouds, to meet the Lord in the air: and so shall we ever be with the Lord.

These verses show clearly that all those who are deemed to be children of God, those who live as Christians, will take place in a resurrection that will involve a transformation from a physical form to a transphysical form, something akin to the nature of Jesus Himself. Such transformation will not be limited to a mere 144,000.

We have already spoken somewhat concerning the belief that Christ and the 144,000 will reign in Heaven over all those on the Earth when we discussed the nature of Kingdom of Heaven in *Plymouth Brethren: The Nature of Christ's Kingdom*, but let us again consider John 18.36:

> Jesus answered, "My kingdom is not of this world: if my kingdom were of this world, then would my servants fight, that I should not be delivered to the Jews: but now is my kingdom not from hence."

The NWT translates this passage as the following:

> Jesus answered, "My kingdom is no part of this world. If my kingdom were part of this world, my attendants would have fought that I should not be delivered up to the Jews. But, as it is, my kingdom is not of this source."

The subtle changes in language made in the NWT serve to allow the Jehovah's Witnesses to say that His Kingdom was not a part of the world in 30 CE, but that it would overtake the world in the years following 1914 CE. The Greek text, however, does not allow for the NWT translation whatsoever: the word "part" has no Greek basis, nor does the idea of "not of this source:" the Greek term *enteuthen*, translated "from hence," denotes a repetition of the concept introduced earlier in the verse, viz., that His kingdom is "not of this world." We see yet again that the Jehovah's Witnesses are forced to manipulate and distort the Scriptures in order to justify their doctrine.

Finally, we have the witness of Christ Himself in Matthew 28.18:

> And Jesus came to them and spake unto them, saying, "All authority hath been given unto me in heaven and on earth."

How, then, can the Jehovah's Witnesses teach that the authority of God has not yet been given to Christ when He has said Himself that all authority has been given to Him in 30 CE? This passage demonstrates clearly that Jesus is presently in control, and that His Kingdom is currently in existence, and that it is represented on earth as His Church, the spiritual Body of Christ that will be resurrected on the last day.

An Earthly Paradise?

The Jehovah's Witnesses teach that this earth will last forever, and it will be populated by those humans deemed righteous along with animals and plants, etc. in "Paradise."[36] They believe that Ecclesiastes 1.4 teaches this:

> One generation goeth, and another generation cometh; but the earth abideth for ever.

Does this verse teach that the earth will exist forever?

Many times in the Old Testament we see that there are ordinances deemed to exist forever, such as Exodus 12.14, Exodus 27.21, and Exodus 31.17:

> And this day shall be unto you for a memorial, and ye shall keep it a feast to the LORD: throughout your generations ye shall keep it a feast by an ordinance for ever.

> In the tent of meeting, without the veil which is before the testimony, Aaron and his sons shall keep it in order from evening to morning before the LORD: it shall be a statue for ever throughout their generations on the behalf of the children of Israel.

> It is a sign between me and the children of Israel for ever: for in six days the LORD made heaven and earth, and on the seventh day he rested, and was refreshed.

Yet we see in the New Testament that the priesthood of Aaron has been superseded by Christ (Hebrews 7.12–14) and that the Sabbath for Christians is the heavenly rest (Hebrews 4.2–11). Have these statues existed forever? Not in the literal sense of time, but for as long as the Israelites were the people of God specifically, these statues did exist. Therefore, we must read the verse in Ecclesiastes understanding that "forever" refers to the purposes of God.

We understand this further because of the words of Peter in 2 Peter 3.10–12:

> But the day of the Lord will come as a thief; in the which the heavens shall pass away with a great noise, and the elements shall be dissolved with fervent heat, and the earth and the works that are therein shall be burned up. Seeing that these things are thus all to be dissolved, what manner of persons ought ye to be in all holy living and godliness, looking for and earnestly desiring the coming of the day of God, by reason of which the heavens being on fire shall be dissolved, and the elements shall melt with fervent heat?

Some Jehovah's Witnesses will argue that only the works of the earth will be burned up, yet the text itself says that both the works and the earth itself will be burned up. Therefore, it is evident that on the day of the Lord, the heavens and the earth as we know them shall be destroyed. Therefore, it is impossible for there to be a paradise on this earth after the "millennium."

The Existence of Hell

Previously we have seen that Jehovah's Witnesses believe that man does not have an eternal soul and that they view eternity in a purely physical way. While they believe that the earth will become a Paradise for some of the faithful, they deny the existence of an eternal place of torment for those consigned to destruction. The Greek word *gehenna*, used often to describe this place, is viewed by Jehovah's Witnesses in its most concrete idea—the Valley of Hinnom with its burning trash near Jerusalem—and does not describe eternal suffering, but a place symbolizing destruction rather than torment.[37] Sheol, or Hades in Greek, is only considered the grave by Jehovah's Witnesses and nothing else.[38] Does the New Testament validate these views?

While it is agreed that Jesus uses the concrete place and function of the Valley of Hinnom to describe a spiritual location, the use of the imagery by Jehovah's Witnesses is inappropriate. While the Jehovah's Witnesses focus on the image of "destruction," consider what both Jesus and James focus upon in Mark 9.47–48 and James 3.6:

> "And if thine eye cause thee to stumble, cast it out: it is good for thee to enter into the kingdom of God with one eye, rather than having two eyes to be cast into hell [Gk *gehenna*]; where their worm dieth not, and the fire is not quenched."

> And the tongue is a fire: the world of iniquity among our members is the tongue, which defileth the whole body, and setteth on fire the wheel of nature, and is set on fire by hell [Gk *gehenna*].

While the Jehovah's Witnesses desire to focus on the "destruction" aspect of the imagery of the Valley of Hinnom, both Jesus and James focus on the "fire" aspect of that imagery. The reasoning of the Jehovah's Witnesses does not follow: Jesus, in Mark, clearly understands that suffering is present in this *gehenna* and uses images accordingly.

It is often argued that since only people who were already dead were cast into the Valley of Hinnom, that *gehenna* can only be the place for the cast-off dead spirits (without any kind of existence as we know it): that is, since no one was cast into the Valley of Hinnom to suffer, *gehenna* or hell is the same way. Jesus, however, says the following in Matthew 10.28:

> And be not afraid of them which kill the body, but are not able to kill the soul: but rather fear him which is able to destroy both soul and body in hell [Gk *gehenna*].

Note that Jesus uses different terms: "kill" the body yet "destroy" the soul and body. Most importantly, *gehenna* is the location in which "both soul and body" will be destroyed. It therefore cannot be envisioned as a place for the "already dead" without any form of existence.

As to Sheol/Hades, it is true that it can often refer to the grave itself. Such is not the only meaning of the term, however, and their use in Isaiah 14.9–11, 15–20, and Luke 16.22–26:

> Hell [Hebr. *Sheol, et al*] from beneath is moved for thee to meet thee at thy coming: it stirreth up the dead for thee, even all the chief ones of the earth; it hath raised up from their thrones all the kings of the nations. All they shall answer and say unto thee, Art thou also become weak as we? art thou become like unto us? Thy pomp is brought down to hell, and the noise of thy viols: the worm is spread under thee, and worms cover thee…Yet thou shalt be brought down to hell, to the uttermost parts of the pit. They that see thee shall narrowly look upon thee, they shall consider thee, saying,
> "Is this the man that made the earth to tremble, that did shake kingdoms; that made the world as a wilderness, and overthrew the cities thereof; that let not loose his prisoners to their home?"
> All the kings of the nations, all of them, sleep in glory, every one in his own house. But thou art cast forth away from thy sepulchre like an abominable branch, clothed with the slain, that are thrust through with the sword, that go down to the stones of the pit; as a carcase trodden under foot. Thou shalt not be joined with them in burial, because thou hast destroyed thy land, thou hast slain thy people; the seed of evil-doers shall not be named for ever.

> And it came to pass, that the beggar died, and that he was carried away by the angels into Abraham's bosom: and the rich man also died, and was buried. And in Hades he lifted up his eyes, being in torments, and seeth Abraham afar off, and Lazarus in his bosom. And he cried and said, "Father Abraham, have mercy on me, and send Lazarus, that he may dip the tip of his finger in water, and cool my tongue; for I am in anguish in this flame."
> But Abraham said, "Son, remember that thou in thy lifetime receivedst thy good things, and Lazarus in like manner evil things: but now here he is comforted, and thou art in anguish. And beside all this, between us and you there is a great gulf fixed, that they which would pass from hence to you may not be able, and that none may cross over from thence to us."

We see in these passages that simple identification of Sheol/Hades as "the grave" does not work. The king in Isaiah 14 is not buried properly, but is in Sheol. Other kings are there also, and it is portrayed as if communication occurs among them. The king in question is not just brought down to Sheol, but even down into "the pit": going lower than the grave is inconceivable if indeed such is what was meant by the author. It is manifest that Isaiah does not consider Sheol only the grave, but some form of afterlife.

As to Luke 16 and the story of Lazarus and the rich man, it is often argued that it represents a parable and cannot be trusted for accurate information. For a parable to have any value, however, it must represent a "true-to-life" situation. If the dead have no consciousness and there is no paradise or torment in the future, why would Jesus act as if there were and use such a story without explanation? We would expect a far different narrative if that were the case!

The Bible makes it clear that there is a place awaiting the unrighteous, and it is not mere annihilation: there will be a resurrection of condemnation (John 5.28–29), and vengeance is reserved for those not knowing God and not obeying the Gospel of our Lord Jesus Christ (2 Thessalonians 1.6–9). This place, Hell, is described in terms of *gehenna*, the burning trash pit, as torment, and as seen in Matthew 8.12:

> "But the sons of the kingdom shall be cast forth into the outer darkness: there shall be the weeping and gnashing of teeth."

If Jesus had simply stopped with the idea of the "outer darkness," we could understand Hell as merely a place of separation from God, perhaps even a way of speaking of nonexistence. Jesus, however, demonstrates that in this place there is "weeping" and "gnashing of teeth," images not describing nothingness or annihilation but torment and suffering. Jesus, therefore, clearly indicates that there is a place of torment and punishment awaiting those who are disobedient to Him, and such a place should not be denied.

Notes

1: *The Truth that Leads to Eternal Life*, Watch Tower Bible and Tract Society, pp. 17–18

2: Ibid., p. 19

3: *Knowledge that Leads to Everlasting Life*, Watch Tower Bible and Tract Society, p. 155

4: Ibid., p. 24

5: In order to make absolutely sure that no one would accidentally attempt to pronounce the Tetragrammaton, the Masoretic scribes would provide the vowel pointings for some of the common terms used in place of the Tetragrammaton: *adonai* (Lord), *ha-Shem* (the Name), or *elohim / eloah* (God). Some "Christian" saw the text YHWH with the vowel markings for *eloah* and attempted to read it like "normal" Hebrew: Ye-HoWaH. Such is meaningless in Hebrew, not correlating to any recognized usage (Consider Brown, Driver, and Briggs, *Hebrew Lexicon of the Old Testament*, pp. 217–218).

6: "Yah" is rather clear from the representation of the vowels with this part of the name of God in Exodus 15.2 and also from names including part of the name of God (e.g. Jeremiah = Hebrew Yirmiyahu). We also have evidence from early Christian authors like Clement of Alexandria, who claim that Jews of his day established that the pronunciation was, as rendered in Greek, "Iaoue" (Clement of Alexandria, *Miscellanies*, 5.6), or, from Epiphanius and Theodoret, "Iabe". Since Greek has no way of rendering "h" internally, and lost its "w" sound, we can see how "Yahweh" would sound like "Iaoue" or "Iabe" to a native Greek speaker.

7: *Knowledge that Leads to Everlasting Life*, Watch Tower Bible and Tract Society, p. 31

8: Ibid.

9: For more on the article, consider Daniel Wallace, *The Elements of New Testament Syntax*, p. 94

10: Regarding John 1.1, ibid., pp. 119–120

11: *The Truth that Leads to Eternal Life*, p. 24

12: *Thayer's Greek-English Lexicon of the New Testament*, p. 288

13: *Knowledge that Leads to Everlasting Life*, p. 66

14: This evidence may be found in Tacitus, *Historiae*, IV, 3, and some works of Seneca. Archaeological evidence may be found in many issues of *Biblical Archaeology Review*.

15: *Knowledge that Leads to Everlasting Life*, p. 31

16: Ibid.

17: Ibid., pp. 81–82

18: Ibid., pp. 87–88

19: Ibid., pp. 83, 87

20: Ibid., p. 88

21: Ibid.

22: Ibid., p. 129

23: Ibid.

24: *The Truth that Leads to Eternal Life*, p. 27

25: Ibid.

26: *Knowledge that Leads to Everlasting Life*, p. 97

27: Ibid.

28: Ibid., p. 96

29: Ibid., p. 99

30: Ibid.

31: Ibid., p. 100

32: Ibid., p. 88

33: Ibid.

34: Ibid.

35: Ibid.

36: Ibid., pp. 7–11

37: *New World Translation of the Holy Scriptures*, Appendix, p. 1641

38: *New World Translation of the Holy Scriptures*, Appendix, p. 1643

The Salvation Army

Overview

The Salvation Army was founded in 1878 by William Booth, a former Methodist minister who began to work among the "unchurched" in London. Many of those who followed his message felt uncomfortable with the standard churches to which they were sent, so Booth began to create "mission centers" for them. These mission centers eventually consolidated into one organization, named the Salvation Army. The Salvation Army is known for its benevolent "missionary" focus along with its military-style hierarchy.

General Considerations

Part I
- *Lutheranism: Faith Alone*
- *Calvinism: T- Total Depravity*

Part II
- *Evangelicalism*

Part III
- *Baptism: Baptism=Immersion; Baptism is for Remission of Sin and is Necessary for Salvation*
- *The Church Treasury, I: Benevolence: Church Benevolence to Non-Saints; The Missionary Society*
- *The Church Treasury, II: Other Considerations: Hospitals; Centers of Education; Kitchens/Fellowship Halls; Gymnasiums; Business Enterprises*

Concerning Observances:
- *Observances Concerning the Lord's Birth: Advent; Christmas*
- *Observances Concerning the Lord's Death: Palm Sunday; Good Friday; Easter*

- *Instrumental Music*

- *The Lord's Supper: When Should the Lord's Supper Be Observed? Part A: Weekly*

- *Positions of Authority: Ordination*

The Church and Military Organization

The Salvation Army is structured like a military organization: there are regular "Salvationists," or members, and then "officers," who represent the hierarchy of the church.[1] This officer system begins with youth at age 7, who are deemed "junior officers" and at that point begin their attempt to live as Christians; they later become "senior soldiers" at 15 or above, affirming that they will follow Jesus and that they have signed the "Articles of War," or a listing of the belief system of the Salvation Army. From this level there is the "officer" class, individuals ordained by the Salvation Army to guide the church; these individuals follow a general military system of ranking. Officers are to marry other officers, and death is deemed "promotion to glory." Do we see this style of organization in the New Testament?

It is true that there are many military type statements and symbols used in the New Testament, such as 2 Timothy 4.7–8 and Ephesians 6.11–17:

> I have fought the good fight, I have finished the course, I have kept the faith: henceforth there is laid up for me the crown of righteousness, which the Lord, the righteous judge, shall give to me at that day; and not to me only, but also to all them that have loved his appearing.

> Put on the whole armor of God, that ye may be able to stand against the wiles of the devil. For our wrestling is not against flesh and blood, but against the principalities, against the powers, against the world-rulers of this darkness, against the spiritual hosts of wickedness in the heavenly places. Wherefore take up the whole armor of God, that ye may be able to withstand in the evil day, and, having done all, to stand. Stand therefore, having girded your loins with truth, and having put on the breastplate of righteousness, and having shod your feet with the preparation of the gospel of peace;

withal taking up the shield of faith, wherewith ye shall be able to quench all the fiery darts of the evil one. And take the helmet of salvation, and the sword of the Spirit, which is the word of God.

These statements, however, are not designed to demonstrate that the church is a military organization with a system of officers and soldiers; this battle is spiritual, and the New Testament betrays no such form of "military" hierarchy of leaders.

In the New Testament, we see a twofold system of leadership, seen in Ephesians 5.23–24 and Philippians 1.1:

For the husband is the head of the wife, and Christ also is the head of the church, being himself the saviour of the body. But as the church is subject to Christ, so let the wives also be to their husbands in everything.

Paul and Timothy, servants of Christ Jesus, to all the saints in Christ Jesus that are at Philippi, with the bishops and deacons.

The purpose of these bishops (or overseers, elders, etc.) is seen in Acts 20.28:

Take heed unto yourselves, and to all the flock, in which the Holy Spirit hath made you bishops, to feed the church of the Lord which he purchased with his own blood.

Therefore, it is evident from the New Testament that the church is to be organized with Christ as its head, elders watching over each individual congregation, and deacons serving within those congregations. There is no evidence in the New Testament of any form of a military hierarchy within the church; it is entirely a nineteenth-century creation.

Notes

1: This information, along with what follows, is from http://www.salvationarmy.org.uk/faqs/ceremonies.html.

Pentecostalism/Charismatic Movement

Overview

Pentecostalism (from Pentecost, the day on which the gift of the Holy Spirit was given to the Apostles) originated from the Wesleyan Holiness movement of the nineteenth century, which emphasized personal faith, proper living, and the imminent return of the gifts of the Holy Spirit. This belief was manifested in Topeka, Kansas, in 1901, where the first "baptism of the Holy Spirit" in modern times was recorded. The movement began to spread; it only gained momentum, however, in 1906, with the Azusa Street Revival in Los Angeles, California. The "massive outpouring of the Holy Spirit" which occurred at Azusa Street gained national notoriety, and the majority of Pentecostal denominations originated in individuals affected by the events of Azusa Street. These first believers in the gifts of the Holy Spirit were not accepted by their denominations, and many therefore began their own or joined such fledgling groups.

Beginning in the 1960s, many members of denominations began to "receive the baptism of the Holy Spirit," and yet did not leave their respective denominations. These individuals began what is deemed as the "Charismatic Movement" (from the Greek *charisma*, or "gift"). Before long, there were Charismatic associations within the Roman Catholic, Lutheran, Anglican/Episcopalian, and Calvinist churches, and the movement spread to encompass almost every denomination within Christendom.

Pentecostalism and the Charismatic Movement are identifiable by their belief in the latter-day outpouring of the Holy Spirit, much like the day of Pentecost. Many of the members experience what is deemed the "baptism of the Holy Spirit," which is supposedly evidenced by the act of speaking in tongues. These groups tend to bring a great deal of emotionalism and activity to their services, generally allow for the full equality of men and women in the activities of the worship service, and focus on the emotional aspects of Christianity.

Variants

The Pentecostal/Charismatic movement is heavily splintered; the number of groups within this movement number in the tens of thousands. We can, however, examine the major groups of the movement. Pentecostalism and its offshoots can be divided into three groups: "Classical" Pentecostals, those who are members of the standard Pentecostal groups, most of which originated in the first quarter of the twentieth century; the Charismatics, or those in other denominations who received the "baptism of the Holy Spirit;" and the so-called "Neo-Charismatics," the groups formed in the last half of the century, most of which are not affiliated with the Pentecostal denominations. We will examine the "classical" Pentecostal groups in more detail; it will suffice to say for the Charismatics that they are present in the majority of the denominations of Christendom, normally having their own associations as part of their denominations.

The chart provided should assist in understanding the creation and organization of the "classical" Pentecostal denominations. Let us speak of them now.

We must first examine the "pre-Pentecostal" era, the time before 1901. Many churches received the message of the Holiness movement, which stemmed from Wesleyan theology. Many of these groups were looking forward to a "renewal of the Holy Spirit," when the gifts present on the day of Pentecost would return to the churches. Many of these Holiness groups became Pentecostal after the turn of the century; others did not accept the message. Therefore, when we discuss a denomination that existed before 1901, we must understand that the denomination was founded first and only later became Pentecostal.

Despite the first demonstration of the "baptism of the Holy Spirit" in 1901, the movement would only begin to take off with the Azusa Street revival five years later. Many of the ministers of the Holiness congregations, along with other interested parties, visited this revival to observe the events and possibly become a part of them.

One of the first denominations to accept Pentecostalism was the Church of God in Christ [COGIC], founded in 1897 by Charles Mason. In 1907, he received the "baptism of the Holy Spirit," and soon the

Pentecostalism/Charismatic Movement

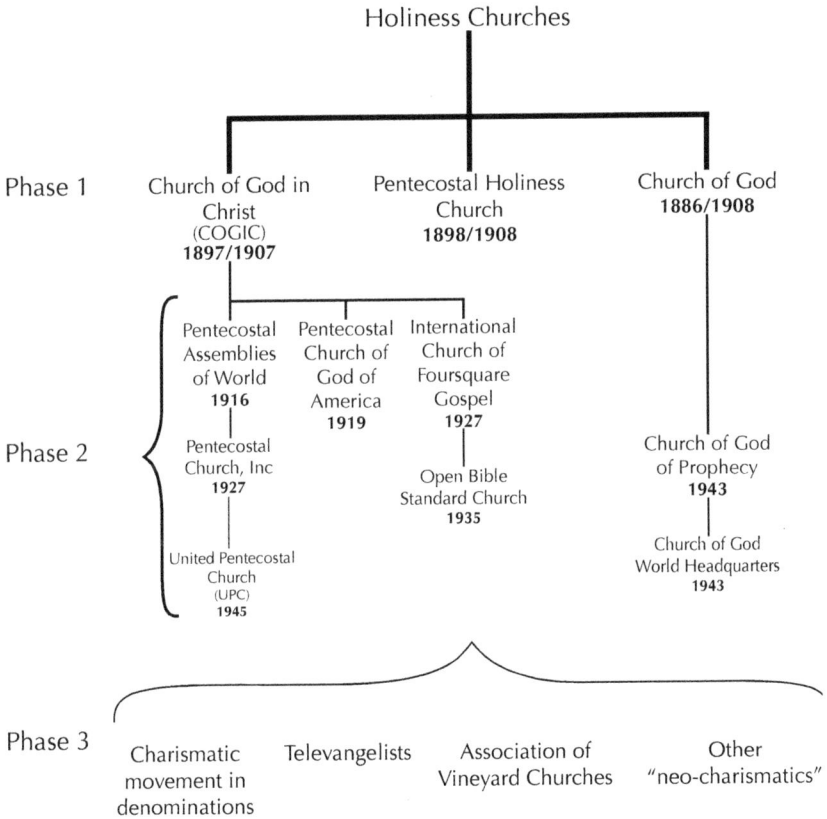

Holiness Churches

Phase 1

Church of God in Christ (COGIC) 1897/1907

Pentecostal Holiness Church 1898/1908

Church of God 1886/1908

Phase 2

Pentecostal Assemblies of World 1916

Pentecostal Church of God of America 1919

International Church of Foursquare Gospel 1927

Pentecostal Church, Inc 1927

Open Bible Standard Church 1935

Church of God of Prophecy 1943

United Pentecostal Church (UPC) 1945

Church of God World Headquarters 1943

Phase 3

Charismatic movement in denominations

Televangelists

Association of Vineyard Churches

Other "neo-charismatics"

majority of his denomination was Pentecostal. This group remains one of the largest denominations within Pentecostalism.

Other denominations also accepted the Pentecostal doctrine. The Pentecostal Holiness Church, founded in 1898, became Pentecostal in 1908. The United Holy Church, founded in 1886, also became Pentecostal.

Another large group that became Pentecostal was the Church of God (Cleveland, Tennessee). This group, founded in 1886, became Pentecostal in 1908, in a large part influenced by A. J. Tomlinson. By 1922, however, the Church of God (Cleveland, Tennessee), could no longer stand the dictatorial nature of Tomlinson; therefore, Tomlinson was removed, and he himself created another Church of God, known first as the "Tomlinson Church of God" until 1943, when Tomlinson died. His two sons, Milton and Homer, began to quarrel over who should take over control of the church. Milton was chosen, and in 1952 he chose the name "Church of God of Prophecy" to replace "Tomlinson Church of God." Homer left that group when he was not chosen and founded his own group, the Church of God, World Headquarters, in 1943.

The denominations listed above are considered the "first wave" of Pentecostalism, since they essentially were Wesleyan Holiness groups who incorporated the *glossolalia* (speaking in tongues) and other gifts into their theology. They believed that one was saved, then sanctified, and then received the baptism of the Holy Spirit. Beginning in the 1910s, however, a new line of theology emerged, known as the "finished work" belief system. These individuals tended to come from outside the Wesleyan Holiness movement, and thus did not share the emphasis on personal sanctification as the Holiness groups did. They believed that sanctification was a gradual process, and that one need not be fully sanctified before one received the baptism of the Holy Spirit. This rift in theology prompted what is known as the "second wave" of Pentecostalism.

One of the largest and best-known churches of this "second wave" is the Assemblies of God [AG or AoG], which divided from the Church of God in Christ in 1914 over the "finished work" theology and also racial issues. The Assemblies of God themselves saw division occur within the next two years over the "oneness" theology, that the name of Jesus was the only name of God, that one needed to be baptized in the name of Jesus alone, and that speaking in tongues was necessary for salvation (more will be discussed about this theology below). This group was eventually cast out of the Assemblies of God in 1916 to form the Pentecostal Assemblies of the World. This group itself divided because of racial differences in 1927, forming a group known as the Pentecostal Church, Incorporated, which later merged with other "oneness" churches to form the United Pentecostal Church (UPC) in 1945.

The Assemblies of God saw further divisions in the next twenty years. The next division occurred in 1919, when John Sinclair of the Assemblies of God became very concerned when the church adopted a "Statement of Fundamental Truths," which went against, in his opinion, one of the founding premises of the denomination to not hold to any doctrinal statements. Therefore, he, along with George Brinkman, left the Assemblies of God to form the Pentecostal Church of God of America.

In 1927, a former Assemblies of God minister named Aimee Semple McPherson founded the International Church of the Foursquare Gospel, a Pentecostal church that grew around the healing and witness of its founder. This church also suffered a division in 1932 with the creation of the Open Bible Evangelistic Association, which eventually merged with another group to form the Open Bible Standard Church in 1935.

Finally, a "third wave" of churches began to form in the later part of the twentieth century, involving many of the mainline evangelicals who had seen and performed the signs and wonders of the Pentecostal movement but did not desire to be labeled with the terms "Pentecostal" or "Charismatic." The foremost group of these individuals is the Association of Vineyard Churches, founded in 1981. These "third wavers" are the ones known as the "neo-Charismatics," and their numbers throughout their many groups are the largest in the Pentecostal movement.

There are many other groups that are part of the Pentecostal/Charismatic movement, including the majority of the televangelists and those who perform "healing revivals." "Charismatic communities" have also been founded, consisting of groups of Charismatics who wish to create their own community of faith.

These are the major groups in the Pentecostal/Charismatic movement; it would be a large task indeed to discuss every little group within this movement. It is believed that for every individual congregation within one of these denominations, there exists one independent Pentecostal/ Charismatic congregation. Let us now examine the general belief systems of these groups.

General Considerations

Part I

- *Lutheranism: Faith Alone*
- *Anabaptism: Nonresistance [some groups]; Ultra-Conservatism [some groups]*
- *Calvinism: T– Total Depravity*
- *Pietism: Foot Washing*
- *Baptists: "Once Saved, Always Saved"*
- *Plymouth Brethren: Dispensationalism; Premillennialism*

Part II

- *Evangelicalism*
- *Fundamentalism*
- *Community Church Movement*
- *House Church Movement*
- *Megachurch Movement*
- *Emergism*

Part III

- *Baptism: Baptism=Immersion; Baptism is for Remission of Sin and is Necessary for Salvation*
- *The Church Treasury, I: Benevolence: Church Benevolence to Non-Saints; The Missionary Society*
- *The Church Treasury, II: Other Considerations: Hospitals; Centers of Education; Kitchens/ Fellowship Halls; Gymnasiums; Business Enterprises*

Concerning Observances

- *Observances Concerning the Lord's Birth: Christmas; Observances Concerning the Lord's Death: Palm Sunday; Good Friday; Easter*
- *Instrumental Music*
- *Judaic Practices: The Ten Commandments and the "Moral Law"*
- *The Lord's Supper: The Bread and the Fruit of the Vine; When Should the Lord's Supper Be Observed? Part A: Weekly*

- *Positions of Authority: Who Is The Pastor?; A Hierarchy of Bishops; Female Deacons [Deaconesses]; Female Elders; Ordination; Synods, Councils, Conventions, and Other Meetings*

Part IV
- *Montanism*

What is the Baptism of the Holy Spirit?

The fundamental premise of the Pentecostal/Charismatic movement is what is deemed the "baptism of the Holy Spirit." It is believed that the "baptism of the Holy Spirit" is given today, and that from this event the ability to speak in tongues, to heal, and possibly to prophecy, is given.[1] They believe that the "outpouring of the Holy Spirit" as seen in the twentieth century is evidence of the "end time" return of the Holy Spirit, believed to have been prophesied by Joel in Joel 2.28–32.[2] The whole Pentecostal/Charismatic belief system requires the baptism of the Holy Spirit to exist for one to be able to speak in tongues, etc. Is this the teaching of the Scriptures concerning the baptism of the Holy Spirit?

The "baptism of the Holy Spirit" is seen twice in the New Testament, and that terminology is only used either before or after the event happens. In Acts 1.4–5, Jesus foretells the baptism of the Holy Spirit for His disciples:

> and, being assembled together with them, He charged them not to depart from Jerusalem, but to wait for the promise of the Father, which, said He,
> "ye heard from me: For John indeed baptized with water; but ye shall be baptized in the Holy Spirit not many days hence."

This was fulfilled on the day of Pentecost according to Acts 2.1–4:

> And when the day of Pentecost was now come, they were all together in one place. And suddenly there came from heaven a sound as of the rushing of a mighty wind, and it filled all the house where they were sitting. And there appeared unto them tongues parting asunder, like as of fire; and it sat upon each one of them. And they were all filled with the Holy Spirit, and began to speak with other tongues, as the Spirit gave them utterance.

The next and last instance of the term "the baptism of the Holy Spirit" in the Scriptures is during Peter's relation to the Christians in Jerusalem concerning what occurred to Cornelius and his men, Acts 11.15–16:

> "And as I began to speak, the Holy Spirit fell on them, even as on us at the beginning. And I remembered the word of the Lord, how he said,
> 'John indeed baptized with water; but ye shall be baptized in the Holy Spirit.'"

This event occurred in Acts 10.44–45:

> While Peter yet spake these words, the Holy Spirit fell on all them that heard the word. And they of the circumcision that believed were amazed, as many as came with Peter, because that on the Gentiles also was poured out the gift of the Holy Spirit.

These two events are the only recorded baptisms of the Holy Spirit within the Scriptures. Many times the gift of the Holy Spirit is given, but it is always done with the laying on of hands, as is evidenced by the example in Acts 8.14–17:

> Now when the apostles that were at Jerusalem heard that Samaria had received the word of God, they sent unto them Peter and John: who, when they were come down, prayed for them, that they might receive the Holy Spirit: for as yet it was fallen upon none of them: only they had been baptized into the name of the Lord Jesus. Then laid they their hands on them, and they received the Holy Spirit.

We see here that when the Spirit was given to men from the Apostles, hands were laid upon them. This action represents the vast majority of the transmission of the Holy Spirit in the Scriptures.

We can therefore see that the baptism of the Holy Spirit was not to be a common event. It was a miraculous event to demonstrate to the people that Jesus Christ was Lord, and that all must obey Him to receive eternal life. In Acts 2, the baptism of the Holy Spirit occurred for the Kingdom of Heaven to be established on Earth in the form of the church. In Acts 10, the baptism of the Holy Spirit served to be a sign to Peter that the Gentiles were to be a part of the Kingdom. These two events signify the fulfillment of the multiple prophecies in the Old Testament concerning the establishment of the heavenly Kingdom and the acceptance of the Gentiles into the fold. There are no Scriptures that would demonstrate that God would bestow any more baptisms of the Holy Spirit beyond the two events in the first century.

It is argued that the prophecy in Joel 2 concerning the dispensation of the Spirit demonstrates that the Holy Spirit would be again poured out upon Christians in the "end times." We have seen, however, in **Plymouth Brethren: Joel 2: The Gift of the Holy Spirit**, that Peter spoke very clearly in saying that the day of Pentecost was the fulfillment of the prophecy given, and thus there does not need to be a later outpouring to make it so. Therefore, we can see that the "baptism of the Holy Spirit" was a miraculous event for the benefit of the Apostles, first to be able to teach and then to show that the Gentiles were to enter the fold, and thus there is no longer a need for such a miracle. The only possible way that the Holy Spirit could be transferred to a Christian would be by the laying on of hands by the Apostles.

Can the gift of the Holy Spirit be imparted today? We can examine the Scriptures to see if it is so. The Scriptures show that only the Apostles were able to transmit the Holy Spirit by means of the "laying on of hands." We do not see anyone else transmitting the gift. This is made manifest by the example of Philip and Peter and John in Acts 8.12–17:

> But when they believed Philip preaching good tidings concerning the kingdom of God and the name of Jesus Christ, they were baptized, both men and women. And Simon also himself believed: and being baptized, he continued with Philip; and beholding signs and great miracles wrought, he was amazed. Now when the apostles that were at Jerusalem heard that Samaria had received the word of God, they sent unto them Peter and John: who, when they were come down, prayed for them, that they might receive the Holy Spirit: for as yet it was fallen upon none of them: only they had been baptized into the name of the Lord Jesus. Then laid they their hands on them, and they received the Holy Spirit.

We see that Peter and John came down from Jerusalem to Samaria in order to give the gift of the Holy Spirit to the Samaritans. Why did Philip not give the gift to them? The only reason that we can accept is that Philip was unable to give the gift since he was not one of the Apostles.

The last Apostle died around the year 100 CE. Therefore, none have been able to give the gift of the Holy Spirit through the laying on of hands since that time. We see, therefore, that the Scriptures teach that not only the baptism of the Holy Spirit but also the laying on of hands are practices not performed today.

Glossolalia: Speaking in Tongues

In the Pentecostal/Charismatic belief system, once one has received the "baptism of the Holy Spirit," the "initial evidence" of this occurrence is the *glossolalia*, or speaking in tongues.[3] The Pentecostals teach that this speaking in tongues is reminiscent of the day of Pentecost in Acts 2. Do the Pentecostals today receive the same gifts as the Apostles and the Christians of the first century received?

A major distinction must be made between the majority of the speaking in tongues today and the speaking in tongues of the first century. The speaking in tongues of today is generally what is deemed a "heavenly language," which is not able to be understood without inspiration and is considered to be "prayer in the Spirit, not linguistic expertise."[4] We read the following in the Scriptures in Acts 2.6–11:

> And when this sound was heard, the multitude came together, and were confounded, because that every man heard them speaking in his own language. And they were all amazed and marvelled, saying, "Behold, are not all these that speak Galilaeans? And how hear we, every man in our own language wherein we were born? Parthians and Medes and Elamites, and the dwellers in Mesopotamia, in Judaea and Cappadocia, in Pontus and Asia, in Phrygia and Pamphylia, in Egypt and the parts of Libya about Cyrene, and sojourners from Rome, both Jews and proselytes, Cretans and Arabians, we hear them speaking in our tongues the mighty works of God."

We therefore see that the Apostles spoke in legitimate tongues (languages), each understood clearly by those who spoke it. The Jews of the various languages did not need special inspiration to understand the language that the Apostles spoke, nor was it a "heavenly language."

It is interesting to note that when missionaries attempted to go to other countries, expecting the Holy Spirit within them to speak in the tongues of the people, they were not able to do so.[5] Instead, it is taught that "speaking in tongues" today refers to the following statement by Paul in 1 Corinthians 14.13–15:

> Wherefore let him that speaketh in a tongue pray that he may interpret. For if I pray in a tongue, my spirit prayeth, but my understanding is unfruitful. What is it then? I will pray with the spirit, and I will pray with the understanding also: I will sing with the spirit, and I will sing with the understanding also.

Does this statement demonstrate that speaking in tongues is prayer? By no means! Paul is saying that if one prays in a tongue, the spirit prays, but the mind is not fruitful! We can see his statement concerning this in verse 16:

> Else if thou bless with the spirit, how shall he that filleth the place of the unlearned say the Amen at thy giving of thanks, seeing he knoweth not what thou sayest?

Therefore, we can see that Paul is advising to not pray in tongues; thus, it is evident that tongues are not "heavenly language" that is "prayer to God" because its chief purpose, edification, was lost when none could understand the meaning of the prayer.

Let us now examine whether or not there are Scriptures that teach that speaking in tongues is the "initial evidence" of the baptism of the Holy Spirit. Do the Scriptures teach that the emphasis is on speaking in tongues? Paul says the following in 1 Corinthians 14.1:

> Follow after love; yet desire earnestly spiritual gifts, but rather that ye may prophesy.

This truth is made evident in verses 2–5:

> For he that speaketh in a tongue speaketh not unto men, but unto God; for no man understandeth; but in the spirit he speaketh mysteries. But he that prophesieth speaketh unto men edification, and exhortation, and consolation. He that speaketh in a tongue edifieth himself; but he that prophesieth edifieth the church. Now I would have you all speak with tongues, but rather that ye should prophesy: and greater is he that prophesieth than he that speaketh with tongues, except he interpret, that the church may receive edifying.

Paul exhorts the Corinthians to recognize that speaking in tongues is not as edifying to the church as prophecy is. Paul says in verse 2 that those who speak in foreign languages really speak to God alone; one can imagine how much edification could be gained in the Greek-speaking church in Corinth if someone began to speak in, say, the language of the Celts. If one prophesies, however, one builds up not only himself but also everyone around him, for all may be convinced of the power of God. Therefore, the Scriptures teach that prophecy is preeminent amongst the gifts of the Holy Spirit, and speaking in tongues comes next. This hierarchy is reversed in modern Pentecostal/Charismatic groups.

Finally, are the gifts of the Holy Spirit, speaking in tongues, prophecy, and knowledge, even for today? Can anyone speak in tongues today moved by the Holy Spirit? We have evidence given to us in 1 Corinthians 13.8–10:

> Love never faileth: but whether there be prophecies, they shall be done away; whether there be tongues, they shall cease; whether there be knowledge, it shall be done away. For we know in part, and we prophesy in part; but when that which is perfect is come, that which is in part shall be done away.

The interpretation of this verse hinges on the "perfect." The exact Greek word in this text for "perfect" is *teleion*, the neuter form of the noun *teleios*, meaning "perfect, complete." The verse could read, therefore, in the following manner: "but when that which is complete comes, the partial will be done away." The Pentecostals and Charismatics argue that the "perfect" refers to Christ and His Second Coming; the text, however, does not support this conclusion. We have stated that the word *teleion* is in the neuter gender; therefore, how can it refer to the masculine Christ? The best interpretation of this verse is to see that "the perfect" refers to the New Testament, the mystery of Christ unfolded. This process ended between 70–100 CE, depending on one's view of Revelation.

We can examine the historical records and see further demonstration that these gifts passed on by 100 CE. We see this is especially true concerning "knowledge." The last book of the New Testament was written most probably around 95 CE, and there has not been any individual since then who has brought forth further revelation that agrees with the gospel of the Apostles. Since the end of the first century, Christians have used the knowledge given to the Apostles and their immediate followers to guide their lives, and have not relied on supposed further revelations. Therefore, it is very accurate to say that the gift of knowledge ceased in the end of the first century.

It is interesting to note the following statement made by a Pentecostal:

> AD 70: After the apostolic age, many small or local renewals or revivals occur, with scores of isolated charismatic believers (often in monasteries) but no global renewal until the 20th century.[6]

This admission, that there was no "global renewal" until the modern day, demonstrates that the Pentecostals admit that a change occurred after the end of the first century. It should also be stated that many of these "small or local renewals or revivals" are either heretical sects (like the **Montanists**) or a re-interpretation of the lives of some monks and nuns based on the current belief in the *charismata* (gifts). Therefore, it is evident that there are only a very few isolated cases of individuals believing in the charismata between 100–1900 CE, with even fewer after 450 CE. The only possible explanation that could be given by the Pentecostals concerning this silent period is that which they give concerning Joel 2 and the supposed "latter day dispensation of the Holy Spirit," which we have shown to be false. Therefore, it is evident from the Scriptures and affirmed by the historical record that the gifts of prophecy, speaking in tongues, and knowledge ceased by 100 CE.

Oneness Pentecostalism

There is a group within the Pentecostal/Charismatic movement known as the "oneness Pentecostals," the origins of which are discussed above. The "oneness" Pentecostals teach that the only valid baptism (the immersion in water, not of the Holy Spirit) is in the name of Jesus alone, and that the "Trinitarian" baptism (Father, Son, Holy Spirit) was forced upon the church by the Nicene Creed.[7] They further believe that the name Jesus was the name of the Father, the Son, and the Holy Spirit, since God is one and thus must have one name, and that name in the new covenant is Jesus.[8] They also believe that speaking in tongues is essential for salvation.[9] Is this what the Scriptures teach?

The Scriptures teach that Jesus is God, but they do not teach that the name of God is Jesus. We have evidence of this in many places, including 1 Timothy 2.5–6:

> For there is one God, one mediator also between God and men, himself man, Christ Jesus, who gave himself a ransom for all; the testimony to be borne in its own times.

There is also the greeting often used by Paul to the churches, e.g. 1 Corinthians 1.3:

> Grace to you and peace from God our Father and the Lord Jesus Christ.

If the name of Jesus refers to the whole God, why does Paul differentiate the two often?

Paul is not alone in doing this; James does the same in James 1.1:

> James, a servant of God and of the Lord Jesus Christ, to the twelve tribes which are of the Dispersion, greeting.

If Jesus were the name of God, would not "a bond-servant of God Jesus" be satisfactory? Yet they all use the term "God" or "God the Father" along with the "Lord Jesus Christ." Therefore, it is evident that the idea of the name of Jesus referring to the whole Godhead is inconsistent with the Scriptures.

Concerning baptism, we are given two Scriptures regarding the specific language of baptism, Matthew 28.18–20 and Acts 2.38:

> And Jesus came to them and spake unto them, saying,
> "All authority hath been given unto me in heaven and on earth.
> Go ye therefore, and make disciples of all the nations, baptizing them into the name of the Father and of the Son and of the Holy Spirit: teaching them to observe all things whatsoever I commanded you: and lo, I am with you always, even unto the end of the world."

> And Peter said unto them, "Repent ye, and be baptized every one of you in the name of Jesus Christ unto the remission of your sins; and ye shall receive the gift of the Holy Spirit."

It is argued by these "oneness" Pentecostals that Matthew 28.19 is a command, while Acts 2.38 demonstrates the command put into action.

The language of the text, however, does not support this: Acts 2.38 is a command in no way different from the command in Matthew 28.19. We see in these two texts that either baptism is valid, for both call upon the authority of God. There is no evidence from the Scriptures that would show that either form of the baptismal formula ought to be bound.

The Oneness Pentecostal view of God is little different from the ancient Modalist/Sabellian heresy and would posit the idea that Jesus spoke to Himself when praying, or the idea that the Father and the Spirit equally suffered with the Son on the cross. This idea of God as one Person is inconsistent with Jesus' testimony in John 8.17–18:

> "Yea and in your law it is written, that the witness of two men is true. I am he that beareth witness of myself, and the Father that sent me beareth witness of me."

Jesus clearly indicates that while He and the Father are one (John 10.30), they are yet distinct in person, enough so to represent two witnesses. Furthermore, manifestations of the triune nature of God, as in Genesis 1.1–2, 26–27 and Matthew 3.16–17, do not lend credence to the modalist view. The Scriptures reveal that God is one in three persons, not three manifestations of one.

Finally, do the Scriptures teach that speaking in tongues is required for salvation? We have already seen above that Paul's directive to the church in Corinth was to prophecy above speaking in tongues; furthermore, we have seen in 1 Corinthians 13 that the gift of speaking in tongues was to cease. There are no Scriptures that show that speaking in tongues is required for salvation; in fact, there is no evidence from the Scriptures themselves that anyone spoke in tongues beyond the Apostles, Cornelius et al, Paul, the Corinthians, and some others. Therefore, it is evident that there is no evidence from the Scriptures that demonstrates that speaking in tongues is required for salvation.

Word of Faith Movement

The "Word of Faith" movement (WOF) is a "neo-Charismatic" movement that teaches that the validity of one's faith is demonstrated by one's material health and wealth.[10] This movement is popularized today by many of the televangelists, including Kenneth Copeland, Joyce Meyer, Benny Hinn, and a multitude of others.[11] They also teach that we are like

God, that God is like us, that Jesus took on the nature of Satan and suffered in Hell to accomplish the work of redemption, and that even humans can be gods.[12] Do the Scriptures agree with these teachings?

We have seen in **Eastern Orthodoxy: Theosis** and **Mormonism, II: Doctrine: Eternal Progression**, that man most assuredly cannot become a god. Concerning the relationship between God and man, we read the following in Isaiah 55.8–9:

> "For my thoughts are not your thoughts, neither are your ways my ways," saith the LORD. "For as the heavens are higher than the earth, so are my ways higher than your ways, and my thoughts than your thoughts."

Therefore, it is evident that there is a wide separation between God and us.

Did Jesus have to go to Hell in order to be saved? As can be seen in **Creeds: The Apostles' Creed**, it is inaccurate to presume that Jesus descended into Hell after His death, for we have the words of David in prophecy concerning Him in Psalm 16.10:

> For thou wilt not leave my soul to Sheol; Neither wilt thou suffer thy holy one to see corruption.

Furthermore, did Jesus Himself need salvation? By no means, for God declared concerning Him the following in Matthew 3.16–17:

> And Jesus when he was baptized, went up straightway from the water: and lo, the heavens were opened unto him, and he saw the Spirit of God descending as a dove, and coming upon him; and lo, a voice out of the heavens, saying,
> "This is my beloved Son, in whom I am well pleased."

Therefore, it is evident that Jesus did not need salvation, for in Him God was "well-pleased."

Finally, there is the doctrine concerning material wealth and health and one's faith. The Scriptures make it evident that our faith is not based in our material possessions, nor are we guaranteed material wealth because of our faith. Let us read the witness of the Scriptures in Matthew 19.21–24, Philippians 4.11–12, and 1 Timothy 6.17–19:

Jesus said unto him, "If thou wouldest be perfect, go, sell that which thou hast, and give to the poor, and thou shalt have treasure in heaven: and come, follow me."
But when the young man heard the saying, he went away sorrowful; for he was one that had great possessions. And Jesus said unto his disciples,
"Verily I say unto you, It is hard for a rich man to enter into the kingdom of heaven. And again I say unto you, It is easier for a camel to go through a needle's eye, than for a rich man to enter into the kingdom of God."

Not that I speak in respect of want: for I have learned, in whatsoever state I am, therein to be content. I know how to be abased, and I know also how to abound: in everything and in all things have I learned the secret both to be filled and to be hungry, both to abound and to be in want.

Charge them that are rich in this present world, that they be not highminded, nor have their hope set on the uncertainty of riches, but on God, who giveth us richly all things to enjoy; that they do good, that they be rich in good works, that they be ready to distribute, willing to communicate; laying up in store for themselves a good foundation against the time to come, that they may lay hold on the life which is life indeed.

These verses do not speak about the wealth one will receive if he or she has faith but the opposite: with faith, one learns to be content with what one is given and should not be seeking for riches on Earth. The Scriptures teach that those who are rich in material wealth are better served to give it to those more needy; in so doing, they store up spiritual wealth. We can see from the Scriptures, therefore, that the faith of Christians is not measured by the size of wealth or the portion of health that they have.

Notes

1: Vinson Synan, *The Century of the Holy Spirit*, p. 3

2: Ibid., p. 71

3: Ibid., p. 3

4: Ibid., pp. 56, 81

5: Ibid., p. 81

6: Ibid, p. 416

7: Ibid., p. 141

8: Ibid., p. 142

9: Ibid., p. 141

10: Ibid., p. 337

11: Ibid.

12: Benny Hinn, TBN, 12/1/1990; Copeland, Kenneth, *Walking in the Realm of the Miraculous* (1979), 77; Copeland, Kenneth, "Believer's Voice of Victory," TBN, 4/21/1991.

International Church of Christ

Overview

The International Church of Christ (also known as the Boston Movement or ICOC; their churches often describe themselves as "church of Christ" without any further designation) began in June 1979 near Boston, Massachusetts, with a Bible study of a few people led by one Kip McKean. McKean had come under the influence of the "Crossroads Movement" in the 1970s at the Crossroads Church of Christ in Gainesville, Florida. The "Crossroads Movement" placed a strong emphasis on the need to "disciple" Christians, especially the new converts, in order to strengthen them and to keep them faithful. McKean believed this principle and then added many of his own tenets. As the Crossroads Movement faded in the 1980s, McKean's new Boston Movement picked up momentum, adding many to its numbers from the old Crossroads movement along with others from denominations and some from churches of Christ. As the 1980s and 1990s progressed, however, McKean's doctrines began to distance themselves from Scripture, adopting a "speak where the Bible is silent and be silent where the Bible speaks" mentality and building an elaborate hierarchical structure within the church.

The International Churches of Christ endured great crisis in 2002 and 2003 (called by some within the movement the "Great Tribulation"), when the central leadership structure of the organization was dissolved, McKean and other top leaders found themselves compelled to resign and disassociated from by other ICOC groups, and the renunciation of two of the main ICOC principles: the hierarchical structure and emphasis on discipling. At that point, many of the different churches comprising the International Church of Christ began to hold meetings designed for reconciliation with "mainline" churches of Christ, while many others remained in a form of suspended animation. The events of the past few years have left many International Churches of Christ as quasi-autonomous groups operating according to some of the originating principles of the movement while having repented of some of the more controversial doctrines associated with the Boston Movement.

While Kip McKean laid low for awhile, he began working with the Portland International Church of Christ, and in October 2005 earnestly began what he now calls the Portland Movement. The Portland Movement is really the Boston Movement with slight adaptations, desiring to be a "restoration movement" within the ICOC churches; McKean and his associates are still drawing in people and some of the ICOC churches have realigned with him. It would seem that churches in the Portland Movement either go by "International Church of Christ" or "International Christian Church" (ICC).[1]

Variants

While it was impossible to speak of variants within the International Church of Christ before 2002, the events of 2002–2003 led to great fragmentation within the movement. As a result of the movement away from Kip McKean, many International Churches of Christ either assimilated with or began to be influenced by "mainline" churches of Christ, and in such groups the distinctive ICOC doctrines have been set aside. While willing to be more accommodative to churches of Christ and other groups, many other International Churches of Christ have continued as distinct entities. The churches remain quasi-autonomous, but the regional divisions seem to remain and the larger metropolitan churches have great influence in those regions. It should be noted that according to McKean, the ICOC as it existed before 2002 was no more after the period of "tribulation" in 2002–2003.[2]

There are also the churches now associated with the Portland Movement, those recently started by McKean and his associates or groups of former ICOC groups that have re-aligned with him. These represent the neo-Boston Movement groups, committed to the same principles as before with only cosmetic changes.

General Considerations

Part III

- *The Church Treasury, I: Benevolence: Church Benevolence to Non-Saints; The Sponsoring Church Arrangement*
- *The Church Treasury, II: Other Considerations: Hospitals; Kitchens/ Fellowship Halls; Gymnasiums*

- *Instrumental Music*
- *Positions of Authority: A Hierarchy of Bishops ["sector leaders" and the like]; Female Evangelists; Synods, Councils, Conventions, and Other Meetings*

Discipleship and Discipling

The International Church of Christ (heretofore referred to as "ICOC") maintains in its teachings that one must be a disciple of Christ, to the extent that one cannot be baptized before he or she decides to be a disciple.[3] The Portland Movement further teaches that one who converts to the faith needs to be "discipled," following supposedly after Matthew 28.19–20, and thus is paired with a "discipler," one who is in charge of the well-being of the new convert.[4] "Discipling" is maintained as a practice in other ICOC groups, although it is no longer made mandatory. Are these principles truly taught in the Scriptures?

We cannot deny that we need to be disciples of Christ; after all, He is the Master Teacher, and we are to heed Him, as is illustrated in Matthew 10.24–25:

> "A disciple is not above his teacher, nor a servant above his lord. It is enough for the disciple that he be as his teacher, and the servant as his lord. If they have called the master of the house Beelzebub, how much more them of his household!"

Therefore, we are to be the disciples of Christ, for He is the Teacher and we must follow Him. The Scriptures do not teach, however, that one must decide to be a disciple before one can be baptized. An example is Acts 2.37–38:

> Now when they heard this, they were pricked in their heart, and said unto Peter and the rest of the apostles, "Brethren, what shall we do?" And Peter said unto them, "Repent ye, and be baptized every one of you in the name of Jesus Christ unto the remission of your sins; and ye shall receive the gift of the Holy Spirit."

We do not hear Peter telling them to "decide to be a disciple, repent, and be baptized," or any such thing. We do see in Acts 2.41–42 that those who were saved did desire to learn the teachings of Christ:

> They then that received his word were baptized: and there were added unto them in that day about three thousand souls. And

> they continued stedfastly in the apostles' teaching and fellowship,
> in the breaking of bread and the prayers.

Therefore, they can be rightly called disciples of Christ and of the Apostles, yet this action is performed after their initial belief and baptism. This is consistent with Jesus' charge in Matthew 28.18–20: indeed, the Apostles were to "go" and "make disciples", but the vehicle of making disciples was to "baptize them" and to "teach them to observe all that [He] had commanded [them]." There is no evidence from the Scriptures that would lead to the conclusion that one must specifically decide to be a disciple before they are baptized: one can only become a disciple by being baptized and being taught the way of Christ.

Do the Scriptures teach that we must disciple new and/or younger members of the faith? Let us again return to Matthew 28.18–20:

> And Jesus came to them and spake unto them, saying, "All authority hath been given unto me in heaven and on earth. Go ye therefore, and make disciples of all the nations, baptizing them into the name of the Father and of the Son and of the Holy Spirit: teaching them to observe all things whatsoever I commanded you: and lo, I am with you always, even unto the end of the world."

We are therefore commanded to "make disciples of all the nations." What does this mean? We may have some pertinent information concerning this in Acts 11.26:

> and when he had found him, he brought him unto Antioch. And it came to pass, that even for a whole year they were gathered together with the church, and taught much people, and that the disciples were called Christians first in Antioch.

From this passage, it appears that Christians were first called simply "disciples," and the name of Christian was added to them later. Therefore, we can read the commandment of Jesus very simply as "Go therefore and make Christians of all the nations…" The Scriptures teach that one is made a Christian by believing in Christ and obeying His Word; this can be performed without a "discipler." The specific need for "discipling" is not necessarily present in Matthew 28.19–20.

Nevertheless, it is evident in the need to teach what Jesus has commanded that a need exists to assist those who are younger in the faith. Is this a job that is to be given to one specific individual? Let us read the Scriptures in Galatians 6.1–2:

> Brethren, even if a man be overtaken in any trespass, ye who are spiritual, restore such a one in a spirit of gentleness; looking to thyself, lest thou also be tempted. Bear ye one another's burdens, and so fulfil the law of Christ.

We are all to "bear one another's burdens;" the task is not limited to, nor is it supposed to be limited to, one individual.

We see in Romans 12.3–8 an important concept:

> For I say, through the grace that was given me, to every man that is among you, not to think of himself more highly than he ought to think; but to think as to think soberly, according as God hath dealt to each man a measure of faith. For even as we have many members in one body, and all the members have not the same office: so we, who are many, are one body in Christ, and severally members one of another. And having gifts differing according to the grace that was given to us, whether prophecy, let us prophesy according to the proportion of our faith; or ministry, let us give ourselves to our ministry; or he that teacheth, to his teaching; or he that exhorteth, to his exhorting: he that giveth, let him do it with liberality; he that ruleth, with diligence; he that showeth mercy, with cheerfulness.

There is an equality of all members in Christianity that the idea of "discipling" violates. We are all equal in Christ; nowhere is any Christian in any way superior to another. The only difference between Christians is of different roles. An elder oversees the congregation; this does not in and of itself mean that the elder is superior to any other Christian. The evangelist brings the word of God to the congregation and the outside world; this does not mean the evangelist is a better Christian than any other member of the congregation. In Christianity, there is a communion of believers assisting each other, thus eliminating the need for one specific individual to watch over another specific individual, a relationship not authorized in the Scriptures. Therefore, the process of growth of an individual in the faith is not dependent on having another individual watch over him, but instead requires the assistance of the whole congregation in building up and strengthening not only the young members and the converts but everyone within that body. The practice of discipling, therefore, is not in accordance with the Scriptures.

Confession of Sin

The ICOC taught, and the Portland Movement maintains, that sin must be confessed often, especially in a system of what is deemed "prayer buddies," two individuals who confess their sins to each other.[5] This is also done with the discipler. Furthermore, many times the ICOC published and circulated to its members lists of individuals and the sins they have confessed, so people can pray for them. Are these practices based in the New Testament?

The ICOC believes that James 5.16 justifies their belief:

> Confess therefore your sins one to another, and pray one for another, that ye may be healed. The supplication of a righteous man availeth much in its working.

Does this verse teach that we must confess our sins to one another? It teaches that confession of sin to one another is beneficial, since the "prayer of a righteous man can accomplish much." The context of the passage, however, demonstrates that James is speaking of a specific situation, James 5.14–15:

> Is any among you sick? Let him call for the elders of the church; and let them pray over him, anointing him with oil in the name of the Lord: and the prayer of faith shall save him that is sick, and the Lord shall raise him up; and if he have committed sins, it shall be forgiven him.

James is therefore making a commandment to those who are sick, that he or she confess their sins so that they may be forgiven, and that this may lead to healing. This passage by no means binds the confession of sins to one another as required.

We are given principles in the New Testament concerning confession to one another in Matthew 18.15–17 and Galatians 6.1–2:

> "And if thy brother sin against thee, go, show him his fault between thee and him alone: if he hear thee, thou hast gained thy brother. But if he hear thee not, take with thee one or two more, that at the mouth of two witnesses or three every word may be

established. And if he refuse to hear them, tell it unto the church: and if he refuse to hear the church also, let him be unto thee as the Gentile and the publican."

Brethren, even if a man be overtaken in any trespass, ye who are spiritual, restore such a one in a spirit of gentleness; looking to thyself, lest thou also be tempted. Bear ye one another's burdens, and so fulfil the law of Christ.

We can see that it is beneficial to confess our sins to one another, that we may receive assistance and prayer, so that we may be built up. We further see that sins that are committed that come to the attention of the church ought to be confessed and repented of, and this is illustrated further in 1 Corinthians 5.

Confession of sin to one another therefore is surely beneficial, but is not to be bound upon any individual. It ought to be an action done on the volition of the one who has sinned so that he or she may be uplifted. There is only one person to whom our confession of sin is required to be given: God, seen in 1 John 1.9:

If we confess our sins, he is faithful and righteous to forgive us our sins, and to cleanse us from all unrighteousness.

Therefore, the Scriptures teach that we must confess our sins to God, and we may confess our sins to each other in order to receive edification.

Notes

1: Much of the information in the above paragraphs comes from http://www.kipmckean.org/the-portland-movement/

2: Kip McKean, "A Concern for all the Churches"

3: Kip McKean, *Revolution Through Restoration, I.*

4: Ibid.

5: Kip McKean, *First Principles.*

Part II: Movements

Evangelicalism

Overview

Evangelicalism, or the Evangelical Movement, represents a potent force in modern "Christendom". A full third of those who would profess Christ in the world fall under the Evangelical umbrella, and most such persons live outside of North America and Europe.[1] As described below, it is often difficult to pin down a specific definition of evangelicalism, but in general, evangelicalism represents a loosely confederated movement of Protestants from the eighteenth century to the present believing in the need for a conversion experience, a personal relationship with Jesus, and relying on the Bible as the standard for faith and practice. Nevertheless, there is great diversity of belief among Evangelicals, and the movement experiences great tension between Calvinist and Arminian (predestination vs. free will), amillennialism and premillennialism, pentecostalism and cessationism, and fundamentalism and post-fundamentalism groups. Many other movements have sprung out of evangelicalism, yet the movement is as alive and as vibrant today as ever.

Origins and History

Evangelicalism (from the Greek *euangelion*, "good news" or "Gospel") emerged out of disparate movements that swept through Protestant churches in the seventeenth and eighteenth centuries. The first, and in many ways the most influential, was the Pietist Movement of the seventeenth century in Germany, a reform movement within Lutheranism which focused on the conversion and regeneration of the "inner man" and the belief that such an experience was necessary for salvation.[2] Such an "experiential" focus would mark later evangelicalism. The second was the Puritan movement which attempted to reform the Anglican church toward Calvinist Protestantism; many such Puritans traveled to America in the early seventeenth century, and their Calvinist Protestantism would impact Evangelical thought.[3] The third group, although starting during the beginning of evangelicalism proper, would greatly impact later evangelical developments: the Wesley brothers and Wesleyanism, whose emphasis on holiness and sanctification would eventually lead to Methodism and Pentecostalism.

The Evangelical movement as such began in the 1730s and 1740s with the first "Great Awakening," involving the preaching of George Whitefield, Jonathan Edwards, and John Wesley, among others, especially in America.[4] This period represented the beginnings of revivalism, when meetings would be held in various communities and many would decide to "accept Christ" in a conversion experience. This "awakening", along with the second "Great Awakening" of the 1820s-1840s, resulted in the "Christianization" of young America and the dominance of evangelicalism over the American religious climate.

The nineteenth century also saw the beginning of the conflict that would engulf evangelicalism for the better part of the twentieth century—the rise of "higher criticism" and evolutionary theory, and their attempts to undermine confidence in the validity of the Biblical account of creation and history. Fundamentalism as a movement began within evangelicalism in the early twentieth century as a reaction against these tendencies in liberal Protestantism and society in general. Until the 1930s, evangelicalism and fundamentalism remained together; the subsequent radicalization and separatism of fundamentalism led to a separation between "mainline" evangelicalism and fundamentalism in the 1930s and 1940s.[5] While fundamentalists may desire to see themselves as evangelicals, other evangelicals would not be very comfortable with them in their fold.

The early twentieth century also saw the explosion of the Pentecostal/Charismatic Movement and its attendant controversies; while some "evangelical" groups did not want to include the Pentecostals in their midst, other voices prevailed, and Pentecostals make up a large proportion of evangelical Christianity.

Modern evangelicalism emerged from the crucible of historic evangelicalism and the fundamentalist schism; it is often called "postfundamentalist" evangelicalism, and it began in 1942 with the creation of the National Association of Evangelicals (NAE).[6] Prominent in postfundamentalist evangelicalism is Billy Graham and his legacy of large meetings and mass conversions; his overall leadership has kept the disparate segments of evangelicalism together.[7] Most recently, there has been a "postconservative" movement within evangelicalism, an attempt to transcend the old "liberal vs. conservative" perspective and return to the spirituality of the days of the "Great Awakenings".[8] These trends have helped to lead to Emergism, or the Emergent movement, in the early twenty-first century.

Who Are the Evangelicals?

In many ways, it is difficult to characterize evangelicalism and the evangelical movement, since its umbrella is vast, and there is little agreement as to what precisely constitutes an "evangelical". This difficulty is compounded by misunderstandings both within and without the movement. It is imperative, therefore, for us to provide a proper definition of whom we speak when we talk of "evangelicals" and the "evangelical movement".

There is no mutually agreed upon single definition, and the term "evangelical" is used in different contexts. The broadest definition represents authentic Christianity based on the Gospel; any group teaching the true Gospel could thus be considered "evangelical". "Evangelical" can also be equivalent to Protestantism, being "Gospel-centered". It can also refer to a group that derives from pietist revivals of Protestant faith in the eighteenth and nineteenth centuries. In the past, evangelicalism has been equated with fundamentalism, although fundamentalism has now become its own subculture. A more modern definition involves post-fundamentalist evangelicalism attempting to return to its pietist, revivalist history. In popular society, it is also equated with any fanatical or aggressive religious group.[9]

For the purposes of our study here of evangelicalism and the evangelical movement, we will define evangelicalism as the movement of the past 270 years blending pietist revivalism with Protestant orthodoxy as manifest in the "Great Awakenings" and in modern post-fundamentalist evangelicalism.

Denominations Involved

Evangelicalism has always been rooted in the individual and his faith; as a result, while many denominations are populated with large percentages of individuals who claim to be evangelicals, few denominations could be considered to be entirely "evangelical". Baptists are prominently featured in evangelicalism, along with Wesleyan and Pentecostal churches (although Oneness Pentecostals are generally excluded, being anti-Trinitarian). The Christian Church (Disciples of Christ) is also in this evangelical mainstream.

Evangelicals can also be found in the midst of Roman Catholicism, Lutheranism, many Anabaptist groups, historic Calvinist churches, Anglicanism/Episcopalianism, some Quakers, Pietist groups, the Plymouth Brethren, and The Salvation Army, although their numbers are fewer among the "liberal Protestant" groups (Lutheranism, Episcopalianism, United Church of Christ, Presbyterians, etc.).[10]

Many movements have developed either from within evangelicalism or under its influence, including Fundamentalism, the Community Church Movement, the House Church Movement, the Megachurch Movement, and Emergism. Evangelicalism, by its very nature, has practiced its own form of ecumenism, although there has been historical skepticism among many evangelicals of the ecumenism of liberal Protestantism.

General Considerations

As with all matters evangelical, there is some level of disagreement about the majority of the matters listed below. They are provided as a general guide for understanding.

Part I

- *Lutheranism: Faith Alone; The Lord's Prayer*
- *Calvinism: TULIP [contested]*
- *Baptists: Once Saved, Always Saved*
- *Wesleyanism: The Church and Social Responsibility*
- *Plymouth Brethren: Dispensationalism; Premillennialism [disputed]*

Part II

- *Fundamentalism*
- *Community Church Movement*
- *House Church Movement*
- *Megachurch Movement*
- *Emergism*

Part III

- *Baptism: Infant Baptism and "Original Sin" [disputed]; Baptism is Immersion [disputed]; Baptism is for Remission of Sin and is Necessary for Salvation*
- *The Church Treasury, I: Benevolence: Church Benevolence to Non-Saints; The Missionary Society*

- *The Church Treasury, II: Benevolence: Hospitals; Centers of Education; Kitchens/Fellowship Halls; Gymnasiums; Business Enterprises*

Concerning Observances:

- *Observances Concerning the Lord's Birth: Advent; Christmas*
- *Observances Concerning the Lord's Death: Palm Sunday; Maundy Thursday; Good Friday; Easter*

- *Creeds: The Apostles' Creed; The Nicene Creed*

- *Instrumental Music*

- *Judaic Practices: The Ten Commandments and the "Moral Law"; Tithing*

- *The Lord's Supper: The Bread and the Fruit of the Vine; When Should the Lord's Supper Be Observed? Part A: Weekly*

- *Positions of Authority: Who is the Pastor?; Female Deacons [Deaconesses]; Female Evangelists; Ordination; Synods, Councils, Conventions, and Other Meetings*

Evangelicals and Society

A general trend that is prevalent in much of evangelicalism involves a high level of interaction with the surrounding secular society. From the 1940s through the 1980s and beyond, "Evangelical culture" grew and developed; since then, it has continually tried to mirror overall societal trends.[11] This is a trend that has been noticeable for even longer, going back to the "missionary" society concept in the nineteenth century. The establishment of church gymnasiums, fellowship halls, church-run "Christian" cafes, coffeehouses, and bookstores and other resources have followed these trends. Modern marketing methods and modern evangelistic methods parallel one another: to suit an entertainment-drenched society, many such evangelical churches have established "seeker-friendly" assemblies designed to entertain. Such methods perhaps have wide appeal among people of the world, but do they represent God's intentions for His people? Let us consider the matter.

Christians always exist in the tension of living in the world while not being of the world, as demonstrated in 1 Corinthians 5.9–10 and James 4.4:

> I wrote unto you in my epistle to have no company with fornicators; not altogether with the fornicators of this world, or with the covetous and extortioners, or with idolaters; for then must ye needs go out of the world.

> Ye adulteresses, know ye not that the friendship of the world is enmity with God? Whosoever therefore would be a friend of the world maketh himself an enemy of God.

While achieving proper balance may not always be easy, many of the trends of evangelicalism seem to violate many Biblical principles in their endeavor to remain "relevant". There is no justification to change the message to make it more appealing to modern man; to speak only of the "positive" matters to be more "seeker-friendly" runs afoul of Galatians 1.6–9 and 2 Timothy 4.2. Likewise, to turn the assembly, which is designed to encourage Christians, into an entertainment service runs afoul of God's intention for the assembly as established in 1 Corinthians 14.26 and Hebrews 10.24–25. It is difficult to see how the operation of various businesses integrates with the role of the church, which is to build itself up in love (Ephesians 4.16).

While such things may make perfect sense to modern Americans, do they make sense according to what God has revealed in the Bible? That must be our primary concern (Romans 12.1–2)!

Political Involvement

Another prominent feature of much of evangelicalism is the high level of political involvement among evangelicals. While some level of political involvement was the norm for various denominations since Constantine, the growth and development of evangelicalism alongside the development of the American state led to a particular political ideology of American evangelicals that is otherwise unparalleled, as evidenced in the following quote by a prominent Evangelical:

> America's uniqueness is in the Christian consensus of the Founding Fathers, who penned documents guaranteeing religious and personal freedom for all. This nation was not founded by atheists, secularizers, or monarchists who thought the elite educated class should rule over the common people. America's founding was based more on biblical principles than any other nation's on

Earth—and that's the reason this country has been more blessed by God than any other nation in history.[12]

American evangelicalism and populist republicanism were ready allies, and there remains to this day an implicit view that America represents the new Israel, the new chosen land and chosen people of God. This sentiment has been exemplified in many social reform movements over the past two hundred years: evangelicals represented strong voices both for abolition and the promotion of Southern slavery, prohibition, and both sides of the mid-20th century civil rights movement. Since 1979 and the founding of the "Moral Majority," evangelical Christians have often been enlisted to promote legislation of moral constraints, and other organizations have developed on the other side of the political spectrum advocating rights for the poor and dispossessed.[13] Underneath all of these sentiments remains a view that Christians and Christian churches have a responsibility to reform or legislate society. Such a view makes sense in a world where Jesus will return to establish an earthly kingdom, or in a world where the division between the old and new covenants is not maintained sharply; however, are these expectations truly manifest in the New Testament?

The New Testament describes the relationship of Christians to the government in passages like Romans 13.1–7 and 1 Timothy 2.1–2:

> Let every soul be in subjection to the higher powers: for there is no power but of God; and the powers that be are ordained of God. Therefore he that resisteth the power, withstandeth the ordinance of God: and they that withstand shall receive to themselves judgment. For rulers are not a terror to the good work, but to the evil. And wouldest thou have no fear of the power? do that which is good, and thou shalt have praise from the same: for he is a minister of God to thee for good. But if thou do that which is evil, be afraid; for he beareth not the sword in vain: for he is a minister of God, an avenger for wrath to him that doeth evil. Wherefore ye must needs be in subjection, not only because of the wrath, but also for conscience sake. For for this cause ye pay tribute also; for they are ministers of God's service, attending continually upon this very thing. Render to all their dues: tribute to whom tribute is due; custom to whom custom; fear to whom fear; honour to whom honour.

> I exhort therefore, first of all, that supplications, prayers, intercessions, thanksgivings, be made for all men; for kings and all that are in high place; that we may lead a tranquil and quiet life in all godliness and gravity.

Peter also provides similar sentiments in 1 Peter 2.13–17. From these passages we see that Christians are to be subject to earthly governments and to pay taxes, along with praying so that Christians may lead tranquil and quiet lives. We do not see any expectations here for Christians or churches to reform or legislate society.

Many will argue that Christians lived under the Roman Empire, which represented a dictatorship, and since America is a republic and its citizens have the opportunity to vote, God's expectations of Christians in America is to be different. We have no Scripture that would validate this type of argument; while it is true that we live under a different form of governance, we still do not see any indication in the New Testament that the Christian is to be devoted to the reformation of society.

Instead, however, we read the following in John 18.36, Philippians 3.20, and 1 John 2.15–17:

> Jesus answered, "My kingdom is not of this world: if my kingdom were of this world, then would my servants fight, that I should not be delivered to the Jews: but now is my kingdom not from hence."

> For our citizenship is in heaven; from whence also we wait for a Saviour, the Lord Jesus Christ.

> Love not the world, neither the things that are in the world. If any man love the world, the love of the Father is not in him. For all that is in the world, the lust of the flesh, and the lust of the eyes, and the vainglory of life, is not of the Father, but is of the world. And the world passeth away, and the lust thereof: but he that doeth the will of God abideth for ever.

God expects that the Christian's primary focus is his spiritual citizenship and the obligations of his spiritual covenant. There is no indication that America is the new Israel or represents God's new chosen people; we certainly hope that at least some Americans are recognized to be God's people by virtue of being His obedient servants (cf. Romans 6.16–23), but it is not on the basis of their being Americans. Galatians 3.28 and Colossians 3.11 indicate that any and all racial or national barriers are broken down in Christ's Kingdom; He remains Lord over all (Matthew 28.18), not merely Lord of America. The appropriation of God's words to Israel to refer to America is misguided: we are under a new covenant with better promises, breaking down such barriers (Ephesians 2.11–18, Colossians 2.14–17, Hebrews 7–9), and the new Israel is represented by those who are known to Christ (Romans 2.28–29).

God does not expect His people to renounce citizenship in an earthly nation. Paul, by virtue of being from Tarsus, was a Roman citizen, and he used his privilege as a Roman citizen whenever necessary so that he could continue to promote the Gospel (Acts 16.37–39, Acts 22.25–30, Acts 23.11, Acts 25.10–12). Christians have the right to use whatever means are legitimate and at their disposal to promote the Gospel, but the focus is always on the salvation of souls, not the preservation of society!

In the end, it remains a personal decision, based on one's understanding of the Scriptures, as to whether he or she should vote and for whom. Nevertheless, the Scriptures demonstrate clearly that the primary goal of Christians and the church is the promotion of God's Kingdom to all men, and not a misguided attempt to force society to conform to Christianity. Christianity is to be promoted through the Gospel, not the legislation of worldly states that are all destined for the historical dustbin (Romans 1.16–17). Earthly authorities have come and gone; Christ's Kingdom remains, and will remain forever (Revelation 1.6).

Notes

1: Philip Yancey in *The Beliefnet Guide to Evangelical Christianity*, x.

2: Roger Olson, *Pocket History of Evangelical Theology*, 22–31.

3: ibid., 41, 45–46

4: ibid., 46.

5: ibid., 87–90.

6: ibid., 92.

7: ibid., 93–94.

8: ibid., 131–138.

9: for all definitions, ibid., 8–12.

10: for many of these, Wendy Zoba in *The Beliefnet Guide to Evangelical Christianity*, 106.

11: ibid., 80.

12: Tim LaHaye, "The American Idea: Godless Society", *The Atlantic Monthly*, November 2007, 44–45.

13: Zoba, *The Beliefnet Guide to Evangelical Christianity*, 93.

Ecumenism

Overview

Ecumenism, or the Ecumenical Movement, represents a modern unity movement seen most prevalently among liberal Protestants, Roman Catholics, and the Eastern Orthodox. After over a millennium of various divisions, members of these churches determined that it was best to attempt a dialogue that would lead to reconciliation and full communion among its constituent members. Unlike other movements, ecumenism has not resulted in any new or different churches or ecclesiastical structures: the movement entirely consists of various member churches communicating and working with one another bilaterally, multilaterally, and within organizations like the World Council of Churches (WCC) and the National Council of Churches of Christ (NCCC).[1] The primary goal of ecumenism is the attainment of full communion of the constituent separated churches within the movement and other ecclesiastical communities, manifest in shared events, collaboration in missions and other activities, and continued dialogue.[2] Ecumenism in the twentieth and now the twenty-first century is greatly responsible for overall attitudes espousing "unity-in-diversity" among different churches and the common appearance that all churches are essentially the same; it has popularized entirely new models of Christian worldview and perspective, recasting "the church" in more expansive terms than ever before.

Origins and History

Ecumenism finds its origins first in the transdenominational movements of the seventeenth and eighteenth century that led to the Evangelical movement (although, as noted below, many evangelicals are cool toward the ecumenical movement proper) and most directly in the missionary society movement in the nineteenth century. The close cooperation of many Protestant denominations in mission work compelled their members to consider their differences and work toward some kind of unity. The beginning of the ecumenical movement is normally reckoned with the 1910 World Mission-ary Conference in Edinburgh, Scotland.[3] Other aspects of the movement soon followed: in 1921, the International Missionary Council was estab-lished, followed by the World Conference on Faith and Order in 1927 (fo-cusing on doctrinal differences); these all led to the establishment of the World Council of Churches (WCC) in 1948.[4] These international develop-ments were paralleled by national movements in many countries, including the United States, where the National Council of Churches of Christ began in 1950. The constituent members of these bodies have met consistently dur-ing their existence, and much discussion and dialogue has taken place re-garding areas of agreement and disagreement among the various groups.

While much of the action of ecumenism has taken place within the na-tional and international ecumenical organizations, other efforts have been undertaken on the denominational level. Roman Catholics have engaged in dialogue with any branch of Christendom willing to converse with them; Lutherans and Anglicans, Anglicans and Eastern Orthodox, and many other such groups have engaged in much dialogue. In 1997, the Episco-pal Church in the United States and the Evangelical Lutheran Church in America established full communion with one another, perhaps one of the greater displays of professed unity within the movement.[5] The conversations and joint participation in matters of agreement continue to this day.

Denominations Involved

The founding members of ecumenism include many Wesleyan churches, pri-marily Methodists, along with Anglicans/Episcopalians and Lutherans. The Christian Church (Disciples of Christ), historic Calvinist churches (United Church of Christ, Presbyterian Church, Reformed churches), many Ana-baptist groups, Pietists, some Quaker groups, and The Salvation Army rep-resent Protestant groups also allied with the ecumenical movement.

While the Roman Catholic Church was leery of the movement from 1919 through 1949, the church reversed itself, and beginning in 1961 fully participated in ecumenism.[6] Eastern Orthodoxy and many of the first millennium splinter groups (Church of the East, Syrian Orthodox Church, Coptic churches) have also participated in the movement.

Many groups aligned with the Evangelical movement (Baptists, some Holiness groups, and many Pentecostal groups) are suspicious of the liberal Protestant-based ecumenical movement and have little to do with the World Council of Churches and its attendant ecumenical dialogues. Such churches, however, practice their own brand of ecumenism among themselves, as discussed within Evangelicalism.

General Considerations

Since ecumenism has not resulted in any new ecclesiastical structure or organization *per se*, it will be sufficient to consider the general considerations listed for its constituent denominational members.

Ecumenical Goals and Methodologies

As we investigate ecumenism in greater detail, we must begin by recognizing that the overall goal of the ecumenical movement is quite noble and excellent: the unity of believers in Christ. Such is the desire of God for those who are indeed His people (1 Corinthians 1.10, Philippians 2.2, John 17.21). Unity of believers is certainly a goal worthy of consideration and diligence.

While unity is a desirable goal, it is important that the unity is indeed the unity that God desires for His people, truly fulfilling the imagery of 1 Corinthians 12.12–28 and Ephesians 5.22–31. A form of unity that is not in accordance with God's will as revealed in the Scriptures is not going to be pleasing to God! Therefore, it is of the greatest importance to consider the smaller goals and methodologies of ecumenism and to compare them with the Scriptures.

One major concern with the methodology of the ecumenical movement is found in its evaluation of its constituent members. One requirement of anyone participating in the ecumenical movement is the confession that the "Church of Christ" is more inclusive than one's own church; it is believed that the Holy Spirit has been working throughout history in each individual denomination and that denominations should learn from the developments in faith that can be found in their ecumenical partners.[7] These views presuppose that all the participants involved in ecumenism represent legitimate and divinely approved expressions of Christianity and that no individual constituent denomination truly manifests the entire truth found in the New Testament.

The New Testament records the following regarding the nature of the church:

> But if I tarry long, that thou mayest know how men ought to be-
> have themselves in the house of God, which is the church of the
> living God, the pillar and ground of the truth *(1 Timothy 3.15)*.

> Beloved, while I was giving all diligence to write unto you of our
> common salvation, I was constrained to write unto you exhorting
> you to contend earnestly for the faith which was once for all deliv-
> ered unto the saints *(Jude 1.3)*.

In both passages the author presupposes that the audience is part of a body that has the truth within itself based upon the revelation of God. 1 Timothy 3.15 may include a challenge for a church (that it will be the pillar and support of the truth), but the fact that Paul can even speak of such a possibility demonstrates that God expects that which is truly the "Church of Christ" will hold firm to the truth as delivered once for all.

By participating in the ecumenical movement, the various members implicitly confess that they are not promoting the Gospel fully as intended by God in the New Testament and somehow expect that the truth will be established by consensus within the movement and its dialogue. Such an implicit admission casts doubt about the legitimacy of the movement and those who would comprise it.

Ecumenism is also marked, even from its origin, by a desire to collaborate in social reform movements and mission work.[8] Indeed, ecumenism attempts to work on the basis of areas of agreement and moves toward areas of disagreement. This kind of methodology, while understandable considering the task that is being attempted, ought to give pause. As can be seen in **The Church Treasury, I: Benevolence, The Church Treasury, II: Other Considerations**, and **Wesleyanism: The Church and Social Responsibility**, church sponsorship of missionary societies, hospitals, centers of education, and the like are without Scriptural authority and that the function of the church is not to push for social reform *per se* but rather the promotion of the Gospel, the building up of itself in love (Ephesians 4.16). If all of these groups are individually acting outside of God's authority for the church, can they truly collectively represent the pillar and support of the truth?

Unity cannot be established on the basis of agreement on certain practices or in collaboration of given works; unity can only be established by the reality of the shared walk in the light of Jesus Christ, and through association with Him (1 John 1.5–7). If a given group or given persons do not have association with Christ, how can those who have association with Christ share in association with them? Such represents the primary concern with the secondary goals and methodologies of ecumenism.

Ecumenical Conceptualizations of the Church

Ecumenism, by its own confession, represents a new and more sophisticated way of attempting to unify disparate parts of Christendom: previous attempts of restoring New Testament Christianity, unity movements, unitary endeavors by various denominations, etc., have been brushed aside in an attempt to foster unity through what is known as *koinonia* fellowship.[9] *Koinonia* is the Greek term for fellowship or association. Ecumenism has disavowed an "institutional merger" form of unity, which looks toward a day in which there is only one church with one structure with various congregations.[10] Since unity is not envisioned in terms of merger, it is viewed in terms of maintaining association with one another in various collaborative endeavors and dialogue.[11] It is Biblically rationalized by appealing to the example of the Jerusalem council of Acts 15, which is believed to represent this *koinonia* of disparate Christian elements.[12]

The ecumenical perspective on interdenominational relationships is entirely a novel thing, diametrically opposed to the historical perspectives of many of the denominations involved. To rationalize and justify this perspective, ecumenism posits a different understanding of the nature of the "universal church". The "universal church," or the Church of Christ according to ecumenism, represents all believers in Christ in all of these denominations, with unity in the basis of faith and baptism, even if its members disagree in the particulars of said faith and baptism.[13] In this model, the different denominations are considered synonymous with the local churches of the New Testament: Corinth, say, would be like a Pentecostal denomination, while Rome might represent Roman Catholicism, and Philippi, Lutheranism. According to this way of thinking, just as these individual local churches were parts of the greater Church, so various denominations are parts of the greater Church.[14] This view attempts to find legitimacy by appealing to the diversity of theology, practice, and church organization in the New Testament.[15] Does the ecumenical movement accurately represent the church in the New Testament?

A Study of Denominations

There is no doubt that the New Testament reveals a variety of beliefs and practices within the various churches. The greater proportion of this variety, however, was not in concordance with God's intentions for the church!

Concerning the organization of the church, we read the following in Acts 14.23 and Titus 1.5:

> And when they had appointed for them elders in every church, and had prayed with fasting, they commended them to the Lord, on whom they had believed.

> For this cause left I thee in Crete, that thou shouldest set in order the things that were wanting, and appoint elders in every city, as I gave thee charge.

Further directives regarding elders are found in 1 Timothy 3.1–8, Titus 1.6–7, and 1 Peter 5.1–4; elders are present in Jerusalem, Philippi, and Ephesus (Acts 11.30, Philippians 1.1, Acts 20.17–38). No other system of governance is divinely approved in the New Testament; the lack of mentioning of elders in other congregations is likely an indication that not enough men were qualified for the task of the eldership rather than an intentionally different system of governance.

As to instruction and truth, the following is recorded in Galatians 1.6–9 and 1 Corinthians 4.17:

> I marvel that ye are so quickly removing from him that called you in the grace of Christ unto a different gospel; which is not another gospel: only there are some that trouble you, and would pervert the gospel of Christ. But though we, or an angel from heaven, should preach unto you any gospel other than that which we preached unto you, let him be anathema. As we have said before, so say I now again, If any man preacheth unto you any gospel other than that which ye received, let him be anathema.

> For this cause have I sent unto you Timothy, who is my beloved and faithful child in the Lord, who shall put you in remembrance of my ways which be in Christ, even as I teach everywhere in every church.

These verses indicate that within the churches of the New Testament there was the expectation that the same Gospel and message would be promoted and taught in all the churches. A Christian could travel to Rome or Ephesus or Antioch and hear the same message being taught. If a different message were being taught, such was considered an *anathema*, an accursed thing! One cannot go to a Roman Catholic church, a Lutheran church, and a Presbyterian church and expect to hear the same Gospel being taught, for the different groups believe vastly different things regarding many of the matters of the faith.

Acts 15 and Romans 14 represent the cornerstones of the ecumenical position, but the texts do not reflect the current position of the ecumenical movement. Yes, Acts 15 represents a council meeting to decide in a dispute regarding circumcision, yet it was hosted by the "source congregation" of the problem, came to a consensus view based upon a mutual understanding of the prophecies of Scripture and recent events, sealed by the Holy Spirit, and was to be considered normative for all the churches. The council did not presuppose the legitimacy of both viewpoints, nor is it assumed that those of the "Judaizing" party actually represent legitimate brethren in Christ (cf. Galatians 2.4). Indeed, those promoting the "Judaizing" view are declared as *anathema* by Paul in Galatians 1.6–9!

Romans 14 represents a text attempting to resolve contention regarding matters of no consequence to God that threatened to divide the church in Rome. The expected conclusion was not that different churches should exist, but that the brethren should maintain association with one another, remain a unified church, and not place any stumbling block in the way of each other. Sacrifices were to be made to establish true, concrete unity; it is not a symbolic event that involves limited participation while the groups involved remain separate entities.

What shall we say to these things? The New Testament reveals that there is but one church (Ephesians 4.4–5) and that the living members of this church, ideally, also constitute local bodies of believers accountable to one another and who assemble to build each other up (Hebrews 10.24–25, 1 Peter 5.1–4). These believers are to be united in the same mind and judgment, believing in the same Gospel and teaching the same things in every church (1 Corinthians 4.7, Galatians 1.6–9, 1 Corinthians 1.10, 1 John 1.6–7). Deviation from this norm is not acceptable or rightly tolerated. The ecumenical perspective on the universal church is unfounded in Scripture.

"Unity-in-Diversity"

Perhaps the hallmark of the ecumenical movement is represented by the concept of "unity-in-diversity". While the ultimate goal of ecumenism is the unity of all its members in all matters of faith and doctrine, it is highly unlikely that such will be realized. Instead, a diversity of theological traditions is seen as acceptable, the various constituent members can work together despite significant disagreement in various matters of faith and practice, and toleration for what is perceived as the "diverse gifts of the Spirit" is mandated.[16] The appeal is made that this unity is possible because of agreement on the "essential" matters—the Trinitarian nature of God, the Chalcedonian understanding of Jesus, practicing many of the same practices, and the like—and that many of the matters of disagreement are "non-essential" matters that ought to be left for liberty.[17] Does this reflect the expectations of God in the New Testament?

We should note that there is an expectation of some level of diversity within the church. Racial, ethnic, cultural, and national diversity is assumed (Galatians 3.28, Colossians 3.11, Revelation 7.9). Differences among the individual members in terms of experiences and talents is also expected (1 Corinthians 12.12–28). There are indeed matters of liberty in the Scriptures, matters of "food and drink," which may allow for divergent practices in some instances (Romans 14.17).

If the matters involved with the ecumenical movement reflected matters of "food and drink," we would have no basis of disagreement with their view of "unity-in-diversity." The ecumenical view of "unity-in-diversity," by necessity, does not correlate with what is presented in Romans 14, for the matters of disagreement among the various bodies involves matters of far greater consequences than mere "food and drink." Differences among the various groups include, but are not limited to: infant baptism versus adult baptism; baptism as sprinkling, pouring, or immersion; the function of baptism; the nature of the elements of the Lord's Supper; bishopric, presbytery, or congregational church organization; the legitimacy or lack thereof of the papacy in Rome; understanding of the roles of the Scriptures and tradition; the role of Petrine authority; the status of homosexuals before God; Calvinist foreordination versus Arminian free will; etc. Who, honestly, can consider these matters of "food and drink" and not matters of "righteousness, peace, and joy in the Holy Spirit" (Romans 14.17)? When we recognize that one who taught that one should be circumcised was accursed (Galatians 1.6–9);

that one who adhered to worldly philosophy violated God's will (Colossians 2.8); and that those who presented stumbling blocks contrary to what was presented to the Christians were to be marked and avoided (Romans 16.16–17, 2 Thessalonians 3.16–17); and then we consider the grave matters of disagreement listed above, how can we say that we can maintain association despite such vast differences in belief and practice?

Such represents the heart of the matter of ecumenism: the boundaries of *koinoinia* or association. Ecumenicalists would claim that any exclusive attitudes are sinful and inherently divisive; nevertheless, what do the Scriptures indicate about the limits of association?

We read the following in 1 John 1.5–7:

> And this is the message which we have heard from him, and announce unto you, that God is light, and in him is no darkness at all. If we say that we have fellowship with him, and walk in the darkness, we lie, and do not the truth: but if we walk in the light, as he is in the light, we have fellowship one with another, and the blood of Jesus his Son cleanseth us from all sin.

We can see clearly that association is to be based in a shared walk with the Lord; one can only walk with the Lord when one does His commandments and walks in the ways that He walked (1 John 2.3–6). Those who do not walk in this way walk in darkness, and there is no ability to have association with such persons.

If God commands that those who are His obedient servants will be immersed in water for the remission of their sins (Acts 2.38, Romans 6.3–7); live by obedient faith (Romans 1.5. James 2.14–26); assemble with fellow Christians in a local congregation (Hebrews 10.24–25, Philippians 1.1); walking by the Spirit and not by the flesh (Galatians 5.17–24); and preaching the one true Gospel (Romans 1.16–17, Galatians 1.6–9); and there are persons who profess Christ but do not do some or all such things, on what basis can there be association? Are all those who profess Christ saved? Not according to Matthew 7.21–23.

The matter of proper association is a difficult matter; God is the ultimate Judge, and He is the only One who truly knows who is His (James 4.12). Nevertheless, Christians are called upon to test the spirits and judge those who are within (1 Corinthians 5, 1 John 4.1). We will be held liable for the decisions we make with our association, whether it be too broad or too restrictive. If our association is too broad, we may give the false impression of a shared walk with the Lord, and disobedience to divine commands (cf. Romans 16.16–17). If our association is too restricted, we will not be building up as we should (Hebrews 10.24–25).

While this is the case, the ecumenical compromise is not Biblically tenable. While there can be toleration of some forms of diversity, the New Testament makes it clear that the Gospel and righteousness, joy, and peace in the Holy Spirit are not up for compromise (Galatians 1.6–9, Romans 14.17). The association of Christians is expected to be meaningful, involving joint participation in matters of the faith, not symbolic gestures with separate structures remaining underneath.

The prayer of unity expressed by Jesus represents the main inspiration for ecumenism, particularly in John 17.20–21:

> "Neither for these only do I pray, but for them also that believe on me through their word; that they may all be one; even as thou, Father, art in me, and I in thee, that they also may be in us: that the world may believe that thou didst send me."

This is a wonderful passage and a message of hope. Notice the basis of the unity: Christians are to all be one, but they are to be one as the Father and the Son are One. The Father and the Son are not in disagreement about the nature of baptism or on the nature of predestination. Christian unity *must* be more than skin deep, as 1 Corinthians 1.10 and Philippians 2.1–2 indicate:

> Now I beseech you, brethren, through the name of our Lord Jesus Christ, that ye all speak the same thing, and that there be no divisions among you; but that ye be perfected together in the same mind and in the same judgment.

> If there is therefore any comfort in Christ, if any consolation of love, if any fellowship of the Spirit, if any tender mercies and compassions, fulfill ye my joy, that ye be of the same mind, having the same love, being of one accord, of one mind.

Joint participation/association is a delusion if there is no substantive agreement and unity among those who work together. We cannot find this unity in the midst of a movement attempting to reconcile denominations with centuries of traditional baggage; we can only find this unity by returning to the standard of faith and practice as embodied in the New Testament, the basis of our shared faith and judgment. Unity is a noble desire, yet the truth in Christ should never be sacrificed for the sake of superficial unity (Galatians 1.6–9, 1 Timothy 3.15)!

Notes

1: Jeffrey Gros et al, *Introduction to Ecumenism*, 12–13, 22, 135.

2: ibid., 38, 53–54, 87.

3: ibid., 23.

4: ibid., 24.

5: ibid., 237.

6: ibid., 25–26, 236.

7: ibid., 95, 138.

8: ibid., 87, 109, 136.

9: ibid., 236, 240.

10: ibid., 236.

11: ibid., 58, 240.

12: ibid., 10–11.

13: ibid., 37.

14: ibid., 10–11.

15: ibid., 120.
16: ibid., 67, 124, 244–245.

17: ibid., 97.

Fundamentalism

Overview

Fundamentalism represents a movement within evangelicalism that began in the late nineteenth and early twentieth centuries as a reaction to two forces that undermined the credibility of the Bible: the "higher criticism" of the Biblical text prevalent in liberal Protestantism and the development of evolutionary theory in science. Many evangelicals began to proclaim the need to establish and defend the fundamentals of the faith against these views.[1] Fundamentalism was equivalent to evangelicalism from the 1920s through the early 1940s, during the highest point of fundamentalism's popularity and presence.[2] Mounting secular opposition to fundamentalism led many within the movement to desire to withdraw from society; this trend led many evangelicals to separate themselves from fundamentalists.[3] Fundamentalism is marked by a passionate defense of that which is perceived to be the "fundamentals" of the faith, including the Trinity, the Incarnation and the Virgin Birth, the death, burial, and resurrection of Jesus, and the creation narrative in Genesis. Fundamentalists also hold to the view of inerrancy of the Scriptures. While many different groups of Christians and denominations agree with fundamentalists on many issues, the anti-intellectual, anti-social, and reactionary tendencies often found in fundamentalism marks it off as a specific subset of evangelicalism.[4]

Origins and History

Fundamentalism developed within evangelicalism, as noted above, as a reaction to the undermining of the credibility of the Bible by liberal Protestantism and the scientific community. The 1878 Niagara Bible Conference established a creed of beliefs akin to fundamentalist concepts; in the 1910s, volumes began to be dispersed regarding "the fundamentals," and this name would eventually attach itself to the entire movement.[5] The term (and the movement) gained great popularity in the 1920s, and at this time, evangelicalism and fundamentalism were all but synonymous.[6]

This popularity would not last long. The Scopes "monkey trial" of 1925, regarding the teaching of evolution in schools, was a Pyrrhic victory for the fundamentalists; while they won the trial, they lost credibility in the eyes of many Americans.[6] Many proponents of fundamentalism began to "circle the wagons", declare dispensational premillennialism as one of the "fundamentals" of the faith, and promote withdrawal from society at large.[7] These tendencies, along with concerns regarding anti-intellectualism and the definition of inerrancy prevalent among many fundamentalists, led to the separation of those who would be deemed "postfundamentalist evangelicals" from fundamentalist evangelicals by the 1940s.[8] From this point on, while most fundamentalists would continue to be evangelicals, not all or even a majority of evangelicals could be considered part of fundamentalism.

Fundamentalism has continued to exist as a subset of evangelicalism. The movement is still marked by a focus on what is deemed the "fundamentals", right wing politics and a "Christian nation" mentality, suspicion of all things intellectual, dispensational premillennial viewpoints, and oftentimes a reactionary zeal.

Who Are Fundamentalists?

Just as with the term "evangelical", the term "fundamentalism" is often used and misused in religious discussions today. It is important for us to understand the meanings of the term and how we shall define the term for the purposes of our study.

One definition of fundamentalism, which is quite popular in modern media today, refers to any or all groups who react to modernism in a militant way. In this light, modern Islamic *jihadists* are described as "Islamic fundamentalists", and many unhelpful comparisons are often made between such persons and Christian fundamentalism. The second definition of fundamentalism involves the conservative Protestant reaction to the rise of liberal Protestantism in the late nineteenth centuries and early twentieth centuries. A third definition, distinct from the second less by belief and more by mood, represents a narrow, more militant separatist movement within conservative evangelical Protestantism emerging in the early twentieth century, after major Protestant denominations embraced many aspects of liberal Protestant ecumenism.[9] Based on the second definition, many times "fundamentalist" also refers to any evangelical or to anyone who believes in the fundamental doctrines of the Christian faith.

We can see, therefore, that while the term "fundamentalist" can be viewed rather broadly, so as to include all "conservative" Christians, such a designation can often be misleading. For the purposes of this study, we will focus upon and use the second and third definitions of fundamentalism, speaking of the movement within evangelicalism that has existed since the beginning of the twentieth century.

Denominations Involved

Fundamentalism, especially in its modern permutation, tends to be found in individuals and in individual congregations of many denominations; there are also many independent fundamentalist churches throughout the country. Denominations that have some fundamentalist factions include Baptists, a few Wesleyan groups, and many Pentecostal churches. There may be a few fundamentalist groups in other Protestant denominations, yet their numbers would be far less.

Fundamentalism, as has been noted, is a subset of evangelicalism. Some fundamentalist trends may be found also in some community churches and house churches.

General Considerations

As with many matters involving fundamentalist groups, there is some level of disagreement about many of the matters listed below. They are provided as a general guide for understanding.

Part I
- *Lutheranism: Faith Alone; The Lord's Prayer*
- *Calvinism: TULIP*
- *Baptists: Once Saved, Always Saved*
- *Plymouth Brethren: Dispensationalism; Premillennialism*

Part III
- *Baptism: Infant Baptism and "Original Sin"; Baptism is Immersion; Baptism is for Remission of Sin and is Necessary for Salvation*
- *The Church Treasury, I: Benevolence: Church Benevolence to Non-Saints*

- *The Church Treasury, II: Other Considerations: Hospitals; Centers of Education; Kitchens/Fellowship Halls; Gymnasiums; Business Enterprises*

Concerning Observances:
- *Observances Concerning the Lord's Birth: Advent; Christmas*
- *Observances Concerning the Lord's Death: Palm Sunday; Maundy Thursday; Good Friday; Easter*

- *Creeds: The Apostles' Creed; The Nicene Creed*

- *Instrumental Music*

- *Judaic Practices: The Ten Commandments and the "Moral Law"; Tithing*

- *The Lord's Supper: The Bread and the Fruit of the Vine; When Should the Lord's Supper Be Observed? Part A: Weekly*

- *Positions of Authority: Who is the Pastor?; Ordination; Synods, Councils, Conventions, and Other Meetings*

Fundamentalism's Reactionary Tendencies

As we have seen, fundamentalism represents a reactionary movement against liberal tendencies in Protestantism. While there is much that is agreeable in an emphasis on the fundamentals of the faith, there is always a concern of going too far when a group is reacting to events in other groups. The majority of concerns that exist regarding fundamentalism, in fact, revolve around some overreactions that have plagued the movement.

One such overreaction has been noted previously: as the fundamentalist movement developed, dispensational premillennialism was added to the list of "fundamental" doctrines. Any "list" or creedal statement is automatically suspicious, as is made clear in **Creeds**. Nevertheless, as is evident from **Plymouth Brethren: Premillennialism**, not only is dispensational premillennialism not a "fundamental" aspect of the faith, but it also represents a false belief system that is not consistent with a holistic understanding of Biblical eschatology. Enshrining dispensational premillennialism as a "fundamental" of the faith demonstrates an instance when a tradition of man is elevated to an improper level.

Another instance of this type of overreaction is seen in the belief system of many fundamentalists regarding women and clothing. Based upon the

Old Testament prohibition of men wearing women's clothing and vice versa in Deuteronomy 22.5, many fundamentalists believe it sinful for a woman to wear pants. Surely it is not sinful for a woman to avoid wearing pants if she is concerned about seeming to look like a man; on the other hand, having such a view and binding it represents an instance where a cultural tradition of a certain time is enshrined as a doctrine of God without any Biblical basis. Sixteenth-century men's clothing looks feminine or effeminate today; similarly, neither men nor women wore pants *per se* in the time of Paul. Regardless, such is an Old Testament proscription; while one may want to avoid cross-dressing on the basis of Romans 1.26–27 and 1 Corinthians 6.9–10, we cannot establish anything as binding today on Christians because it was established in Deuteronomy (Ephesians 2.11–18, Colossians 2.14–17). If it is culturally acceptable for women to wear pants and there is no perception that by doing so they look like men, it is inappropriate for us to instead bind a tradition of fifty to a hundred years ago against such a view.

Not all fundamentalists practice such things, but most who do could be classified as fundamentalists. Such views and doctrines demonstrate the stumbling block inherent in reactionary movements: they oftentimes go beyond what is written in the other direction (cf. 2 John 1.9). Such is a trap which ought to be avoided!

KJV Onlyism

Another manifestation of this reactionary tendency within fundamentalism is seen within the King James Version (KJV) Onlyism. While not all fundamentalists are KJV onlyists, most KJV onlyists are fundamentalists. KJV onlyism represents a spectrum of views favoring the King James Version over any and all other versions. In the "mildest" cases, a person simply prefers the KJV over other versions. Others believe that the *Textus Receptus* (TR), the Greek text upon which the KJV was translated, was in fact inspired by God; some go so far as to say that the KJV itself is the inspired word of God, and any alterations to the KJV are reckoned as anathema.

Such a view has been promoted for as long as fundamentalism has existed, ever since Westcott and Hort came out with a Greek text based upon the more ancient manuscripts of the New Testament in the nineteenth century. These manuscripts—the basis of the modern translations and versions—differed from the TR in many ways. Since Westcott and Hort were both scholars associated with liberal Protestantism, fundamentalists were automatically suspicious of their activities. Many fundamentalists made no distinction between "higher" and "lower" forms of textual criticism and considered the endeavor to present the Biblical text as represented by the oldest and most superior witnesses as equivalent to the literary criticism that was undermining faith in the Biblical text. Some began to defend the KJV and its text base, the TR, strongly against the American Standard Version (ASV) and later versions based on these older manuscripts.

KJV onlyists will often point to various New Testament passages as rendered in the KJV versus modern versions, note various contrasts, and then charge the translators of the modern versions with either denigrating Jesus' divinity, denying His substitutionary atonement, or some other doctrine. They will claim that the name of God is removed thousands of times from the Bible. Many other serious claims will be made in an attempt to demonstrate the legitimacy of the King James Version over the more modern versions.

The underlying difficulty with all of the arguments made by KJV onlyists is that they use the KJV or the TR as the standard of judgment. If the KJV or the TR represent the standard by which all other versions are judged, then certainly they will all fall short. Should the KJV or the TR be considered the standard?

Desiderius Erasmus, the editor of the *Textus Receptus*, did not consider either himself or his text as inspired. The members of the translation committee of the King James Version did not claim that they or their translation were inspired. In fact, both Erasmus and the translators of the KJV used many of the same textual critical and translational methods as modern scholars. Furthermore, the King James Version was "authorized" not by God but by the King of England!

What, then, should be the standard? In 2 Timothy 3.15–17, Paul establishes that all Scripture is inspired; Peter speaks of men who spoke as they were moved by the Holy Spirit in 2 Peter 1.21. We have no doubt, based upon these passages, that the original texts of the New Testament were inspired; there is no indication that any later changes or errors that crept in during the transmission process are also "inspired". The KJV and the TR, or the modern versions or the present Greek texts of the New Testament, do not represent the standard of judgment: the original texts ought to represent the standard of judgment!

Unfortunately, we do not have possession of the original texts of the New Testament. That is why textual critics seek to use the oldest and most superior manuscripts—they attempt to return to be as close to the original texts as we can be allowed.

In this way, the majority of the arguments made by KJV onlyists are untenable: modern functional equivalence translations do not "change" the Bible inasmuch as get us closer to the original text. If anything, the KJV represents the text with the most "changes" of the Bible!

Likewise, the charge that modern versions attempt to subvert various doctrines is simply untenable. All modern versions, in appropriate passages, affirm the Deity of Christ, the substitutionary atonement of Christ, and all other appropriate truths of the Gospel. Just because certain other verses read differently does not mean that their translators are denying core doctrines!

It is a task suited for its own book to systematically analyze all of the arguments of KJV onlyism; it is sufficient for our purposes to demonstrate how KJV onlyism represents another reactionary tendency in the fundamentalist movement. In part, KJV onlyism represents the suspicion of any intellectual endeavor: textual criticism is guilty by association with literary criticism, even though the two do not always meet. KJV onlyism also represents enshrining a given later tradition—in this context, a seventeenth century English translation of the Bible—as itself a fundamental, even though there is no Biblical basis for such a view. Finally, KJV onlyism represents the attempt to resolve a theological conundrum regardless of what reality may dictate: many fundamentalists do not want to imagine that the Word of God was altered or changed even to the smallest jot or tittle, and therefore it is easier to consider the KJV inspired than to believe that errors crept into the text, and that textual criticism is necessary to provide a text closely related to the original New Testament.

There are many times when there is good reason to disagree with a given textual critical decision, or to favor one way of translating a given passage over another. Such represents the natural discussion that takes place within the textual critical and translational communities, which ought to involve normal Christians whenever possible. Such discussions, however, provide no justification of elevating one translation as the "inspired Word of God" above any other translation. Translations are the work of men; while they are quite accurate these days, they all have their strengths and weaknesses. Any Bible translation can lead a person to enough understanding of the faith so as to be saved; there are enough tools available to assist any Christian who seeks to grow in his or her faith to understand any difficulties that are present within the Bible.

There is no difficulty in someone preferring the KJV as his or her translation of choice. On the other hand, it is also important to not bear false witness toward God in claiming that He inspired something that He did not inspire, and to elevate a given translation or version as authoritative when God has not given us any ground upon which to do so. It is important to avoid overreacting and "going beyond Jerusalem," so to speak, and ending up in another kind of error (cf. 2 John 1.9–10)!

Notes

1: Roger Olson, *Pocket History of Evangelical Theology*, 85–88.

2: ibid.

3: ibid., 88–90

4: ibid., 100–101

5: ibid., 85

6: ibid., 86

7: ibid., 88

8: ibid., 90

9: For all these definitions, cf. ibid., 83–84

Community Church Movement

Overview

The Community Church Movement originates in the early twentieth century as a highly evangelical attempt at realizing practical ecumenism: groups of Christians who leave denominationalism and engage in non-denominational Christianity. The movement attempts to support community churches in many locations. Community churches are difficult to characterize, since each congregation represents a different dynamic and perhaps different doctrinal emphases. Regardless, while community churches are "nondenominational," the doctrines espoused tend to be consistent with conflated denominational teachings.

Origins and History

The earliest origins of the community church movement are likely from the nineteenth century and the practical concerns of many small American communities: there were not enough members of individual denominations to each have a congregation, and many times such Protestants would come together to establish a community church of sorts.

The community church movement began in the early twentieth century alongside ecumenism and represented an attempt to aspire to the ideal of that movement: Christians, mostly Protestant and Evangelical, coming out of denominations and being unified in a community church concept.

Community churches are now quite popular, and they exist in almost every community in America.

Denominations Involved

Since the community church movement is, generically, a marriage of evangelicalism and ecumenism, community churches strive to be either nondenominational or even postdenominational. Regardless, most of its members come either from the world or the "evangelical" denominations, and doctrine follows accordingly.

There is a body, the *International Council of Community Churches*, which represents an organization of various community churches, but by no means is every community church affiliated with that council.

General Considerations

Since community churches are extremely diverse, it is impossible to make entirely accurate characterizations of any individual congregation. The list below represents a likely range of doctrines consistent with community churches.

Part I

- *Lutheranism: Faith Alone; The Lord's Prayer*
- *Calvinism: TULIP*
- *Baptists: Once Saved, Always Saved*
- *Wesleyanism: The Church and Social Responsibility*
- *Plymouth Brethren: Dispensationalism; Premillennialism*

Part II

- *Evangelicalism*
- *Ecumenism*
- *Fundamentalism*
- *Emergism*

Part III

- *Baptism: Infant Baptism and "Original Sin"; Baptism is Immersion; Baptism is for*
- *Remission of Sin and is Necessary for Salvation*
- *The Church Treasury, I: Benevolence: Church Benevolence to Non-Saints; The Missionary Society*
- *The Church Treasury, II: Other Considerations: Hospitals; Centers of Education; Kitchens/Fellowship Halls; Gymnasiums; Business Enterprises*

Concerning Observances:

- *Observances Concerning the Lord's Birth: Advent; Christmas*

- *Observances Concerning the Lord's Death: Palm Sunday; Maundy Thursday; Good Friday; Easter*

- *Creeds: The Apostles' Creed; The Nicene Creed*

- *Instrumental Music*

- *Judaic Practices: The Ten Commandments and the "Moral Law"; Tithing*

- *The Lord's Supper: The Bread and the Fruit of the Vine; When Should the Lord's Supper*

- *Be Observed? Part A: Weekly*

- *Positions of Authority: Who is the Pastor?; Female Deacons [Deaconesses]; Female Evangelists; Ordination; Synods, Councils, Conventions, and Other Meetings*

House Church Movement

Overview

Christians have assembled in houses since the beginning of Christianity; the house church movement began in the 1960s as an attempt at reformation of the structure of "church" as it was commonly practiced in almost all of the denominations of the day. Its followers attempt to return to New Testament norms and believe that house churches represent a superior way to achieve the goals of the church according to the New Testament. Groups within the house church movement are noted for networking, various doctrinal stands, a charismatic influence, and multiple models and patterns of their own particular house church practices. While there is no inherent Biblical difficulty with meeting in homes, the theology of the house church movement, along with their understanding of the church, assemblies, and the Lord's Supper, marks it off as its own movement worthy of consideration.

Origins and History

As has been said above, Christians have met in houses throughout time; many groups did so during times of persecution or where it was not practical to use another facility. As will be seen, throughout the majority of this time, there was no house church theology *per se*: Christians simply met in homes when such was necessary or desirable, but did not attach much significance to it.

Beginning in the 1960s, and especially in the 1970s, a concerted movement began, especially among evangelicals, to return to the structure of New Testament churches and thus established house churches.[1] Such, in many ways, was a reaction to perceived failures and abuses within the "institutional" church organization. House church movement participants began establishing a theology of the house church, combining certain scholastic interpretations of history with aspects of New Testament belief and practice, and this endeavor continues to this day. The movement remains small but is growing throughout the country and the world.

Denominations Involved

Many house churches exist outside of any specific denominational structure; they represent nondenominational groups having association with one another. All kinds of models for house churches exist.

There are many movements within various denominations that are somewhat similar to the house church movement, especially the "cell church movement" present within many denominations. Small group tendencies within denominations are also similar to the house church concept, but do not go to the same lengths, nor represent singular cohesive units as do house churches.

Furthermore, house churches can be found within almost every denomination and/or movement; many Anabaptist and Pietist groups are known for having many house churches.

Many of those in the house church movement would consider themselves evangelicals; house churches often manifest ecumenical tendencies in their associations and networks.

General Considerations

Since house churches are extremely diverse, it is impossible to make entirely accurate characterizations of any individual congregation. The list below represents a likely range of doctrines consistent with many in house churches.

Part I

- *Lutheranism: Faith Alone; The Lord's Prayer*
- *Calvinism: TULIP*
- *Pietism: Foot Washing; Love Feast; The Holy Kiss*
- *Baptists: Once Saved, Always Saved*
- *Wesleyanism: The Church and Social Responsibility*
- *Plymouth Brethren: Dispensationalism; Premillennialism*
- *The Charismatic Movement*

Part II
- *Evangelicalism*
- *Ecumenism*

Part III
- *Baptism: Infant Baptism and "Original Sin"; Baptism is Immersion; Baptism is for Remission of Sin and is Necessary for Salvation*
- *The Church Treasury, I: Benevolence: Church Benevolence to Non-Saints; The Missionary Society*
- *The Church Treasury, II: Other Considerations: Kitchens/Fellowship Halls; Business Enterprises*

Concerning Observances:
- *Observances Concerning the Lord's Birth: Advent; Christmas*
- *Observances Concerning the Lord's Death: Palm Sunday; Maundy Thursday; Good Friday; Easter*
- *Creeds: The Apostles' Creed; The Nicene Creed*
- *Instrumental Music*
- *Judaic Practices: The Ten Commandments and the "Moral Law"; Tithing*
- *The Lord's Supper: The Bread and the Fruit of the Vine; When Should the Lord's Supper Be Observed? Part A: Weekly*
- *Positions of Authority: Who is the Pastor?; A Hierarchy of Bishops [singular elder over house church in some models]; Female Deacons [Deaconesses]; Female Evangelists; Ordination; Synods, Councils, Conventions, and Other Meetings*

House Churches or Churches Assembling in Houses?

As we begin, it is important that we establish that early Christians in the New Testament did indeed assemble in houses, and that there is nothing wrong *per se* with Christians assembling in a house. The house church movement came quite a bit later than the New Testament and has developed a "theology of the house church": it is now posited that the house church represents the fundamental building block to corporate Christian life and is superior to churches meeting in buildings in almost every way.[2] Many in the house church movement, therefore, believe that early Christians deliberately chose to meet in houses and that God expects house churches to remain normative. This belief is justified by appealing to the family imagery used in relation the church in passages such as Matthew 12.46–50 and the idea that the house church is the base unit in passages like 1 Corinthians 11.18, 33.[3] Do the Scriptures teach that house churches were established, or did churches simply assemble in houses?

As we have said, Christians met in houses, but the New Testament betrays no indication that the presence of the church in a house was considered important or critical. Christians also assembled in the Temple/Solomon's Portico (Acts 2.46, 5.12; house church movement perspectives on these assemblies will be spoken of below) and in schools (Acts 19.9). Such locations are mentioned quite simply; to believe that the early Christians placed great value in meeting in houses *per se* goes beyond the evidence provided by the New Testament.

This is clearly seen in the argumentation (or lack thereof) regarding this principle. Indeed, Jesus uses the imagery of church as family in Matthew 12.46–50, among other places; yet there is also imagery of church as Israel (Galatians 6.16), church as body (1 Corinthians 12.12–28), church as wife (Ephesians 5.22–33), etc. While it is true that families live in houses, a house does not inherently define a family. No application is made of the image of church as family to the idea of the "house church". Likewise, we can read the following in 1 Corinthians 11.18 (v. 33 will be spoken of below with the Lord's Supper):

> For first of all, when ye come together in the church, I hear that divisions exist among you; and I partly believe it.

Paul here indicates the quality of assembling—"come together in the church". While it is most likely true that the Corinthians met in a house, specifically the house of Gaius (Romans 16.23), there is no mention of this here. All that is important is that the church "comes together"; extrapolating that the location of the coming together is significant reads too much into the text.

We can clearly see, therefore, that the assumption that the "house church" was God's deliberate intention for the church comes without Biblical merit. Based upon the New Testament evidence, all that can be firmly established is that most often, early Christians assembled in houses.

House Churches and the Nature of the Church

Many in the house church movement also posit a different perspective regarding the nature of the local church in the New Testament. In this view, house churches of between 12–20 (the size based upon the assumption of what an average Roman house could fit) would assemble frequently; there would be many such house churches in a given city or region. These house churches would occasionally come together for a "celebration" as what is often called a home church-based congregation.[4] According to this view, when Paul writes to the church in, say, Rome, he is writing to the "home church-based congregation" of the city or the network of house churches in Rome. This view is justified by interpretation of historical data, along with Romans 16.15, 1 Corinthians 16.19, Colossians 4.15, and Philemon 1.1–2; Acts 2.42–47 is the quintessential example of the "house church" and the "celebration" of the "home church-based congregation."[5] Let us consider the matter.

If the Scriptures ever indicated that there was more than one "house church" per city, then the argument would be valid. The difficulty is that the Scriptures indicate no such thing; when Paul speaks of "the church in x house" in Romans 16.15, 1 Corinthians 16.19, Colossians 4.5, and Philemon 1.1–2, such seems to represent the only "house church" in the city. Romans 16.23 speaks of this clearly:

> Gaius my host, and of the whole church, saluteth you. Erastus the treasurer of the city saluteth you, and Quartus the brother.

Here Gaius is called the "host of the whole church". House church movement advocates may attempt to say that such represents the "celebration" of the "home church based congregation", but such an entity must be first proved to actually exist before it can be considered evidence. What is stopping Gaius from continually being the host of the whole church?

In the rest of the passages, an interesting trend exists. In Romans 16, the brethren are to salute the church that is in the house of Aquila and Priscilla (Romans 16.4–5), yet the "households" of Aristobulus and Narcissus are to be greeted (Romans 16.10–11). Why are they not listed as having "churches" in their houses? It may be argued that it is odd for Paul to tell the church in Rome to greet the "church in the house" of Aquila and Priscilla if they all represent that church. Is it not just as odd, however, if the "church in the house" of Aquila and Priscilla represents a constituent part of the church in Rome and no other such "church" is mentioned?

1 Corinthians 16.19 is also instructive in this regard:

> The churches of Asia salute you. Aquila and Prisca salute you much in the Lord, with the church that is in their house.

When Paul speaks of the "churches in Asia", would anyone think that he refers to individual house churches or the collective churches in the various cities in Asia (cf. Revelation 2–3)? Why would he speak of the "home church-based congregation" and then turn around and speak of the "church" in the house of Aquila and Prisca, a house church, using the same terminology? Such is entirely inconsistent with the evidence.

The whole basis of this delineation derives from Acts 2, which is considered the normative pattern for the church by many adherents to the house church movement.

> And they continued stedfastly in the apostles' teaching and fellowship, in the breaking of bread and the prayers. And fear came upon every soul: and many wonders and signs were done by the apostles. And all that believed were together, and had all things common; and they sold their possessions and goods, and parted them to all, according as any man had need. And day by day, continuing stedfastly with one accord in the temple, and breaking bread at home, they did take their food with gladness and singleness of heart, praising God, and having favour with all the people. And the Lord added to them day by day those that were being saved.

Many things are immediately apparent in this passage: no collective is called "the church" in this passage, and the breaking of bread was done "at home", not indicating the pluralities assumed by house church movement advocates. This interpretation is based on assumptions about Roman houses and the inference that the Christians in Jerusalem met in multiple homes and then came together in the Temple as one. Even if it were true that they met to eat meals in various houses, such is not called "the church" or even an "assembly". Their assemblies, in reality, took place in the Temple, as established in Acts 2.46, with the events of Acts 2.42 dictating much of what was done in those assemblies. There is no indication that the Christians in Jerusalem perceived themselves as being part of "house churches" at home and then part of a "home church-based congregation" when meeting in the Temple.

The belief that Acts 2–7 is considered normative for Christians also should be challenged. Selling of all possessions, the unity of the accord of the brethren, and their level of togetherness (Acts 2.42–47, 4.32) are not seen in any other church. Paul must tell Timothy to counsel the rich among the brethren regarding how they should conduct themselves (1 Timothy 6.17–19); James and John both speak regarding Christians who do not help their own in need (James 2.1–9, 1 John 3.17). Christians assembled on the first day of the week (Acts 20.7, 1 Corinthians 16.1–3); there is no indication of daily assemblies as in the early church in Jerusalem. When we see these contrasts and examine the context, we can see that the early church in Jerusalem did extraordinary things on account of extraordinary circumstances: many from all over the world had been converted and needed support, and the foundation of the church led to great zeal and determination to follow in the footsteps of the Christ. The fact that the example of Jerusalem is not enjoined on later churches—weekly assemblies are not condemned for being too infrequent, James and John do not indicate that selling all one has is normative—indicates that the situation is not expected to represent the norm. Christians should be willing to do everything that the early Christians in Jerusalem did if circumstances demand it. When circumstance provides no such demand, there is more liberty. There is no basis, in the New Testament, to consider the situation of the early church in Jerusalem as being the norm.

When Paul writes to various churches, and later Jesus through John in the Revelation, the authors do not betray the idea that the local church represents multiple house churches as a home church-based congregation. In all circumstances, the authors speak of a coherent church: they address the strengths and weaknesses of the brethren, even speaking of different factions within a given church. Are we to believe that in a given city, each individual house church had the same strengths and weaknesses as its fellow house churches? No two New Testament city churches are the same—how then are we expected to believe that Paul, John, and others can write to multiple individual house churches in such a way that we only see a coherent unity within the church of that city, whether for good or ill? That is indeed too much to swallow! The New Testament makes it clear that there was normally one church per city and that when Paul wrote to Rome or John to Ephesus, they were writing to one coherent body that very well might have met in the house of one of the brethren. The house church movement view of the churches of the New Testament is without Biblical foundation.

Many in the house church movement, in various ways, overemphasize the role of the church and particularly that of the local church. Some go so far as to say that Paul only speaks of local churches in the New Testament.[6] Others have such an exalted view of the local church that the individual has no room for existence: the focus is not to be on Christian growth as much as multiplication of churches, mission is seen as the church sending itself out in a multipliable unit, the church is the good news (the Gospel), and the church must be part of everyday life.[7] Do the Scriptures support these assertions?

While Paul often speaks of churches in a local sense, there are other times where such an identification is not so simple. Paul speaks of "the church" in Ephesians 5.22–32, going so far as to call "the church" the "body" of Christ (Ephesians 5.29–30). A chapter before, in Ephesians 4.4–5, the same author confidently establishes that there is "one body". It is manifest that there are many local churches and yet the "body" under discussion is clearly singular. Paul does not speak only of the local church; he also has the "universal church" in view in many passages.

As can be seen in detail in **The Church Treasury, I: Benevolence: The Individual and the Church**, 1 Timothy 5.16 indicates that there are responsibilities that individuals should bear so that the church would not be burdened. This principle illustrates the reality that while the church consists of its constituent individuals, each individual is more than the church. Christians went out and promoted the Gospel (Acts 8, 13.1–3), and the Gospel was always the "good news" about Jesus Christ and His redemptive work for man, not the church *per se* (Romans 1.16, 2.16, 1 Corinthians 1.17). The individual Christian, not the church, represents the basic unit of Christianity (e.g. James 1.27). A strong emphasis on the collective to the exclusion of the individual is not Biblically justifiable.

Since the house church movement is a reaction to the perceived failings of "institutional" churches, it should not be surprising to find some elements in the movement going beyond the Scriptures in their opposition to those failings. Many house church movement advocates will present a dichotomy between "church as life" and "church as meeting," contrasting "family fellowship" with "impersonal structures."[8] Is this a legitimate dichotomy?

There is no doubt that institutional structures have often hindered family-type fellowship which ought to exist among brethren. On the other hand, we must remember that the Greek word translated as church is *ekklesia*, which has a base meaning of "assembly". The "assembly" could be as disorganized as a mob or as organized as a legislative body (Acts 19.32, 39), but they are all marked by a group of people "coming together" or "assembling". If we speak of "assemblies" and not "churches," the ludicrousness of the statement is clear: "the assembly is not a series of assemblies". Yes, the members of the church should interact with one another, both inside and outside of the assemblies (cf. Acts 2.42, 1 Peter 4.9). There is no Biblical justification, however, for the dichotomy. Christianity can be a way of life that involves assemblies with other Christians. Christians can share in family-type fellowship and assemble in buildings with a structured service. Responding to excess with excess is not finding the truth!

House Churches and the Lord's Supper

The hallmark of many house churches within the house church movement is the focus upon what is called the Lord's Supper. Many believe that the Lord's Supper was originally a meal; many, in fact, do not see the Lord's Supper as a separate ritual, but "an ordinary meal with extraordinary significance." They justify this with Acts 2.46 and 1 Corinthians 11.33.[9] This has led many to abandon bread and fruit of the vine entirely, considering whatever is eaten during the meal to be the "Lord's Supper".[10] This represents a focus entirely on the "communion" aspect of the Lord's Supper. Is this the way that the Lord's Supper is presented in the Scriptures?

We have already examined the concept of the *agape*, or "love feast," in **Pietism: Love Feast**. There we saw that the church in Corinth was not approved in how they partook of the Lord's Supper; with 1 Corinthians 11.33 should also be quoted verse 34:

> Wherefore, my brethren, when ye come together to eat, wait one
> for another. If any man is hungry, let him eat at home; that your

coming together be not unto judgment. And the rest will I set in order whensoever I come.

This is no mere condemnation of "excess"; if any is "hungry," they should eat at home. If the Lord's Supper in the assemblies of the saints was supposed to represent a full meal, why would anyone need to "eat at home" if they were "hungry"? Would they not eat fully at the meal?

The Lord's Supper was never designed to be a full meal to satisfy the physical appetite, but a ritual meal shared together to remember the Lord. This is first seen in its inauguration in Luke 22.19–20:

> And he took bread, and when he had given thanks, he brake it,
> and gave to them, saying,
> "This is my body which is given for you: this do in remembrance of me."
> And the cup in like manner after supper, saying,
> "This cup is the new covenant in my blood, even that which is
> poured out for you."

Notice that Jesus takes the cup "after supper". The Lord's Supper was inaugurated in the context of the Passover meal (Luke 22.15), yet it was not the Passover meal. It was a ritual act done after the actual meal was eaten, and it was designed to have significance.

The emblems are also of great import. Even if the identification is symbolic, Jesus still identifies the bread as His body and the fruit of the vine as His blood (Luke 22.19–20). The association makes sense: one could perceive bread like a body, and fruit of the vine like blood. That association is important in terms of remembering the death of our Lord, important enough that Paul reiterates its inauguration in 1 Corinthians 11.23–25, concluding with 1 Corinthians 11.26:

> For as often as ye eat this bread, and drink the cup, ye proclaim
> the Lord's death till he come.

If Christians do not eat "this bread", and do not drink "the cup", do they still proclaim the Lord's death?

There is certainly the aspect of communion within the Lord's Supper: it is to be shared together (1 Corinthians 10.16–17). "Communion," however, is not the only aspect involved in the Lord's Supper. Paul has provided an explicit tradition that he enjoins upon the Corinthians, and we by all means should observe it likewise. The Lord's Supper represents a ritual meal designed to bring Christians together in a memorial of the sacrifice which reconciled them to God and the resurrection which gives us hope, and it should not be confused with a common meal.

The "Apostolic-Prophetic" House Church Model

Different house churches and house church networks maintain varying structures of leadership. One model of the house church promotes a "fivefold ministry" concept based on Ephesians 4.11–13, with apostles, prophets, evangelists, pastors, and teachers working with house church networks.[11] The "apostles" and "prophets" are recognized as leaders, moved by God to establish vision and purpose, seeking others to train to be "apostles" and "prophets". The presence of apostles today is justified by Ephesians 2.20 and Revelation 2.2.[12] Do the Scriptures teach a continuing line of apostles and prophets within the church?

Such a view has many affinities with Pentecostal doctrines and represents another manifestation of the charismatic movement within the house church movement. Many of the comments made previously are relevant here. Regardless, let us examine the nature of the apostles and prophets further.

Ephesians 2.20 and Revelation 2.2 read as follows:

> Being built upon the foundation of the apostles and prophets, Christ Jesus himself being the chief corner stone.

> I know thy works, and thy toil and patience, and that thou canst not bear evil men, and didst try them which call themselves apostles, and they are not, and didst find them false.

Do these passages indicate that there are more apostles and prophets than present in the first century? Do false apostles in the 90s mean that more true apostles than John were around, too? What do the Scriptures teach about the apostles?

We must first recognize that there are two uses of the word "apostle". The word means, quite simply, "one sent out". Therefore, anyone "sent out" is an "apostle". The word has a distinctive meaning, however, in terms of the Twelve and Paul, as seen in Acts 1.20–22 and 1 Corinthians 15.3–9:

> For it is written in the book of Psalms,
> "Let his habitation be made desolate, And let no man dwell therein:"
> and,
> "His office let another take."
> Of the men therefore which have companied with us all the time
> that the Lord Jesus went in and went out among us, beginning from
> the baptism of John, unto the day that he was received up from us, of
> these must one become a witness with us of his resurrection.

> For I delivered unto you first of all that which also I received, how
> that Christ died for our sins according to the scriptures; and that
> he was buried; and that he hath been raised on the third day ac-
> cording to the scriptures; and that he appeared to Cephas; then
> to the twelve; then he appeared to above five hundred brethren
> at once, of whom the greater part remain until now, but some are
> fallen asleep; then he appeared to James; then to all the apostles;
> and last of all, as unto one born out of due time, he appeared to
> me also. For I am the least of the apostles, that am not meet to be
> called an apostle, because I persecuted the church of God.

One was not automatically made an apostle because of one's faith or
training; the Twelve and Paul were especially chosen by God, saw the
risen Christ, and met certain standards. These standards are impossible to achieve after the first century. This, along with the lack of any
evidence of succession of apostles or prophets (along with the confession that the apostolic ministry needs "restoration"[13]), provides ample
evidence to see that the apostolic office was held by a few select men in
the first century to meet a specific purpose of God (cf. Matthew 18.18).
Their office was not to be taken over by any other.

Ephesians 2.20 is still true: for a church to represent a New Testament
church, it must be built upon the foundation of the apostles and prophets.
We all have that foundation from the writings of the Scripture, whereby
we may have confidence that the apostolic doctrine is still able to be taught
from its pages (Acts 2.42, 2 Timothy 3.16–17). We can see, therefore, that
it is sufficient to trust in the apostles and prophets of the New Testament
era, and that we must continue to devote ourselves to their doctrines.

Notes

1: Wolfgang Simson, *Houses That Change the World*, 72

2: Robert and Julia Banks, *The Church Comes Home*, 96

3: ibid., 26, 30

4: Simson, xvii, 37–38; Banks, 29

5: Simson, xvii; Banks, 28

6: Banks, 28

7: Simson, 16, 31, 43

8: ibid., xv, 28

9: Banks, 46

10: ibid., 51, 166

11: Simson, 110–124

12: ibid., 119

13: ibid., 117

Megachurch Movement

Overview

By definition, megachurches have always existed; the church in Jerusalem represents the first "megachurch" (Acts 2.42–47). Nevertheless, a few particular brands of megachurches began to develop in the middle of the twentieth century as modern Americans became used to large structures and large crowds in other venues; such a trend is now recognized as the megachurch movement. Megachurches are defined by their oversized organizational structures that developed to meet the needs of their vast numbers of members, focus on small groups, use of contemporary imagery and technology, and the innovative individuals who begin and promote such organizations.

Origins and History

While, by definition, many individual congregations have been "megachurches," the megachurch movement proper has its precedents in many of the large Protestant congregations of the nineteenth and early twentieth centuries.[1] Beginning in the 1950s, and especially toward the end of the twentieth century, as Americans became used to large venues and institutions, extremely large congregations became appealing to many. Some churches, based upon charismatic leadership, location, and other factors, started to grow exponentially, and felt compelled to develop new structures and organization styles to meet the needs of their congregations. It is the organizational structures necessary, more than anything, that provide coherence to the megachurch movement.[2] The movement is growing, and congregations worldwide continue to grow to the "megachurch" level.

What is a Megachurch?

Confusion often exists in understanding precisely what a megachurch is. Strictly speaking, a megachurch is any single Protestant congregation averaging over 2,000 people attending weekly services.[3] By necessity, such groups exhibit a high level of structure, with nothing being left to chance; indeed, they are probably over-structured.

This represents a very broad definition that can include many different types of churches. Four distinct types of megachurches exist today: old-line or program-based, represented by some traditional Protestant denominational congregations that exceed 2,000; "seeker" churches, megachurches focusing on "seeker services" and bringing in the "unchurched"; charismatic, pastor-focused churches, having been built up largely on the charisma of the founding pastor; and new-wave or re-envisioned megachurches, an emergent set of megachurches attempting to reach a younger demographic.[4] These four approaches lead to much variety among megachurches; nevertheless, we will focus primarily on the second and third varieties, since they represent the commonly understood paradigms for the "megachurch movement".

Denominations Involved

Many Protestant denominations are able to number megachurches in their ranks, including Baptists, Methodists, and some Pentecostal groups. Some Roman Catholic parishes number in excess of 2,000, but are normally not considered part of the "megachurch movement".

Most megachurches are within the main evangelical stream. Many megachurches not affiliated with denominations are part of the community church movement. As noted above, at least one stream of megachurches is part of the emergent movement.

General Considerations

Megachurches reflect the same variety seen consistently in movements. The list below represents many features consistent with most megachurches.

Part I
- *Lutheranism: Faith Alone; The Lord's Prayer*
- *Baptists: Once Saved, Always Saved*
- *Wesleyanism: The Church and Social Responsibility*
- *Plymouth Brethren: Dispensationalism; Premillennialism*
- *The Charismatic Movement*

Part II

- *Evangelicalism*
- *Community Church Movement*
- *Emergism*

Part III

- *Baptism: Infant Baptism and "Original Sin"; Baptism is Immersion; Baptism is for Remission of Sin and is Necessary for Salvation*
- *The Church Treasury, I: Benevolence: Church Benevolence to Non-Saints; The Missionary Society*
- *The Church Treasury, II: Other Considerations: Hospitals; Centers of Education; Kitchens/Fellowship Halls; Gymnasiums; Business Enterprises*

Concerning Observances:

- *Observances Concerning the Lord's Birth: Advent; Christmas*
- *Observances Concerning the Lord's Death: Palm Sunday; Maundy Thursday; Good Friday; Easter*
- *Creeds: The Apostles' Creed; The Nicene Creed*
- *Instrumental Music*
- *Judaic Practices: The Ten Commandments and the "Moral Law"; Tithing*
- *The Lord's Supper: The Bread and the Fruit of the Vine; When Should the Lord's Supper Be Observed? Part A: Weekly*
- *Positions of Authority: Who is the Pastor?; A Hierarchy of Bishops; Female Deacons [Deaconesses]; Female Elders; Female Evangelists; Ordination; Synods, Councils, Conventions, and Other Meetings*

"Seeker Friendly" Assemblies

One innovation developed among many megachurches, especially of the "seeker" strain, involves the concept of the "seeker friendly" assembly. In their attempt to reach the "unchurched" among them, such groups design Sunday assemblies entirely around this group, intentionally directing all programming, messages, and focus upon the unbeliever.[5] Separate assemblies, usually in the middle of the week, focus on the members and their development, including observing the Lord's Supper.[6] Is this consistent with the New Testament?

While there is certainly value in attempting to promote Christianity among unbelievers, and there may be appropriate times set aside to promote the faith among such persons, the Scriptures indicate a quite different story for the regular assemblies of the churches of the New Testament, especially the assemblies on the Lord's Day. In Acts 20.7, we see that the disciples met that day to "break bread"; 1 Corinthians 16.1–3 indicates that such was also the day for the collection. Paul provides a glimpse into such assemblies in 1 Corinthians 14; we will focus upon 1 Corinthians 14.22–26:

> Wherefore tongues are for a sign, not to them that believe, but to the unbelieving: but prophesying is for a sign, not to the unbelieving, but to them that believe. If therefore the whole church be assembled together, and all speak with tongues, and there come in men unlearned or unbelieving, will they not say that ye are mad? But if all prophesy, and there come in one unbelieving or unlearned, he is reproved by all, he is judged by all; the secrets of his heart are made manifest; and so he will fall down on his face and worship God, declaring that God is among you indeed. What is it then, brethren? When ye come together, each one hath a psalm, hath a teaching, hath a revelation, hath a tongue, hath an interpretation. Let all things be done unto edifying.

Paul speaks about the "unlearned" or "unbeliever" who happens to be in the assembly in verses 24–25, but such persons are by no means the focus; the focus, as indicated in verse 26, is the edifying of the brethren, consonant with Hebrews 10.24–25:

> And let us consider one another to provoke unto love and good works; not forsaking the assembling of ourselves together, as the custom of some is, but exhorting one another; and so much the more, as ye see the day drawing nigh.

The assemblies of the saints in the New Testament, especially on the first day of the week, were designed for the edification of the saints. The concept of the "seeker-friendly service" as envisioned in many megachurches and others who adhere to the philosophy is rather backwards: let the Lord's Day be spent on the Lord's Supper and the edification of brethren

(1 Corinthians 11, 14), and use other opportunities to preach the Gospel to the unbelievers!

Multi-site Congregations

Another recent development, particularly among some megachurches, involves the concept of a multi-site congregation. As many buildings and facilities strain to contain the numbers involved, many are electing to follow a "franchise" type of model, having one church that just happens to meet in different locations.[7] The different locations may have satellite uplink to the "main church" or have their own pastoral system preaching the same type of message as presented in the "main church". The same leaders have oversight of both the main church and the "satellite" churches. Is this a system consistent with what the Scriptures teach?

The New Testament certainly demonstrates the existence of multiple local churches, but never do the Scriptures indicate any such "multi-site" system. Each individual local church was to represent a community of God's people, shepherded by elders and served by deacons (Acts 2.42–47; 14.23, Philippians 1.1). We do not see any system in the New Testament where elders have oversight of more than one local congregation at a time.

Likewise, God expects the local church to function like a body where its members are accountable to each other and are to encourage one another (1 Corinthians 12.12–28, Galatians 6.1–2, Hebrews 10.24–25). How can this truly be accomplished when brethren in the same "church" do not even assemble together?

The "multi-site" model looks more like a "mini-denomination" than a truly Biblical model for a growing church. If a local congregation grows and multiplies, each congregation should maintain its autonomous status, patterned after the New Testament rather than modern American trends!

Notes

1: Thuma and Travis, *Beyond Megachurch Myths*, 24

2: ibid., xxi

3: ibid., xviii

4: ibid., 31

5: Hybels and Hybels, *Rediscovering Church*, 73

6: ibid., 176

7: Thuma and Travis, 40

Emergism

Overview

Emergism, or the emergent movement/emergent churches, represents a variety of groups attempting to work within postmodernist society to establish viable faith communities, beginning in the late 1990s. Because it is a marriage of most of the movements considered previously, emergism takes many forms and it is quite difficult to make any generalized statement that is truly inclusive of all groups. Regardless, most of the emergent movement focuses on attempting to grow their view of God's Kingdom by working within existing culture, to deconstruct previous traditions, and to be willing to experiment with new ways of performing Christianity.

Origins and History

Emergism is the offspring of postmodern philosophy and the modern movements within "Christendom," particularly evangelicalism, the charismatic movement, ecumenism, the community church movement, the house church movement, and the megachurch movement. Many emergent groups grew out of "Generation X" style churches of the 1980s; the movement gained its name around 1999, even though many would not wish to be so identified.[1] The movement has continued to grow since, especially in the United States and the United Kingdom. While there is no formal organization of emergism or any such thing, most involved in the emergent movement are online and continually interact through that medium.

Denominations Involved

Emergism is not affiliated with any particular denomination, yet most Protestant denominations (Lutheranism, Calvinism, Anglicanism/Episcopalianism, Baptists, Wesleyanism, Christian Church, many Pentecostal churches) have some "emerging" congregations in their midst. Many of those within emergism came from such denominational backgrounds.

Emergism has a strained relationship with evangelicalism overall, since many would consider themselves "post-evangelical"; nevertheless, emergism does represent an offshoot of evangelicalism. Many involved in emergism maintain an ecumenical viewpoint, and some consider themselves as community churches. While many emergent groups have small group meetings in houses, and share many common beliefs, there is no formal connection to the house church movement or its theology. Many emergent thinkers and emerging churches were or are also part of the megachurch movement. Quite a few emergent groups, however, have no denominational affiliation and stand on their own.

General Considerations

Emergism reflects the same variety seen consistently in movements. The list below represents many features consistent with many strands of emergism.

Part I
- *Lutheranism: Faith Alone; The Lord's Prayer*
- *Baptists: Once Saved, Always Saved*
- *Wesleyanism: The Church and Social Responsibility*
- *Plymouth Brethren: Dispensationalism; Premillennialism*
- *The Charismatic Movement*

Part II
- *Evangelicalism*
- *Ecumenism*
- *Community Church Movement*
- *House Church Movement: House Churches and the Lord's Supper*
- *Megachurch Movement*

Part III
- *Baptism: Infant Baptism and "Original Sin"; Baptism is Immersion; Baptism is for Remission of Sin and is Necessary for Salvation*
- *The Church Treasury, I: Benevolence: Church Benevolence to Non-Saints; The Missionary Society*
- *The Church Treasury, II: Other Considerations: Business Enterprises*
- *Concerning Observances: Observances Concerning the Lord's Birth: Ad-*

vent; Christmas; Observances Concerning the Lord's Death: Palm Sunday; Maundy Thursday; Good Friday; Easter

- *Creeds: The Apostles' Creed; The Nicene Creed*

- *Instrumental Music*

- *Judaic Practices: The Ten Commandments and the "Moral Law"; Tithing*

- *The Lord's Supper: The Bread and the Fruit of the Vine; When Should the Lord's Supper Be Observed? Part A: Weekly*

- *Positions of Authority: Who is the Pastor?; Female Deacons [Deaconesses]; Female Elders; Female Evangelists; Ordination; Synods, Councils, Conventions, and Other Meetings*

Emergism and Postmodernism

Emergism has developed entirely within the postmodern world, and perhaps the most unifying concept among the various strands of emergism is the conviction of the need to work within postmodernist society using the ideology of postmodernist society.[2] Postmodernism, in this context, is the philosophical reaction to what is commonly called "modernism", which was the primary philosophy in Western culture from at least 1750 to 1950. Modernism was marked by a desire for objectivity, rationalism, and the triumph of human ability, among other matters. Postmodernism, born in the tempest following two destructive world wars, challenged all the assumptions of the modernist viewpoint, marked by subjectivism, relativism, and a much more limited view of human ability, especially in being able to discern truth. There is no doubt that we currently live in a time of great change and fluctuation, as modernism and postmodernism collide, and humans are left to sort out what to believe. In this climate, should we as Christians embrace either such philosophy? What do the Scriptures teach?

Paul bears witness in Colossians 2.6–10:

As therefore ye received Christ Jesus the Lord, so walk in him, rooted and builded up in him, and established in your faith, even as ye were taught, abounding in thanksgiving. Take heed lest there shall be any one that maketh spoil of you through his philosophy and vain deceit, after the tradition of men, after the rudiments of the world, and not after Christ: for in him dwelleth all the fulness of the Godhead bodily, and in him ye are made full, who is the head of all principality and power.

God's wisdom as established here is important for us to remember: we should not be taken captive by any individual philosophy, according to the traditions of men, but always to be rooted and established in Jesus Christ. We must recognize that modernism and postmodernism both provide support for—as well as particular stumbling blocks against—Christian beliefs. Modernism recognized the existence of absolute truth and provided a rationalist framework through which much could be understood; on the other hand, it fostered an overly scientific viewpoint and went too far in compartmentalizing the world. Postmodernism corrects some of these tendencies, and yet as a reaction poses its own difficulties. In postmodernism, truth is quite relative, and any concept of "absolute truth" is *anathema*; in Christianity, such truth exists (John 14.6). Postmodernism eschews structure; while this nicely corrects many excessive structures within "Christendom," some structure is still necessary (Acts 14.23 et al). Postmodern tolerance and ecumenical concepts come together; the Scriptures, however, establish a level of exclusivity that makes many today uncomfortable (John 14.6, Galatians 1.6–9, 2 Thessalonians 1.6–9).

Christians, therefore, are not to be "modern," "postmodern," or whatever new fad philosophy may come into place. Christians are to be just that—followers of Christ—and put that allegiance first. Where modernism or postmodernism is conducive to the truths of Scriptures, we freely promote such truths. When the Scriptures present concepts that do not sit well with philosophies, we must still hold fast to what God has taught. Human philosophy is insufficient in expressing the will of God; whenever anyone tries to profess a given philosophy while trying to follow Christ, such a conflicting perspective limits that person's ability to understand what God has revealed and can lead his/her understanding of God—in light of such changing philosophies—to become irrelevant when the prevailing philosophy changes. Perhaps many denominational structures conformed to modernist thinking and need reformation; such does not justify establishing postmodern structures that may need reformation when the next philosophical change takes place. We are not to conform to the world or its philosophies, but rather to be transformed by the renewal of our minds in Christ (Romans 12.2)!

As postmodern philosophy represents a reaction to modernism, so too emergism often represents a reaction to various structures present within denominations. We may sympathize with many of the tenets of emergism and agree about the errors plaguing many denominations; nevertheless, emergism also often goes too far in its postmodern thinking, as will be seen below.

Emergism and Culture

As established earlier, emergism finds its greatest voice in its attempt to present the Gospel within postmodern American and British culture of the twenty-first century. Those in the emergent movement attempt to be followers of Jesus, faithful "in their place and time".[3] This endeavor is particularly marked by "alternative worship," which represents attempts to worship God "native" to the culture of those involved, even if that culture involves bars or nightclubs.[4] The "embodied Gospel" in postmodern culture may include the club scene, dance music, and Gregorian chants: this is consonant with many emergent churches' view of their role in culture, being high-profile, youth-oriented congregations who gain attention because of their rapid growth and ability to attract twenty-some-things.[5] Previous notions of church are deemed "not viable" for postmodern culture, and many within emergism point to the decline in historical churches over the past few years.[6] It is claimed that the differences between emergism and historic Christianity, especially in "alternative worship," are "cultural" and not doctrinal.[7] Finally, emergism often points to the example of Jesus, who was incarnated in a particular culture, that of first-century Palestinian Judaism, and we must do the same in the twenty-first century.[8] Are these claims true?

There is no doubt that there are many traditions within churches that are more cultural than doctrinal; these represent liberties and can easily be questioned. Are all such things liberties? If a given culture or sub-culture involves things like clubs or other such places, should we automatically embrace such things within that culture?

Paul establishes the following in Colossians 3.8–11:

> But now put ye also away all these; anger, wrath, malice, railing, shameful speaking out of your mouth: lie not one to another; seeing that ye have put off the old man with his doings, and have put on the new man, which is being renewed unto knowledge after

the image of him that created him: where there cannot be Greek and Jew, circumcision and uncircumcision, barbarian, Scythian, bondman, freeman: but Christ is all, and in all.

In Christ's Kingdom, all persons can be reconciled to Him; in a very real sense, therefore, Jesus transcends culture. Culture in and of itself cannot be the standard: Jesus must remain the standard.

In any culture, tendencies will exist that are consonant with Christianity; there will also be tendencies that are against the principles of Christianity. Yes, Jesus was a first-century Jew in Palestine; the Jews of Palestine were God's people attempting to live according to God's standards, and whenever traditions or sin were getting in the way, Jesus would rebuke those elements (Matthew 23, John 8.11). It is manifest that we must live within the world, and that will mean that we will have to understand the culture around us, as Jesus did His own—but does this justify radically changing Christian practice?

Paul's words in 1 Corinthians 9.19–22 are instructive:

For though I was free from all men, I brought myself under bondage to all, that I might gain the more. And to the Jews I became as a Jew, that I might gain Jews; to them that are under the law, as under the law, not being myself under the law, that I might gain them that are under the law; to them that are without law, as without law, not being without law to God, but under law to Christ, that I might gain them that are without law. To the weak I became weak, that I might gain the weak: I am become all things to all men, that I may by all means save some.

Here we see that Paul is willing to "become all things to all men," but notice that to those "without law," he was "as without law," yet "not being without law to God, but under law to Christ" (1 Corinthians 9.21). We are to do what we can to communicate the Gospel of Christ to all men, and that may mean that we must wear different "hats"; it does not require embracing all aspects of culture!

Paul was willing to enter synagogues and teach the Gospel (Acts 17.1–3), and yet we never see him entering a pagan ritual ceremony, a symposium, or other revelrous festivity. Jesus was willing to eat with sinners and prostitutes, but never justified their behavior (cf. Matthew 9.9–13).

Yes, we must interact with postmodern, twenty-first century culture, but we must never conform to the culture entirely in order to do so (Romans 12.2). We must avoid that which is revelry and all things contrary to God's Word and instead strive to present normative New Testament Christianity to the twenty-first century. Christianity must dictate our relationship to culture; culture has no right to dictate how we must act as Christians!

Emergism and the Church

Great deliberation has occurred within emergism on the church, and while some of their views are consistent with the New Testament, many overreach and go beyond what the Scriptures present. Emergism, in general, takes a "Kingdom" view of matters, and places the church within that view: great focus is placed on the church as a community.[9] This focus is so preeminent, however, that many groups feel no need to have weekly assemblies; because "traditional Christianity" has become so building and assembly focused, many in emergism shift entirely to a "community" view of the church.[10] The church becomes paramount; most of the distinction between an individual and the church are lost, and one's life of practicing Christianity is considered one's "church life," in effect. Within many emergent churches, distrust of historical systems along with democratic concepts have led to "leaderless" churches or churches where "leaders" relinquish most order and control to the group.[11] Emergent churches wish to be "new expressions" of church that will be relevant to the modern day.[12] Are these views consistent with what is seen in the New Testament?

As in much of what has been seen before, balance in all things is essential. Many churches have become too focused on the building and the Sunday assembly and have not focused on the building of the community that was present in the New Testament church (cf. Acts 2.42–47). Nevertheless, New Testament churches met on the first day of the week to break bread, have a collection, and other acts of encouragement (cf. Acts 20.7, 1 Corinthians 16.1–3; likely 1 Corinthians 14). *Ekklesia*, the Greek word translated as "church," properly means "assembly"; what kind of assembly can there be when its members do not assemble? The *ekklesia* of Christ is to be both an assemblage of persons and also a group of persons with shared identity that share in *koinonia*, or association/community (1 John 1.5–7). Both are essential aspects of the faith.

While postmodernism may eschew leadership, the New Testament affirms the need for some structure and leadership in local churches. Elders were installed to oversee and shepherd the congregations of which they were a part, both Jewish and Greek, on three continents (cf. Acts 14.23, Acts 15.2, Philippians 1.1). Such are to "rule" the members, guiding them in the ways of God (1 Peter 5.1–4).

While the individual is part of the church, and the church represents a collective of individuals, we each represent individual children of God, who will individually stand or fall before our Master (Romans 14.12). The collective is not to be burdened when the individual has the resources available (1 Timothy 5.16). The Christian is part of the church, but the Christian is also more than the church, and is to shine the light of Jesus to all men with whom he comes into contact (cf. Matthew 5.13–16). We should not so over-emphasize the church (the collective body) so as to miss the individual parts that comprise it!

Reactions rarely serve to achieve true Biblical faith. Let us maintain a balanced view of our lives, faith, and practice, gaining our understanding from Jesus over culture, philosophy, or any other such thing!

Notes

1: Gibbs and Bolger, *Emerging Churches*, 30

2: ibid., 28

3: ibid.

4: ibid., 39, 84, 87

5: ibid., 41, 87

6: ibid., 28

7: ibid., 72

8: ibid., 118

9: ibid., 61

10: ibid., 61, 90–91, 96, 99

11: ibid., 109–110, 119

12: ibid., 235

Part III: Doctrines

Baptism

Statement of Belief

The Scriptures say that baptism is a commandment of God,

> "He that believeth and is baptized shall be saved; but he that disbelieveth shall be condemned" *(Mark 16.16)*,

being the immersion in water for the remission of sins,

> And Peter said unto them, "Repent ye, and be baptized every one of you in the name of Jesus Christ unto the remission of your sins; and ye shall receive the gift of the Holy Spirit" *(Acts 2.38)*,

that allows one to be buried with Christ,

> having been buried with him in baptism, wherein ye were also raised with him through faith in the working of God, who raised him from the dead *(Colossians 2.12)*,

and leads to salvation,

> which also after a true likeness doth now save you, even baptism, not the putting away of the filth of the flesh, but the interrogation of a good conscience toward God, through the resurrection of Jesus Christ *(1 Peter 3.21)*.

The Need for Baptism

There are some denominations today that teach that baptism is not a physical action that should be performed; instead, they teach that when Jesus and the Apostles mention baptism, they are speaking about a "spiritual" act. This "spiritual" act is not physical nor has any form of physicality. Do the Scriptures teach that baptism is only a "spiritual" action?

Let us consider the example of Philip and the Ethiopian eunuch from Acts 8.38:

> And he commanded the chariot to stand still: and they both went down into the water, both Philip and the eunuch; and he baptized him.

By all accounts, Philip physically went down into the water with the eunuch and the eunuch was physically baptized. The example of Peter in Acts 10.47–48 is also telling:

> For they heard them speak with tongues, and magnify God. Then answered Peter, "Can any man forbid the water, that these should not be baptized, which have received the Holy Spirit as well as we?"

If Peter were speaking about a "spiritual" baptism that does not involve one getting into the water, why would he speak about the physical substance into which one is baptized? How could water factor into Peter's mind if baptism were simply some "spiritual" act? Further, what need would there be for any Christian to assist another in some "spiritual" act, yet we see in the Scriptures countless times that a Christian baptizes someone into Christ (cf. above, Acts 16.31–33, Acts 19.1–9, etc.)?

Therefore, we can see from the Scriptures that baptism is a physical action that takes place when one desires to become a Christian.

Infant Baptism and "Original Sin"

Many denominations today teach that children and even infants must be baptized in order to be cleansed of sin. Let us examine the progression of this belief and to see what the Scriptures teach.

The first premise for baptizing infants is an inference based on the content of some of the Scriptures. The argument, generally, goes as follows:

Argument: When Cornelius and the Philippian jailer believed, their whole households were baptized. Thus, children were probably baptized also.

Answer: This argument is based upon an assumption about the term "household." Within the texts in question, Acts 10 and Acts 16.24–38, we also read the following about these families:

a devout man, and one that feared God with all his house, who
gave much alms to the people, and prayed to God always *(Acts 10.2).*

And they said, "Believe on the Lord Jesus, and thou shalt be saved,
thou and thy house."
And they spake the word of the Lord unto him, with all that were
in his house. And he took them the same hour of the night, and
washed their stripes; and was baptized, he and all his, immediately *(Acts 16.31–33).*

We can see in Acts 10.2 that "all the house" of Cornelius is said to fear
God. Regarding the house of the jailer in Acts 16.31, we can safely say
that the jailer's household also must believe if its constituents will be
saved, considering that no other Scripture witnesses that an entire family
can be saved on account of the belief of one member. This evidence allows us to reach two possible conclusions:

1. Everyone in the households of Cornelius and/or the jailer were
    old enough to understand the Gospel and believe in its message,
    and therefore every single person believed and was baptized.

2. Luke expects his audience to understand that his use of the term
    "all" involves some hyperbole: he is not trying to say that literally ev-
    ery member of the house of Cornelius and/or the jailer believed and
    were baptized, but that everyone in those houses who were of suffi-
    cient age to understand the Gospel believed in it and were baptized.

Either option demonstrates that the inference made concerning these
two texts is not valid: just because a "household" is baptized does not
mean that any and all children present are baptized.

As the years progressed, it became clear that a compelling reason
needed to be found to justify the baptism of infants, and the doctrine of
"original sin" fit the bill. "Original sin" is defined somewhat differently by
different denominations, but the basic idea is that sin is inheritable. Most
denominations do not teach that individuals inherit specific sins from
their parents, but instead believe that children are born with a sinful nature and therefore are sinners requiring baptism.

The main difficulty with "original sin" is found in the way Jesus speaks about children in Matthew 18.1–4 and Mark 9.35–37:

> In that hour came the disciples unto Jesus, saying, "Who then is greatest in the kingdom of heaven?"
> And he called to him a little child, and set him in the midst of them, and said, "Verily I say unto you, Except ye turn, and become as little children, ye shall in no wise enter into the kingdom of heaven. Whosoever therefore shall humble himself as this little child, the same is the greatest in the kingdom of heaven."

> And he sat down, and called the twelve; and he saith unto them, "If any man would be first, he shall be last of all, and minister of all." And he took a little child, and set him in the midst of them: and taking him in his arms, he said unto them, "Whosoever shall receive one of such little children in my name, receiveth me: and whosoever receiveth me, receiveth not me, but him that sent me."

Jesus indicates that if anyone desires to enter the Kingdom of Heaven, he or she must be like a little child. It is well-known that if an example is not valid, an argument cannot be supported by it. Therefore, if children have sin against them that requires baptism, how can it be that Jesus presents a child as an example of one who would enter the Kingdom of Heaven? If we are to aspire to be as a child, but a child is still in sin, how can we enter the Kingdom? How can it be that receiving a little child is as receiving the Son and the Father if the little child is in his sins? The conclusion is clear: children do not have sin against them. They are in a state of innocence.

Nevertheless, to defend original sin, many will first turn to passages describing how God will visit the iniquity of fathers upon children (cf. Exodus 20.5). Regardless, the Scriptures show also that the punishment of sin is only for those who sin:

> "The fathers shall not be put to death for the children, neither shall the children be put to death for the fathers: every man shall be put to death for his own sin" *(Deuteronomy 24.16)*.

> "The soul that sinneth, it shall die: the son shall not bear the iniquity of the father, neither shall the father bear the iniquity of the

son; the righteousness of the righteous shall be upon him, and the wickedness of the wicked shall be upon him" *(Ezekiel 18.20).*

It would appear on the surface that we have a contradiction between these passages: some say that sons suffer the iniquities of their father, and some say that each soul suffers for their own sins. We can, however, reconcile these passages in one of two ways:

1. God perhaps does not visit the iniquity on the first generation of sinful people, but perhaps on a later generation of sinful people. Notice, for instance, that the exile of Israel and Judah are carried out not under faithful kings like Hezekiah or Josiah, but unfaithful kings, Hoshea and Zedekiah (2 Kings 17–18, 25).

2. God describes the propensity of children to follow in their parents' footsteps. Do we not even today say, "The apple does not fall far from the tree?" If the fathers involve themselves in some sin, it is very likely that children will also. This is not an absolute and hard and fast rule, but nevertheless often accurate.

Regardless, we do not need to infer from these passages that there is some form of "original sin" that each generation inherits from their forefathers. Many will then cite Psalm 51.5:

Behold, I was shapen in iniquity; and in sin did my mother conceive me.

When we look at the evidence we have seen above from Jesus' words in the Gospels, we get the strong impression from the whole of the Scriptures that children do not inherit sin. Since we know that the sum of God's word is true (Psalm 119.160) and without contradiction, we must consider the context of the passage and see whether there are some mitigating circumstances. Psalm 51 represents a psalm, a form of poetry, and a psalm which was written by David after his sin with Bathsheba had been made known (cf. 2 Samuel 12). His great grief, no doubt, led to the use of hyperbole, thinking himself so sinful that he was born that way. As we will see, many other passages that are not written in poetry declare children to be without sin. It is also possible to read "in iniquity" and "in sin" in Psalm 51.5 as David saying that he was born in a sinful world, not that he himself actively had sin against him from birth.

It is also argued when people read the declarations of Paul in Romans 3.10 and 3.23 that because "all" are not righteous and "all" have sinned, therefore, children are also a part of this group:

> as it is written, "There is none righteous, no, not one."

> for all have sinned, and fall short of the glory of God.

Do these verses teach that children are sinners? Let us examine the passage that Paul quotes in Romans 3:10ff, Psalm 53.1–3:

> The fool hath said in his heart, "There is no God." Corrupt are they, and have done abominable iniquity; There is none that doeth good. God looked down from heaven upon the children of men, to see if there were any that did understand, that did seek after God. Every one of them is gone back; they are together become filthy; there is none that doeth good, no, not one.

We see here that not only do none do good, none even know God. Do children "know" God? Can children understand fully the precepts of the Lord, especially infants? By no means! They are not capable of understanding such things. Therefore, are we to believe that God includes them in the category of those who choose to not do God's will nor to know Him?

We can understand, then, that Paul uses a bit of hyperbole to make his point. The "all" of Romans 3.10 and 3.23 refers to all people who are capable of knowing good from evil, and not every creature. This is comparable to Matthew's use of "all" in Matthew 3.5:

> Then went out unto him Jerusalem, and all Judaea, and all the region round about Jordan.

Shall we believe from this that every single inhabitant of Jerusalem, Judea, and the Jordan river area came to John? That is not the intent; the point is to show that a large number of people came out to see John. We use the term in the same way today. Therefore, considering the evidence in Matthew 18.1–4 and Mark 9.35–37, we can see that Paul is not referring to every single human ever but all who are capable of knowing good from evil.

Romans 5.12–17 is often used to try to show that we have inherited sin from Adam:

Therefore, as through one man sin entered into the world, and
death through sin; and so death passed unto all men, for that
all sinned—for until the law sin was in the world: but sin is not
imputed when there is no law. Nevertheless death reigned from
Adam until Moses, even over them that had not sinned after the
likeness of Adam's transgression, who is a figure of him that was
to come. But not as the trespass, so also is the free gift. For if by
the trespass of the one the many died, much more did the grace
of God, and the gift by the grace of the one man, Jesus Christ,
abound unto the many. And not as through one that sinned, so
is the gift: for the judgment came of one unto condemnation, but
the free gift came of many trespasses unto justification. For if,
by the trespass of the one, death reigned through the one; much
more shall they that receive the abundance of grace and of the gift
of righteousness reign in life through the one, even Jesus Christ.

While this passage may give the impression that we inherit sin from
Adam, when we read it closely, we see that Paul says no such thing. The
text never says directly that anyone inherits actual sin from Adam; it
does say that sin entered the world because of the transgression, and that
death was its consequence, but never that we actually inherited sin. Yes,
we die because sin entered the world through Adam, but that does not
mean that we actually inherit Adam's sin. We can read this passage consistently with the rest of Scripture: sin is not only present but also per-
meates the world, death is present in the world because of sin, and that
climate will compel all capable persons to sin, but sin is not inherited.

"Original sin," then, is not consistent with the entire witness of the
Scripture (Psalm 119.160). The main justification of infant baptism, then,
is without Scriptural merit. When, then, should one be baptized? The
Scriptures testify that one submits to baptism having believed in Jesus
Christ, confessing His name, and repenting of one's sins (cf. Acts 16.31,
Romans 10.9, and Acts 2.38), and that one is baptized for the remission of
one's sin (Acts 2.38). A person must be baptized when they have sinned,
are separated from God (cf. Isaiah 59.1), and come to the realization of
their need for salvation in Christ Jesus. As we have seen, in order to sin,
one must need to know the difference between good and evil and choose
the evil. Only then is one under the sentence of judgment. This moment
varies by the individual, and some who have mental handicaps may never

reach that moment. Baptism, then, should be done when one is mentally capable of doing so, realizing one's sin and need for salvation in Christ.

It should also be noted that since "infant baptism" is indeed of no value, since an infant has no sins to remit, infants are not really baptized but simply get wet. The Scriptures give no reason for confidence for anyone who would rely on their "baptism" as an infant. Such persons ought to consider the Scriptures discussed in this lesson and be immersed in water for the remission of their sin.

Baptism is Immersion

Many in denominations teach that baptism need not be immersion, but can be sprinkling or pouring; all three are considered "modes" of baptism.

The main difficulty in this argument is found in the meaning of the Greek word *baptizo*:

> to immerse, submerge, to make overwhelmed (i.e. fully wet) *(Strong's Dictionary of Hebrew/Greek Words).*

> to dip repeatedly, to immerse, to submerge (of vessels sunk); to cleanse by dipping or submerging, to wash, to make clean with water, to wash one's self, bathe; to overwhelm *(Thayer's Greek Lexicon).*

The definition of "baptism" then, according to its use in the New Testament, does not allow for the idea of "sprinkling" or "pouring" or any idea of "modes" of baptism. Baptism is immersion. This reality is illustrated, in particular, by Paul in Romans 6.4:

> We were buried therefore with him through baptism into death: that like as Christ was raised from the dead through the glory of the Father, so we also might walk in newness of life.

While we realize that Paul is using the metaphor baptism as burial, the metaphor only makes sense if we realize that baptism is immersion. When we bury bodies, we do not sprinkle or pour dirt on them; we cover them in dirt. Baptism cannot be a burial unless one is covered in water. It is clear, then, that New Testament baptism is immersion.

Tripartite Baptism

In some denominations, baptism is administered in three parts: one is dipped three times under the water, once each in the name of the Father, the Son, and the Holy Spirit.

While there is nothing particularly wrong with baptizing in this way, the Scriptures nowhere demand it. By all accounts, baptism was a singular immersion done in the name of (or by the authority of) the Father, the Son, and the Holy Spirit (Matthew 28.18–20). Sometimes baptism is mentioned as done in the name of Jesus (Acts 2.38), and therefore it is entirely possible that some were baptized with only Jesus' name mentioned and therefore one immersion.

Baptism in Running Water

There are some who would claim that baptism is only legitimate if it is done in running water. The fact that Jesus and many others were baptized in rivers and other such sources of moving water is cited as evidence (cf. John 1.30–34, John 4.1–2).

While there is certainly nothing wrong with being baptized in running water, we see no such requirement in the Scriptures. Furthermore, it is likely that the Ethiopian eunuch in Acts 8.36–39 was baptized in some pool of water in the desert that would not really be "running water". The only requirement in the Scriptures is for a person to be immersed in water—it is a liberty as to whether one is immersed in moving or non-moving water.

Baptism is for Remission of Sin and Necessary for Salvation

The major difference between New Testament teachings and the teachings of many denominations concerns the nature of baptism. Most do not believe that baptism is the act that causes the remittance of sins and allows one to be saved; more often than not, denominations teach that believing—or believing and repentance, or some other action—allows one to be saved. Let us examine these arguments, beginning with disputations about the Scriptures involved:

Mark 16.16:

> "He that believeth and is baptized shall be saved; but he that disbelieveth shall be condemned."

Argument: Mark 16.16 does not say that you must be baptized to be saved; after all, it only says that those who disbelieve are condemned. Nothing is said about those who believe yet are not baptized.

Answer: This argument "does not follow" (the official term used for this is *non sequitur*). Why would someone who disbelieves be baptized? They would not consider it! Furthermore, why would anyone who believed not be baptized? Every detailed account of conversion in the book of Acts includes a baptism. Ultimately, we are not out to speculate about what the text does not say, but to establish what the text does say is necessary: belief and baptism. To "believe and not be baptized" is to tread in very dangerous water.

Argument: Mark 16.16 is invalid because textual evidence shows the text to possibly be a later addition.

Answer: It is true that a few very old manuscripts of the Gospel of Mark do not include Mark 16.9–20; many important witnesses, however, do contain the passage, and the passage is questioned more on subjective grounds. Furthermore, the antiquity of the text is verified by its use by Irenaeus in the late second century (*Apostolic Constitution 6.83*). The feeling that it should be omitted comes, on admission, only on doctrinal evidence from scholars, that, "well, baptism for salvation is not spelled out anywhere else, hence, this is a later addition." In the end, all New Testament textual critics will be forced to admit that the argument against the text is without sufficient evidence, and that there is little reason to believe that the text is false.

Acts 2.38:

> And Peter said unto them, "Repent ye, and be baptized every one of you in the name of Jesus Christ unto the remission of your sins; and ye shall receive the gift of the Holy Spirit."

Argument: Luke uses the Greek word *eis* in Acts 2.38. This word does not necessarily mean "for;" it could also mean "since," and thus read, "be baptized since you have been forgiven of your sins."

Answer: Greek prepositions can mean a whole host of possibilities based on context and usage. The above is highly unlikely, especially in view of Matthew 26.28:

"For this is my blood of the covenant, which is shed for many unto remission of sins."

"Unto remission of sins" in the above is the exact same phrase as used in Acts 2.38, and *eis* is indeed the preposition rendered "unto". No one would argue that Jesus is saying here that His blood is shed "because your sins have been remitted." Why, then, should Acts 2.38 be any different?

It is also telling that every single translation, even the interpretive translations, translate Acts 2.38 as "for" as a statement of purpose. The argument does not stand.

Argument: Peter is preaching to the Jews, and his message is only relevant for the Jews.

Answer: While it is true that Jews are the direct audience of Peter in Acts 2, the conclusion is not valid.

Peter's message is directed towards the Jews, yes, and uses themes familiar to the Jews. The Scriptures do show that the presentation of the Gospel varies based on the audience: consider Paul's preaching in Acts 13.16–41 to a Jewish audience versus Acts 17.22–31 to a Gentile audience. The substance of the message, however, remains the same, and Paul affirms that he preaches the same message as Peter in Galatians 2.6–9:

> But from those who were reputed to be somewhat (whatsoever they were, it maketh no matter to me: God accepteth not man's person)—they, I say, who were of repute imparted nothing to me: but contrariwise, when they saw that I had been intrusted with the gospel of the uncircumcision, even as Peter with the gospel of the circumcision (for he that wrought for Peter unto the apostleship of the circumcision wrought for me also unto the Gentiles); and when they perceived the grace that was given unto me, James and Cephas and John, they who were reputed to be pillars, gave to me and Barnabas the right hands of fellowship, that we should go unto the Gentiles, and they unto the circumcision.

If the message is the same, so would be the response to the message. Furthermore, the idea that baptism was required for Jews but not for Gentiles is at odds with Acts 10.47–48, Acts 16.31–33, and 1 Corinthians 1.14–16, all of which show that Gentiles also were baptized.

1 Peter 3.21:

> which also after a true likeness doth now save you, even baptism, not
> the putting away of the filth of the flesh, but the interrogation of a
> good conscience toward God, through the resurrection of Jesus Christ.

Argument: Peter does not say that baptism saves you, but your clean conscience is what saves you.

Answer: 1 Peter 3.21 is yet another explicit statement showing the need for baptism, therefore, to refute it, one must turn to the manipulation of the text.

Peter here is saying that baptism is not a bath. Its intent is not to purge someone of dirt, but to clean one's conscience; after all, immediately after baptism, one is sinless. This clean conscience is the direct result of the remission of sin granted in baptism. Peter in fact affirms the efficacy of baptism. No one believes that there is any power in the water, the *ad hominems* constantly used against us notwithstanding; the power is in Christ's blood and the appeal being made to God by being immersed in water for remission of sin. This is the immersion that saves.

Now that we have looked at the Scriptures, let us look at other arguments that are used against baptism:

Argument: Jesus, and only Jesus, has performed the work of salvation. We cannot add to His work, and baptism is an addition to His work.

Answer: No one would deny that the agent of salvation is Jesus the Christ. However, the letter to the Hebrews makes it clear that Jesus took our sins upon Him on the cross (Hebrews 9.12–15). Paul says this much about Christ's actions,

> Have this mind in you, which was also in Christ Jesus: who, being in
> the form of God, counted it not a prize to be on an equality with God,
> but emptied himself, taking the form of a servant, being made in the
> likeness of men; and being found in fashion as a man, he humbled
> himself, becoming obedient even unto death, yea, the death of the
> cross. Wherefore also God highly exalted him, and gave unto him the
> name which is above every name; that in the name of Jesus every knee
> should bow, of things in heaven and things on earth and things under
> the earth, and that every tongue should confess that Jesus Christ is
> Lord, to the glory of God the Father, *(Philippians 2.5–11).*

Therefore, we see that Christ died on the cross for our sins and to perform the Father's will, which was for His Son to humble Himself so that He may be exalted and given all authority. This is important; since He has this authority, the terms of salvation come through Christ. Paul continued in his letter with Philippians 2.12:

> So then, my beloved, even as ye have always obeyed, not as in my presence only, but now much more in my absence, work out your own salvation with fear and trembling.

After a discussion of Christ's authority, Paul says that we must continue to obey! Obedience is central to the reception of the work which Christ has done; we are only able to receive the salvation that comes through Christ when we are obedient to His will, as said in 2 Thessalonians 1.6–9,

> If so be that it is a righteous thing with God to recompense affliction to them that afflict you, and to you that are afflicted rest with us, at the revelation of the Lord Jesus from heaven with the angels of his power in flaming fire, rendering vengeance to them that know not God, and to them that obey not the gospel of our Lord Jesus: who shall suffer punishment, even eternal destruction from the face of the Lord and from the glory of his might.

Without obedience, one is lost. Baptism is submissive obedience to Christ, commanded by Him, and we must follow through. To deny the need for obedience for salvation is to deny the New Testament plan of salvation.

Argument: Baptism is symbolic. Since God symbolically remits your sin, baptism is not necessary for salvation.

Answer: We recognize that the power in baptism is not in the water, but in the appeal in faith to God for the cleansing from sin (cf. 1 Peter 3.21). We also recognize that the New Testament provides illustrations of the significance of baptism, as can be seen in Romans 6.3–7:

> Or are ye ignorant that all we who were baptized into Christ Jesus were baptized into his death? We were buried therefore with him through baptism unto death: that like as Christ was raised from the dead through the glory of the Father, so we also might walk in

newness of life. For if we have become united with him in the likeness of his death, we shall be also in the likeness of his resurrection; knowing this, that our old man was crucified with him, that the body of sin might be done away, that so we should no longer be in bondage to sin; for he that hath died is justified from sin.

Baptism is likened to a death and resurrection, the end of the man of sin and the raising of the new man. Does the fact that baptism can be understood in symbolic terms mean that we can dispense with the actual physical baptism? An appropriate parallel is the Lord's Supper: the bread and the fruit of the vine represent the body and blood of our Lord, but no one would say that we are not to physically partake of these emblems because they have symbolic value. As with the Lord's Supper, so with baptism: both of these events are rich in symbolic value, but we nevertheless need to physically engage in them.

Argument: Baptism does not automatically mean that one is immersed in water; it can mean, and does for Christians, that one is baptized in the Holy Spirit.

Answer: Much has been said regarding the baptism of the Holy Spirit in Pentecostalism/TheCharismatic Movement: What is the Baptism of the Holy Spirit?. There the evidence for the baptism of the Holy Spirit is considered: it is seen that the "baptism of the Holy Spirit" is only mentioned in connection with two specific events for two specific purposes, and both times it was done by God alone: on the day of Pentecost, as a fulfillment of the prophecies of Joel (cf. Acts 1.4–5, Acts 2.1–36, Joel 2.28–32), and when God showed Peter that Gentiles were to receive the Word of life (Acts 10.44–45, 11.15–16). It is also seen that the usual means of receiving the Holy Spirit was to have the "laying on of hands" from an Apostle (Acts 8.14–17, Acts 19.1–6).

Baptism in water, however, is explicitly identified in Acts 8.36–39 and also in Acts 10.47–48, right after Cornelius was baptized with the Holy Spirit. Since baptism in water was the standard form of baptism, and the baptism of the Holy Spirit was only given in special circumstances by God for specific purposes, we can see clearly that baptism in water is the "one baptism" in Ephesians 4.5.

Retort: Many times baptism is mentioned without water.

Answer: Indeed, many times we read of someone being baptized with nothing stating that it was "in water". The passages likewise do not state that they were baptized in the Spirit, either. We must look at the passages and see if there are any indicators regarding what is under discussion.

In many passages it is clear that baptism in the Spirit is not under consideration. In Acts 2.38, baptism precedes the "gift of the Holy Spirit", and therefore the baptism is not in the Holy Spirit. The Samarians in Acts 8.5–17 and the disciples of John in Acts 19.1–6 are said to have first been baptized and then later had hands laid on them so as to receive the Holy Spirit, demonstrating that their baptism was not in the Spirit.

Furthermore, God is the only one who administers the baptism of the Holy Spirit, and is done not by the intent of man but by the intent of God, as seen in Acts 2 and 10. Therefore, other examples in the Scripture when persons submit to baptism (cf. Acts 9.18, Acts 16.15, Acts 16.33, Acts 18.18, etc.), all indications show that they were baptized in water, not in the Spirit.

We can see, then, that even if immersion in water is not explicitly mentioned, all evidence points to that conclusion in all the passages cited.

Retort: 1 Corinthians 12.13 indicates that we are all baptized in the Spirit.

Answer: Let us consider 1 Corinthians 12.13:

> For in one Spirit were we all baptized into one body, whether Jews or Greeks, whether bond or free; and were all made to drink of one Spirit.

The question we must ask is whether Paul is trying to show that our baptism was in the Spirit or whether our baptism in water was done in accordance with the one Spirit. The context demonstrates that Paul's point is about the unity of Christians, how Christians are to work together in one body; therefore, Paul is not speaking about the nature of baptism *per se*, but that when we were immersed in water, we did so by one Spirit and were brought into one Body. We cannot understand this verse to be in contradiction with the mountain of evidence for immersion in water (cf. Psalm 119.160).

Argument: The Apostles were not baptized, yet they were certainly saved.

Answer: This argument presupposes that since the baptism of the

Apostles is not revealed in the Scriptures that it did not happen. Such is not a wise presupposition; we are told that not everything that was done during Christ's ministry is revealed, nor could it really ever be (John 20.30–31, 21.25). It is entirely possible, therefore, that the Apostles were baptized and yet such was not revealed.

Furthermore, the idea that the Apostles were baptized is rendered more plausible by the evidence in John 4.1–2:

> When therefore the Lord knew that the Pharisees had heard that Jesus was making and baptizing more disciples than John (although Jesus himself baptized not, but his disciples).

If the disciples were out baptizing people during Christ's ministry, it is very likely that they had already been baptized as well.

Argument: Cornelius was saved before baptism. Baptism, then, is not necessary to be saved.

Answer: Since no statement to this effect can be found in Acts 10 or any other passage, to understand and respond to this argument, we must understand the underlying assumption driving it: if one has the Holy Spirit, one must be in a saved state. Is this assumption true?

While this assumption may have merit in the majority of cases, nevertheless, there are times when the Holy Spirit is upon a person who is not saved so as to effect God's will. As it is written in 2 Peter 1.21:

> For no prophecy ever came by the will of man: but men spake from God, being moved by the Holy Spirit.

Peter makes no exception: if a man provides a prophecy, it is not by his will, but by God through the Holy Spirit. Having understood this, let us see what John says regarding Caiaphas in John 11.49–52:

> But a certain one of them, Caiaphas, being high priest that year, said unto them, "Ye know nothing at all, nor do ye take account that it is expedient for you that one man should die for the people, and that the whole nation perish not."
> Now this he said not of himself: but being high priest that year, he prophesied that Jesus should die for the nation; and not for the

nation only, but that he might also gather together into one the children of God that are scattered abroad.

John clearly says that Caiaphas "prophesied" regarding Jesus, since he was High Priest that year. Since no man can speak of himself when prophesying, but is guided by the Holy Spirit (2 Peter 1.21), Caiaphas must have spoken by the Holy Spirit, and therefore the Holy Spirit was with him. Yet who would claim that Caiaphas was saved?

It should be manifest, then, that God can provide the Holy Spirit to a person, even if not saved, to fulfill His purposes. Since God desired for Peter and the other disciples to understand that Gentiles were to hear the Word of life, God poured out His Spirit onto Cornelius and his men to be a sign for Peter, and Peter then understood and had divine testimony to prove it to others (Acts 10.44–47, Acts 11.15–18).

In reality, the fact that Peter's immediate response was to baptize Cornelius and his men after God poured out His Spirit onto them indicates the importance and need for baptism (Acts 10.47). Cornelius and his men, in truth, show that we do require immersion in water!

Argument: Baptism in water was only under John the Baptist, and was for repentance; Christ's baptism is "with fire."

Answer: This argument attempts to make a firm distinction between the natures of the baptisms of John and Jesus (Luke 3.16, Acts 1.5). This argument would perhaps have merit if it were not for Paul's discussion with some of John's disciples in Acts 19.1–6:

> And it came to pass, that, while Apollos was at Corinth, Paul having passed through the upper country came to Ephesus, and found certain disciples: and he said unto them, "Did ye receive the Holy Spirit when ye believed?"
> And they said unto him, "Nay, we did not so much as hear whether the Holy Spirit was given."
> And he said, "Into what then were ye baptized?"
> And they said, "Into John's baptism."
> And Paul said, "John baptized with the baptism of repentance, saying unto the people, that they should believe on him which should come after him, that is, on Jesus."
> And when they heard this, they were baptized into the name of the

Lord Jesus. And when Paul had laid his hands upon them, the Holy Spirit came on them; and they spake with tongues, and prophesied.

We can see, then, that the issue was not the nature of the baptism but the purpose of the baptism. John's baptism was for repentance; the baptism in the name of Christ is for the remission of sin through His blood. We see that the disciples of John were baptized again, this time in the name of Jesus, and then they had hands laid on them and received the Spirit. There is no reason, then, to allege that Christ's baptism is not in water.

Argument: 1 Corinthians 1.14–17 shows that baptism is not valid for today: Paul did not baptize, and Paul said to imitate him as he imitated Christ.

Answer: We can see here a classic example of inferring an answer despite the fact that one has been given. Let us consider 1 Corinthians 1.14–17:

> I thank God that I baptized none of you, save Crispus and Gaius; lest any man should say that ye were baptized into my name. And I baptized also the household of Stephanas: besides, I know not whether I baptized any other. For Christ sent me not to baptize, but to preach the gospel: not in wisdom of words, lest the cross of Christ should be made void.

It would be rather odd to try to argue here that Paul does not value baptism, considering that he confesses that he baptized no fewer then three persons in Corinth. The reason for his hesitance in baptizing people is found in verse fifteen:

> lest any man should say that ye were baptized into my name.

Paul had a peculiar problem when preaching to the Gentiles; they had a tendency to worship a man with supernatural powers as a god. Consider what occurred in Lystra in Acts 14.11–18:

> And when the multitude saw what Paul had done, they lifted up their voice, saying in the speech of Lycaonia, "The gods are come down to us in the likeness of men."
> And they called Barnabas, Jupiter; and Paul, Mercury, because he was the chief speaker. And the priest of Jupiter whose temple was before the city, brought oxen and garlands unto the gates, and would have done sacrifice with the multitudes. But when the apostles, Barnabas

and Paul, heard of it, they rent their garments, and sprang forth among the multitude, crying out and saying,
"Sirs, why do ye these things? We also are men of like passions with you, and bring you good tidings, that ye should turn from these vain things unto a living God, who made the heaven and the earth and the sea, and all that in them is: who in the generations gone by suffered all the nations to walk in their own ways. And yet He left not himself without witness, in that he did good and gave you from heaven rains and fruitful seasons, filling your hearts with food and gladness."
And with these sayings scarce restrained they the multitudes from doing sacrifice unto them.

We can see, then, that Paul has previously been elevated beyond his position. Even in Corinth, there was division over to whom people owed their allegiance- to Apollos, Cephas, Paul, and/or Christ (1 Corinthians 1.12). Paul did not wish to baptize the Corinthians so that no one would think that there was any power in Paul, since the power was in Christ. Paul asked the Corinthians in verse 13, just before the discussion of baptism, the following:

Is Christ divided? Was Paul crucified for you? Or were ye baptized into the name of Paul?

The difficulty, then, is not that the Corinthians were baptized or not baptized, or that Paul was to baptize or not to baptize, but the attitudes of the Corinthians and their tendency to exalt the men who worked with them. The fact that so many Corinthians were said to be baptized confirms the need for all to be baptized.

Argument: The thief on the cross was saved, and he was not baptized.
Answer: The thief on the cross died with a special promise from Jesus:

But the other answered, and rebuking him said, "Dost thou not even fear God, seeing thou art in the same condemnation? And we indeed justly; for we receive the due reward of our deeds: but this man hath done nothing amiss."
And he said, "Jesus, remember me when thou comest in thy kingdom."
And he said unto him, "Verily I say unto thee, today shalt thou be with me in Paradise," *(Luke 23.40–43)*.

Christ had not yet died, nor was raised; the work of salvation had not yet been completed (cf. Psalm 22, Isaiah 53). The thief died under the old covenant with a personal guarantee from Christ, realities that are not present for us today. We could say in response, "If Christ comes down and says to you that He will see you in Paradise today, then good, you do not need to be baptized. Otherwise, the need for baptism still stands."

Retort: The thief died after Christ did.

Answer: While it is probably true that the thief outlasted Jesus, the full redemptive work (let alone the inauguration of the Kingdom) required the resurrection, and it is certain that the thief was dead by then. As it is written:

> After two days will he revive us: on the third day he will raise us up, and we shall live before him, *(Hosea 6.2).*

Likewise, Paul establishes that if the resurrection is not true, then our faith in Christ is in vain, and we are still in our sins (1 Corinthians 15.12–18). The resurrection, therefore, is as important as the cross in our salvation, and no change in covenant occurred before that point.

Argument: Romans 10.9–10 says that belief and confession save. Belief and confession, then, and not baptism, save.

Answer: Romans 10.9–10 does indeed say that belief and confession are necessary:

> Because if thou shalt confess with thy mouth Jesus as Lord, and shalt believe in thy heart that God raised him from the dead, thou shalt be saved: for with the heart man believeth unto righteousness; and with the mouth confession is made unto salvation.

As good students of God's Word (2 Timothy 2.15), we must always remember that the sum of God's Word is truth (Psalm 119.160), and we ought not to introduce contradiction into the text. Note that Paul does not say here that belief and confession "alone" save. Consider Luke 13.5:

> I tell you, "Nay: but, except ye repent, ye shall all likewise perish."

Would we say that this verse denies the need for belief and confession, because it only mentions repentance? By no means! We learn that belief and confession are necessary for salvation in Romans 10.9–10 and repentance is necessary for salvation in Luke 13.5 and Acts 2.38. If Acts 2.38, Romans 6.3–7, and 1 Peter 3.21 affirm the need for baptism to be saved, we recognize that all of these aspects, not just one or two, are necessary. Therefore, the absence of the term "baptism" in Romans 10.9–10 does not negate the need for baptism.

It should be noted that this same type of argument will also use belief from Acts 16.31 or another passage, and one can respond in a similar way as above.

Argument: Jesus did not baptize anyone; therefore, why don't we follow His example?

Answer: As seen from John 4.1–2 above, the disciples did baptize people as disciples of Christ with Christ present. If Christ disapproved of this example, would He not have stopped it then? This is actually a confirmation of the need for baptism: Christ used Himself as an example for baptism and people were baptized in His name with His approval while present on the earth.

Argument: Baptism requires a baptizer. If you make baptism a requirement for salvation, you also require a baptizer, adding someone to the salvation that comes through Christ alone.

Answer: First of all, we should note that the term "baptizer" is foreign to the New Testament after discussion of John the Baptist. The focus is never on the baptizer, but that one is baptized.

Nevertheless, the foundation of this argument—the idea that needing a baptizer adds a person to salvation—is undermined by Romans 10.14:

> How then shall they call on him in whom they have not believed?
> And how shall they believe in him whom they have not heard?
> And how shall they hear without a preacher?

Every group recognizes the need for belief, and Paul says that belief can come only when one "hears" the Word of God. Is Paul "adding" someone to the salvation that comes through Christ alone by positing that someone must preach the Word? Absolutely, because it makes little sense to posit that the understanding and eventual salvation through Christ is done in a vacuum, without any human intervention. If the Word is spread through the preaching of men, then there is no problem with men baptizing others so that they can be saved.

Argument: Well, if baptism is what gives remission of sins, wouldn't you need to be baptized every time you sin?

Answer: Baptism is a one-time act that transforms the individual into a new creature, described as being "born again of the water" in John 3.4. After being born again, we must confess our sins, and by doing so, we are forgiven, as John says in 1 John 1.9:

> If we confess our sins, he is faithful and righteous to forgive us our sins, and to cleanse us from all unrighteousness.

The Scriptures do not require continual baptism for remission of continual sin.

Argument: What if an airplane crashes into the desert, and a Christian on that plane converts everyone but cannot baptize them, and they all die without water. Are they saved?

Answer: This is one of many kinds of such arguments: it may involve different details, but the idea is the same: a person is hindered from being baptized and dies.

All of these arguments are really *argumenta ad absurdum*. They posit unlikely situations, and are really self-defeating. One could simply change some of the details and return the argument, using belief, repentance, or something else of the sort. "Well, what if someone is hearing the Gospel, sees that Christ is Lord and that He died for his sins, but just before he could repent, he is struck by lightning and dies. Is he saved?"

The answer, invariably, is, "God will decide." If that is true in the circumstance of one before repentance, so it is with the one before baptism. God said that we should be baptized for remission of sins, and that is the rule. We are to preach the rule, not dwell on some ludicrous exceptions. After all, it is likely that the one with whom you speak is near plenty of water, and the only hindrance would be a lack of faith or understanding in his or her need to be immersed in water for the remission of their sin.

The Church Treasury, I: Benevolence

Statement of Belief

The Scriptures teach that the church is to give benevolence to any needy saint:

> Now concerning the collection for the saints, as I gave order to the churches of Galatia, so also do ye. Upon the first day of the week let each one of you lay by him in store, as he may prosper, that no collections be made when I come *(1 Corinthians 16.1–2)*.

And also to provide for evangelism:

> And ye yourselves also know, ye Philippians, that in the beginning of the gospel, when I departed from Macedonia, no church had fellowship with me in the matter of giving and receiving but ye only; for even in Thessalonica ye sent once and again unto my need *(Philippians 4.15–16)*.

It is also the responsibility of the individual Christian to help saints in need:

> If any woman that believeth hath widows, let her relieve them, and let not the church be burdened; that it mat relieve them that are widows indeed *(1 Timothy 5.16)*.

But the duty of assisting any others in need falls upon the individual Christian:

> Pure religion and undefiled before our God and Father is this, to visit the fatherless and widows in their affliction, and to keep oneself unspotted from the world *(James 1.27)*.

The Scriptures do not teach that the church may fund evangelism through the use of an extra-church organization or for a group of churches to fund evangelism through one church alone.

The Individual and the Church

When discussing the responsibilities of the church and the individual in regards to benevolence, there often seems to be confusion regarding the relationship of the individual and the church. Many feel that since the church is made up of individual Christians, whatever the individual is commanded to do is something the church is allowed to do. Does Scripture show this to be true?

While it is certainly true that the church is the collective of individual Christians with Christ at its head (Colossians 2.18), we see that the roles of individual and collective are differentiated in 1 Timothy 5.16:

> If any woman that believeth hath widows, let her relieve them, and let not the church be burdened; that it may relieve them that are widows indeed.

The individual first has the responsibility, and only when there are no individuals to assist, then the church is to step in and care for widows. If the church had the same responsibility as the individual, this distinction in 1 Timothy would not be necessary.

Furthermore, we have the example of the Judgment scene in Matthew 25.31–40:

> "But when the Son of man shall come in his glory, and all the angels with him, then shall he sit on the throne of his glory: and before him shall be gathered all the nations: and he shall separate them one from another, as the shepherd separateth the sheep from the goats; and he shall set the sheep on his right hand, but the goats on the left.
> Then shall the King say unto them on his right hand, 'Come, ye blessed of my Father, inherit the kingdom prepared for you from the foundation of the world: for I was hungry, and ye gave me to eat; I was thirsty, and ye gave me drink; I was a stranger, and ye took me in; naked, and ye clothed me; I was sick, and ye visited me; I was in prison, and ye came unto me.'

Then shall the righteous answer him, saying, 'Lord, when saw we
thee hungry, and fed thee? or athirst, and gave thee drink? And
when saw we thee a stranger, and took thee in? or naked, and
clothed thee? And when saw we thee sick, or in prison, and came
unto thee?'
And the King shall answer and say unto them, 'Verily I say unto
you, Inasmuch as ye did it unto one of these my brethren, even
these least, ye did it unto me.'

As we can see, the sheep collectively represent the church, yet the judgment is based on how each person as an individual helped those in need.

The church exists for the assistance of its members, spiritually, physically, and emotionally (Hebrews 10.25, 1 Corinthians 16.1–2). Yet, as we
have seen from the above in Matthew 25, the saints are saved not by virtue of the church with whom they assemble, but because they have been
found righteous in the eyes of the Lord. We work as a collective to assist
each other in this walk, but in the end, the judgment shall be made on
an individual basis, as seen clearly from Romans 14.10:

But thou, why dost thou judge thy brother? Or thou again, why
dost thou set at nought thy brother? For we shall all stand before
the judgment-seat of God.

Therefore, as we have seen, the individual has more responsibility than
the collective church, for the individual can act in one of three ways:

1. Individual as an individual [i.e. evangelizing (Matthew 28.18),
   being an example (Matthew 5.13–16)]

2. Individual as part of the collective church [i.e. Lord's Supper
   (Acts 20.7), collection (1 Corinthians 16.1–2)]

3. Individual as either an individual or as a part of the collective
   church [i.e. singing (Colossians 3.16/James 5.13), praying (1
   Thessalonians 5.17)]

All of these acts, done in accordance with the Scriptures, will lead to the
building up of the individuals and the Body of Christ. When we blur
or destroy the lines that God has made, we place ourselves in danger of
apostasy (2 John 9).

Church Benevolence to Non-Saints

Many groups and denominations teach that the church is authorized to use part of its treasury to assist non-saints in some way, either through direct subsidy or through some institution established for this purpose. Do the Scriptures teach that the church is allowed to assist non-saints through benevolence? Let us examine the Scriptures.

Scriptural Considerations

Many arguments are made using the Scriptures to justify the use of the funds of the Lord's treasury to assist non-saints. Let us examine these now.

Argument: 2 Corinthians 9.12–14 shows that the church gave to more than just saints.

Answer: The passage in question:

> For the ministration of this service not only filleth up the measure of the wants of the saints, but aboundeth also through many thanksgivings unto God; seeing that through the proving of you by this ministration they glorify God for the obedience of your confession unto the gospel of Christ, and for the liberality of your contribution unto them and unto all; while they themselves also, with supplication on your behalf, long after you by reason of the exceeding grace of God in you.

This passage does say that the church gave to "them and to all," but who is contained in the "all?" We know from verse 14 that "they" (referring back to the phrase "to them and to all") were "pray[ing] on [their] behalf." Who prays but the believers? Therefore, it is certain from this passage that Paul is referring to the giving to the saints, and to the saints alone.

Argument: We are to do good to "all men" in Galatians 6.10. The letter to the Galatians is written to the churches of Galatia, therefore, the church is to do good to "all men."

Answer: The text in question:

> So then, as we have opportunity, let us work that which is good toward all men, and especially toward them that are of the household of the faith.

When considering this verse, we must examine the context of the letter to the Galatians, especially around the sixth chapter. Throughout the sixth chapter, Paul makes reference to individuals, that they should bear one another's burdens (verse 2), each bearing his or her own burden (verses 3–5), that the individual should teach the things of Christ (verse 6), that one will reap what he sows (verses 7–8). Therefore, as we can see, the individual Christian is the focus of this portion of the Galatian letter; it stands to reason that verse 10 thus also refers to the work of the individual, and not the work of the church.

Argument: James 1.27 shows that we are to help orphans and widows; why can't we as a church?

Answer: The text:

> Pure religion and undefiled before our God and Father is this, to visit the fatherless and widows in their affliction, and to keep oneself unspotted from the world.

James is very specific in this passage as to whom the burden of visiting the orphans and widows falls upon: "oneself." Since these two principles consist of "pure and undefiled religion," and one is qualified as to be done as "oneself" and the other shows no qualification, it is clear that James intends this pure and undefiled religion to be practiced by the individual.

Retort: Are you saying that the church cannot practice pure and undefiled religion?

Answer: James 1.27 is not discussing the church in any way, shape, or form. James is making no comment toward the nature of the church or its function. We learn the following from Ephesians 5.27:

> That he might present the church to himself a glorious church, not having spot or wrinkle or any such thing; but that it should be holy and without blemish.

We see that the church is holy and blameless, thus "pure and undefiled... unstained from the world." The need for "practicing religion" as seen in James 1.27 needs not be a burden placed upon the church, and thus neither is it to be burdened with the assistance of non-saints.

Expediencies?

Argument: We give to the church so that the church can give to the poor as an expedient for us to fulfill our commands.

Answer: As discussed in **Instrumental Music**, an expedient is the way that one fulfills a command. Expedients are surely to be used when a command has been given, i.e. a songbook so that we know what to sing, a car to transport ourselves to assembly and back, and such things, but there is no Scriptural right to have an expedient for a command which has not been made. An expedient in the case of benevolence for a non-saint would be if a Christian financially supported an institution that assists the poor and needy (if that were a profitable way to go about assisting the poor). Involving the church constitutes an addition not sanctioned in the Scriptures.

Distinctions Between Responsibilities

Some, when discussing this issue, wish to cloud the matter under consideration by attempting to discuss orphans in general. The church has the responsibility to help anyone who is a saint no matter what he or she happens to be, a widow, a mother, a father, a child, or an orphan. If they have called upon the name of the Lord and have been added to His church (Acts 22.16), the church is under obligation to help them in any need. The church, however, has no such responsibility to anyone who is a non-saint, be they mothers, fathers, widows, children, or orphans, for this is the responsibility of the individual Christian (as discussed above; James 1.27, Galatians 6.10).

The Ends Justify the Means?

When discussing giving benevolence to non-saints, some will argue that the church can give money to non-saints in order to help convert them. They argue since some of these individuals will convert, what could be wrong with assisting them beforehand?

It is very true that we are to convert any and everyone we can (Matthew 28.18–20), and that the church ought to support evangelism (Philippians 4.15–16), yet does anything go when converting people? Should we do whatever we can to convert people? For instance, if a Christian would go into a bar to spread the Word and he buys a prospective Christian a drink, and the prospect later converts, does this justify the purchase of the alcohol? By no means! We are to lead others to Christ by our example (Matthew 5.7–13); what kind of example do we set when we implicitly approve things which God has not? We must always strive to evangelize and help those in the lost world, but we must not do so at the expense of our own purity and holiness, as evidenced in James 1.27.

Furthermore, to what are we converting people if we use benevolence? Are we converting people to the spiritual Kingdom of God or to a handout? Let us consider the example of John 6 and see that we need to preach the Gospel to convert people to the Gospel, and that we ought not to preach food or benevolence.

The Missionary Society

Many denominations have established what are called "missionary societies," institutions established to fund the needs of missionaries throughout the world. These missionary societies generally receive funding from individual churches within the denomination or denominations and distribute the funds to the missionaries. Do the Scriptures allow for such a practice?

There is no command or example in the Scriptures of any church or churches giving to a separate institution to support missionaries. It is argued, however, that since evangelists were funded in many different ways in the Scripture, by their own work (Acts 18.3), by the church they are currently working with (2 Corinthians 11.7–10), or by different churches supporting them (Philippians 4.15–17), that God has established a liberty in the way that missionaries may be funded.

It would be possible to justify a group of Christians coming together to pool their resources to fund an evangelist/missionary with the argument given above, yet, as we have seen earlier, the individual and the church are different entities. The difficulty within the Scriptures concerning the establishment of the missionary society is not in how the missionaries are funded but because of the means by which they are funded. A church is required to give up its funds into the hands of a different organization which determines who shall receive the funding in the missionary society system; where is the Scriptural pattern for a liberty in this regard?

The Scriptures teach that each individual congregation of the Lord's people is an autonomous entity: it is self-governed. Each congregation is to have its own elders shepherding the flock and deacons to serve its needs. We read the following in Acts 20.28 and Titus 1.5:

"Take heed unto yourselves, and to all the flock, in which the Holy Spirit hath made you bishops, to feed the church of the Lord which he purchased with his own blood."

For this cause left I thee in Crete, that thou shouldest set in order the things that were wanting, and appoint elders in every city, as I gave thee charge.

It may be noted here that Paul's words in Acts 20.28 are directed to the elders of the church in Ephesus, and the elders of the church in Ephesus only (Acts 20.17). We have no evidence in the Scriptures that any of these churches were governed by any higher official of any kind.

Therefore, since each individual congregation is an autonomous entity, each congregation is responsible for encouraging and edifying one another and supporting evangelism. There is no pattern or example in the Scriptures of churches combining their efforts into a separate institution to fund evangelism. How can a local church wield any form of control over the funds they send to the society? If their funds go to pay for the support staff of the institution, have they fulfilled the commandment to fund evangelism or have they spent the money improperly? The local congregation evidently has no control over where the money goes, and if asked cannot definitively claim that their funds were spent directly on evangelism nor can they affirm the soundness of those to whom funds were given. Thus, the "missionary society" is an institution without Scriptural foundations, and churches which fund these societies violate the Scriptural pattern of local church autonomy.

The Sponsoring Church Arrangement

There have been some, especially in some congregations of churches of Christ, who do not have missionary societies but instead fund evangelists through a "sponsoring church arrangement," where one local church supports a missionary in a given place and all other churches who desire to fund that missionary send aid to that church. Is this a pattern established in the Scriptures?

The idea is quite similar to the missionary society, with a local church taking over the responsibility of the society. While this system would have less bureaucracy, there is still no Scriptural support for such an arrangement. The local church would still not be directly funding the evangelist, and the pattern of the autonomy of the local church would again be violated.

It is argued by some that such an arrangement was in place with Paul and the church of Jerusalem in Acts 15.22 and Acts 16.4–5 with the churches of Antioch and Asia Minor. Since the church in Jerusalem gave a message of truth to Paul to proclaim to these churches, it is argued that this is an example of the church in Jerusalem assisting the other churches in evangelism. What do the Scriptures say?

We read the following in Acts 15.22 and Acts 16.4–5:

> Then it seemed good to the apostles and the elders, with the whole church, to choose men out of their company, and send them to Antioch with Paul and Barnabas; namely, Judas called Barsabbas, and Silas, chief men among the brethren.

> And as they went on their way through the cities, they delivered them the decrees to keep which had been ordained of the apostles and elders that were at Jerusalem. So the churches were strengthened in the faith, and increased in number daily.

It is difficult not to notice that the Apostles factor heavily in this episode; but why are the elders in Jerusalem involved? The reason is made clear in Acts 15.1:

> And certain men came down from Judaea and taught the brethren, saying, "Except ye be circumcised after the custom of Moses, ye cannot be saved."

This matter was discussed by not only the Apostles but also the elders of the church in Jerusalem because the source of the conflict came from this area. We know from 2 Corinthians 3.1–2 that the men teaching this error would come with letters of commendation, and since they were at least formerly part of the church in Jerusalem (Acts 15.5), the elders of that church stood up for the truth of the Gospel because the error originated in their own congregation.

The source of the authority of the message proclaimed by letter through Paul and the others is the approval of the Holy Spirit, understood by the apostles and the elders of the church of Jerusalem. This decision was not proclaimed by the church in Jerusalem to the churches in Asia Minor: the decision was proclaimed through Paul and the others with the approval of the other Apostles and the elders of the church in Jerusalem by the authority of the Holy Spirit.

Further, no funds or any other form of aid was given on the basis of this matter, nor did all the churches look up to the church in Jerusalem for this decision: the elders of the church in Antioch thought it wise to send Paul and the others to Jerusalem to discuss the matter with the Apostles, the men inspired by the Holy Spirit, along with the elders of Jerusalem, the authorities over the congregation from which the source of the conflict arose. There is no hint in these passages of the modern "sponsoring church arrangement."

The main argument given is that benevolence and evangelism are tied together, and since none disagree that a local church has the authority to send benevolence to another local church to disperse to others, this means that a local church can send funding for evangelism to another local church to disperse to others. What Scripture, however, states definitively that benevolence and evangelism are tied together? There is evidence in the Scriptures to the contrary, seen in Acts 6.1–4:

> Now in these days, when the number of the disciples was multiplying, there arose a murmuring of the Grecian Jews against the Hebrews, because their widows were neglected in the daily ministration.
> And the twelve called the multitude of the disciples unto them, and said, "It is not fit that we should forsake the word of God, and serve tables. Look ye out therefore, brethren, from among you seven men of good report, full of the Spirit and of wisdom, whom we may appoint over this business. But we will continue stedfastly in prayer, and in the ministry of the word."

Here we have evidence of benevolence and evangelism separated quite clearly: the Apostles did not find it proper to leave the preaching of the Word of God to assist the brethren at that time. If benevolence and evangelism are tied together, why would the Apostles separate them?

It is further argued that Paul was the beneficiary of a "sponsoring church arrangement" according to Philippians 4.15–16 and 2 Corinthians 11.8–9:

And ye yourselves also know, ye Philippians, that in the beginning of the gospel, when I departed from Macedonia, no church had fellowship with me in the matter of giving and receiving but ye only; for even in Thessalonica ye sent once and again unto my need.

I robbed other churches, taking wages of them that I might minister unto you; and when I was present with you and was in want, I was not a burden on any man; for the brethren, when they came from Macedonia, supplied the measure of my want; and in everything I kept myself from being burdensome unto you, and so will I keep myself.

Paul, in the letter to the Philippians, declares quite plainly in verse 15 that the church in Philippi was the only one supporting him when he left Macedonia! The account in 2 Corinthians is most probably about a similar event, but at this time many churches were supporting him—but the Scriptures do not give an account of in what way. "Churches" supporting Paul can be seen in one of two ways:

1. Individual churches sent to Paul individual contributions
2. Individual churches all gave resources to one church to send to Paul as a collective contribution

The second inference requires much stronger of an implication than the first, and without other sufficient Scriptural support, does not suffice as Scriptural evidence for the claim made. The first inference is simpler, and harmonizes better with the text.

Many other such texts exist, including Romans 15.29 and texts in 2 Corinthians 8 and 9, and all require the same idea of inference. In the end, the entire "sponsoring church arrangement" rests only on inference, and all of the Scriptures are more easily explained by individual churches contributing directly to evangelists. There remains no Scriptural authority to have a "sponsoring church arrangement," and such an idea violates the Scriptural principle of the autonomy of the local congregation.

The Church Treasury, II: Other Considerations

General Considerations

As we have seen in The Church Treasury, I: Benevolence, many denominations burden the church with responsibilities it has not been called upon to bear, especially in terms of benevolence to non-saints and the creation of unnecessary institutions to facilitate benevolence and evangelism.

Many denominations also burden the collective with other responsibilities, including healing the ill, educating children, and feeding people, among other things. We will investigate many different aspects of these responsibilities below. Before we do, however, it is important that we remind ourselves of two important principles that we establish in other sections.

In **Instrumental Music: Silence Considerations**, it is established that silence does not authorize or condemn in and of itself, but that there must be either corresponding generic authority to establish liberty, or specific authority to establish prohibition. The following practices come with no New Testament command that the church should engage in them; it is hard to say, therefore, how they could in any way be authorized and profitable for the church.

In **The Church Treasury, I: Benevolence: The Individual and the Church**, it is established that the individual and the church, while often sharing obligations, are not interchangeable. 1 Timothy 5.16 provides the principle that the individual is not the same as the church, for the individual is to be burdened with a believing widow so that the church can help others. Many of the practices concerning which we will speak are profitable for individuals to do; there is no evidence from the Scriptures, however, that the church has been burdened with these responsibilities.

Nevertheless, many times when people are questioned about many of the practices mentioned below, especially in terms of where the church is authorized to erect buildings for the purposes of healing, fellowship, exercise, etc., they will respond by wondering what authority exists for a church building at all.

It is a good question, indeed; there are no church buildings in the New Testament, nor is there ever a command to build one. The church building is really a liberty: an expedient for the assembling of the saints. The expedient is authorized from the New Testament by the clear commandment to assemble in Hebrews 10.25:

> ...not forsaking our own assembling together, as the custom of some is, but exhorting one another; and so much the more, as ye see the day drawing nigh.

The command establishes that we are to assemble; we have examples in Acts 20.7 and 1 Corinthians 16.1–2 that Christians assembled on the first day of the week to break bread and to have a collection, and that further assemblies could also be held daily if one so desired (Acts 2.46). Nevertheless, what do we see in regards to where we should assemble in the New Testament?

We see the following three examples in the New Testament:

1. The Temple, from Acts 2.46:

> And day by day, continuing stedfastly with one accord in the temple, and breaking bread at home, they took their food with gladness and singleness of heart.

2. Solomon's Portico, from Acts 5.12:

> And by the hands of the apostles were many signs and wonders wrought among the people; and they were all with one accord in Solomon's porch.

3. Houses of Christians, from Philemon 1.2:

> ...and to Apphia our sister, and to Archippus our fellow-soldier, and to the church in thy house.

We see from these three examples that Christians met wherever they could, and that because of the varying places, God has shown through

His Word His indifference to where His saints meet. Thus, since we have generic authority concerning our meeting place, we have authority to build a building for that purpose.

Hospitals

Some denominations create and support hospitals to care for the sick. Oftentimes it is argued that since Jesus healed the sick, the church can help to heal the sick. Is this what we see established in the Bible?

As individuals, if we have the opportunity to help some people who are ill, by all means we should do so. Such is what James expects in James 5.14:

> Is any among you sick? Let him call for the elders of the church;
> and let them pray over him, anointing him with oil in the name
> of the Lord: and the prayer of faith shall save him that is sick,
> and the Lord shall raise him up; and if he have committed sins, it
> shall be forgiven him.

It is interesting to see that James expects the elders to pray over the ill person, and that it is the prayer of faith that shall save. James does not expect the church to build hospitals for this purpose; instead, the elders and the sick person are to trust in God.

Does the fact that Jesus heals people mean that we should build hospitals? It is clear that part of Jesus' ministry did include healing the sick (Matthew 4.24), yet what was the primary mission of Jesus while on the earth? Jesus Himself establishes His purpose in Luke 19.10:

> For the Son of man came to seek and to save that which was lost.

Jesus' purpose, then, was to "seek and save the lost"—not from their illnesses *per se*, but from their sins! Healing the sick was a sign for the people to realize that Jesus was the Christ. Many who were healed realized in the process the need to follow Jesus (cf. John 9). Nevertheless, Jesus' primary purpose has always been to redeem lost souls, and the church is to carry on that mission (Matthew 28.18–20, Philippians 4.15–17). The church has nowhere been burdened with the responsibility of building and funding hospitals.

Centers of Education

Many churches today fund centers of education, be it for primary or secondary education, private colleges, or schools for religious instruction. Do the Scriptures indicate that the church has been so burdened?

Christians have the right to be educated; Luke himself was a physician (Colossians 4.14). We are also to be educated in religious matters, as Paul says to Timothy in 2 Timothy 2.15:

> Give diligence to present thyself approved unto God, a workman that needeth not to be ashamed, handling aright the word of truth.

We are to teach and to learn (Colossians 3.16), but we never see a church erecting a facility for the purpose of educating anyone. The only New Testament examples of religious instruction involve the regular teaching and preaching in the assemblies of the saints (Cf. Acts 2.42) and Paul and Timothy, Titus, and others, when the more experienced preacher (Paul) continually taught Timothy and Titus while they worked with him in the churches and by letter (cf. 1 Timothy, 2 Timothy, and Titus).

The primary responsibility for the education of children lay with the parents of the child (Ephesians 6.4). If the parents decide to send their child to a public or private school to learn of secular matters, and instruct in religion in their home, or if they decide to home school in both secular and religious matters, well and good; they have liberty in that matter. Nevertheless, the church has not been burdened with the responsibility of training up children in secular matters, nor to create and/or fund an institution to teach children in any way, shape, or form.

Kitchens/Fellowship Halls

Many churches today have built kitchens and/or fellowship halls to encourage fellowship amongst the saints. While it may seem like a good idea, has the church been so burdened?

Christians certainly should get together and have association with one another; hospitality involving the saints is commanded by Peter in 1 Peter 4.9. While we have examples of Christians getting together for social reasons, including the eating of meals (cf. Acts 2.46), nowhere do we see that the corporate church has in fact facilitated such association with a building or any other such thing. Further, we read the following in 1 Corinthians 11.19–22:

For there must be also factions among you, that they that are approved may be made manifest among you. When therefore ye assemble yourselves together, it is not possible to eat the Lord's supper: for in your eating each one taketh before other his own supper; and one is hungry, and another is drunken. What, have ye not houses to eat and to drink in? Or despise ye the church of God, and put them to shame that have not? What shall I say to you? Shall I praise you? In this I praise you not.

Clearly, the church in Corinth had division fostered within itself, and it would seem from this passage that some of this division was being caused by eating and drinking during their assembly. Paul here is delineating between activities while assembled and activities to be done at home: partake of the Lord's Supper together; eat and drink at home.

Individuals are to open their homes and share meals with brethren; the church has not been so burdened.

When the matter of the fellowship hall or the kitchen is discussed, many times people will ask what is wrong with "eating in the building". The matter is not about "eating in the building," so to speak. Many times children require food during a long assembly; some people for other health reasons need to eat at specified times. There may be a time when people are working on the building and it is convenient to eat there. Nevertheless, there is a vast difference between an individual or two eating in the building for some necessary purpose and setting aside space in the church building or erecting another building for the sole purpose of preparing food and/or eating within. The issue is not about "eating in the building," *per se*, but whether or not the Scriptures have burdened the church with the obligation of facilitating the association of its constituents; no such authorization has been put forward.

Argument: The fellowship hall is an expedient for us to have fellowship.

Answer: As we have seen previously in **The Church Treasury, I: Benevolence: Expediencies?**, if one is going to have an authorized "expedient," the expedient must be facilitating the fulfillment of a command. As with giving benevolence to non-saints, so it is with association: nowhere is the church commanded do such things. Yes, there are examples of the church getting together for a social function, but where do we see that examples are to be expedited? Where has the church been burdened with the responsibility of expediting the God-given obligations of the individual? The Scriptures indicate no such burden!

Gymnasiums

There are many denominations and churches that have built gymnasiums. Such facilities are designed to help better the physical bodies of the members and to provide association.

While 1 Corinthians 6.19 indicates that our bodies are the "temple of the Holy Spirit," and therefore that it would be a good idea to keep the body in good shape, the Scriptures nowhere command physical exercise, even for the individual. Paul does establish that physical exercise does profit a little in 1 Timothy 4.8, and therefore a Christian certainly has the right to exercise. Nevertheless, since physical exercise is nowhere commanded, even for the individual, in the Scriptures, how can a church building a gymnasium for that purpose be justified Biblically? It is clear that the church has nowhere been so burdened!

Business Enterprises

In many larger churches today, it is popular for various kinds of businesses to be run within the church campus, somehow or another connected to that particular church. These businesses include coffee shops, bookstores, and other enterprises. Some denominations even serve as landlords or run investment corporations and may perhaps own and run facilities in no way connected to any religious purpose.

While it may be profitable for individuals to engage in business and to support their families (1 Timothy 5.8), the church has nowhere been burdened with the responsibility of operating or overseeing business enterprises. The Bible indicates that the church is to support its work by the freewill contributions of its members (1 Corinthians 16.1–3, 2 Corinthians 9), or in times of distress, money for benevolence from other churches (2 Corinthians 8–9). There is no other Biblically-approved way for the church to make money. We see no indication that the church ought to be involved in coffee houses, bookstores, real estate, or any other such thing.

Evangelism?

Sometimes one or more of the above practices will be defended in the name of evangelism: the fellowship hall or the gymnasium or the bookstore or some other such thing may lead someone to Christ. Is such a sufficient justification for these practices?

We have previously discussed a similar matter in **The Church Treasury, I: Benevolence: The Ends Justify the Means?**. One of the important points mentioned regarded to what you convert people when you use food or medical care or a gym or other such things. Are such persons being converted to Jesus and His truth or to the various services provided?

Jesus provides a helpful illustration in John 6. After He has fed the five thousand, and the people have followed after Him, He says the following to them in verse 26:

> Jesus answered them and said, "Verily, verily, I say unto you, Ye seek me, not because ye saw signs, but because ye ate of the loaves, and were filled."

While it is true that Jesus fed the multitude, the multitude was converted to bread, not Jesus. As Jesus preaches some difficult truths in verses 27 through 65, this fact becomes apparent. In John 6.66, it is clear that only the original twelve disciples remain with Him. Of the five thousand who ate bread, how many were converted to serve Jesus? Not one. If such was the result for our God and Savior, how should we expect to fare any better?

To build and maintain such facilities is by no means a profitable form of evangelism, and such is indicated by the example of our Lord Himself. We ought to preach the Gospel of Christ by promoting His spiritual truth, and not to try to attach the Gospel to some form of a gimmick or "bait and switch" concept.

.

Concerning Observances

Statement of Belief

In general, the Scriptures indicate no specific festivals or specific observances for Christians save the assembly on the first day of the week to break bread (Acts 20.7).

The Scriptures make no commandment or memorial to honor the birth of our Lord; the Scriptures do not even mention the date of His birth.

Concerning the Lord's death, the only memorial He has established for it in the Scriptures is the Lord's Supper,

> And He said unto them, "With desire I have desired to eat this passover with you before I suffer: for I say unto you, I shall not eat it, until it be fulfilled in the kingdom of God."
> And He received a cup, and when he had given thanks, He said, "Take this, and divide it among yourselves: for I say unto you, I shall not drink from henceforth of the fruit of the vine, until the kingdom of God shall come."
> And He took bread, and when He had given thanks, He brake it, and gave to them, saying, "This is my body which is given for you: this do in remembrance of me."
> And the cup in like manner after supper, saying, "This cup is the new covenant in my blood, even that which is poured out for you." *(Luke 22.15–20).*

Observances and the "Church Year"

Over the course of the history of "Christendom," many special observances in many forms have been established. These observances, in theory, attempt to celebrate many events in the life and death of Jesus, the founding of the church, and celebrations of various individuals over time. In many cases, these observances represent a "Christianizing" of previously pagan festivals: since the pagans would not give up their festivals, religious authorities simply provided a new Christian veneer.

None of the observances concerning which we are about to speak derive from the New Testament. We see no evidence from the New Testament that the Christians observed any of the observances described below. This silence is quite telling, especially considering their modern popularity.

In discussions such as these, however, it is important to remember Romans 14.5–6:

> One man esteemeth one day above another: another esteemeth every day alike. Let each man be fully assured in his own mind. He that regardeth the day, regardeth it unto the Lord: and he that eateth, eateth unto the Lord, for he giveth God thanks; and he that eateth not, unto the Lord he eateth not, and giveth God thank.

While we find no Scriptural reason to observe many of these festivals and other observances, the vast majority of them most likely fit into the description here in Romans 14.5. Taking out particular days to remember events in the life of our Lord are not wrong or sinful; they are not, however, to be bound upon others.

The collection of most of the popular observances (Advent, Christmas, Epiphany, Annunciation, Ash Wednesday, Lent, Palm Sunday, Good Friday, Easter, Ascension, Pentecost) comprise what is often called the "church year" in many denominations. Since these observances normally fit between November and July, they do not represent much of a substantive year. Nevertheless, such a concept is not grounded in the Scriptures, and we see no reason to limit remembrance of various aspects of the Lord's life and death to particular times of the year.

Observances Concerning the Lord's Birth

Advent

In some denominations, a season called Advent is observed. It begins either on November 11 or on the fourth Sunday before Christmas, and it is a season to meditate upon the prophecies concerning the Christ. Many times, the observers will have calendars for Advent and will read certain Scriptures concerning the prophecies as outlined by their denomination.

While it may be beneficial to spend some time considering the prophecies regarding the Christ, the Scriptures teach nothing concerning doing so. We are to always remember the Lord's life and His deeds on our behalf, especially in the observation of the Lord's Supper (1 Corinthians 11.26).

Christmas

In many denominations, December 25 is observed as Christmas (from the Old English *christes maesse*, "festival of Christ"). Christmas has its roots in pagan festivals, notably the Saturnalia of the Romans and concerning Mithras of the Persians, as a celebration of the winter solstice and the "rebirth" of the Sun. Read what Tertullian, a "church father," has to say of such things:

> The Saturnalia, New Year, Midwinter festivals, and Matronalia are frequented by us! Presents come and go! There are New Year's gifts! Games join their noise! Banquets join their din! The pagans are more faithful to their sect...For, even if they had known them, they would not have shared the Lord's Day or Pentecost with us. For they would fear lest they would appear to be Christians. Yet, we are not apprehensive that we might appear to be pagans! *(On Idolatry 14).*

The pagan origin of this festival, then, is confirmed, and that Christians were observing such things to their shame is also attested. The date of December 25 was arbitrarily fixed to coincide with these festivals in order for them to be "Christianized." Clement of Alexandria has the following to say concerning the birth date of Christ:

> Therefore, from the birth of Christ to the death of Commodus [Ed. note: Commodus was emperor of Rome in the second century] are a total of one hundred ninety-four years, one month, and thirteen days. There are those who have calculated not only the year of our Lord's birth, but also the day. They say that it took place in the twenty-eighth year of Augustus, on the twenty-fifth day of Pachon [May 20]...Others say that He was born on the twenty-fourth or twenty-fifth day of Parmuthi [April 19 or 20] *(Stromata, 1.21).*

The Scriptures do not fix the specific day of the birth of our Lord, nor even its season. We do not know when He was born, but all evidence we do have points to either spring or fall. December 25 surely is not the day of the birth of our Lord.

The fact that Scripture does not teach the day on which our Lord was born is significant: it demonstrates clearly that we have no commandment, example, or inference that we ought to celebrate the day of the Lord's birth over any other day. There is no authorization for the religious observance of Christmas.

Binding No Observance of Christmas?

There are some today who will even bind that no one should celebrate Christmas in any form, even the social and secular aspects of it. Do the Scriptures justify such a stand?

First, it must be said that Christmas is not today nor has it ever been a "Christian" holiday. It has never fully divested itself of much of its pagan origins, and most of the traditions we associate with Christmas actually derive from only the past two hundred years. Furthermore, our modern culture has embraced Christmas as a secular holiday, a time to come together with family and to exchange gifts. Even the court system these days finds no difficulty with state recognition of Christmas; it surely is not "only" religious!

We have previously seen what Paul said about observances in Romans 14.15–16; he also says the following in Colossians 2.16–17:

> Let no man therefore judge you in meat, or in drink, or in respect of a feast day or a new moon or a sabbath day: which are a shadow of the things to come; but the body is Christ's.

As we can see, Paul says that we are not to condemn or be judged based on the observation (or lack thereof) of any day or any festival. We would do well to remember this in the context of this lesson: while these observances are not authorized in Scripture, we cannot condemn their observation as sin. Therefore, no one has the right to bind the lack of observation of any holiday on another who feels that the holiday is acceptable. Furthermore, no one who observes a holiday has the right to bind that holiday on anyone who does not agree with it.

Therefore, while we ought to respect the convictions of those who do not observe Christmas in any way, and ought not put a stumbling block in their way, such persons also ought to respect the liberty of their brethren to observe the day in a secular manner, and not be quick to condemn (cf. Romans 14.3–21).

Observances Concerning the Lord's Death

Ash Wednesday

Toward the end of February, approximately forty days before Easter, the observance of Ash Wednesday is performed in some denominations. Often, the ashes of palm fronds used in the previous year's Palm Sunday (see below) are placed on the observer's forehead as a sign of penitence and the cognizance of the mortality of man. This observance is the beginning of the season of Lent.

There are no Scriptures that demonstrate the use of this observance, nor is it ever commanded in Scripture.

Lent

In some denominations, a season of Lent is observed between Ash Wednesday and Easter. The season lasts forty days, and is designed for observers to imitate Christ in the desert (Matthew 4.1–2). In earlier times, observers would fast completely; later, observers would only have to sacrifice any unnecessary indulgences. Today, many are content with sacrificing one or more pleasures. Often, the observers will abstain from the eating of meat, at least on Fridays.

Although the desire to sacrifice and to fast is admirable and is Scriptural (Acts 13.3), we have no Scriptures that authorize such practices for forty days before Easter. It is important to remember that binding abstinence from food was one of the marks of the falling away that was to come (1 Timothy 4.3). There is no doubt that we ought to sacrifice for our Lord; nevertheless, the Scriptures attest that our sacrifices ought to be complete and constant, and not a trifle for a short period of time (cf. Romans 12.1, Galatians 2.20).

Palm Sunday

In many denominations, the Sunday before Easter is celebrated as Palm Sunday. This observance is done as an imitation of the arrival of our Lord in Jerusalem a week before His crucifixion, as seen in John 12.12–15:

> On the morrow a great multitude that had come to the feast, when they heard that Jesus was coming to Jerusalem, took the branches of the palm trees, and went forth to meet him, and cried out, "Hosanna: Blessed is he that cometh in the name of the Lord, even the King of Israel."

> And Jesus, having found a young ass, sat thereon; as it is written, "Fear not, daughter of Zion: behold, thy King cometh, sitting on an ass's colt."

Palm fronds are given to each observer in memory of this event. It is good to remember the events surrounding the arrival of our Lord in Jerusalem and the other events leading up to his death, but we have no indication from the Scriptures that such things are to be re-created or observed in any special way.

Maundy Thursday

Also called Holy Thursday, this day is observed by many denominations as the day before Good Friday, the day in which the Lord instituted the Lord's Supper (Matthew 26.20–29). The Lord's Supper is therefore partaken on this day.

The Scriptures do mention the need to partake of the Lord's Supper (see above), but our only example of Christians doing so after the death and resurrection of our Lord is on the first day of the week (Acts 20.7; see **The Lord's Supper**). The Lord's Supper takes on an aspect of also remembering the Lord's resurrection on the first day of the week, and it is telling that there are no examples from the Scriptures of anyone observing the Lord's Supper on any Thursday. Again, while it may be beneficial to remember the events leading up to the Lord's death, we find no evidence from the Scriptures that such are to be done on a consistent yearly basis.

Good Friday

Good Friday is observed on the Friday before Easter in many denominations. This recognizes the day in which Christ was crucified, and died. There is much speculation as to whether Christ was crucified on a Thursday or a Friday; it depends if the sign of Jonah as discussed in Matthew 16.4 and the "three days" of John 2.19 are either three full days Thursday/Friday, Friday/Saturday, Saturday/Sunday) or the "third" day (first day Friday, second day Saturday, third day Sunday). Regardless, we have never been given a command to observe the Lord's death on the Friday before Easter in the Scriptures; we have been commanded to observe the Lord's death on the first day of every week by partaking of the Lord's Supper (Acts 20.7, 1 Corinthians 11.23–29; for more regarding this observance, see **The Lord's Supper**).

Easter

Easter is observed between the end of March and the middle of April each year on a Sunday by many denominations as the day of the resurrection of our Lord, as seen in the Gospels (cf. Matthew 28.1–9). The date is supposed to be parallel with the Passover and Feast of the Unleavened Bread observance of the Jews, and therefore falls on the Sunday two weeks after the first new moon on or after the vernal equinox.

While we have no dispute that Jesus did indeed die and was resurrected in the midst of the Passover and Feast of the Unleavened Bread observance, the Scriptures never indicate that Christians are to specifically observe this event at this time nor does it provide any examples of Christians doing so. Moreover, the origin of the Easter observance does not come only from the tradition of the death of Christ; the pagans had many festivals concerning the spring equinox, for it is at this time that the Earth becomes green and alive again. The term "Easter" itself comes from the Teutonic [a German tribe] goddess *Eaestre*, who was a goddess of fertility. The pagan traditions of the rebirth of the land and the Christian tradition of the rebirth of Christ were thus joined by the denominations in the celebration of Easter. The fact that the Lord's Supper is on Sunday, the "Lord's day" (Revelation 1.10), indicates that Christians are to observe and celebrate the resurrection of our Lord on every first day of the week.

Other Observances

Ascension-Pentecost

Some denominations also observe the forty days between Easter and Christ's Ascension (Acts 1.9) and the following ten days until Pentecost (Acts 2). These observances serve to remember the power of Christ and the genesis of the church on Earth. Again, the Scriptures never teach any commandment or example to observe these days.

There are some who may attempt to establish that Christians did indeed observe Pentecost based on Luke's description of events in Acts 20.16:

> For Paul had determined to sail past Ephesus, that he might not have to spend time in Asia; for he was hastening, if it were possible for him, to be at Jerusalem the day of Pentecost.

While it is interesting that Luke records the events in terms of this observance, we must also note that he speaks of the "days of unleavened bread" in Acts 20.6. Since Paul so often associated with Jews (cf. Acts 17.1–3), and he was returning to the Jewish heartland, it should perhaps not surprise us that Luke is telling time on the basis of these observances. We see no indication that Luke or Paul or anyone else is actually observing either the days of unleavened bread or Pentecost; these seem to be used simply as time markers. Furthermore, we have no idea whether Pentecost is being mentioned in terms of the Jewish festival itself or in a "Christianized" form. Despite this use of the term "Pentecost," the Scriptures still remain silent on whether early Christians observed this day as the founding of the church or in any way whatsoever.

Epiphany

According to some denominations, January 6 is observed as Epiphany. This day is considered by these observers to be the day in which Christ was baptized by John (Matthew 3.13–17). This is the beginning of Christ's ministry on Earth; therefore, the Eastern Orthodox celebrate Epiphany at the same level as the Roman Catholics and some Protestant denominations celebrate Christmas. Epiphany is also known as the Twelfth Day, and is observed by some denominations as the day on which the Magi from the East visited Christ (Matthew 2). On a secondary level it is also the observation of the deeds of Christ at the wedding feast in Cana (John 2.1–11).

While it is good to remember these events, the specific day of Christ's baptism, the day of the wedding feast in Cana, nor the day of the arrival of the Magi are precisely fixed in Scripture, and no commandment or example exists for their observance.

Annunciation

Some denominations observe the feast of the Annunciation, or the day wherein Gabriel announced to Mary that she would be impregnated by the Holy Spirit (Luke 1.26–38). This feast is observed on March 25, corresponding to the belief that Christ was born on December 25 (exactly 9 months later). Since the Scriptures are silent on when Jesus was born, by necessity the Scriptures are also silent on when Gabriel visited Mary. It is good for us to remember how Gabriel visited Mary, but the Scriptures make no command or show any example of observing this event.

Days Concerning Saints

In some denominations, days are observed for "saints." A church, like the Roman Catholic Church, will determine what day of the year a certain "saint" (for the purposes of this discussion, the "saint" is one considered canonized by the Roman Catholic Church and/or other denominations) will be honored. Furthermore, November 1 is considered to be All Saints' Day, a day wherein all such "saints" are honored. Concerning saints, please consider **Roman Catholicism, II: Traditions Concerning Saints;** since the modern definition of "saint" does not concord to the Scriptural definition of "saint," neither should we expect the Scriptures to endorse the celebration of days regarding them. It can be good to consider the struggles of faith of faithful Christians that have lived since the cross; nevertheless, the Scriptures do not show that we should venerate them in any special way.

Creeds

Overview

Many denominations hold to creeds, or statements of faith, written in ages past. Many feel that these creeds represent a summation of the faith outlined in the Scriptures, or a concise statement of their belief system. While many denominations have their own creeds, we will now examine three creeds more widely used among denominations, the Apostles' Creed, the Nicene Creed, and the Athanasian Creed.

The Apostles' Creed

Even though many may believe legends that the Apostles' Creed was developed by the Apostles themselves on the Day of Pentecost or some such time, this is not so. The earliest complete text of the creed is from the eighth century; many believe that it has its origins in certain litanies performed in the second century. Regardless of its historicity, many denominations accept it as a concise summation of the Gospels; Luther went so far as to declare it **the** statement of faith. The following is the text of the Apostles' Creed, with notes describing the variants in the text:

> I believe in God, the Father Almighty, creator of Heaven and Earth.
> I believe in Jesus Christ, His only Son, our Lord.
> He was conceived by the power of the Holy Spirit and born of the Virgin Mary.
> He suffered under Pontius Pilate, and was buried.
> He descended into Hell.[1]
> On the third day He rose again.[2]
> He ascended to Heaven and is seated at the right hand of the Father.
> He will come again to judge the living and the dead.

I believe in the Holy Spirit, the holy catholic Church,[3] the communion of saints, the forgiveness of sins, the resurrection of the body, and the life everlasting.
Amen.

1: Anglicanism (original is also used, but this variant is accepted): "...was crucified, died, and was buried. He descended to the dead."

Calvinism: "...was crucified, died, and was buried. He descended into Hell."

2: Calvinism adds "from the dead."

3: Lutheranism: "the holy Christian church."

As we have seen, many consider the Apostles' Creed to sum up the message of the Gospel. There is one aspect of this creed that does not entirely fit the message of the Gospel, however—the idea that "He descended into Hell." Those who adhere to the creed say that this is in conformity with the teaching in 1 Peter 3.18–19:

> Because Christ also suffered for sins once, the righteous for the unrighteous, that he might bring us to God; being put to death in the flesh, but made alive in the spirit; in which also he went and preached unto the spirits in prison.

Does Peter say that Christ descended into Hell? By no means! Peter is saying that Christ preached to those *now* in prison; Peter makes no comment as to where they were when Jesus preached to them.

We can be sure that Christ did not descend to Hell during His time between the crucifixion and the resurrection because David prophesied the following of Him in Psalm 16.10:

> For thou wilt not leave my soul to Sheol; Neither wilt thou suffer thy holy one to see corruption.

How could Jesus descend to Hell if He is prophesied to not be abandoned to Sheol, or Hell? The Apostles' Creed would not have Jesus fulfill prophecy! Therefore, we can see that the Apostles' Creed does not entirely sum up the Gospel.

The Nicene Creed

The Nicene Creed is a specific statement of faith that had a specific purpose. In 325, the Roman emperor Constantine called together a council of all the bishops in the "catholic" church to come together in the city of Nicaea in modern day Turkey to resolve the conflict that had begun concerning the relationship of the Father to the Son. The Arians had determined that the Son was always subservient to the Father, yet the majority of the "catholic" church held to their equality, in nature and in position. This is the creed determined by this council:

> We believe in one God, the Father, the Almighty, Maker of Heaven and Earth, of all there is, seen and unseen.
> We believe in one Lord, Jesus Christ, the only Son of God eternally begotten of the Father, God from God, Light from Light, true God from true God, begotten, not made, one in Being with the Father. Through Him all things were made.
> For us men and our salvation He came down from Heaven: by the power of the Holy Spirit He was born of the Virgin Mary, and became man.
> For our sake He was crucified under Pontius Pilate;
> He suffered, died, and was buried.
> On the third day He rose again according to the Scriptures;
> He ascended into Heaven and is seated at the right hand of the Father.
> He will come again in glory to judge the living and the dead, and His Kingdom will have no end.
> We believe in the Holy Spirit, the Lord, the giver of life, who proceeds from the Father.[1]
> With the Father and the Son He is worshiped and glorified.
> He has spoken through the Prophets.
> We believe in one holy catholic and apostolic Church.
> We acknowledge one baptism for the forgiveness of sins.
> We look for the resurrection of the dead, and the life of the world to come.
> Amen.

1: The Roman Catholic church and the denominations of western Europe add: "…and the Son."

Such is the Nicene Creed, a summation of faith, but as we will see in the conclusion, is it necessary?

The Athanasian Creed

The name of the Athanasian Creed is derived from Athanasius, "bishop" of Alexandria in the mid-fourth century CE, yet the creed itself was most likely written sometime during the seventh or eighth century CE, likely in Spain. This creed is also written against Arianism.

> Whosoever will be saved, before all things it is necessary that he hold the catholic faith.
> Which faith except every one do keep whole and undefiled, without doubt he shall perish everlastingly.
>
> And the catholic faith is this, that we worship one God in Trinity, and Trinity in Unity;
> Neither confounding the Persons, nor dividing the Substance.
> For there is one Person of the Father, another of the Son, and another of the Holy Ghost.
> But the Godhead of the Father, of the Son, and of the Holy Ghost is all one: the glory equal, the majesty coeternal.
> Such as the Father is, such is the Son, and such is the Holy Ghost.
> The Father uncreate, the Son uncreate, and the Holy Ghost uncreate.
> The Father incomprehensible, the Son incomprehensible, and the Holy Ghost incomprehensible.
> The Father eternal, the Son eternal, and the Holy Ghost eternal.
> And yet they are not three Eternals, but one Eternal.
> As there are not three Uncreated nor three Incomprehensibles, but one Uncreated and one Incomprehensible.
> So likewise the Father is almighty, the Son almighty, and the Holy Ghost almighty.
> And yet they are not three Almighties, but one Almighty.
> So the Father is God, the Son is God, and the Holy Ghost is God.
> And yet they are not three Gods, but one God.
> So likewise the Father is Lord, the Son Lord, and the Holy Ghost Lord.
> And yet not three Lords, but one Lord.

For like as we are compelled by the Christian verity to acknowledge every Person by Himself to be God and Lord,

So are we forbidden by the catholic religion to say,

There be three Gods, or three Lords.

The Father is made of none: neither created nor begotten.

The Son is of the Father alone; not made, nor created, but begotten.

The Holy Ghost is of the Father and of the Son: neither made, nor created, nor begotten, but proceeding.

So there is one Father, not three Fathers; one Son, not three Sons; one Holy Ghost, not three Holy Ghosts.

And in this Trinity none is before or after other; none is greater or less than another;

But the whole three Persons are coeternal together, and coequal: so that in all things, as is aforesaid, the Unity in Trinity and the Trinity in Unity is to be worshiped.

He, therefore, that will be saved must thus think of the Trinity.

Furthermore, it is necessary to everlasting salvation that he also believe faithfully the incarnation of our Lord Jesus Christ.

For the right faith is, that we believe and confess that our Lord Jesus Christ, the Son of God, is God and Man; God of the Substance of the Father, begotten before the worlds; and Man of the substance of His mother, born in the world;

Perfect God and perfect Man, of a reasonable soul and human flesh subsisting.

Equal to the Father as touching His Godhead, and inferior to the Father as touching His manhood;

Who, although He be God and Man, yet He is not two, but one Christ:

One, not by conversion of the Godhead into flesh, but by taking the manhood into God;

One altogether; not by confusion of Substance, but by unity of Person.

For as the reasonable soul and flesh is one man, so God and Man is one Christ;

Who suffered for our salvation; descended into hell, rose again the third day from the dead; He ascended into heaven; He sitteth

on the right hand of the Father, God Almighty; from whence He
shall come to judge the quick and the dead.
At whose coming all men shall rise again with their bodies, and
shall give an account of their own works.
And they that have done good shall go into life everlasting; and
they that have done evil, into everlasting fire.

This is the catholic faith; which except a man believe faithfully
and firmly, he cannot be saved.

The Athanasian Creed would seem to negate the many statements of Jesus showing that there is some aspect of hierarchy in the Godhead, the Father, then the Son, then the Holy Spirit (John 14.16–17, 1 Corinthians 15.24–28). How meaningful such a "hierarchy" is when God is One in essence and purpose is of course worthy of discussion, but it is present within the Scripture. The Athanasian Creed also affirms Jesus having gone into hell, discussed above. These issues, therefore, lead us to question the legitimacy of such a creed.

Conclusion

There are many other creeds, conciliar decisions, and confessions made that denominations hold to, but these three are the most common. What do we learn from them?

We can see that they are not the inspired Word of God, for not one of them comes with any authority from God at all. This is clear in how the wording is changed in them: Luther changes the Apostles' Creed to sound less Roman Catholic, and the Roman Catholic and the Eastern Orthodox churches are still divided over the former's addition of "and the Son" to the Nicene Creed. No one believes that any of these creeds actually go back to the Apostles; they are all additions of men.

We must ask the question: why creeds? We see a great emphasis placed on such statements of faith within denominations, and yet the Scriptures never provide us with any explicit examples of them. Granted, many members of denominations who believe in creeds find creedal statements all over the place in the New Testament, but such represent interpretations of the data; we must wonder if they would "see" these creeds in the text if they themselves did not hold to creeds. Why are creeds even necessary? If they represent in substance the message of the Gospel, are God's words in the Scriptures not sufficient enough to speak and to which to adhere? If they are not substantively within the Scriptures, but represent our interpretations of various doctrines based upon what the Scriptures say, on what basis can we formulate them into statements and require universal adherence to them? How can we be sure that such statements are approved by God? Creeds, in the end, are entirely unnecessary; adherence to the Word of God as revealed in the Scriptures should be sufficient (2 Timothy 2.15, 2 Timothy 3.16–17). We must remember the words of Paul in Galatians 1.6–9, and always make sure that we hold to the Gospel which he delivered along with the other Apostles:

> I marvel that ye are so quickly removing from him that called you in the grace of Christ unto a different gospel; which is not another gospel, only there are some that trouble you, and would pervert the gospel of Christ. But though we, or an angel from heaven, should preach unto you any gospel other than that which we preached unto you, let him be anathema. As we have said before, so say I now again, if any man preacheth unto you any gospel other than that which ye received, let him be anathema.

Let us hold to the true Gospel, delivered to us in the Word of God, and not to the creeds and confessions of men.

Instrumental Music

Statement of Belief

The Scriptures teach that Christians are to sing in praise of their God:

> ...speaking one to another in psalms and hymns and spiritual
> songs, singing and making melody with your heart to the Lord
> *(Ephesians 5.19).*

> Let the word of Christ dwell in you richly; in all wisdom teaching
> and admonishing one another with psalms and hymns and spiritual
> songs, singing with grace in your hearts unto God *(Colossians 3.16).*

> Is any cheerful? Let him sing praise *(James 5.13).*

The Scriptures make no mention of the use of instrumental music for
Christians.

Silence Considerations

Many who use instrumental music first defend their practice by saying,
"Well, God never said **not** to use instruments!" Do the Scriptures establish this as a legitimate defense?

We must always remember the purpose of God's Word. The Word of
God is our guide to life; within its pages, we have all of the knowledge
that we need to live a life pleasing to God, as shown in 2 Timothy 3.16–17:

> Every scripture inspired of God is also profitable for teaching, for
> reproof, for correction, for instruction which is in righteousness.
> That the man of God may be complete, furnished completely unto
> every good work.

The Bible does not, however, lay out explicitly every little thing that is sinful. The Law was good at demonstrating what the Jews were not to do—however, thanks be to God, we are no longer under that bondage, for we are freed in Christ Jesus from such a Law (Colossians 2.14–17, etc.). We have an important principle established in Romans 14.23:

> But he that doubteth is condemned if he eat, because he eateth not of faith; and whatsoever is not of faith is sin.

Note that Paul does not say that whatsoever is not of sin is of faith; indeed, what is not of faith is sin. We recognize the nature of faith from Hebrews 11.1:

> Now faith is the assurance of things hoped for, the proving of things not seen.

Faith is not just some "feeling"; proper faith will have some substance and assurance. If we are going to engage in a practice, we need some legitimating evidence from the Scriptures. Therefore, we are to do what we see in the Bible according to valid principles. Nevertheless, some will question whether or not the idea of God's silence as being prohibitive is a valid principle. For them we appeal to Hebrews 7.13–14:

> For He of whom these things are said belongeth to another tribe, from which no man hath given attendance at the altar. For it is evident that our Lord hath sprung out of Judah; as to which tribe Moses spake nothing concerning priests.

In this situation, we see that God previously had made a specific command that the tribe of Levi officiate as priests (cf. Numbers 3.6–9). Christ, therefore, cannot be a priest according to the tribe of Levi because He descended from the tribe of Judah. God did not speak about the tribe of Judah officiating as priests because He gave commandment of the tribe of Levi, and to no other. Likewise, we have been given a specific command to sing; to use instrumental music would be adding where God has not said to add, and using the principle demonstrated in Hebrews 7.13–14, we see that the practice is wrong.

Others will say that God's silence shows indifference toward practices. In some cases, this can be true: when God has made a command to do something, but not about how to go about fulfilling the command, we have liberty to perform the command in any way we wish. A good example is assembling: we see that we are commanded to assemble (Hebrews 10.25), but God never said specifically where we were to assemble. The early Christians met in various places as they could. Thus, we are left to conclude that where Christians meet is of no consequence to God, as long as they are meeting.

This condition does not exist with instrumental music, however, since God has made a specific command to sing. Since the specific command has been given, we must not add anything to it, as shown above. We can establish, then, that when God establishes generic authority and is silent about specific means, there is liberty; where God establishes specific authority and is silent about any other practice, there is prohibition.

Old Testament Considerations

Argument: David used instruments, and David found favor with God, so instruments are acceptable.

Answer: This would be so, if it were not for the change of covenant that divides David and us as Christians today.

We read in Colossians 2.14 that the Law was nailed to the cross and in Galatians 3.24–25 that the Law was a tutor, no longer necessary when we have the fullness of Christ. Hebrews 7.12 is very specific on the subject:

> For the priesthood being changed, there is made of necessity a change also of the law.

Finally, Hebrews 9.15 captures the essence of the distinction:

> And for this cause he is the mediator of a new covenant, that a death having taken place for the redemption of the transgressions that were under the first covenant, they that have been called may receive the promise of the eternal inheritance.

We can see, therefore, that a change of law has occurred. When change occurs, the change runs throughout the law—if there is a practice performed in the Old Testament that is not done in the New, we have no right to perform that practice. This goes for the Sabbath as well as for instrumental music. Until we see a verse in the New Testament that shows that instrumental music is authorized, we must assume that it was done away with at the cross.

Retort: David's use of instruments was not commanded by the Law; we can therefore use instruments today.

Answer: While many try to present this view, the Scriptures actually show that God did provide commands for the use of instruments in the Temple, as can be seen from 2 Chronicles 29.25, among other places:

> And he set the Levites in the house of the LORD with cymbals with psalteries, and with harps, according to the commandment of David, and of Gad the king's seer, and Nathan the prophet: for the commandment was of the LORD by his prophets.

While some may attempt to say that the command comes from David, the text is very specific that the command is prompted by the LORD Himself. We must not consider this command to be against the Law or adding to it, for Miriam the sister of Moses used a tambourine to praise the LORD in Exodus 15.20, and instruments seem to be an aspect of service to the LORD in the old covenant.

The argument is not valid, nevertheless, even if instruments were not directly commanded. David lived under the covenant between God and Israel; his actions are either legitimated or condemned by the terms of that covenant. We are under a new covenant, as seen above from Hebrews 9.15. Our actions will be legitimated or condemned by the terms of this new covenant between God and all mankind through Christ Jesus. Even if a given practice is not specifically required by the Law of Moses, it nevertheless is authorized or unauthorized under the terms of the covenant between God and Israel, and cannot be forced onto the new covenant. We have as much right to use instrumental music as we would to slaughter Philistines, to offer a heifer without blemish on an altar, or to require circumcision; just because God approved something under a previous covenant does not mean that we today have the right to do the same!

New Testament Considerations

Argument: Paul says that we are to sing psalms. Psalms were sung with instruments, therefore, instruments are acceptable.

Answer: This argument posits an inference that may not be in the text. While psalms were certainly sung with instrumental accompaniment in the Old Testament, where do we see any such thing in the New?

Although uninspired, we have the witness of one Clement of Alexandria, who lived a century after the Apostles, and explains an interpretation of David's statements in the Psalms:

> If people occupy their time with pipes, psalteries, choirs, dances, Egyptian clapping of hands, and such disorderly frivolities, they become quite immodest…Let the pipe be resigned to the shepherds, and the flute to the superstitious ones who are engrossed in idolatry. For, in truth, such instruments are to be banished from the temperate banquet…Man is truly a peaceful instrument. However, if you investigate, you will find other instruments to be warlike, inflaming to lusts, kindling up passion, or rousing wrath…The Spirit, distinguishing the divine service from such revelry, says, "Praise Him with the sound of trumpet."
> For with the sound of the trumpet, He will raise the dead. "Praise Him on the psaltery."
> For the tongue is the psaltery of the Lord. "And praise Him on the lyre."
> By the lyre is meant the mouth struck by the Spirit *(The Instructor, 2.4)*.

Here we see early witnesses that interpreted the Psalms in a way that rendered them usable for the voice and the voice only. Since early Christians could obviously sing psalms without using musical accompaniment, nothing hinders us from doing the same.

Argument: Ephesians 5.19, Colossians 3.16, and James 5.13 are all talking about playing instruments in the Greek.

Answer: The Greek word translated "sing" is the word *psallo*. *Psallo* meant "to pluck" when it was first used by the Greeks, but later the meaning of the word shifted, so that by the time of Christ, the term meant "to sing." All translators and Greek scholars confirm this fact. A more modern example of the shift in meanings of word can be seen with "gay". A term that once was used to describe one who is happy, by various means, now more often is used to describe one who is a practicing homosexual. Words, therefore, can often change in meaning as time goes on, and therefore we have every confidence that the translators of the New Testament have it right.

Argument: Early Christians met in the Temple (Acts 2.42–46), and we know that instrumental music was played in the Temple (Psalm 150, Ezra 3.10). Therefore, early Christians praised God with instruments.

Answer: While it is true that early Christians did meet in the Temple, a significant leap is required to establish that they used instruments in their praise to God. First of all, the Temple was a vast complex encompassing a large part of the city; it is unlikely that the sounds of instruments could be heard in every part of it. Furthermore, the presence of instruments in another part of the Temple does not mean that the early Christians were actively using them or working with them to praise God. This inference is not required from the account in Acts, and there is no good reason to believe that the Christians in Jerusalem used instruments in their praise to God.

Argument: Instruments are used in Revelation, so they are authorized.

Answer: The texts in question:

> And when he had taken the book, the four living creatures and the four and twenty elders fell down before the Lamb, having each one a harp, and golden bowls full of incense, which are the prayers of the saints *(Revelation 5.8)*.

> And I saw as it were a sea of glass mingled with fire; and them that come off victorious from the beast, and from his image, and from the number of his name, standing by the sea of glass, having harps of God *(Revelation 15.2)*.

Notwithstanding that no one is actually "playing" a harp in these texts, but merely holding them, we must recognize that the book of Revelation is full of figurative language. If we are to be consistent in literalizing the passage, the harps that would be held in the assembly must be held by beasts, or one must stand on a sea of glass mixed with fire. Who, however, would argue that such could be done? Instead, just as the incense in Revelation 5.8 represents the prayers of the saints, we can posit that the harps would represent the praise of the saints. The figurative language of the Revelation in no way authorizes any New Testament practice; even if the harps are used in Heaven, when did God make any comment on their usage here on Earth?

Retort: The examples in Revelation show that God obviously approves of instruments in these happy examples. You must show where God disapproves of instruments.

Answer: Does God show His approval of instruments using Revelation? In Revelation 8, we read of trumpets heralding eight events, of which five bring about death and destruction to the Earth. Now, the destruction will be just and right, but can any Christian who purports to love his fellow man say that the destruction is positive or happy? No real pronouncement as to the feelings of God toward instrumental music can be made because of the figurative nature of the language of Revelation, let alone the varying ways in which instruments are used. Otherwise, if figurative language can be used to justify a practice, should we plunder the strong man's house, as Jesus alludes to in Matthew 12.29? By no means! Therefore, let us keep figurative language exactly as it is—figurative, understanding the spiritual message that is being proclaimed and not reading too much into the physical examples used to present them.

As for showing disapproval of instruments, where in the Scriptures do we see that God must show approval or disapproval of practices to make them right or wrong? We see in Matthew 19.7–8 that God allowed the Jews to divorce their wives, even though God hates divorce (Malachi 2.16). God disapproved of the practice, yet it was allowed. Furthermore, do we read anywhere of God showing disapproval of observing the Sabbath under the Law of Moses? Only when the people were otherwise disobedient (cf. Isaiah 1.10–18)! Yet we do not observe the Sabbath today, not because God disapproves of it, but because the covenant has changed, and the Sabbath rest is now our hope laid up in Heaven (Hebrews 4.1–11). Likewise, God does not need to explicitly disapprove of instrumental music for us to recognize that it comes without authority.

Other Considerations

Argument: We still fulfill the command, because we sing: we just have an instrument accompanying the singing.

Answer: If you tell me to go to the store to get bread, and I get bread and a candy bar, did I fulfill your command?

I certainly did what you asked me to do, but I did more than that, and thus violated your commandment. The same goes for the instrument— you may still be singing, but the singing is no longer akin to singing in the New Testament, for it is done with an addition concerning which He spoke nothing. We are to make melody with our heart, not with a piano.

Furthermore, the "addition" is hindering the God-given purpose for singing. In Ephesians 5.19 and Colossians 3.16 we see that our singing is to represent speaking to, teaching, and admonishing one another. How do instruments assist in our "conversation" with one another? It adds nothing to the substance of the message; it only aids in production. Where in the Scriptures do we see that the focus of singing is on the production? God is more pleased with a joyful noise done to build up according to Ephesians 5.19 and Colossians 3.16 than a perfect performance that does not lead to teaching and admonishment. Those who would emphasize instruments seem to put production over the message, and reverse God's established priorities!

Argument: Well, if instrumental music is an addition, what about songbooks, song leaders, and pitch pipes?

Answer: There is a fundamental difference between an expedient and an addition. An expedient helps to facilitate the completion of a commandment, while an addition changes the nature of the completion.

Song books, song leaders, and pitch pipes are all used to fulfill the command to sing, and that it should be done orderly, as seen in 1 Corinthians 14.40:

But let all things be done decently and in order.

Without a song leader, who would determine when we begin singing and at which tempo and pitch? Without the songbook, how would we know what we are singing? And without the pitch pipe, how will the song leader know what pitch to use?

None of these changes the command given to us in the Scriptures, but rather help us fulfill the command. Instrumental music alters the purity of the human voice praising its Creator, and is done without God having spoken to its effect.

Argument: Well, God gave me the talent to play instruments; why can't I use that talent He gave me?

Answer: God gives talents, yes, but does He give specific talents?

For instance, does a con man get the ability to deceive others from God? Should he engage in deceptive behaviors for God? Should a thief do so for the Lord, since God gives talents?

I am sure that there is agreement that God gives us talents, and that we can use them in proper and improper ways. There is, however, a proper way to use all talents; a con man, which generally is very persuasive, could change his life and persuade people to follow Christ. Likewise, one who has a talent playing an instrument has some music ability, and thus could sing and lead singing very well. God gives talents, and we need to use them as He has directed, not according to our own whims.

Early Witnesses Concerning Instrumental Music

I have added this section to provide earlier witnesses to the lack of instrumental music within "Christian" churches. It must be remembered that instruments were only first used in the seventh century and were only popularized in the nineteenth. I do not present this material thinking that its authors are infallible, nor should it be assumed that I accept all things that these individuals wrote. The following represent witnesses to the practices of the early "Christendom."

> The one instrument of peace, the Word alone, by whom we honor God, is what we employ. We no longer employ the ancient psaltery, trumpet, timbrel, and flute. For those expert in war and scorners of the fear of God were inclined to make use of these instruments in the choruses at their festive assemblies *(Clement of Alexandria, The Instructor, 2.4)*.

> What trumpet of God is now heard—unless it is in the entertainments of the heretics? *(Tertullian, Against Marcion, 5.24.13)*.

> One imitates the hoarse, warlike clanging of the trumpet. Another with his breath blowing into a pipe regulates its mournful sounds… Why should I speak of…those great tragic vocal ravings? Why should I speak of strings set with noise? Even if these things were not dedicated to idols, they should not be approached and gazed upon by faithful Christians *(Novatian, On the Public Shows, 7)*.

> [Satan] presents to the eyes seductive forms and easy pleasures, by the sight of which he might destroy chastity. He tempts the ears with harmonious music, so that by the hearing of sweet sounds,

he may relax and weaken Christian vigor *(Cyprian, Treatise X: On Jealousy and Envy, 2).*

Sometimes I avoid [the error of listening to melodies more than the words] in an intemperate fashion, and I err by an excess of severity. Then I strongly desire that all the melodies and sweet chants with which David's psalter should be banished from my ears and from the Church itself. Then I think that the safer course is what I remember has often been related to me about Athanasius, bishop of Alexandria. He made the reader of the psalm utter it with so slight a vocal inflection that it was more like speaking than singing *(Augustine, The Confessions, 16.33.50).*

I am inclined rather to approve the practice of singing in church, although I do not offer an irrevocable opinion on it, so that through the pleasure afforded the ears the weaker mind may rise to feelings of devotion. However, when it so happens that I am moved more by the singing than by what is sung, I confess that I have sinned, in such wise as to deserve punishment, and at such times I should prefer not to listen to a singer...*(Augustine, The Confessions, 16.33.50).*

While such persons are not inspired, their collective witness demonstrates clearly that the use of instruments in the assembly was foreign to "orthodox Christianity" in its first few hundred years. The practice, therefore, does not originate either in the New Testament or in early Christianity.

Judaic Practices

Statement of Belief

The Scriptures teach that the Law of Moses was to pass away in favor of the covenant with Christ:

> In that he saith, "A new covenant," he hath made the first old. But that which is becoming old and waxeth aged is nigh unto vanishing away *(Hebrews 8.13)*.

This covenant was done away with because it was written against us and served as a tutor to lead to Christ:

> ...having blotted out the bond written in ordinances that was against us, which was contrary to us: and he hath taken it out that way, nailing it to the cross *(Colossians 2.14)*.

> So that the law is become our tutor to bring us unto Christ, that we might be justified by faith. But now faith that is come, we are no longer under a tutor *(Galatians 3.24–25)*.

And it was therefore replaced,

> For the priesthood being changed, there is made of necessity a change also of the law *(Hebrews 7.12)*.

> And for this cause he is the mediator of a new covenant, that a death having taken place for the redemption of the transgressions that were under the first covenant, they that have been called may receive the promise of the eternal inheritance *(Hebrews 9.15)*.

The Ten Commandments and the "Moral Law"

Many denominations teach that we as Christians are under the Ten Commandments today, and that the "moral law" established by it represents the unchanging law of God. Let us examine how and why this conclusion was reached and then examine if the Scriptures teach if this is so.

This belief system began as a response to a question brought about by a seeming contradiction within the Scriptures: how can we have "liberty in Christ," set free by His death on the cross and the grace made manifest in that act, and yet still maintain a moral/ethical standard by which a Christian might live? Verses like Romans 8.2, Romans 3.20, and Romans 5.20–21 are compared in this viewpoint:

> For the law of the Spirit of life in Christ Jesus made me free from the law of sin and of death.

> …because by the works of the law shall no flesh be justified in his sight; for through the law cometh the knowledge of sin.

> And the law came in besides, that the trespass might abound; but where sin abounded, grace did abound more exceedingly: that, as sin reigned in death, even so might grace reign through righteousness unto eternal life through Jesus Christ our Lord.

The conclusion reached by these denominations is that knowledge of sin comes through the Law of Moses, and that we receive our redemption through the "law of grace" of Jesus Christ. Therefore, the "Law" as described by Moses is the "law" under which we are to live.

It was understood, however, that the death of Christ demanded the end of certain parts of the Law; these are described as the "ceremonial" or "ritual" portions of the Law along with the "dietary laws" in the Law. By necessity, therefore, these denominations distinguish the "moral law," the principles of which are clearly illustrated in the Ten Commandments and are to be followed, from these other groups. Do we see this distinction in the Scriptures?

We do not see within the Scriptures concerning the Law any distinction between the "moral" law, the "ceremonial" law, and the "dietary" law. It is considered to be the same law. Furthermore, the concept of the "moral law" brings about many questions: upon what standard is the "moral law" determined? The Ten Commandments alone? The specific instructions given by God concerning each of these commandments? The Scriptures do not give any such instruction.

The Scriptures themselves demonstrate that Christians are not under the "moral law" of the Law of Moses; this is seen in Matthew 19.7–9, Ephesians 2.13–16, and Colossians 2.14–16:

> They say unto him, "Why then did Moses command to give a bill of divorcement, and to put her away?"
> He saith unto them, "Moses for your hardness of heart suffered you to put away your wives: but from the beginning it hath not been so. And I say unto you, Whosoever shall put away his wife, except for fornication, and shall marry another, committeth adultery: and he that marrieth her when she is put away committeth adultery."

> But now in Christ Jesus ye that once were far off are made nigh in the blood of Christ. For he is our peace, who made both one, and brake down the middle wall of partition, having abolished in the flesh the enmity, evem the law of commandments contained in ordinances; that he might create in himself of the two one new man, so making peace; and might reconcile them both in one body unto God through the cross, having slain the enmity thereby.

> Having blotted out the bond written in ordinances that was against us, which was contrary to us: and he hath taken it out that way, nailing it to the cross; having despoiled the principalities and the powers, he made a show of them openly, triumphing over them in it. Let no man therefore judge you in meat, or in drink, or in respect of a feast day or a new moon or a sabbath day.

Each of these examples refer to one of the commandments within the Ten Commandments and what would be deemed the "moral" law. According to Jesus, laws concerning divorce were different from the beginning than they were under Moses; divorce under the Law of Moses was granted for many more reasons than in the beginning and under Christ. Therefore, someone who divorced his mate legally under the Law of Moses in many cases could not do so legally either in the beginning or under the covenant in Christ. It may be argued, however, that since the commandment says simply to not commit adultery, this commandment is still in effect. This cannot be, however, since the whole thrust behind a commandment is in how the language is defined. If adultery is defined differently in the Old Testament than it is in the New (as has been demonstrated), the commandment to not commit adultery in the Old Testament will be examined differently than it is in the New. Since the meaning of the term "adultery" changed between the Law of Moses and the covenant of Christ, we cannot be under the commandment as it was given to the Israelites by Moses.

Paul explains in the Colossian letter how the Law has passed away, having been "nailed to the cross." It is argued by many that this verse does not refer to this "moral law" seen in the Ten Commandments, but rather the "ceremonial" and "dietary" portions of the Law. The text itself, however, shows that this is not the case in verse 16:

> Let no man therefore judge you in meat, or in drink, or in respect of a feast day or a new moon or a sabbath day.

"Therefore" is always used to demonstrate a conclusion: because A is so, therefore B is its consequence. Paul refers to the fact that the "certificate of debt" was taken from us, "nailed to the cross." He concludes from this premise that no one is to judge a Christian on the basis of food and drink, a festival, a new moon, and a Sabbath. The first refers to the "dietary law," and the second two the "ceremonial law," yet what other conclusion can we draw concerning the Sabbath save that it refers to the "moral law," considering that the fourth commandment was to observe the Sabbath (Exodus 20.8)? In order to extricate themselves from this difficulty, some would posit that the "Christian Sabbath" is Sunday, and therefore wholly transport the legislation regarding the Sabbath observance for the Jews onto Sunday for Christians. The Scriptures, however, say nothing regarding this; furthermore, the Sabbath rest for Christians is portrayed in terms of Heaven, not Sunday, in Hebrews 4.1–11! We therefore may conclude that the common practice in the denominations that believe that we must use the Ten Commandments, that Sunday is the "new Sabbath," in which no work may be done, does not conform to the message of Paul in the Colossian letter.

The message of Paul in the Ephesian letter confirms the lessons we have found in the Colossian letter, for he tells those who are of the Gentiles that

Jesus, through His death upon the cross, destroyed the wall dividing Jew from Gentile and did so by removing the "law of commandments contained in ordinances." What else could this be but the "moral" law of Moses, enjoined upon the Jew but not upon the Gentile? This law had to be done away with in order for the Jew and the Gentile to each become part of one new group, those following Christ. We see, therefore, that the New Testament explains very clearly that there is a distinction between the "moral law" of the Old Covenant through Moses and the New Covenant through Christ.

What, then, can we say about the Law? There are multiple verses that show clearly that the Law has passed away. Many are given above; others include Galatians 3.19 and Galatians 4.21–26:

> What then is the law? It was added because of transgressions, till the seed should come to whom the promise hath been made; and it was ordained through angels by the hand of a mediator.

> Tell me, ye that desire to be under the law, do ye not hear the law? For it is written, that Abraham had two sons, one by the handmaid, and one by the freewoman. Howbeit the son by the handmaid is born after the flesh; but the son by the freewoman is born through promise. Which things contain an allegory: for these women are two covenants; one from mount Sinai, bearing children unto bondage, which is Hagar. Now this Hagar is mount Sinai in Arabia and answereth to the Jerusalem that now is: for she is in bondage with her children. But the Jerusalem that is above is free, which is our mother.

Therefore, we can see that the Law had a purpose: that humans may know of sin and understand the redemption in Jesus Christ. This point is demonstrated fully in Galatians 4.4–9, which also explains how Christians are free today:

> But when the fulness of the time came, God sent forth his Son, born of a woman, born under the law, that he might redeem them that were under the law, that we might receive the adoption of sons. And because ye are sons, God sent forth the Spirit of his Son into our hearts, crying, "Abba, Father."
> So that thou art no longer a bondservant, but a son; and if a son,

then an heir through God. Howbeit at that time, not knowing God, ye were in bondage to them that by nature are no gods: but now that ye have come to know God, or rather to be known by God, how turn ye back again to the weak and beggarly rudiments, whereunto ye desire to be in bondage over again?

Paul explains that the Law is a form of bondage, committing one to slavery. This same metaphor is used and emphasized in Romans 6.17–18:

But thanks be to God, that, whereas ye were servants of sin, ye became obedient from the heart to that form of teaching whereunto ye were delivered; and being made free from sin, ye became servants of righteousness.

The word translated as "servants" has two meanings in Greek: servant and slave. I believe that the passage above is best served reading as the following:

But thanks be to God, that, whereas ye were slaves of sin, ye became obedient from the heart to that form of teaching whereunto ye were delivered; and being made free from sin, ye became servants of righteousness.

I believe this is so because of the connotation of the terms "slave" and "servant;" one is forced to be a slave, yet one chooses to be a servant. This is the demonstration of how we as Christians are "free." Thanks to the sacrifice of Jesus on the cross, we have been given an opportunity to believe in Him and be freed from the slavery of sin and now allowed to choose to serve righteousness through Jesus Christ. Likewise, the world was bound to be slaves of the Law, since one was born into the Law and would die in the Law. Jesus set the world free from that Law, allowing all men the opportunity to choose to be servants of righteousness.

The fact that we are not compelled from birth to follow Christ, unlike Israelites under the Law, affirms that the practice of denominations of equating the Old Testament circumcision with New Testament baptism is not from the Scriptures. The premise of infant baptism because of the Old Testament circumcision is Scripturally unjustifiable and demonstrably wrong since we are no longer under such bondage, as is made clear in **Baptism: Infant Baptism and "Original Sin"**.

Therefore, we see clearly that the Law is a form of bondage, just like sin also is a form of bondage. Neither justifies us, and according to Galatians 5.4, the Law can only ruin us:

Ye are severed from Christ, ye would be justified by the law; ye are fallen away from grace.

Seeing, then, that the Law of Moses is in no way bound upon Christians today, the question is begged: is there a law for Christians today? Let us examine the Scriptures.

John defines what sin is in 1 John 3.4:

Every one that doeth sin doeth also lawlessness; and sin is lawlessness.

If sin is "lawlessness," by necessity that which is not sin is "lawful". Therefore, there must be some form of law that guides Christians today. A possible idea of this law is given to us in Galatians 6.2:

Bear ye one another's burdens, and so fulfill the law of Christ.

We may call this law the "law of Christ," and examine its contents. We see that Jesus often ratified many of the commandments that God gave to Moses, yet He also pointed to the narrower way concerning these values, as is evidenced in the Sermon on the Mount. The "law of Christ" therefore consists of the commandments given to Christians by Christ and His Apostles throughout the New Testament.

Many will argue that it is a semantic game to affirm that the Law of Moses was passed away yet many parts were ratified by Christ for the New. This distinction is critical, however, so that we may understand from whom we should receive our laws: Christ or Moses. The laws in the old covenant ratified in the new are binding because Christ and His Apostles gave them that authority, not because they had that authority within themselves.

A parallel example would be the formation of the United States in the late eighteenth century. When the laws and guidelines for the creation and execution of the government and the obligations of the people were written, many times the authors used the laws that governed the colonies under British rule, and in many other places those laws were adapted to conform to the desires of the citizens of the United States. Could someone argue in 1789 that Americans ought to follow a law that was in effect when Britain ruled simply because the United States incorporated many of the rules of England and that the "basic laws" of the law of England did not change? This would be considered preposterous; the new country would set new precedents with every law created. A rule had authority not because it was first an English rule, but because it was declared proper for the United States. Likewise, a commandment that originated in the Law of Moses does not have authority today because it comes from Moses, but because Christ and His Apostles affirmed it as true.

Ultimately, the example of America also demonstrates our freedom in Christ. In America, we consider ourselves to be "free persons," living under liberty. We still have many laws guiding our conduct, however, and if we do not follow these laws, we lose our freedom. Essentially, by declaring ourselves citizens of the United States, we affirm the responsibility of having liberty and freedom, for having liberty and freedom necessitates protecting the liberty and freedom of every other citizen of the United States. The laws exist to protect each individual's liberty. In the same manner, when we declare ourselves citizens of Heaven by believing in and obeying Christ, we affirm the responsibility of having liberty and freedom from sin by not performing it. If we perform those sins, and we do not follow God's guidelines concerning repentance, we lose the liberty from sin that we initially desired. We are free because we have chosen Christ not by compulsion but with our own will, and therefore we must now follow the guidelines given to us that we may continue to live in Christ Jesus. This is how we are free yet under the law of Christ, and this belief does not necessitate the use of the Law of Moses.

Tithing

Many denominations teach that Christians today are to tithe, just like the Israelites did under the Law of Moses. A tithe refers to ten percent of one's income to be given; under the Law of Moses, the Israelites were told to give one-tenth of their gain, be it by funds or animals, to God (Leviticus 27.30–33) and another tenth to the Levites (Numbers 18.21). These denominations teach that since this was the demand of God in the Old Testament, this demand is still binding in the New. Do the Scriptures teach this?

The New Testament does not command a tithe, nor is it given as an example. The word itself is only used five times in the New Testament, and every time it refers to either individuals under the Law of Moses or past historical events. Furthermore, the Scriptures do not give an exact number or figure for our giving; it is given to the individual to decide, as is evidenced in 2 Corinthians 9.6–7:

> But this I say, He that soweth sparingly shall reap also sparingly; and he that soweth bountifully shall reap also bountifully. Let each man do according as he hath purposed in his heart: not grudgingly, or of necessity: for God loveth a cheerful giver.

The giving in the New Testament is to be done by the purpose of the heart over a specific quantity. The concept of the tithe can be a good guideline, and may be used by an individual if he purposes to do so; this guideline, however, is by no means bound in the New Testament.

Let us not be deceived, however, that since no specific guideline has been given that Christians are not expected to give as the Israelites did. All examples of giving that we see in the New Testament—Acts 2–6, 2 Corinthians 8–9—would indicate that Christians were giving far more than 10% when there were times of need. Since we are under a better covenant with better promises (cf. Hebrews 7.19, 22), we are set free from the tithe so that we may give **more**, not less, to God and to build up His Kingdom!

Jesus taught concerning giving in Mark 12.41–44:

> And He sat down over against the treasury, and beheld how the multitude cast money into the treasury: and many that were rich cast in much. And there came a poor widow, and she cast in two mites, which make a farthing. And He called unto Him His disciples, and said unto them,
> "Verily I say unto you, This poor widow cast in more than all they that are casting into the treasury: for they all did cast in of their superfluity; but she of her want did cast in all that she had, even all her living."

The principle taught by Jesus in this passage demonstrates the attitude that a Christian ought to have in his giving. It should not be compulsory, nor should it be out of one's excess: it should be a form of sacrifice, the demonstration of one's concern with the things of God over all else. This sacrifice cannot be measured in a number or a percent, for there are many who can live comfortably without 10% of their income, and yet there are far more for whom every extra dollar is a luxury. Jesus demonstrates here the concern of God: one's desire to serve God, not percentages and numbers.

Conclusion

We have seen that many denominations attempt to justify either practices or laws on the basis of their usage in the Law of Moses, despite the fact that Paul speaks often about how the law brings one under bondage. Let us heed these words, remembering foremost the rhetorical question Paul asks of all those who would bind any of the Law in Galatians 4.9:

> But now that ye have come to know God, or rather to be known by God, how turn ye back again to the weak and beggarly rudiments, whereunto ye desire to be in bondage over again?

Let us press on for the freedom in Christ, and avoid the bondage of the Law.

The Lord's Supper

Statement of Belief

The Lord's Supper was instituted by Christ on the evening of His arrest:

> And as they were eating, Jesus took bread, and blessed, and brake
> it; and he gave to the disciples, and said, "Take, eat; this is my body."
> And he took a cup, and gave thanks, and gave to them, saying,
> "Drink ye all of it; for this is my blood of the covenant, which is
> shed for many unto remission of sins. But I say unto you, I shall
> not drink henceforth of this fruit of the vine, until that day when
> I drink it new with you in my Father's kingdom" *(Matthew 26.26–*
> *29).*

He desired that it should be done to commemorate His death:

> For I received of the Lord that which also I delivered unto you,
> how that the Lord Jesus in the night in which he was betrayed
> took bread; and when he had given thanks, he brake it, and said,
> "This is my body, which is for you: this do in remembrance of me."
> In like manner also the cup, after supper, saying, "This cup is the
> new covenant in my blood: this do, as oft as ye drink it, in re-
> membrance of me."
> For as often as ye eat this bread, and drink the cup, ye proclaim
> the Lord's death till he come *(1 Corinthians 11.23–26).*

And that it ought to be commemorated weekly,

> And upon the first day of the week, when we were gathered to-
> gether to break bread, Paul discoursed with them, intending to
> depart on the morrow; and prolonged his speech until midnight
> *(Acts 20.7).*

The Need for the Lord's Supper

There are some denominations who teach that the Lord's Supper is not a physical event, but is a "spiritual" communion, not requiring actual bread and fruit of the vine. Is the Lord's Supper in the Scriptures a physical act or a uniquely "spiritual" one?

We can see that physical bread and fruit of the vine was taken by Christ in Luke 22.19–20:

> And he took bread, and when he had given thanks, he brake it, and gave to them, saying, "This is my body which is given for you: this do in remembrance of me."
> And the cup in like manner after supper, saying, "This cup is the new covenant in my blood, even that which is poured out for you."

Paul confirms that the Lord revealed the same to him in 1 Corinthians 11.23–26, and even speaks in detail concerning the nature of the Lord's Supper in 1 Corinthians 11.27–29:

> Wherefore whosoever shall eat the bread or drink the cup of the Lord in an unworthily, shall be guilty of the body and the blood of the Lord. But let a man prove himself, and so let him eat of the bread, and drink of the cup. For he that eateth and drinketh, eateth and drinketh judgment unto himself, if he discern not the body.

If the Lord's Supper does not involve physical elements, why does Paul speak of "eat[ing] the bread" and "drink[ing] the cup" of the Lord? If the Lord's Supper is only a spiritual communion, why does Luke speak of the original Lord's Supper in the context of the Passover meal? The Scriptures indicate clearly that the Lord's Supper is most certainly a physical act that Christians ought to perform.

The Nature of the Emblems

There are many denominations that teach that the bread and the fruit of the vine are literally the body and blood of Christ. There are two streams of thought concerning how this comes about: transubstantiation and consubstantiation.

Transubstantiation is taught by some denominations, including the Roman Catholic Church and many in the Eastern Orthodox Church; it holds that the bread and the fruit of the vine literally turn into the body and blood of Christ after it is blessed and a Christian partakes of it. The metaphors used in the Gospels and by Paul in 1 Corinthians are essentially literalized. What do the Scriptures say concerning this?

The New Testament—in fact, the whole Word of God—teaches that the eating of literal blood is an abomination to God. This has been so from the beginning: when God first commanded man to eat the flesh of animals, after the flood in Genesis 9, the only stipulation He made was in verse 4:

> "But flesh with the life thereof, which is the blood thereof, shall ye not eat."

This teaching is carried down through the Law of Moses (cf. Leviticus 3.17) and then in the covenant under Christ, when the Apostles proclaim it as part of their edict in Acts 15.29:

> That ye abstain from things sacrificed to idols, and from blood, and from things strangled, and from fornication; from which if ye keep yourselves, it shall be well with you. Fare ye well.

Therefore, we have seen that from the beginning and even through the time of the Apostles, it has been forbidden for man to drink of blood. If the early Christians understood the fruit of the vine to literally become the blood of Christ, why do we see no exception in the prohibition in Acts 15.29? All evidence, therefore, demonstrates that the emblems do not actually become flesh and blood.

Argument: Jesus says explicitly that we must eat His body and drink His blood if we want eternal life. Therefore, the elements of the Eucharist are literally His body and blood.

Answer: Jesus indeed says such things in John 6.53–57:

> Jesus therefore said unto them, "Verily, verily, I say unto you, Except ye eat the flesh of the Son of man and drink his blood, ye have not life in yourselves. He that eateth my flesh and drinketh my blood hath eternal life; and I will raise him up at the last day. For my flesh is meat indeed, and my blood is drink indeed. He that eateth my flesh and drinketh my blood abideth in me, and I

in him. As the living Father sent me, and I live because of the Father; so he that eateth me, he also shall live because of me."

This is said to the Jews long before Jesus establishes the Lord's Supper, and yet He says that they must (presently) "eat His flesh" and "drink His blood". Since He is physically alive at this moment, how can it be possible for them to eat His literal flesh and drink His literal blood?

These questions are easily understood when we consider how Jesus often teaches in the Gospel of John: He constantly uses physical elements to refer to spiritual things, and the people constantly do not understand. Jesus tells the Samaritan woman that she should have requested from Him "living water" (John 4.10), and she continues to think that He refers to physical water (John 4.11, 15). Yet we see the following in John 4.13–14:

> Jesus answered and said unto her, "Every one that drinketh of this water shall thirst again: but whosoever drinketh of the water that I shall give him shall never thirst; but the water that I shall give him shall become in him a well of water springing up unto eternal life."

We understand that the water of which Jesus speaks is the Gospel, the Word of life that leads to salvation. There is further evidence of the figurative use of this type of language earlier in John 6: the people seek physical bread, and Jesus explains their spiritual needs using the same image in John 6.33–35:

> "For the bread of God is that which cometh down out of heaven, and giveth life unto the world."
> They said therefore unto him, "Lord, evermore give us this bread."
> Jesus said unto them, "I am the bread of life: he that cometh to me shall not hunger, and he that believeth on me shall never thirst."

Would we say from this passage that Jesus is speaking any more "literally" than in John 4? By no means; from Jesus, the Word of God (John 1.1, 14), comes the Gospel and eternal life, and such is the "bread" and "water" of which Jesus speaks. Since Jesus teaches in this way in John 4.10–14 and 6.33–35, why should we expect anything different in John 6.53–57? The image of eating His flesh and drinking His blood is certainly visceral, but it communicates the essential spiritual message: those who seek eternal life must partake of the salvation that comes forth from Jesus. This is certainly symbolized in the Lord's Supper, but it is an abuse of these passages to deduce that the Lord's Supper is literally the body and blood of Jesus.

Others, including some Lutherans and Eastern Orthodox, accept the consubstantiation view. They affirm that the bread is the literal body of Christ and that the fruit of the vine is the literal blood of Christ, but yet the emblems physically remain as bread and as the fruit of the vine. This approach seems to take a "middle way" that is rather inconsistent: either the bread and fruit of the vine are literally Christ's body and blood or they figuratively/symbolically are His body and blood. This doctrine seems to be an attempt to avoid any negative implications of a symbolic association between bread/fruit of the vine as body/blood while not going so far as the "Real Presence" belief of transubstantiation. Since it is either literal or symbolic, there is no room for the position of consubstantiation!

Furthermore, when we consider the Gospel accounts of the Lord's Supper (Matthew 26.26–30, Mark 14.22–26, Luke 22.15–20), we see that it makes the most sense for Jesus to be speaking in figurative language; after all, how can He determine that bread is His body when He is physically present? How can the fruit of the vine be determined as His blood while the blood of Christ still runs through His veins? The bread and the fruit of the vine were to represent for the disciples His body and blood, and they are to represent the same for His disciples today. Representation and actualization, however, remain entirely different matters, and there is no good reason to accept the idea of the actualized body and blood of Christ in the Lord's Supper.

The Bread and the Fruit of the Vine

Many denominations teach that the Lord's Supper can be made up of leavened bread and wine. Is this what the New Testament shows?

We must remember that the Lord's Supper was instituted during the Passover. When God commanded the Passover in Exodus 13, He mandated that the bread be unleavened in verse 3:

> And Moses said unto the people, "Remember this day, in which ye came out from Egypt, out of the house of bondage; for by strength of hand the LORD brought you out from this place: there shall no leavened bread be eaten."

Thus, the bread that Jesus broke was unleavened, since it was eaten during the Passover. Concerning the "fruit of the vine," the text itself shows what should be used: the fruit of the vine! In the Greek, the phrase used is *genematos tes ampelou*; this refers to grape juice, not wine (which is more consistently rendered in Greek by *oinos*). While some may deny that the ancients had the ability to stop fermentation, ancient literature does attest to the consumption of unfermented grape juice. Therefore, there is no reason to deny the New Testament example for the Lord's Supper being unleavened bread and grape juice.

When Should the Lord's Supper Be Observed?

Part A: Weekly

Many denominations teach that the Lord's Supper ought to be observed four times yearly, or maybe monthly; some even believe it ought to be observed daily. How often do we see the Christians in the New Testament observing the Lord's Supper?

We see the example of Paul and other Christians in Acts 20.6–7:

> And we sailed away from Philippi after the days of unleavened bread, and came unto them to Troas in five days; where we tarried seven days. And upon the first day of the week, when we were gathered together to break bread, Paul discoursed with them, intending to depart on the morrow; and prolonged his speech until midnight.

Let us consider what we can learn from this text:

1. Paul stayed for seven days; of those seven, the Christians gathered on the first day of the week. The stay of seven days is significant, for we read in verse 16 that Paul was hastening to return to Jerusalem.
2. This particular first day of the week does not seem to have any special connotations; it is a first day of the week that comes between the Passover and Pentecost (cf. Acts 20.6, 16).
3. Their purpose for gathering was to break bread.

"Breaking bread" is metonymy for an entire meal; while it can refer to a common meal (cf. discussion of Acts 2.46 below), it also can refer to the Lord's Supper (1 Corinthians 10.16). The purpose of this assembly, as we have seen, was to have this meal. Furthermore, we see that after Paul preaches, he "breaks bread" in Acts 20.11:

And when he was gone up, and had broken the bread, and eaten,
and had talked with them a long while, even till break of day, so
he departed.

There is no reason to assume that anyone else is eating except for Paul,
and that this breaking of bread is not the purposed meal of verse 7.
Based on all of this evidence, the best conclusion is that the "breaking of
bread" in Acts 20.7 refers to the Lord's Supper, and not a common meal.
Likewise, since there is no evidence that this particular first day of the
week had any special meaning, we can deduce that the disciples were in
the habit of partaking of the Lord's Supper on each first day of the week.

Argument: In Acts 2.46, we see the first disciples breaking the bread
daily. This validates the need of partaking on a daily basis.

Answer: First, the text:

And day by day, continuing stedfastly with one accord in the
temple, and breaking bread at home, they did take their food with
gladness and singleness of heart.

Context is the best way of deciding whether "breaking bread" refers
to the Lord's Supper or a common meal. In this context, the wording
shows that these Christians were not partaking the Lord's Supper daily,
but eating their meals together daily: "breaking bread…,they did take
their food…". The Lord's Supper is most probably in view in Acts 2.42,
where the discussion focuses on more spiritual events.

Argument: Paul establishes that the Lord's Supper can be partaken at
any time based on 1 Corinthians 11.26.

Let us consider 1 Corinthians 11.26:

For as often as ye eat this bread, and drink the cup, ye proclaim
the Lord's death till he come.

Paul is not here telling the Corinthians how often to partake; instead,
he is telling them what happens when they partake. "As often as" does
not determine how often one actually partakes: it simply establishes
that whenever the Lord's Supper is taken, the death of the Lord is proclaimed. We have to look elsewhere to determine how often is "as often
as", and the best evidence comes from Acts 20: they met on the first day

of the week, which by all evidence seems to be their normal assembly time (Acts 20.7, cf. 1 Corinthians 16.1–3), and by all accounts they assembled weekly for that purpose. 1 Corinthians 11.26 complements, and does not contradict, the message from Acts 20.

Part B: On the First Day of the Week

In many churches of Christ today, there is some controversy over how often the Lord's Supper ought to be observed during the first day of the week. There is agreement that it is not a question of when the Lord's Supper should be taken on Sunday; the question is over whether or not it should be offered more than once during the same day. The arguments on both sides have some merit, so let us present them:

Only one observance. The Christians of the New Testament gathered for the purpose of partaking of the Lord's Supper as we see in Acts 20.7. They were to do this "together," signifying unity. If most partake in the morning and merely sit and observe in the evening, the unity is lost. Nowhere in the Scriptures is there any evidence for a "second serving".

Two observances. Yes, the Christians met to partake on the first day of the week; however, if one person does not partake, the unity that is sought is not existent. The Lord's Supper is manifestly an individual action done collectively, else why is there a command to "prove" oneself before partaking (1 Corinthians 11.27–28)? One could, conceivably, judge oneself not worthy to partake at a given assembly. Where do we see in the New Testament any regulations concerning what percentage of members is necessary to achieve "unity?" Is there a quorum for observance in the New Testament? If the focus is on the unity, where do we see how "unified" the church must be? If all meditate on spiritual things while some partake in the morning and while some partake in the evening, the unity is still in mind, especially when it cannot be in body. This is further established in 1 Corinthians 10.16–17, where Paul speaks in the first person plural ("we") when he is in Ephesus (cf. 1 Corinthians 16.8) and they are in Corinth. How can they partake of the "one bread" when they are in different places unless the communion is spiritual? If one assembles with the purpose to partake of the Lord's Supper, who are we to hinder such a one (Acts 20.7)?

It is up to each individual Christian to weigh out the evidence on either side and to be convinced of what he ought to do (Hebrews 11.1, Romans 14.23).

The Number of Loaves and Cups

There are some groups that believe that Christians only have authority to partake of the Lord's Supper with one loaf and one cup. The Scriptures certainly allow this belief; there is no sin in partaking with only one loaf and one cup. Unfortunately, however, many of these groups wish to bind this idea, and condemn any who would partake of the Lord's Supper with more than one loaf and using multiple cups as sinning. What do the Scriptures say about this?

All of the Scriptures concerning the bread and the cup in the Lord's Supper can be viewed in a literal or a metaphorical way. As good Bible students, we realize that we should interpret literally unless there is a compelling reason otherwise. In terms of the elements of the Lord's Supper, the main reason why "the bread" and "the cup" are to be seen as accommodative or metonymical is based in the example of Acts 2.41–47:

> They then that received his word were baptized: and there were added unto them in that day about three thousand souls. And they continued stedfastly in the apostles' teaching and fellowship, in the breaking of bread and the prayers. And fear came upon every soul: and many wonders and signs were done by the apostles. And all that believed were together, and had all things common; and they sold their possessions and goods, and parted them to all, according as any man had need. And day by day, continuing stedfastly with one accord in the temple, and breaking bread at home, they did take their food with gladness and singleness of heart, praising God, and having favour with all the people. And the Lord added to them day by day those that were being saved.

This shows that the first Christians did all things together, and thus they would have partaken of the Lord's Supper together. How can one loaf and one cup be used to feed over 3,000 people?

Argument: You are making an assertion the text never makes.

Answer: This text does show that the first Christians used more than one loaf of the unleavened bread and one cup of the fruit of the vine by necessary inference on account of the fact that they devoted themselves to the "breaking of bread" (Acts 2.42) used in Acts 20.7 to denote the Lord's Supper, and they did all things together (Acts 2.44). Therefore, if they did all things together, then they would have all broken bread together. If they all partook of the Lord's Supper together, how would they all have partaken of one loaf and one cup? This idea remains inconsistent with the text.

Argument: The first Christians would have met in smaller groups in households on the Lord's Day.

Answer: This is an assertion not borne out by the text. In three places, once in verse 44 ("all those who had believed were together") and twice in verse 46 ("continuing with one mind in the temple...taking their meals together"), Luke demonstrates the togetherness of the first Christians. To say that the first Christians did not partake of the Lord's Supper together is to brand Luke a liar and make the Scriptures void; for if they partook in separate houses, how could Luke say that all those who believed were together?

Again, I want to reiterate that it is not wrong to partake of the Lord's Supper with one loaf and one cup, but to bind such practice when the Scriptures allow for the liberty is sin. However, those who know that we are allowed to partake with multiple cups must not offend those who do not see this liberty, and we must bend not to cause offense if the need arises (Romans 14.13–23).

Argument: The Scriptures show that Jesus used one loaf and one cup. Thus, we must also.

Answer: The Scriptures shed some doubt on this idea in Luke 22.17:

And he received a cup, and when he had given thanks, He said, "Take this, and divide it among yourselves."

The cup was divided before the Lord's Supper was instituted. The Gospels then show that the cup was "divided"; therefore, Christ and His disciples may have used more than one cup. Furthermore, the usage of the term "cup" is most certainly metaphorical, being metonymy, as shown below.

Argument: As seen in 1 Corinthians 11.23–34 and in other places, the "cup" is used. Where is their authority for more than one cup when the text says "cup?"

Answer: Let us consider how the cup is described in 1 Corinthians 11.25–26:

> In like manner also the cup, after supper, saying,
> "This cup is the new covenant in my blood: this do, as often as ye
> drink it, in remembrance of me."
> For as often as ye eat this bread, and drink the cup, ye proclaim
> the Lord's death till he come.

The term "cup" cannot be used literally here because no one literally drinks a cup. One drinks the contents of the cup; the cup is used to describe its contents, a commonly used figure known as metonymy. Would any consider the new covenant in the blood of Christ to be a literal cup? If so, we ought to go and seek the Holy Grail! Most recognize, however, that the blood of Christ represents this new covenant, and thus it is the contents of the cup, not the cup itself, which signifies the new covenant. Therefore, the nature of the container is of no relevance to the Lord's Supper; only its contents matter.

Argument: 1 Corinthians 10.16–17 show the need for one loaf and one cup: unity amongst Christians.

Answer: The text in question:

> The cup of blessing which we bless, is it not a communion of the
> blood of Christ? The bread which we break, is it not a communion
> of the body of Christ? Seeing that we, who are many, are one
> bread, one body: for we are all partake of the one bread.

Nowhere in this text is the bread limited to one loaf, nor is the fruit of the vine limited to one cup. As we have seen above, Paul is in Ephesus and the Corinthians in Corinth, and yet Paul includes himself in the discussion—how can it be that they all share one loaf and one cup when they are separated by the Aegean Sea? We all partake of the "one bread", just not the same loaf; the "one cup", just not in the same cup. The emblems themselves, not the containers, are the thrust of the Lord's Supper, and the fact that we partake of the same type of emblems across the world is the basis of the communion in Christ.

We can see, therefore, that there is no Scriptural basis by which to bind one loaf and one cup for the Lord's Supper. God has established the number of loaves and cups as a liberty for His disciples.

Positions of Authority

Statement of Belief

The Scriptures teach that elders were appointed in the churches:

> And when they had appointed for them elders in every church, and had prayed with fasting, they commended them to the Lord, on whom they had believed *(Acts 14.23)*.

They were instructed to oversee their church:

> "Take heed unto yourselves, and to all the flock, in which the Holy Spirit hath made you bishops, to feed the church of God which he purchased with his own blood" *(Acts 20.28)*.

These elders should meet certain qualifications:

> Faithful is the saying, If a man seeketh the office of a bishop, he desireth a good work. The bishop therefore must be without reproach, the husband of one wife, temperate, soberminded, orderly, given to hospitality, apt to teach; no brawler, no striker; but gentle, not contentious, no lover of money; one that ruleth well his own house, having his children in subjection with all gravity; (but if a man knoweth not how to rule his own house, how shall he take care of the church of God?) not a novice, lest being puffed up he fall into the condemnation of the devil. Moreover he must have good testimony from them that are without; lest he fall into reproach and the snare of the devil *(1 Timothy 3.1–7)*.

Deacons were also appointed in the churches, and are expected to conform to certain qualifications:

Deacons in like manner must be grave, not double-tongued, not given to much wine, not greedy of filthy lucre; holding the mystery of the faith in a pure conscience. And let these also first be proved; then let them serve as deacons, if they be blameless…Let deacons be husbands of one wife, ruling their children and their own houses well. For they that have served well as deacons gain to themselves a good standing, and great boldness in the faith which is in Christ Jesus, *(1 Timothy 3.8–10, 12–13).*

Who is the Pastor?

Many denominations today have one pastor or a staff of pastors having various functions who serve as church officers and as evangelists/ministers in some form. Do we see that ministers are equivalent to pastors in the New Testament?

We have seen above in 1 Timothy 3.1–8, Acts 14.23, and Acts 20.28, along with many other places, that the New Testament establishes an office for one called either an "elder" or a "bishop" (also translated "overseer"). Acts 20.28 demonstrates that the "elders" have been made "overseers" of the flock by God; this indicates that "elder" and "bishop/overseer" represent the same office. In Greek, the terms involved are *episcopos* for "bishop" and *presbuteros* for "elder". The former term is used above in 1 Timothy 3.1; the latter term, most often used to refer to this position, is used in Titus 1.5 and 1 Peter 5.1, among others.

The term "pastor" is derived from the Greek *poimon*, which is literally a "shepherd." We understand from Acts 20.28 that the elders are to be shepherds of the flock. Therefore, we can also see that this term refers to the elder or the overseer. This term is not used in the New Testament to refer to one who is an evangelist or minister.

Therefore, we can see that the Scriptures do teach that there are persons charged to shepherd God's flock, having met certain qualifications. These individuals are called elders, overseers, bishops, presbyters, shepherds, and pastors. We do not see in the New Testament anyone who is simply an evangelist referred to as one of these elders (or pastors). Now, an evangelist can be an elder if he is sufficiently qualified; Peter was one, as seen in 1 Peter 5.1:

The elders therefore among you I exhort, who am a fellow-elder, and a witness of the sufferings of Christ, who am also a partaker of the glory that shall be revealed.

An evangelist is not automatically a pastor/elder on account of his position; he must reach the same qualifications as any other elder. The only authority that an evangelist has is the ability to appoint elders, as seen in Titus 1.5:

For this cause left I thee in Crete, that thou shouldest set in order the things that were wanting, and appoint elders in every city, as I gave thee charge.

Therefore, using the term "pastor" to refer to any evangelist is not in harmony with God's concept of offices within the church.

A Hierarchy of Bishops

Some denominations teach that the church should be overseen by bishops, with one bishop presiding over a set of churches. Those bishops tend to be overseen by an archbishop, who himself oversees a large geographic area. In some instances, there are even higher authorities. Do we see such a hierarchy in the New Testament?

There is no example in the New Testament of any positions of authority existing over more than one church. Furthermore, as far as we are able to see from the Scriptures, each church had a plurality of elders, not just one over many, as seen in Philippians 1.1:

Paul and Timothy, servants of Christ Jesus, to all the saints in Christ Jesus that are at Philippi, with the bishops and deacons.

Beyond the elders in the local congregation, the only presently living authority is the head of the Body, Christ Jesus:

…and Christ also is the head of the church, being himself the saviour of the body *(Ephesians 5.23)*.

We also should heed the authority of the Apostles of old (Matthew 18.18, Ephesians 4.11) through their instruction in God's Word.

Furthermore, some of these denominations have bishops that do not even conform to the New Testament standards, for they are required by their denominations to be unmarried. Paul, however, speaks to the contrary when discussing the qualifications of elders in 1 Timothy 3.2, 4–5:

> ...the husband of one wife...one that ruleth well his own house, having his children in subjection with all gravity; (but if a man knoweth not how to rule his own house, how shall he take care of the church of God?)

It is clear that the bishop/overseer (elder/presbyter/pastor) must have a wife and a family so that his ability to effectively shepherd the church of Christ is made evident.

The hierarchical concept of authority was a progressive apostasy from New Testament teaching, beginning with one "bishop" over "presbyters" over a congregation, then progressing to having a bishop over other bishops in a larger metropolitan area, and then developed into the various systems seen today. We have seen that such was not God's intention, in the New Testament, for the oversight of His church.

Elders Determining Doctrine?

There are some who teach today that elders have the responsibility to determine doctrine through their examination of the Scriptures. Do the Scriptures teach this?

When we read in the Scriptures concerning the duties of elders, we see nothing of them being told specifically to determine doctrine or to interpret Scripture as an authority for a congregation. We are told, in fact, that we are all to examine ourselves and our beliefs in 2 Corinthians 13.5:

> Try your own selves, whether ye are in the faith; prove your own selves. Or know ye not as to your own selves, that Jesus Christ is in you? Unless indeed ye be reprobate?

Paul further states in 2 Timothy 2.15 that we must be diligent to make sure we are handling God's Word properly:

> Give diligence to present thyself approved unto God, a workman that needeth not to be ashamed, handling aright the word of truth.

The elders of a congregation are bound just as the members themselves are to examine themselves according to the Word of God and to make sure that their doctrines conform to the word of truth.

The only persons in the New Testament church vested with the ability to establish doctrine are the Apostles, and indeed whatever they established had been previously established by God in Heaven, as is made clear in a proper translation of Matthew 18.18 (seen here in the NASU):

> "Truly I say to you, whatever you bind on earth shall have been bound in heaven; and whatever you loose on earth shall have been loosed in heaven."

We have no indication that this authority was transferred to anyone else. We can see, then, that elders have no authority to establish doctrine. As shepherds of the flock they perhaps will be called upon to establish a practice of the church in regards to a matter of liberty, and such is within their right; to establish any such thing as doctrine, however, has not been given to them.

Widowed or Childless Elders?

Some have argued that an elder who is widowed or who loses his children in some way or another can still serve as an elder, especially since the death of his wife and/or children is something beyond his control and does not speak against his character. Is this idea and reasoning acceptable in the Scriptures?

When we look at the qualifications of elders in 1 Timothy 3.1–8 and Titus 1.5–7, the Greek is very specific about the nature of those qualifications. As Paul begins the listing of qualifications in 1 Timothy 3.2, he begins by saying, quite literally, "it is necessary for the overseer to be…". The verb "to be" here is the Greek *einai*, which is a present active infinitive. The present tense, especially in an infinitive, carries with it a "progressive" or "repeated" aspect. An expanded, but no less accurate, translation would be "it is necessary for the overseer to be being," or "to continually be." Paul, therefore, specifically charges that elders continually be qualified. An elder, therefore, must continually be the husband of one wife, and must continually have faithful children.

While it is lamentable when good elders, by no fault of their own, are no longer qualified, we must remember one of the preeminent qualifications: an elder is to be above reproach. The presence and good standing of an elder's wife and children demonstrate that he is above reproach; without their presence, there are many aspects of the work of the elder that would be near impossible to do and questions could be raised about his competence in shepherding. It is perhaps for this reason that Paul requires that elders continually meet the qualifications; regardless, the Scriptures are clear that any elder who is widowed or becomes childless or whose children fall away is no longer qualified for that position.

The Deacon

The deacon is a servant; this is the exact definition of its Greek word, *diakonos*. Nowhere in the New Testament do we see that the position of the deacon is vested with any authority, nor is it called a position for "elders in training." We must remember this when we consider the position of the deacon.

Deacons Without Elders?

There are some who believe that churches may have deacons even if there are no men qualified to be elders. The Scriptures never speak of any such situation; nevertheless, considering that those serving in the office of a deacon are only mentioned in the context of elders, we have no reason to conclude that God has authorized any church to have deacons without elders. As long as the men of the congregation are willing to perform the tasks that are required for the church to go on, there should be no need for an official position.

Female Deacons [Deaconesses]

Some assert that females can be deacons, citing the example of Phoebe in Romans 16.1:

> I commend unto you Phoebe our sister, who is a servant of the church that is at Cenchreae.

In some translations, she is called a "deaconess." Does this mean that she holds the office of the deacon?

It must be first stated that the Greek term *diakonos*, or its feminine counterpart, *diakona*, means literally "a servant." As with the term "elder" (Greek *presbuteros*), that means either one serving in the office of an elder (Acts 14.23) or simply one who is an old man (1 Timothy 5.1), so "deacon" can refer to either to one serving in the office of a deacon

(1 Timothy 3.8–10, 12), or simply as a servant. The term *diakona* in Romans 16.1 does not describe the office of the deacon, but simply the idea that Phoebe is a servant. This also is the same idea in Acts 6.1–6, when Stephen and the others are appointed as servants to assist the widows in need. We can determine this to be true because neither Phoebe nor Stephen *et al.* meet the qualifications in 1 Timothy 3.8–13:

> Deacons in like manner must be grave, not double-tongued, not
> given to much wine, not greedy of filthy lucre; holding the mys-
> tery of the faith in a pure conscience. And let these also first
> be proved; then let them serve as deacons, if they be blameless.
> Women in like manner must be grave, not slanderers, temperate,
> faithful in all things. Let deacons be husbands of one wife, rul-
> ing their children and their own houses well. For they that have
> served well as deacons gain to themselves a good standing, and
> great boldness in the faith which is in Christ Jesus.

We see that a deacon must be the husband of one wife, and the Greek term is specific for "wife," *gunaikes*. Therefore, Phoebe cannot be one who holds the position of a deacon, for she surely cannot be the husband of one wife. Furthermore, we know nothing of the families of Stephen *et al.*; even if they perhaps met these qualifications, these men were given a certain task at a certain time for a certain purpose, and nothing in the New Testament associates them with the office of the deacon described later.

We can see, therefore, that while *diakonos* or a similar term is used often to describe servants of the church, not every use of *diakonos* refers to one holding the office of a deacon.

Female Elders

Some denominations have elders or other similar persons vested with authority who are female. Does such a practice originate in the New Testament?

Paul writes to Timothy the following in 1 Timothy 2.12:

> But I permit not a woman to teach, nor to have dominion over a
> man, but to be in quietness.

This, along with the requirement that the elder be the "husband of one wife" in 1 Timothy 3.2, demonstrates that elders can only be men.

Female Evangelists

There are many denominations today (and the list of denominations grows ever longer) who now teach that women may perform the same evangelistic duties as men. Are these teachings in harmony with the Scriptures?

We do see that females were present in the work of evangelism, as seen with the example of Priscilla in Acts 18.26:

> But when Priscilla and Aquila heard him, they took him unto them, and expounded unto him the way of God more accurately.

We have no reason to doubt that Priscilla took on some form of assistance in teaching Apollos, but it is also notable to see that her husband Aquila was also present.

We must always strive diligently to maintain the harmony of the Scriptures, and there is no exception when speaking concerning female evangelists. We have seen in 1 Timothy 2.12 above that a woman is not to have any form of dominion over a man, and this must be considered in our discussion: a woman may teach and preach to other women, certainly, and perhaps even a man according to the example of Priscilla and Aquila, but we do not see any evidence from the Scriptures that any woman took it upon herself to preach to a man. While women can assist in teaching the Gospel, women would be contradicting Paul's exhortation for women to not teach and usurp authority over men if they were to fulfill the normal responsibilities of evangelists to exhort and preach.

Argument: Junia was a female and she was counted among the Apostles. **Answer:** We read about Junia in Romans 16.7:

> Salute Andronicus and Junias, my kinsmen, and my fellow-prisoners, who are of note among the apostles, who also have been in Christ before me.

We see that "Junias" (Junia) was "of note" among the Apostles; while it is possible that Andronicus and Junia were considered "apostles," this need not be so. It is just as possible that they were simply well-respected by the Apostles. Even if they are to be considered "apostles", the term is just like "elder" and "deacon" in that it can refer to a specific office or simply as a term referring to a person having been "sent out". Nevertheless, this verse does not demonstrate that Junia herself was an Apostle or taught men: she is mentioned along with Andronicus, who is most probably her husband, and they probably worked together in the same manner as Aquila and Priscilla did. Therefore, there is no conclusive evidence that Junia was an Apostle or a servant of Christ different in any way from Priscilla.

Homosexual Evangelists

There are many denominations today that not only accept practicing homosexuals into their groups but are even allowing them to perform the functions of the evangelist. Some are even installing homosexuals as bishops! What do the Scriptures say about homosexuals and evangelism?

The Scriptures are silent about homosexuals evangelizing, and this is not surprising since the Scriptures teach clearly that homosexuality is a sin in Romans 1.27 and 1 Corinthians 6.9–10:

> ...and likewise also the men, leaving the natural use of the woman, burned in their lust one toward another, men with men working unseemliness, and receiving in themselves that recompense of their error which was due.

> Or know ye not that the unrighteous shall not inherit the kingdom of God? Be not deceived: neither fornicators, nor idolaters, nor adulterers, nor effeminate, nor abusers of themselves with men, nor thieves, nor covetous, nor drunkards, nor revilers, nor extortioners, shall inherit the kingdom of God.

Therefore, we can see that the homosexual lifestyle is condemned as sinful in the Scriptures, and we cannot expect that one who is flagrantly violating God's Word would be vested with the authority to teach it or to shepherd God's flock!

Argument: Romans 1.27 and 1 Corinthians 6.9–10 denounce the promiscuous homosexual lifestyle; those homosexuals living in a monogamous relationship are not condemned in these passages!

Answer: This type of distinction is not even seen in the text. There are no words spoken by Paul that condemn a "promiscuous" homosexual lifestyle as opposed to a "monogamous" homosexual lifestyle—Paul condemns the act of homosexuality itself. Therefore, attempting to make a distinction such as this has no merit within the pages of the New Testament.

Argument: But these homosexuals in these committed monogamous relationships have love—and love cannot be wrong!

Answer: This type of answer comes from a mentality foreign to the Scriptures but common in America, where almost anything is possible in the name of "love". The Scriptures distinguish between different forms of love, however, and the Scriptures do not teach that every form of love is justified.

Furthermore, the idea of "love" justifying what God has called sin is not universally applied. Perhaps there is a man who feels that he has just "too much love" for just one woman and needs to "love" two or more, despite the fact that he is only married to one and the other relationships are adulterous! Are his actions of unfaithfulness justifiable because he has so much "love?" By no means! Just because there is a feeling of "love" between two individuals does not mean that their actions are justified by the New Testament. Therefore, homosexuality is still a sin, and thus no one who performs homosexuality can be an evangelist for Christ.

Priests

Some denominations have individuals who are deemed as priests, who fulfill various duties. Is this a Scriptural designation?

In the New Testament, we do not see anyone specifically being referred to as a priest. In fact, Peter says that we are all priests in 1 Peter 2.5 and 9:

> Ye also, as living stones, are built up a spiritual house, to be a holy priesthood, to offer up spiritual sacrifices, acceptable to God through Jesus Christ.

> But ye are a elect race, a royal priesthood, a holy nation, a people for God's own possession, that ye may show forth the excellencies of him who called you out of darkness into his marvelous light.

The only other priest we are told of is the High Priest, who is Christ Jesus (Hebrews 7). All Christians, therefore, represent a priesthood of believers under the High Priest Jesus Christ, who is of the order of Melchizedek.

Ordination

Many denominations go through the process of "ordaining" their evangelists and ministers. Is this a Scriptural practice?

We do not see anyone being "ordained" in the New Testament. Often we will see individuals being given the "laying on of hands," but this appears to be a blessing more than an ordination. In the New Testament, Christians evangelized without needing any special ordination or license. They would only be accepted if they taught the plain truth of Scripture, if the brethren were noble minded (Acts 17.11).

The idea of "ordination," therefore, is not explicitly established in the New Testament, and the idea of evangelists being accredited as such by some form of governing authority, be it a denominational council or center of education, is foreign to the Scriptures.

Synods, Councils, Conventions, and Other Meetings

Many denominations today have meetings wherein representatives of many geographical areas and/or congregations come together at some location to discuss issues within their denomination, and very often decisions will be made at these meetings about where the denomination will stand doctrinally. These meetings have many names in different denominations, including synods, councils, and conventions. Are these types of meetings seen as a function of the church of the New Testament?

When we read the New Testament, we see that there is no such "church cooperation," for every local congregation in the New Testament is autonomous (i.e. making decisions for itself). We see this because the "governing" body of the church, a plurality of elders, was instituted at the level of the local church (cf. Philippians 1.1, Titus 1.5). We do not see any form of governing body beyond the local church.

Many will turn to the council of Acts 15, however, to attempt to justify their synods, councils, meetings, etc., by saying that in this instance the "church universal" met to discuss doctrine. Let us examine Acts 15 to see if this is so.

We see in Acts 15.2–6 the origin of this meeting:

> And when Paul and Barnabas had no small dissension and questioning with them, the brethren appointed that Paul and Barnabas, and certain other of them, should go up to Jerusalem unto the apostles and elders about this question. They therefore, being brought on their way by the church, passed through both Phoenicia and Samaria, declaring the conversion of the Gentiles: and they caused great joy unto all the brethren. And when they

were come to Jerusalem, they were received of the church and the apostles and the elders, and they rehearsed all things that God had done with them. But there rose up certain of the sect of the Pharisees who believed, saying, "It is needful to circumcise them, and to charge them to keep the law of Moses."

And the apostles and the elders were gathered together to consider of this matter.

While Paul and Barnabas were certainly commissioned by the church in Antioch to discuss this matter with the other Apostles and the elders in Jerusalem, we see that Paul and Barnabas were certainly not the "delegation" from Antioch, but represented themselves. The council was comprised, as seen in verse six, of the Apostles and the elders in Jerusalem. We do not see any evidence that anyone else was involved with this meeting. It was natural for the meeting to be held in Jerusalem because such was the origin of the dispute: men from Judea had come to Antioch and had brought this teaching, and therefore it should be in Judea that the matter be settled (cf. Acts 15.1). The situation, then, regards persons somewhat associated with one local church visiting another local church to discuss a matter of doctrine perpetuated by members of that latter church.

We see in Acts 15.23, 28 the results of this meeting:

and they wrote thus by them, The apostles and the elders, brethren, unto the brethren who are of the Gentiles in Antioch and Syria and Cilicia, greeting...For it seemed good to the Holy Spirit, and to us, to lay upon you no greater burden than these necessary things.

We see here that the decision was made with the guidance of the Holy Spirit and made specifically by the Holy Spirit, the Apostles, and the elders of Jerusalem.

Now, let us return to the question: does the conciliar meeting of Acts 15 justify the modern synods, councils, and conventions of denominations today? By no means! The meeting in Acts 15 consisted of the church of Jerusalem and the Apostles—not delegations from all churches that existed at that time. The decisions made were made on the basis of the determination of the Holy Spirit and the approval of the Apostles and the elders of the church in Jerusalem, not by a majority vote of all members present. Therefore, it is evident that the meeting in Jerusalem seen in Acts 15 cannot justify the modern synods, councils, conventions, etc., of modern denominations.

It may be argued by some of these denominations that their councils and synods are guided by the Holy Spirit and are convened by the successors of the Apostles. The difficulty with this argument is that the meeting in Acts 15 was still not a meeting of all the "bishops" of the region, but only of the church of Jerusalem along with the Apostles. The belief of inspiration by the Holy Spirit and the belief of the bishopric still do not harmonize with Acts 15. Therefore, we may see that such synods, councils, conventions, and so forth are not practices performed in the New Testament.

Part IV: Early Movements in Christianity

The "Judaizers"

Overview

The "Judaizers" seem to be a group of Jewish Christians in the first century CE who preached to the recently founded churches of the Gentiles the need to conform to the Law of Moses, even after the death and resurrection of Jesus Christ. This group originated in Jerusalem; we know little about them, only that at least some are likely Pharisees (Acts 15.5). We do not know how organized they were or any names of any individuals within the movement. They are called the "Judaizers" for lack of a more official term; they attempted to make Jews out of Gentile Christians.

The importance of this group comes not from what they teach but by the reaction given to their teachings. The letters of Paul to the churches affected show that Christ has instituted a new covenant, and therefore the activities performed under the Law of Moses are made null and void. Let us now examine the history of this movement and the reaction to it.

Jewish Christians in Jerusalem

Before we begin to examine the impact of the "Judaizers" in the churches of Asia Minor and Greece, let us look at the church in Jerusalem.

The church in Jerusalem seems to consist of a large number of converts from Judaism, hereafter "Jewish Christians." These Christians seemed to have been very zealous for the traditions of their forefathers, as is evidenced by Acts 21.20:

> And they, when they heard it, glorified God; and they said unto him, "Thou seest, brother, how many thousands there are among the Jews of them that have believed; and they are all zealous for the Law."

The significant thing about these former Jews is that they do not seem to be condemned for still holding to the Law of Moses. Luke tells the story in Acts 21.18–26:

And the day following Paul went in with us unto James; and all the elders were present. And when he had saluted them, he rehearsed one by one the things which God had wrought among the Gentiles through his ministry. And they, when they heard it, glorified God; and they said unto him,

"Thou seest, brother, how many thousands there are among the Jews of them that have believed; and they are all zealous for the Law: and they have been informed concerning thee, that thou teachest all the Jews who are among the Gentiles to forsake Moses, telling them not to circumcise their children neither to walk after the customs. What is it therefore? They will certainly hear that thou art come. Do therefore this that we say to thee: We have four men that have a vow on them; these take, and purify thyself with them, and be at charges for them, that they may shave their heads: and all shall know that there is no truth in the things whereof they have been informed concerning thee; but that thou thyself also walkest orderly, keeping the Law. But as touching the Gentiles that have believed, we wrote, giving judgment that they should keep themselves from things sacrificed to idols, and from blood, and from what is strangled, and from fornication." Then Paul took the men, and the next day purifying himself with them went into the temple, declaring the fulfilment of the days of purification, until the offering was offered for every one of them.

We see here that Paul performs the actions according to the Law, even though he has preached vehemently against binding the Law of Moses. How can this be?

We must see that the Jewish Christians in Jerusalem were not yet condemned for holding to the Law of Moses because of the hardness of their hearts. For a period of time, God overlooked their ignorance, for the Jewish people were proud of their heritage, very zealous for their traditions (Romans 10.2), and bore great resentment towards the Gentiles. It was very difficult for these Jews, having heard the good news of Christ, to forsake the traditions handed down from their forefathers. There is further evidence of this period in the letter to the Hebrews, Hebrews 8.13:

> In that he saith, "A new covenant," he hath made the first old.
> But that which is becoming old and waxeth aged is nigh unto
> vanishing away.

The first covenant had not yet fully disappeared, but was passing away.

Jesus had predicted these things and the end of this period in Matthew 24.3–41, the great destruction of Jerusalem in 70 CE. With the destruction of the Temple, the service of God as prescribed in the Law of Moses was rendered impossible, and by this it was understood that the last vestiges of the old covenant had finally faded away.

Therefore, when Paul went to Jerusalem in Acts 21, he understood the difference in covenants, although his Jewish brethren did not. He heeded his own words in 1 Corinthians 8 and 9 and performed the actions of service in the Temple to avoid causing strife in the church there.

What, then, is to be said about Paul's conformity to the Law in Acts 21 but his insistence on the removal of the Law from the Galatians, Corinthians, Thessalonians, and Colossians? The answer lies in the audience. For those who were Jews and had converted to Christ, their conformity to the Law was for a time overlooked. For those who were Gentiles, however, who had neither heard the Law nor were ever under any compulsion to follow the Law, it had seemed good to the Holy Spirit and the Apostles not to burden them with the Law in Acts 15.

Therefore, the "Judaizers" seem to be those Christians from Jerusalem who wish to compel the Gentile converts to Christianity to follow the Law of Moses as they do.

The Beginning: Antioch and the Conference in Jerusalem

The first time the activities of the "Judaizers" are mentioned is in Acts 15.1:

> And certain men came down from Judaea and taught the brethren,
> saying, "Except ye be circumcised after the custom of Moses, ye
> cannot be saved."

Paul and Barnabas then debated these men concerning these things, and the brethren of Antioch determined that the best course of action was to have Paul and Barnabas travel to Jerusalem to inquire of the apostles and elders there concerning this issue. Paul and Barnabas went, and the meeting between them and the apostles and elders began.

It is at this time that we are informed that these "Judaizers" seem to be Pharisees, for Luke says that it is they who stood and declared that the Gentiles who had heard the message of Christ from Paul needed to be circumcised and to hold to the Law of Moses (Acts 15.5). There is then much discussion, but the end comes with the words of James, quoting the Old Testament prophets concerning the Gentiles, showing clearly that they are not to be bound according to the Law. The proclamation of the apostles and elders is seen in Acts 15.23–29:

> and they wrote thus by them, "The apostles and the elders, brethren, unto the brethren who are of the Gentiles in Antioch and Syria and Cilicia, greeting: Forasmuch as we have heard that certain who went out from us have troubled you with words, subverting your souls; to whom we gave no commandment; it seemed good unto us, having come to one accord, to choose out men and send them unto you with our beloved Barnabas and Paul, men that have hazarded their lives for the name of our Lord Jesus Christ. We have sent therefore Judas and Silas, who themselves also shall tell you the same things by word of mouth. For it seemed good to the Holy Spirit, and to us, to lay upon you no greater burden than these necessary things: that ye abstain from things sacrificed to idols, and from blood, and from things strangled, and from fornication; from which if ye keep yourselves, it shall be well with you. Fare ye well."

We also learn in Paul's letter to the Galatians that during his stay in Jerusalem, Paul discussed privately with James, Peter, and John, the nature of the Gospel which was being spread; Paul said they "contributed nothing" to the message which he preached, and that they saw that he was "entrusted with the gospel to the uncircumcised" (Galatians 2.1–8). The three extended to Paul "the right hand of fellowship," demonstrating clearly that the gospel preached by Paul was valid and in accordance with the will of God (Galatians 2.9–10).

The "Judaizers" vs. Paul: Galatia

Despite the decree of the apostles and elders of the church in Jerusalem, the "Judaizers" continued to preach the need of the Gentiles to conform to the Law of Moses. Within a few years of the conference in Jerusalem, the "Judaizers" are seen actively in the areas of Asia Minor and Greece. We see this concern manifest in Paul's letter to the Galatians, written to churches in south central Asia Minor around 55–57. In this letter, Paul first defends his apostleship and declares his authority (Galatians 1.11–2.10), demonstrating that the message he preaches comes from God. He then speaks of the hypocrisy of Peter in Antioch, who first fellowshipped with the Gentile Christians but then became aloof when some Jewish Christians from Jerusalem came (Galatians 2.11–21). Paul then chides the Galatians, calling them "foolish" (Galatians 3.1), demonstrating very clearly that the original covenant made was made with Abraham looking toward Christ (Galatians 3.2–14). The Law of Moses was therefore designed to be a tutor, leading men to the knowledge of sin and death to be ready for the coming of the faith through Christ, in whom all men are now equal (Galatians 3.15–29). Finally, Paul makes a plain declaration to the Gentile Christians in Galatians 5.1–6:

> For freedom did Christ set us free: stand fast therefore, and be not entangled again in a yoke of bondage. Behold, I Paul say unto you, that, if ye receive circumcision, Christ will profit you nothing. Yea, I testify again to every man that receiveth circumcision, that he is a debtor to do the whole law. Ye are severed from Christ, ye would be justified by the law; ye are fallen away from grace. For we through the Spirit by faith wait for the hope of righteousness. For in Christ Jesus neither circumcision availeth anything, nor uncircumcision; but faith working through love.

It is abundantly clear: salvation comes through Christ and Christ alone. The Law of Moses can do nothing for the Christians in Galatia.

The "Judaizers" vs. Paul: Corinth

The "Judaizers" seem to enter Corinth in around 57, between the writing of the first and second Corinthian letters. They seem to have been accepted rather quickly, leveling charges against Paul: that he was not a true apostle, having no commendation from Jerusalem, as they did (2 Corinthians 3.1–2); that he was not a qualified speaker (2 Corinthians 10.10); and that since he did not take assistance from the Corinthian brethren, this was somehow a detriment to his validity as an Apostle (2 Corinthians 12.13).

Paul writes a very strong rebuttal to these charges. He establishes that his letters of commendation are the members of the church in Corinth, for whom Paul worked diligently (2 Corinthians 3.1–3). He then demonstrates how the Spirit is much more powerful than the Law written on tablets is (2 Corinthians 3.4–18). Later, he describes himself as meek when present, but bold through his letters (2 Corinthians 10.1–3), that he is the same person in present as in his letters (2 Corinthians 10.11–12), and is equal to many of the most eminent apostles in knowledge (2 Corinthians 11.5–6). He then says that he robbed from other churches to work with the Corinthians (2 Corinthians 11.7–9), and says the following concerning a comparison of himself and these "Judaizers," in 2 Corinthians 11.22–28:

> Are they Hebrews? So am I. Are they Israelites? So am I. Are they the seed of Abraham? So am I. Are they ministers of Christ? (I speak as one beside himself) I more; in labors more abundantly, in prisons more abundantly, in stripes above measure, in deaths oft. Of the Jews five times received I forty stripes save one. Thrice was I beaten with rods, once was I stoned, thrice I suffered shipwreck, a night and a day have I been in the deep; in journeyings often, in perils of rivers, in perils of robbers, in perils from my countrymen, in perils from the Gentiles, in perils in the city, in perils in the wilderness, in perils in the sea, in perils among false brethren; in labor and travail, in watchings often, in hunger and thirst, in fastings often, in cold and nakedness. Besides those things that are without, there is that which presseth upon me daily, anxiety for all the churches.

Paul speaks about the reaction of the Corinthians regarding his lack of receiving any assistance from the Corinthians in 2 Corinthians 12.11–13:

> I am become foolish: ye compelled me; for I ought to have been commended of you: for in nothing was I behind the very chiefest apostles, though I am nothing. Truly the signs of an apostle were wrought among you in all patience, by signs and wonders and mighty works. For what is there wherein ye were made inferior to the rest of the churches, except it be that I myself was not a burden to you? Forgive me this wrong.

Finally, Paul asks the Corinthians if he or Titus had taken advantage of the Corinthians in any way or if their conduct was anything but befitting a servant of Christ (2 Corinthians 12.14–18). We have no information about any changes made in the church at Corinth because of Paul's exhortation, but we do see that no more rebuke or defense was necessary from him.

The "Judaizers" vs. Paul: Colossae

We cannot be sure if it is the same group of "Judaizers" who impacted the church in Colossae in Asia Minor around 60–61. This group seemed to focus on the festivals and the food proscriptions of the Law of Moses. Let us hear the words of Paul in Colossians 2.16–23:

> Let no man therefore judge you in meat, or in drink, or in respect of a feast day or a new moon or a sabbath day: which are a shadow of the things to come; but the body is Christ's. Let no man rob you of your prize by a voluntary humility and worshipping of the angels, dwelling in the things which he hath seen, vainly puffed up by his fleshly mind, and not holding fast the Head, from whom all the body, being supplied and knit together through the joints and bands, increasing with the increase of God. If ye died with Christ from the rudiments of the world, why, as though living in the world, do ye subject yourselves to ordinances, "Handle not, nor taste, nor touch,"
> (all which things are to perish with the using), after the precepts and doctrines of men? Which things have indeed a show of wisdom in will-worship, and humility, and severity to the body; but are not of any value against the indulgence of the flesh.

It appears that some had taught those in the church of Colossae to follow the commandments of Moses not to eat certain foods and to observe the Sabbath and other holy days. Paul says that no one has the right to judge on the basis of such things, for they are a shadow of what is to come and not the truth in Christ.

Conclusion

The last impact of the "Judaizers" can be seen in Ephesus, with those who "pay attention to...endless genealogies" in 1 Timothy 1.4, but we cannot know if this was due to an external force (such as the "Judaizers") or some strange idea brought forth within the church in Ephesus itself. Regardless, the "Judaizers" seem to be in decline by the time of Paul's death in 64, and after the destruction of Jerusalem in 70, with the Temple and many of the other vestiges of the Law of Moses destroyed, the movement loses most of its impetus. There are later indications of "Ebionite", or "Hebrew", Christians, but these groups are small and few, and do not pose much of a concern.

We can learn much from the impact of the "Judaizers" on the churches of the Gentile world, specifically, the changes between the Law of Moses and the Law of Christ. It is made evident by Paul in his letters that the Old Covenant is to be done away with, that it can do no good for us under the mediation of the man Christ Jesus. There is no better way to describe this change than to read the words of Paul concerning Christ in Colossians 2.13–14:

> And you, being dead through your trespasses and the uncircumcision of your flesh, you, I say, did he make alive together with him, having forgiven us all our trespasses; having blotted out the bond written in ordinances that was against us, which was contrary to us: and he hath taken it out that way, nailing it to the cross.

The Law has been nailed to the cross, and Christ now reigns. Let us endeavor to seek His will and His commandments, and forsake any commandment not in harmony with His teachings.

Gnosticism

Overview

Gnosticism (from the Greek word *gnosis*, meaning "knowledge") is the term given to a philosophical movement that flourished between the second century BCE and the fourth century CE. Gnosticism placed the emphasis of life and salvation upon the obtaining of knowledge (Greek *gnosis*), which was deemed Truth, and removing ignorance or error. The movement itself was very splintered and had multiple schools: Gnostic groups incorporated Platonic and Zoroastrian philosophies, and in the late first century CE, many of these groups incorporated Christian and Jewish thought and practice into their philosophies. For the purposes of our discussion, we will concentrate on "Christian" Gnosticism, or, those Gnostics who believed in Jesus Christ in some form or another.

This "Christian" Gnosticism is known for its multiple divisions, with some groups practicing certain elements of Christianity, and others forsaking such practices. With all the division in Gnosticism, it is exceedingly difficult to make general statements that will be universally accurate, but it can be said that Gnostics attempted to incorporate many facets of Christian belief into the philosophical beliefs of the Greeks. Many Gnostic groups attempted to remove Christianity from its Judaic foundation, rejecting the God of the Israelites as an arrogant, presumptuous deity, one out of many. It is for this reason that Gnosticism represents the opposite pull from the "Judaizers" on the early church: as the "Judaizers" attempted to make Christianity into a form of "fulfilled Judaism," so the Gnostics attempted to meld Christianity into Greek philosophy. True Christianity emerged out of this conflict as neither Judaic nor Hellenic, but as what it really is, a new covenant between God and all people on earth through His Son Jesus Christ.

Let us now examine the forms of Gnosticism that we see discussed in the Scriptures, and then examine the points in which Gnosticism attempted to place Christ in a Hellenic philosophical mold.

Paul: Proto-Gnosticism in Colossae and Hymenaeus and Philetus

The philosophy of Gnosticism existed before Christianity, dating back to the last centuries before Christ, as a philosophy incorporating the Greek philosophy of Plato and others along with the Persian philosophy of Zoroaster. It did not take long after the Hellenistic world was exposed to Christianity for many groups of Gnostics to begin to incorporate Christ into their philosophy. The first such example may have been in the church of Colossae, to which Paul writes the following in Colossians 2.8–9:

> Take heed lest there shall be any one that maketh spoil of you through his philosophy and vain deceit, after the tradition of men, after the rudiments of the world, and not after Christ: for in him dwelleth all the fulness of the Godhead bodily.

This text would demonstrate to us that a form of Gnosticism, probably a proto-Gnosticism, had come forth in the church of Colossae, for Paul does give a hint of what this "philosophy" entails: the concept that Christ did not come in the flesh. Many Gnostic groups, following after the dualism of flesh and spirit of Plato, accepted the idea of Christ but not that He came to Earth in the form of a man. They believed that He came in the appearance of a man, what we would call today a hologram, but could not have possibly humiliated Himself to the point of becoming human. We see, however, that Paul affirms this very thing, here and also in other places, especially Philippians 2.5–10.

The other possible demonstration of Gnosticism becoming apparent in the churches in Paul's writing concerns two individuals, Hymenaeus and Philetus, of which the following is written in 2 Timothy 2.16–18:

> But shun profane babblings: for they will proceed further in ungodliness, and their word will eat as doth a gangrene: or whom is Hymenaeus and Philetus; men who concerning the truth have erred, saying that the resurrection is past already, and overthrow the faith of some.

We do see that there were many forms of Gnosticism that recognized that the "resurrection" occurred at the moment that one recognized his mortality and thus transcended it.[1] It could very well be that Hymenaeus and Philetus accepted this belief and left the faith for a form of Gnosticism.

John: Adversary of Gnosticism

The Gnostic form of Christianity is considered to be "proto-Gnostic" in the time of Paul because the evidence that we have demonstrates that the belief system was only beginning to take form during his years of service, between 41–67 CE. We can see from the writings of John in the latter part of the first century CE that by this time "Christian" Gnosticism had taken root and was probably one the largest sources of doctrinal disputation at that time. This is made evident by the large number of references to the bodily existence of Jesus (John 1.1–18; 1 John 1.1; 1 John 4.2–3; 2 John 1.7–11), a good example of which is 2 John 1.7–11:

> For many deceivers are gone forth into the world, even they that confess not that Jesus Christ cometh in the flesh. This is the deceiver and the antichrist. Look to yourselves, that ye lose not the things which we have wrought, but that ye receive a full reward. Whosoever goeth onward and abideth not in the teaching of Christ, hath not God: he that abideth in the teaching, the same hath both the Father and the Son. If any one cometh unto you, and bringeth not this teaching, receive him not into your house, and give him no greeting: for he that giveth him greeting partaketh in his evil works.

Here John refers to those of the Gnostic persuasion as the "deceiver" and the "antichrist," and true Christians should provide no greeting or blessings for such persons. We see, therefore, that John did not mince words concerning the fruit of the Gnostics, and refuted them in his works.

Gnosticism versus Judaism

Unlike the "Judaizers," who faded from history after the destruction of Jerusalem in 70 CE, the Gnostics remained and even grew after the time of the Apostles, going fully underground only in the fourth or fifth centuries CE and active in other belief systems until the thirteenth century CE. Therefore, much of the information that we have about the Gnostics came from sources who lived after the apostolic era, mostly by those generally deemed the "church fathers." In 1945, however, a discovery was made in Nag Hammadi, Egypt, of twelve codices containing many Gnostic works. These works have helped to illuminate many of the doctrines and beliefs held by the Gnostics.

One significant belief held by the Gnostics concerned the God of the Israelites, YHWH. The Gnostics developed a mythology concerning the creation of gods and of the world in which the Father is the "Spirit," from whom emanated many other gods, known as aeons.[2] One of these aeons was known as Sophia, and when she created things with the Spirit, all was well. One day, however, she desired by thought to create a likeness of herself without the approval of the Spirit, and the thought became reality, and she called this likeness Yaltabaoth (or Yaldabaoth).[3] This Yaltabaoth was hidden from the other aeons, and he began to establish authorities on his behalf and created the heavens and the earth.[4] He then in his "arrogance" proclaimed himself the only god and a jealous one at that.[5] It is also believed by the Gnostics that Jesus Christ was a spirit of a higher level of understanding and awareness than this Yaltabaoth, and thus superior to him. The allusions to the God of the Israelites cannot be ignored in this mythology, and it is made evident that the Gnostics desired to separate Jesus Christ from Judaism and to incorporate Him into the pantheism of the Greeks. This philosophy, however, has no place in the Scriptures, and it represents the lengths the Gnostics went to deny the mission of the Lord Jesus.

Greek Influences Within Gnosticism

Many of the departures of the Gnostics from the truth are derived from the Greek philosophical foundations of Gnosticism. The Gnostics were heavily influenced by Plato, a fourth century BCE Greek philosopher. Plato's philosophy was heavily dualistic, positing two opposing forces working within humanity: flesh and spirit. In Plato's world, the spirit represented everything good and wholesome; the flesh, everything evil and degenerative. Gnosticism accepts this dualism wholeheartedly, yet within the movement there were divisions over how the dualism was applied. The majority of Gnostics accepted the fact that the flesh was evil and the spirit was good, and therefore took great pains to supplant all fleshly desires, even to the point of renouncing women and marriage.[6] There were other groups, however, who believed that since the flesh was inferior to the spirit, the deeds of the flesh were irrelevant as long as the spirit aimed for higher knowledge. This group was therefore known for its widespread immorality.

The Gnostics also accepted other tenets of Platonic philosophy, especially his attitude concerning women. Plato found little use for women since they lead men toward a family life, forcing the male to make a living away from the cultivation of his mind. The Gnostic attitude towards women, therefore, was exceedingly negative, portraying all forms of evil as "becoming female"[7] and even going as far as the following from the Gospel of Thomas:

> Simon Peter said to them, "Let Mary leave us, for women are not worthy of life."
> Jesus said, "I myself shall lead her in order to make her male, so that she too may become a living spirit resembling you males. For every woman who will make herself male will enter the kingdom of heaven."[8]

These concepts are far from Scriptural and demonstrate the permeation of Greek philosophy into the Gnostic theological system.

Conclusion

We have seen that the Gnostics in many ways represented a pull on Christianity in the opposite direction of that of the "Judaizers," away from the practices of Judaism (in fact, completely renouncing the God of the Jews as the only God) and toward the philosophies of the Mediterranean world, especially that of the Greeks. The "early church" was able to stand up to the forces of Gnosticism; today, however, many denominations have brought back many of the tenets of Gnosticism, including dualism and asceticism, and have incorporated these philosophies into their belief systems. We must recognize this neo-Gnosticism and be as diligent to refute it as Paul and John and others did all those centuries ago.

Notes

1: "The Treatise on the Resurrection," from *The Nag Hammadi Library*, ed. by James Robinson, p. 56

2: "The Apocryphon of John," p. 106

3: Ibid., p. 110

4: Ibid., p. 112

5: Ibid., p. 113

6: "The Testimony of Truth," pp. 452–453

7: "The Dialogue of the Savior," p. 254; "The Second Treatise of the Great Seth," p. 369

8: "The Gospel of Thomas," (114) p. 138

Montanism

Overview

Montanism is derived from Montanus, a "monk" who was a former priest of Cybele in Asia Minor in either 156 or 172. He claimed that he was given the gift of speaking in tongues, and proceeded to give many revelations concerning the "end of the world." We do not have much information on this group, but the little that we do have is very enlightening, and sheds light on the modern Pentecostal/Charismatic movement.

The Gift of the Spirit and Revelation

There is nothing mentioned about Montanus and his group in the Scriptures since they originated at least 50 years after the end of the Apostles. We do have information concerning them from those that are deemed the "church fathers": one of them, Tertullian, even joined Montanism.

From the information preserved in the records of these "church fathers," we see that Montanus described himself as the inspired instrument of the Holy Spirit, even going so far as to claim that he was the "Father and the Son and the Paraclete."[1] The movement was also known for two women, Prisca (or Priscilla) and Maximilla; the latter declared that "after me, there will be no more prophecy, but the End."[2]

The Montanists' main theology was that the end of the world was soon to come and that the "heavenly Jerusalem" would soon come to earth in Phrygia, in the little town of Pepuza.[3] They were known for their "ecstatic outbursts," losing possession of their faculties, and their insistence that their words were the actual words of God Himself.[4]

Let us examine the testimony of Eusebius of Caesarea concerning this group:

> In a certain village in that part of Mysia over against Phrygia, Montanus, they say, first exposed himself to the assaults of the adversary

through his unbounded lust for leadership. He was one of the recent converts, and he became possessed of a spirit, and suddenly began to rave in a kind of ecstatic trance, and to babble in a jargon, prophesying in a manner contrary to the custom of the Church which had been handed down by tradition from the earliest times.[5]

If we remove the more virulent language to see the nature of the history that Eusebius recounts, we see that Montanus believed in the gift of speaking in tongues and did so not in accordance with the speaking in tongues of Pentecost, but as a form of babble.

Conclusion

Montanism no longer exists today; the movement continued into the third century, but died out not long after its three founders did. The "heavenly Jerusalem" did not fall to Pepuza in Phrygia, and 1,800 years later, the millennium they imagined has not begun. Therefore, can anyone say that these individuals were truly given the Spirit?

The Pentecostal/Charismatic movement looks back and sees a bit of itself in the Montanism of the second century. Montanism, however, represents an Achilles' heel to the Pentecostals: if it were a true movement, how can the gifts still be around when one of its members declared that "after [her], there will be no more" ? Furthermore, why did the world not end in the second or even third century? If we accept, therefore, that the Montanists were deluded by false spirits, why does the Montanist experience correlate so well with the Pentecostal/Charismatic experience of the twentieth century, with the emphasis on emotionalism, loss of possession of faculties, and the "utterance of the Spirit"?

The debacle that was Montanism thus demonstrates that the Spirit of God is not poured out in such a way that causes the high emotionalism and the "ecstasy" that has been purported first in Montanism and later in Pentecostalism. The Montanists help affirm the truth of the fulfillment of the prophecy given by Paul in 1 Corinthians 13.8–10:

Love never faileth: but whether there be prophecies, they shall be done away; whether there be tongues, they shall cease; whether there be knowledge, it shall be done away. For we know in part, and we prophesy in part; but when that which is perfect is come, that which is in part shall be done away.

Since the experience of Montanism has been proven false by the passing of time, why should we believe that the experiences of the Pentecostal/ Charismatic movements fall into any other category when the same nature of experience existed in both groups? Therefore, it is evident that the gifts of the Spirit mentioned in 1 Corinthians 13.8 are not present today, just as they were not present in the second and third centuries CE.

Notes

1: Bruce Metzger, *The Canon of the New Testament*, pp. 100–101

2: Ibid.

3: Henry Chadwick, *The Early Church*, p. 52, and *The Canon of the New Testament*, p. 100

4: *The Early Church*, p. 52

5: Eusebius of Caesarea, *History of the Church*, v. xvi. 7

Bibliography

The Book of Discipline of the United Methodist Church, 1996. Nashville, Tennessee: The United Methodist Publishing House, 1996.

The Book of Mormon, The Doctrines & Covenants of the Church of Jesus Christ of Latter-Day Saints, The Pearl of Great Price. Salt Lake City, Utah: The Church of Jesus Christ of Latter-Day Saints, 1995.

The Book of Resolutions of the United Methodist Church, 1996. Nashville, Tennessee: The United Methodist Publishing House, 1996.

Carpenter, Gilbert Sr. and Jr. *Mary Baker Eddy: Her Spiritual Footsteps.*

Carroll, B. H. *Baptists and their Doctrines.* Nashville, Tennessee: Broadman and Holman Publishers, 1999.

Catechism of the Catholic Church. New York, New York: Image Books, 1995.

Chadwick, Henry. *The Early Church.* London, England: Penguin Books, 1993 [1967].

Dyck, Cornelius. *An Introduction to Mennonite History,* Third Edition. Scottdale, Pennsylvania: Herald Press, 1993 [1967].

Dowley, Tim, ed. *Introduction to the History of Christianity.* Minneapolis, Minnesota: Fortress Press, 2002 [1977].

Eddy, Mary Baker. *Science and Health with Key to the Scriptures.* The Mary Baker Eddy Foundation: 1986 [1910].

Edwards, David. *What Anglicans Believe in the Twenty-First Century.* London, England: Mowbray, 2000.

The Episcopal Church. *The Book of Common Prayer.*

Fox, George. *The Journal.* London, England: Penguin Books, 1998.

God's Kingdom of a Thousand Years. Brooklyn, New York: Watchtower Bible and Tract Society, 1973.

Good, Merle and Phyllis. *20 Most Asked Questions about the Amish and Mennonites.* Intercourse, Pennsylvania: Good Books, 1995 [1979].

An Invitation to Faith. The Mennonite Fellowship. Scottdale, Pennsylvania: Herald Press, 1972 [1957].

Johnson, Kevin. *Why Do Catholics Do That?* New York, New York: Ballantine Books, 1994.

Knowledge That Leads to Everlasting Life. Brooklyn, New York: Watchtower Bible and Tract Society, 1995.

Kuyper, Abraham. *Lectures on Calvinism.* Grand Rapids, Michigan: Eerdmans Publishing Company, 1999 [1931]. Luther, Martin. *The Large Catechism.* Philadelphia, Pennsylvania: Fortress Press, 1959.

LaHaye, Tim and Jenkins, Jerry. *Are We Living in the End Times?* Wheaton, Illinois: Tyndale House Publishers, 1999.

_____. *Luther's Small Catechism with Explanation.* St. Louis, Missouri: Concordia Publishing House, 1991.

McConkie, Bruce. *Mormon Doctrine.* Salt Lake City, Utah: Bookcraft, 1999 [1966].

New World Translation of the Holy Scriptures. Brooklyn, New York: Watchtower Bible and Tract Society, 1984.

Nolt, Steven. *A History of the Amish.* Intercourse, Pennsylvania: Good Books, 1992.

Presbyterian Church (USA). *Book of Catechisms*, Reference Edition. Louisville, Kentucky: Geneva Press, 2001.

_____. *Book of Confessions*, Study Edition. Louisville, Kentucky: Geneva Press, 1996.

Rhodes, Ron. *The Complete Guide to Christian Denominations.* Eugene, Oregon: Harvest House Publishers, 2005.

The Truth that leads to Eternal Life. Brooklyn, New York: Watchtower Bible and Tract Society, 1968.

Ware, Timothy. *The Orthodox Church.* London, England: Penguin Books, 1997 [1963].

West, Jessamyn. *The Quaker Reader.* Wallingford, Pennsylvania: Pendle Hill Publications, 1962.